Real-Time Cameras

Real-Time Cameras: A Guide for Game Designers and Developers

Mark Haigh-Hutchinson

ELSEVIER

AMSTERDAM • BOSTON • HEIDELBERG • LONDON • NEW YORK
OXFORD • PARIS • SAN DIEGO • SAN FRANCISCO
SINGAPORE • SYDNEY • TOKYO

Morgan Kaufmann Publishers is an imprint of Elsevier

MORGAN KAUFMANN PUBLISHERS

Morgan Kaufmann Publishers is an imprint of Elsevier.
30 Corporate Drive, Suite 400, Burlington, MA 01803, USA
This book is printed on acid-free paper.

Library of Congress Cataloging-in-Publication Data

ISBN: 978-0-12-311634-5

For information on all Morgan Kaufmann publications, visit our Web site at www.mkp.com or www.elsevierdirect.com

Printed in the United States of America

Transferred to Digital Printing, 2011

Contents

Foreword

Paul Tozour

When Mark Haigh-Hutchinson mentioned to me in late 2006 that he was starting to write a book on real-time game camera systems, I was thrilled. As the creator of the camera systems in all of the games in the *Metroid Prime* trilogy and a longtime industry veteran who played a major role in the development of many of the industry's most beloved classics, I knew that Mark was uniquely qualified to write such a book.

Videogames have long had problems with camera systems. A surprising number of games have delivered high quality graphics and game play and yet fallen victim to inadequate camera control systems. Any number of game reviews bemoan cameras that stutter, lag, shake the player's viewport violently, pass through walls, or point in the wrong direction.

I knew that if anyone could show us the way toward fixing all of these problems, it was Mark "H-H." His dedication to the task, his relentless perfectionism, and his boundless energy affected everything he touched. I enthusiastically urged him to write the book.

Mark began working on the manuscript shortly after our conversation. Like all of our fellow employees at Retro Studios, Mark and I were very busy finishing *Metroid Prime 3: Corruption*, a flagship title for the Nintendo Wii gaming console. Mark often stayed late and worked weekends, only to spend several hours later that evening and several more in the morning working tirelessly to finish the book. He often sent me chapters for review as he finished them, and I was astonished by his continuous progress.

No one could have foreseen what would happen next. As the game drew nearer to completion, Mark mentioned health problems, which were diagnosed as inflammation of the digestive tract. Only days after Retro Studios shipped *Metroid Prime 3* in August 2007, Mark's diagnosis was changed to pancreatic cancer and he was admitted to the hospital immediately.

Devastated, we found ourselves at his funeral in late January.

Mark's wife Melanie asked me to speak. I was honored to have had the opportunity to say a few words:

> *I'm deeply grateful for having been able to know Mark as a colleague and as a friend.*
>
> *When I think of Mark, I will always think of him as a man who gave of himself.*
>
> *Mark gave us his time, his unstoppable energy, and his boundless enthusiasm. He gave to us from his endless knowledge and his rich imagination — sometimes more than we could handle, always more than we deserved. He gave to us his deep and genuine warmth, which came from a heart even bigger than his extraordinary intellect. Mark gave us three games that will always be remembered, one book that will change our industry, and countless memories of a great friend. He gave us more than we could ever hope to repay.*
>
> *Mark never acted out of ambition or self-interest. He gave of himself, and he gave because he had a vision for Retro and for the industry. He gave because of that vision, out of a genuine desire to help move all of us forward to that better place.*
>
> *I offer my condolences to Mark's family. I offer my condolences to everyone who considered Mark a friend. But I especially offer my condolences to those in our industry who never had the opportunity to work with Mark, to learn from him, and to know him as a friend, and will never know what they have missed.*

Mark is survived by his loving wife of 14 years, Melanie, and two adoring daughters, Emma and Rachel.

Although Mark's book was not yet completed, those who knew him knew how important it was, both to Mark and to the industry, and could not let it disappear. In the summer and fall of 2008, a number of Mark's friends and colleagues came together in loving memory of this extraordinary individual to complete this essential book.

The following individuals contributed to the completion of *Real-Time Cameras*:

> *Ryan Cornelius, Software Engineer*
> *Mark DeLoura, Videogame Technology Consultant*
> *Jim Gage, Senior Software Engineer*
> *Jack Mathews, Technical Director*
> *Steve McCrea, Senior Engineer*

Akintunde Omitowoju, Software Engineer
Eric Rehmeyer, Software Engineer
Marco Thrush, Engineer
Paul Tozour, Independent Consultant

Mark, you are always in our thoughts. We will never forget the extraordinary contributions you have made, or the joy of knowing you, our dear colleague, mentor, and friend.

We offer this completed book in sincere gratitude for having had the opportunity to live and work alongside the inestimable Mark H-H.

Preface

"You should write a book on cameras."

It didn't sound *that* difficult.

Four years since starting. Desire to improve camera standards, too many great games spoilt by poor camera usage. Own frustration with games I wanted to enjoy but couldn't.

25+ years of game development.

Writing this book, as many authors will attest, has been a labor of love.

Acknowledgements

Akintunde Omitowoju (it was all his fault)
Ryan Harris (co-conspirator)
John Giors
Kynan Pearson
Aaron Walker
Colleagues at Retro Studios, previous colleagues
Nintendo
Michael Kelbaugh

Original encouragement:

Andrew Glassner (introduced to Morgan Kaufman)
Eric Haines

Reviewers:

Fred Ford, in particular
Jim Van Verth
Ed Rotberg
Peter Lipson
Jon Knoles
Ryan Harris

Morgan Kaufman publishers:

Laura Lewin
Georgia Kennedy
Denise Penrose
Tim Cox
Dave Eberly
Jessie Evans

Personal:

Melanie
Emma
Rachel
Ronnie and Diana
Martin and Rosemary Wright
Costa and Luke

About the author

Mark Haigh-Hutchinson was a Senior Software Engineer at Retro Studios Inc., based in Austin, Texas. Originating from Halifax in the North of England, Mark designed and programmed video games professionally starting in 1984 and as a hobby since 1979. He contributed to over 40 published video games in roles as varied as programmer, designer, and project leader. Some of the more notable titles that he worked on included several *Star Wars* games: *Rogue Squadron, Episode 1: Racer, Shadows of the Empire,* and *Rebel Assault,* as well as many other games including *Zombies Ate My Neighbors, Sam and Max Hit The Road,* and *Alien Highway.* Most recently, Mark was responsible for the camera system and player controls in *Metroid Prime 3: Corruption* in addition to its prequels *Metroid Prime 2: Echoes* and the award-winning *Metroid Prime.*

Introduction

Video games and other interactive real-time applications are often required to present a view of a virtual world in a manner that is both contextually appropriate and aesthetically pleasing. The internal mechanism responsible for this process is colloquially known as a *virtual camera system*. As the main avenue through which the viewer interacts with the virtual world, the effectiveness of the camera system at presenting such a view has a major influence on the viewer's satisfaction and enjoyment of the experience. A poorly implemented camera system will likely cripple the application to such an extent that excellence in graphical presentation or interactive mechanics may be insufficient to overcome it. A brief perusal of video game reviews, for example, will reveal common problems such as poor framing, cameras passing through environmental features, and so forth. These recognized problems will have a negative effect on the rating that the game receives. On the other hand, a well-designed camera system — one that presents the virtual world in an unobtrusive and easy to understand manner — allows a great interactive design to become fully realized. In light of this, it is surprising that there is so little information available to the designers and implementers of interactive camera systems.

Real-Time Cameras is aimed at expanding the knowledge of designers and programmers regarding this crucial yet often overlooked topic. While there is common ground between traditional cinematography techniques and virtual camera systems (especially, of course, with respect to non-interactive movie sequences), the dynamically changing nature of video games and other interactive real-time applications demands different approaches and solutions. Interactive application design lags behind traditional movie making in that the underlying principles of real-time camera design are still in their formative process. However, enough information is now available to establish a set of ground rules that should apply regardless of the genre or presentation style.

The fundamental design philosophy upon which this book is based may be stated quite simply:

> *An ideal virtual camera system, regardless of the genre, is notable by the lack of attention given to it by the viewer.*

If the camera system is able to present views of the virtual world that allow viewers to completely immerse themselves within the experience, it may certainly be considered successful.

Camera system design is so fundamental to the application design process that there should be production resources dedicated solely to this aspect during the application's initial design, throughout the prototyping phase, and into its final implementation. This book aims to increase awareness of the importance of this aspect of the development process, and in doing so to raise the bar for camera system quality.

The role of the camera system is to enhance the viewer's experience through its management of the camera's position, orientation, and other properties during interactive sequences, in addition to presenting non-interactive (or *cinematic*) sequences as desired by the designer or artist. Designing and engineering a general-purpose camera system capable of presenting the most varied and demanding of interactive situations in a consistently unobtrusive and appropriate manner is a demanding task indeed. It should be noted that simple changes to the position or orientation of the camera might greatly influence the viewer's perception of the virtual world; the relative size and position of characters or objects within the scene will often influence the importance given to these objects by the observer. If the viewer is unable to discern how their presence in the virtual world (sometimes referred to as an *avatar* or *player character*) will interact with other elements of the scene, the result will likely be frustration and dissatisfaction.

Thus, we may state a second maxim concerning real-time camera systems, namely:

> *Successful presentation of an interactive application is directly dependent upon the quality of the design and implementation of its camera system.*

The focus of this book is *real-time, interactive* camera systems. A clear distinction is made here between *non-interactive movies* and camera usage during actual viewer interactions. Cinematographic techniques are covered extensively elsewhere; nonetheless, knowledge of cinematography is often both desirable and pertinent. However, these techniques must be applied carefully to real-time situations.

There are two main components to virtual camera systems, interaction design and engineering design. The former is often established by a dedicated designer but must be tempered by the practicalities of the virtual environment, engine capabilities, and toolset. The latter is dependent upon the ability of the engineering staff to alter the existing technology or to create new camera systems within the usual constraints of time, quality, and performance. Regardless, the engineering tasks must take into account the interactive requirements specified by the designer; the camera system is a critical part of the interactive design and should enhance the viewer's experience rather than be seen as a technical exercise.

Much of the content of this book refers to video games and the usage of camera systems within that context. However, it should be noted that both camera design and user control play an important role in many different forms of interactive computing, not only game applications. Real-time medical imaging, virtual reality, robotics, and other related fields often require navigation through virtual environments in ways that are required to be meaningful to the observer; much of the information presented here is equally applicable to these pursuits. Indeed, even traditional movies are adopting techniques pioneered in games for pre-visualization techniques and shot composition or special effects planning. The key element of these differing fields is that they are all *interactive*, which leads us to a third maxim:

> *Real-time camera systems implicitly affect the viewer's perception of the controls used to interact with the virtual world.*

The interactions between the camera system and viewer control are important because many viewers have difficulty in understanding the spatial relationship between the projected view of the virtual world and their representation within it. The natural separation between the viewer and the projected view of the game world is difficult to overcome. However, these elements must be considered during all aspects of development to alleviate this potential problem.

Who should read this book?

Real-Time Cameras has a broad scope; it aims to cover both design and implementation issues associated with the use of cameras in games and other real-time applications. It should be noted that a successful camera system is dependent upon collaboration between designers, artists, and programmers. Each discipline is required to participate in the presentation of the game to satisfy the competing constraints of game play design, aesthetics and technical limitations.

A large portion of this book covers the theory of camera design, and while most relevant to game designers, it should prove useful to programmers involved in implementing camera systems or player control. Cinematography issues are discussed to a lesser degree, nonetheless, designers and artists may also find useful information regarding combining these techniques with real-time game play. World construction techniques that may be used to avoid potential camera implementation problems are also described. Programmers charged with implementing camera systems in both games and other real-time interactive applications should find enough information upon which to base their designs.

How to read this book

This book is divided into three main parts: Core Concepts, Design Principles, and Camera Engineering. Core Concepts provides a foundation of how virtual cameras are used within real-time applications such as video games. Design Principles expands upon this knowledge and details both the requirements and rules of thumb applicable to camera design. Camera Engineering examines individual properties of virtual cameras, including both theory and practical issues involved in camera system implementation.

Each chapter of *Real-Time Cameras* is usually divided into two types of sections: design and technical. The design sections cover the principles and theories of camera design with some light technical information where appropriate. If pertinent, detailed technical explanations are placed within a technical section as a highlighted block and may be consulted for further information if so desired. The design sections are of most interest to designers and artists, though engineers should benefit greatly from a good understanding of the theory and requirements behind camera design. The technical sections delve into the practicalities of camera system implementation by means of algorithms, pseudo-code, and some C++ code examples. Some knowledge of programming techniques will be helpful in gaining the most from these sections. Anecdotal notes on practical camera issues discovered during actual game development may be found throughout the text.

Thus, the early chapters of this book are more concerned with introductory topics and camera design principles, whereas the later chapters become generally more technical in nature, allowing the reader to tailor their reading experience as desired.

PART ONE: CORE CONCEPTS Chapter 1: Game Overview explains the basics of a typical video game update loop, and how the camera system functions within the context of the entire game. Chapter 2: Camera Fundamentals describes the basic definition of real-time cameras and how they compare to their real-world counterparts. There is a brief explanation of how the camera properties are used to generate the desired view of the game world in addition to an overview of game camera design guidelines. Although this book is primarily concerned with real-time cameras, knowledge of cinematic theory and conventions often proves useful. This is especially true since camera systems in real-time applications often have to deal with cinematic concerns whether in regular usage or within *cut-scenes* (i.e., non-interactive movie-like sequences). Chapter 3: Cinematography briefly discusses some of the main cinematographic conventions and how they may be applied within real-time applications.

PART TWO: DESIGN PRINCIPLES

The design of a camera system must take into account the desired feature set and preferred presentation style balanced with the requirements of viewer interaction. Chapter 4: Camera Design describes the factors that must be considered when determining the feature set for a camera system. The production process for designing a camera system is often quite involved, and typically requires collaboration between the disciplines of design, engineering, and art. A suggested approach for the camera design process is given, including a set of questions that may be used to guide its development. Emphasis is given to the inclusion of camera design as part of the initial interactive design, regardless of application genre. Certain types of presentation style have become associated with a particular video game genre. Chapter 5: Camera Solutions enumerates some of the more common solutions for a selection of game genres and their particular benefits. It should be noted that many of these approaches are equally valid for applications other than video games. There is also discussion of the differences in presenting single or multi-player games on a single display device. Camera scripting refers to a collection of techniques used to control the activation and timing of behavioral changes to real-time camera systems within either interactive or non-interactive sequences. These changes often correspond to pre-defined events that occur at specific times within the application. Camera scripting is also used to define and react to dynamically changing interactive elements to provide the most appropriate view of the virtual world at all times. A variety of potential solutions and functionality requirements for camera and player control scripting will be explored in Chapter 6: Camera Scripting.

PART THREE: CAMERA ENGINEERING

The desired position and orientation of the camera are major components of any camera system as they dictate the generated view of the virtual world. Chapter 7: Position and Orientation discusses a variety of ways in which these properties may be defined according to game play and aesthetic considerations. Virtual cameras are often required to move within complex environments. Determining how the camera should negotiate through these environments while balancing the game play requirements of presenting a target object in an appropriate manner is a demanding task. Chapter 8: Navigation and Occlusion discusses dynamic and pre-determined methods of achieving these goals, referred to here as *navigation*. A related topic concerns ensuring that an element of the virtual world (such as the viewer's avatar or player character, for example) remains in a viewable position regardless of how the camera is required to move. Several possible methods of both determining and avoiding this problem, known as *occlusion*, are also discussed here. Chapter 9: Motion and Collision describes ways in which the movement of the camera through the virtual world may be achieved while maintaining both continuous and smooth motion. However, such motion of the camera may still result in its collision with environmental elements. This chapter therefore covers common collision avoidance techniques as well as collision detection and resolution. The implementation of real-time cameras requires an understanding of a variety of mathematical techniques. While Chapter 10: Camera Mathematics is not a tutorial, it covers the practical use of mathematics to solve a selection of problems encountered within typical camera systems. The architectural issues involved in an actual camera system implementation, including methods that might be used to dynamically alter camera behavior according to interactive requirements, will be discussed in Chapter 11: Implementation.

APPENDICES

While cinematography has developed a language and set of terminology that is both widely used and well understood, the same is not yet true of camera usage within real-time applications. Appendix A: Glossary provides a basis for real-time camera definitions and thus hopes to improve communication between different disciplines. Appendix B: Extras includes several extra items of additional interest to readers, including a discussion of human visual perception and how it pertains to real-time camera design.

REFERENCES AND BIBLIOGRAPHY

The amount of literature available concerning camera usage in real-time applications is small but growing. Given the similarities between cameras and logic used to control other video game objects (collectively referred to as Artificial Intelligence or AI), common research into areas such as navigation and collision avoidance may be found. Indeed, robotics research from the 1980s and 1990s provides some fertile ground for exploration, especially regarding autonomous navigation through complex environments. Similarly, the medical-imaging industry has also dealt with issues regarding user interfaces and camera manipulation. Papers concerning camera usage have appeared over the years at SIGGRAPH (www.siggraph.org), usually concerning non-interactive movies or cinematography-related issues; more recently the Game Developers Conference (www.gdconf.com) has featured presentations concerned with real-time camera systems. References to relevant literature (including online resources) are provided, divided into specific categories.

ACCOMPANYING MATERIAL

Source code for a simple camera system has been developed for the Windows XP and OS X operating systems. This camera system should provide a useful test bed for developing camera theories or for a more thorough understanding of the basic principles of camera system development.

The reader is directed to the companion Web site to this book, www.realtimecameras.com. This site provides movie examples, source code, analysis of camera design in existing games, and further information regarding camera system design and implementation.

Comments regarding this book or any aspects of interactive camera systems are always welcome; contact details may be found on the companion Web site.

Core Concepts

As far as I'm concerned, if something is so complicated that you can't explain it in 10 seconds, then it's probably not worth knowing anyway.

— Calvin from "Calvin and Hobbes," January 5, 1989 (Bill Watterson).

The first three chapters of this book lay the foundations of how to describe and design camera systems for real-time applications. They provide a common vocabulary that may be used in specifying both design elements and implementation details. The first chapter gives an overview of game applications and how camera systems function within them. The second chapter examines the basic constructs used to define game cameras and their generation of a view of the game world. The third chapter lightly examines the basics of cinematography and how it might be applied to real-time applications.

Game overview

This chapter describes a broad view of the role played by a camera system within real-time applications with the example of a typical video game update cycle used for illustrative purposes. There is a brief description of the mechanisms typically used to update the game state and how a camera system integrates into the other game systems. Readers familiar with the basic concepts of a game update loop may skip this chapter.

REAL-TIME APPLICATIONS

Modern interactive real-time applications such as video games present their users with dynamic, varied experiences in a virtual world seemingly conjured out of thin air. Most users, of course, have little conception of the complex and difficult tasks involved in developing these applications. Underneath the surface, there are myriad different aspects to real-time applications, all of which must function both efficiently and in concert to present the user with a satisfying experience. Games are one of the most demanding of such applications, typically requiring both rapid updating of the game world (hence the real-time moniker), responsive player controls, and smooth, flicker-free updating of the display device. Additionally, the game world must be presented in a manner that is both appropriate to the game play requirements specified by the designer and meaningful to the player. Even more important is that the game should be *fun*.

GAME SYSTEMS

A common approach to such a large and multifaceted problem as the design and implementation of real-time applications is decomposition. It is usually possible to break the application into a number of components, each of which is of a more manageable size. Within the context of a video game, these components are often referred to as *game systems*; they each control individual aspects of the application and are collectively referred to as a *game engine*. A typical game engine might include systems such as:

- Resource management (memory usage, game state saving and restoring, model management, animation management, texture management, level data loading, etc.)
- Player control (e.g., converting controller hardware data into game commands)
- Physics simulation (a mathematical representation of physical forces and their effect on game objects, this may also encompass collision detection and resolution)
- Game object logic (the actual processes that define game play mechanics)
- Graphical user interface (the visual interface of the game information to the player)
- Camera and viewport management (controls the generation of the displayed view into the game world)
- Network communication (i.e., communication with external entities including other games or hardware devices, match-making services, and much more)
- Artificial intelligence (the mechanisms dictating game object logic; autonomous, pre-defined, or dynamic responses to game events or player input)
- Game event management (controls the designer-specified sequence of game play elements)
- Rendering (the actual process of generating the displayed view of the game world)
- Inter-object communication (used by event management and game object logic)
- Audio (management of audio-related processes varying from simple playback through effects processing and spatial positioning)
- Task management (allocates tasks to multiple processors, thread management, etc.)
- And so forth…

Several of these systems are of particular interest; namely the *camera*, *player control*, and *scripting* systems. These systems interact and combine in ways that will greatly influence the player's perception of the game. *Rendering* is a related system to the camera, but will only be covered here in light detail; the reader is referred to [Foley90] and

TECHNICAL

More details regarding the practicalities of camera system implementation can be found in Chapter 11, but a brief summary is useful here. Each of the game systems mentioned above typically has a separate implementation, sometimes referred to as a *manager*. In one form of game system, these managers may be arranged hierarchically, with an overriding game manager or *system manager* in command of all the others. This system manager typically organizes the update loop and is the central access point for the other managers; it usually tracks the elapsed time between updates and supplies that value to the other managers as required. Each manager implements and organizes everything related to that aspect of the game; an obvious example is the *camera manager*. The camera manager is the game implementation of the camera system and provides interfaces to allow other game systems to obtain information about the current state of the active camera, provide basic data used by the renderer, and so on. Each manager executes its logic to update the game objects under its control at least once per update loop. An overview of typical game system managers, showing some of their complex relationships, is shown in Figure 1.1.

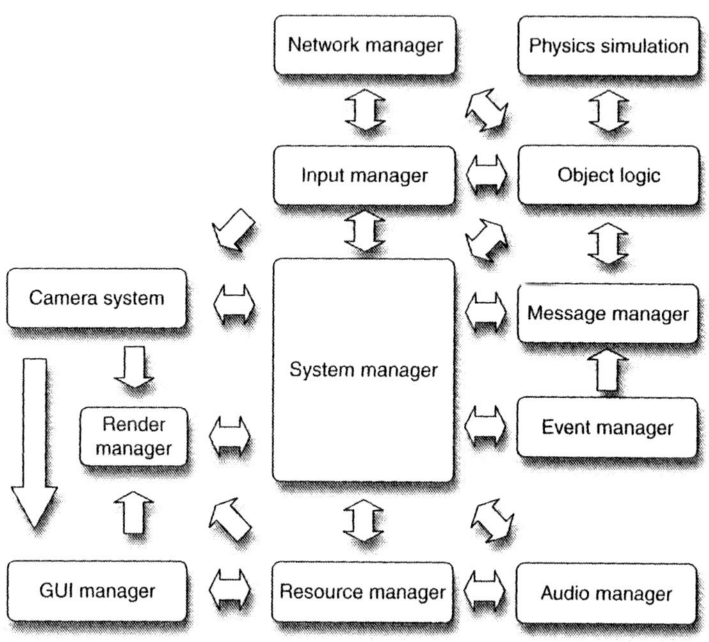

■ **FIGURE 1.1** Overview of typical game system managers and their intercommunication.

[Akenine-Möller02] for a more thorough explanation of the rendering process. A more comprehensive analysis of game architectures may be found in [Eberly04].

Before discussing the specifics of these systems, a brief overview of the methods used to update and display a real-time game may be in order. Readers familiar with these concepts may wish to skip ahead to the General Performance Issues section.

GAME UPDATE LOOP

A typical video game executes a relatively standard series of actions repeatedly during its operation; these actions may be grouped together into larger *steps* or *phases*. The activities performed within each step will vary according to changing game play requirements (and may result in dividing each step into smaller sections), but the ordering of the steps will usually remain constant (though some may be omitted at times). The complete sequence of steps to be performed is colloquially known as the *update loop*. The steps within an update loop may vary considerably depending upon the hardware and software environment provided.

One such example is network communication; for multi-player games, it is sometimes necessary to receive (or transmit) player input or positional information across a network connection. This may introduce a *network* step directly after, or as part of, the *input* step. Other console hardware may require that the graphics data be updated during a short period when the display device is not being updated (also known as the *vertical blanking* period). It may otherwise require a separate step to execute in parallel with those mentioned earlier.

There are also occasions where the steps will vary during the actual execution of the game; for example, while the game is paused or within some forms of menu display (such as the interface shown before the main game begins) it may no longer be necessary to perform object movement or logic.

While there are too many permutations to enumerate all possibilities, a high-level view of a typical update loop sequence is illustrated in Figure 1.2.

The update loop continues to repeat these steps throughout game execution, although individual steps may vary in their activities as required by the game state (e.g., actual game play vs. the game selection menu). Let us briefly examine each of these steps in turn.

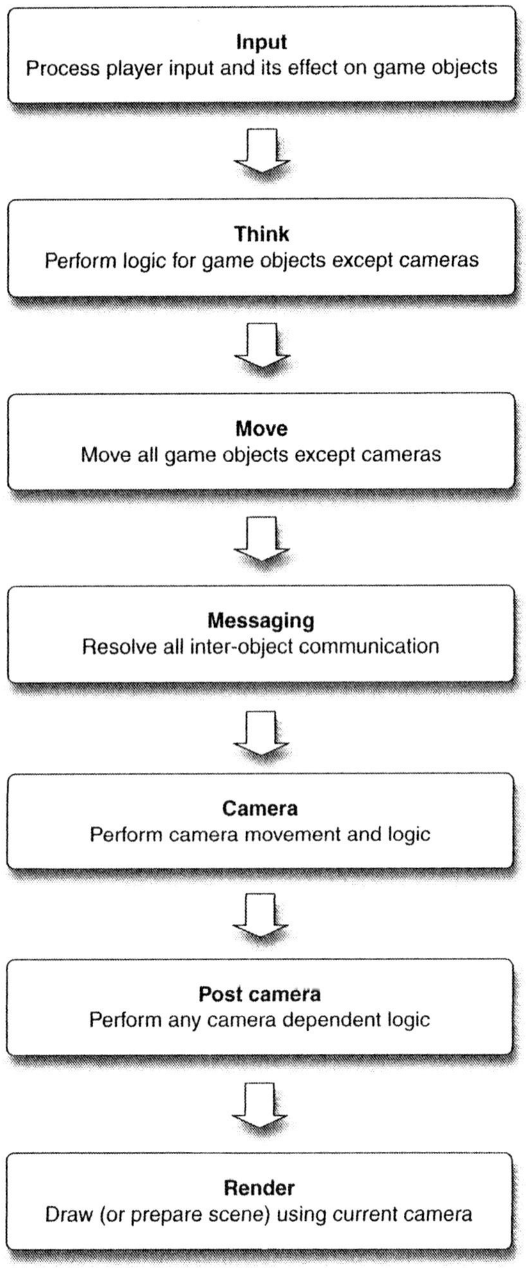

■ **FIGURE 1.2** An example of a typical game update loop.

TECHNICAL

It is important to note that the camera logic is usually executed after most other game logic within the game update loop. This ordering may be required to ensure that the camera position and orientation may correctly reflect the most up-to-date positions of game objects, especially when the camera derives its properties from another game object. However, there may still be dependency problems related to the order of operations. For example, if the message processing stage causes the game to start a "cinematic" sequence, the camera logic will be run with the new state active whereas previous game objects have yet to run their logic in that state. This effectively means that the cameras are one update in advance of the other game objects; this can be a problem when it is important that game object logic is initialized (for example, their position within the game world) before a cinematic sequence begins. There are several possible solutions for this scenario. One option might be to defer the cinematic state change until after both the camera logic and rendering has occurred (or has been initiated if executing in parallel). This solution may be generalized to include processing of all camera-related messages as the final step in the update loop (after render initialization). An alternative solution is deferring message handling until the end of the update loop.

Input

In the *input* step, controller values are read (or collated from other sources where the hardware access occurs during an interrupt handler, for example) and converted by the game engine logic into commands for the game, such as moving the player character, pausing the game, choosing menu options, and so forth. Usually the controllers are only read once per update loop, sometimes due to hardware constraints but also because typically the game logic and player movement is only performed once per frame. However, some games actually analyze the player input multiple times during the same update loop. This is only feasible (or useful) when the hardware is capable of supplying the information at a higher frequency than once per update loop. In such a situation, higher fidelity information regarding the player's intended actions might be ascertained; this information could be used to better predict player motion or simply to allow the movement or control logic of the player to run multiple times per update and thus allow finer movement or action control. The latter scheme may improve player control even if the update rate of the game is low, perhaps due to network latency.

TECHNICAL

A game system manager (referred to here as the *game object manager*) usually controls the execution of game object logic, including any prioritization or dependency determination and resolution. Two common methods used by the game object manager for amortization of game logic are *cooperative* and *preemptive multitasking*. In the former method, each game object is responsible for the amount of processor time it utilizes in any given update, and voluntarily returns control to the game object manager when it determines this has occurred. Thus it may be required that a game object must run its logic several times before making game play decisions. Alternatively, or as an additional amortization step, the game object manager may decide which game objects actually execute their logic on any given update (this is usually referred to as *load balancing*). This often requires knowledge of the relative performance cost of differing game objects. Such cost determinations may be ad hoc, pre-calculated, or dynamically analyzed and adjusted as the game executes (e.g., tracking the average amount of time required by individual game objects of a particular type or instance).

In preemptive multitasking, the game object manager interrupts the execution of a particular game object after a pre-determined period; this requires the state of the game object to be preserved and restored upon its next execution. Difficulties may arise from this approach as the state of the object is not guaranteed to be completely valid at the point that its execution is halted (for example, the position of a tracked object may have subsequently changed between logic updates on this object).

Although the logic cost of an object may be amortized over a number of update loops, the movement and collision testing of the object must still be performed at every iteration to maintain coherent motion. Parallel processing capabilities or multi-threading of tasks may introduce even more complexity and order-dependency issues.

Think

The *think* step is where a large amount of the game logic is performed. This would include any player logic dictated by the input step, artificial intelligence (AI) logic determinations for game objects, generation of game events (and possibly their handling), and so on. This step is often very processor intensive and great efforts are normally expended to find ways to amortize the cost of such game logic over successive update loops. A good example of this is AI logic. It is unusual for a game object such as an enemy character to require its behavior to change every time the game update loop is processed.

This is mainly because the enemy object is typically not required to react with this level of fidelity to be a challenging or interesting opponent; by comparison, in the real world reaction times for humans are typically measured in tenths of a second or faster, depending on the activity. Since game update loops are usually updated at least fifty or sixty times a second, we may reduce the number of times per second that each game object has its logic performed and still maintain believable reactions and behavior.

Move

The *move* step updates the physical simulation used to control changes in position and/or orientation of game objects; this step also includes collision detection and resolution. Many games use very simple techniques to derive the motion of their characters so that the performance costs may be reduced to a manageable level; even so, collision detection in particular remains a complex and difficult problem to solve efficiently. Mathematically based physical simulations of real-world behavior (that is, ones using a programmatic model of forces acting on game objects, such as gravity) are often complex and computationally expensive; they are also deeply meshed with the problems of collision detection and resolution. Yet, the rewards are often worth this cost; high visual fidelity, realistic or "expected" behavior from object interactions, plus generalized handling of movement and collisions are some of the potential benefits. As processor performance has improved, this approach has become both feasible and popular. However, care must be taken when using physical simulations to ensure that game play is not adversely affected in the quest for a realistic simulation of physical properties. Truth be told, realism does not always equate to *fun*.

Messaging

Messages are a generalized mechanism typically used to communicate between game objects and either other game objects or game system managers. They are frequently used to signify an important game event has occurred that requires changes to the state of objects or the game itself. Typical examples might include the player character becoming submerged (and thus changing its movement characteristics or camera behavior), activation of a new game object, unlocking a door, death of an enemy, completion of resource loading, animation events (such as a footstep), collisions between game objects, and so forth. Often these messages are controlled and specified via a *scripting system*; in this way

TECHNICAL

Messages are also a mechanism to ensure that game events do not change game state until a specified time or until they are synchronized with other game events. Some object state changes must occur immediately within the *think* step as they are used to alter the game logic of the object in question; others must be deferred until all game objects have performed their logic (to ensure consistent behavior of all objects during that update loop). Theoretically, each game object should run its logic and move in parallel with all other game objects; but the practicalities of computer representation mean that an implicit (or sometimes explicit) ordering of these operations occurs. The order in which game objects execute their logic therefore imparts a default ordering to messages queued for delivery. Alternatively, this ordering may be specified by a prioritization value for each message; the queued messages may then be sorted before delivery as appropriate. Some game engines eschew staged delivery of game messages and instead process all pending messages directly after the game logic for each object has been executed. More information regarding messaging may be found in Chapter 6.

game designers may specify and control the behavior of objects to shape game play elements such as puzzles, lay out cinematic sequences, and so forth. Naturally, messages may also be generated directly via the game code or object logic; for example, when two game objects collide.

The *messaging* step is not always present in the update loop; messages may sometimes be handled immediately upon being sent (usually during the *think* step) or may be deferred until after the game logic has been executed, when all pending messages will be delivered. Messages can be useful in resolving problems regarding the sequence in which game objects have their logic performed. The order in which objects have their game logic executed in the *think* step is not always explicitly specified, and may in fact be based upon the time when the game objects were created. Additionally, messaging systems may allow easier decoupling of interfaces between different game systems; they may also simplify recording of game events that are sometimes used for demo replaying, remote duplication during multi-player games, or simply for debugging purposes.

Camera

The *camera* step is of the most interest to readers of this book because it concerns the majority of all camera logic in the game. During the camera step, each of the active game cameras will be allowed to execute the logic required to update its position and orientation, as dictated by its behavior and specified properties. Changes to the current behavior of the camera, or activation of a different camera type, will be handled here before the current scene is rendered. A brief summary of this step might include the following actions:

- Remove any inactive cameras.
- Activate new cameras as required by game state changes (e.g., player mode) or scripting choices.
- Determine if the camera used to render the world should change due to scripting or game logic.
- Perform logic for currently active cameras, including all movement and reorientation.
- Initiate changes to the main camera, including starting or completing interpolation if required.
- Update the player *control reference frame* (used to dictate the relationship between player controls and movement of the player character, see Chapter 2), based on the main camera position and orientation.
- Construct the transformation matrices required to render the views of the game world, including any special effects such as camera shaking, field of view, or aspect ratio changes, etc.

The final goal of the camera logic is to construct the information necessary to produce one or more views of the game world. Additionally, it must supply data to other game objects that may be required to perform logic relative to the orientation and position of the active cameras. Note that camera logic may still be performed even if the camera in question is not directly used to generate a rendered view of the game world; a typical situation where this might occur would be during interpolation between two active cameras.

Post-Camera

After the camera logic has been executed, there is often a need to update game elements that are dependent upon changes to the camera system state. An example of this might be the depiction of a player's weapon in a first person game. In such a game, the weapon is often positioned and oriented relative to the viewpoint of the player character; thus, it is dependent upon the position and orientation of the first person camera. Therefore, any camera transform dependent logic is executed after the cameras have been updated to avoid any potential *lag* (i.e., a discrepancy in position and/or orientation) that would otherwise be introduced.

Render

Usually the last step in the update loop, the *render* step, will actually produce the view of the world appropriate to the current game state or send data to the hardware to allow this rendering to take place. Thus, it must occur after all other game and camera logic has taken place; even so, the view that is generated on the display device will actually be seen during the *next* update loop. The player's view of the game is therefore *delayed by one update* from the time it actually happened.

The render step may involve the updating of several views of the game world; one form these may take is independent *viewports*, as typically used in multi-player games. Each viewport represents a portion of the output device used to display a view of the game world associated with a game camera. These may overlap (for example, to display a picture-in-picture effect such as a rear-view mirror in a racing game) and thus require an explicit ordering to their rendering.

Rendering of a camera view is not always output in the form of a distinct viewport (whether full-screen or not). Sometimes it is required to render a view into a *texture*; that is, a camera view is used within the generation of a different camera view of the game world. One example of this technique occurs when a player character is observing a view of the game world on a display device within the game environment such as a computer monitor. The view on the monitor is formed by rendering into the texture used by its game model, creating the effect of a real-time view of the game world within the viewport used to display the player character. This technique is usually computationally expensive, as it requires the traversal of two scene hierarchies to determine what parts of the game world should be rendered (assuming that the views differ, of course); it should therefore be used sparingly. More details on the process of constructing a view of the game world are covered in Chapter 2.

GENERAL PERFORMANCE ISSUES

Game applications continue to demand high levels of performance in many aspects of their presentation including the graphical approach used as well as the numbers of seemingly autonomous game objects that are used to populate the game world, whether or not they directly interact with the player character. Given the limited resources available, programmers and designers are constantly working to balance the demands of creating a believable, fun experience for the player with the practicalities of implementation within real-time limitations. Common constraints found in real-time game applications include:

- Memory restrictions
- Processor performance
- Graphical processing capabilities
- Display device resolution
- Controller functionality
- Network latency and bandwidth

A full discussion of all of these issues is beyond the scope of this book; however, it is true to say that simpler solutions typically cost less in performance (there are naturally technical exceptions to this). Camera systems may easily become very demanding in terms of performance, especially because of their propensity to test the game environment to solve navigation problems.

For camera design concerns, *Occam's Razor* certainly applies; this may be paraphrased as *the simplest camera solution is usually the best*. Aesthetically, simpler camera movement or orientation changes are easier for the viewer to understand. Simpler here does not necessarily imply simpler to implement, although that may indeed follow. Rather, the concern is that viewers should easily understand the relationship between the camera presentation of the world and game play requirements, such as the control of their character. Additionally, simpler camera solutions hopefully have less special situations that must be handled and may be easier to formulate, test, and debug.

THE CAMERA SYSTEM

The camera system is typically responsible for management of all camera-related features of the game. This often encompasses both cinematic sequences and real-time game play. Depending upon the particular game architecture, it may also involve the drawing (or *rendering*) of the game world. More succinctly, the camera system defines how the game world is presented to the player under a variety of different situations.

The camera system works with other game systems and may well provide or modify information used by other systems including rendering of the current world view, mapping of controller input to player motion, and so forth. Additionally, the camera system often provides mechanisms

TECHNICAL

The performance demands of a camera system may vary considerably upon the chosen presentation style or behaviors. First person cameras, for example, typically have very low performance requirements as their testing of the game environment is usually limited. Third person cameras, on the other hand, often have significant processor usage when navigating through complex environments, or testing for potential collisions with other game objects or the environment. Ways to reduce these costs are discussed in the third part of this book. The amount of expected performance usage for a camera system is debatable and subject to the requirements of the game design; a reasonable rule of thumb might be that no more than 5 percent of the processor time should be devoted to camera logic. Your mileage will certainly vary. Alternatively, consider the camera system as a complex game object akin to those executing specialized AI functionality (aka a "Boss" creature), and use their performance costs as an approximate guide. Since camera systems are active throughout the game's execution, their performance requirements should be considered as significant and frequently reassessed.

by which the designers may dynamically alter camera behavior according to game play or player requirements. Such behavioral variations are often required by player character state changes (e.g., the character alters its size or movement characteristics), environmental changes (e.g., moving from open to confined spaces), and so forth. Altering the camera behavior dynamically also requires that the camera system manage prioritization of competing camera behavior requests.

To summarize, the responsibilities of the camera system are included in the list below.

- Management of all active cameras and ensuring their logic is updated regularly, prioritization is observed, etc.
- Control the addition or removal of new cameras, as required by scripting or other game state changes.
- Allow the overriding of camera behavior or properties as they may vary according to the changes in game play.
- Provide reference frames used for player control.
- Handle all aspects of non-interactive cinematic movie sequences.
- Provide control over camera display properties that affect rendering including field of view, aspect ratio, and so forth.
- Manage and update viewport data as required by the graphical user interface.

- Gather view frustum information used by the render engine to display the current worldview(s).
- Offer optional debugging capabilities including camera status information, user control over an independent debugging camera, or to replay a sequence of events viewed from a variety of positions.

The design and implementation of such camera systems is the focus of this book, and will be covered in detail in later chapters.

CONTROLS

The interpretation of how the game controller is used to determine the motion or actions performed by the player character is of great importance. As one of the main interaction mechanisms between the player and the game, the control system should ideally provide a consistent and meaningful interface to the player. Controller hardware may vary considerably in the functionality provided or physical arrangement of the controls, both of which add to the challenge of determining an appropriate usage of the controller.

Player control is often closely connected to the camera system as the spatial relationship between the player and the camera greatly influences the players' perception of how their character is controlled. This, of course, is dependent upon the genre and presentation style of the game. Games that offer a third person viewpoint, for example, are prone to difficulties whenever the camera position is instantaneously repositioned. First person games often have to determine control schemes that allow for player movement at the same time as manipulating the orientation of the camera (often referred to as *free-look*). One of the more common game play techniques combining camera orientation changes with player movement is that of *circle strafing*, a method of moving around an opponent's position in a circular arc while maintaining an orientation toward them (thus allowing the player to shoot toward or ahead of their opponent). This movement is achieved by combining a sideways motion (i.e., a sidestep) with a turn in the opposite direction, as shown in Figure 1.3. By varying the ratio of these controls, it is possible to vary the radius of the arc of motion. This relatively advanced technique requires a degree of finesse from the player; it is necessary to coordinate manipulation of the controls with the reaction of the player character (and camera) provided by the game engine.

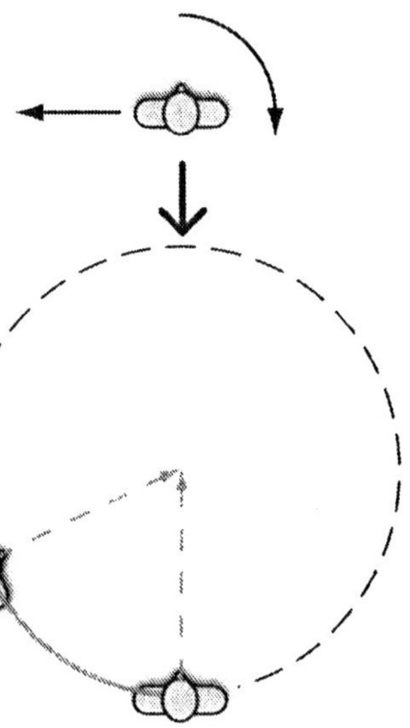

■ **FIGURE 1.3** Circle strafing allows movement of the player character relative to another object or position in the game world.

Similarly, many third person games also offer the ability for players to dynamically influence the position and/or orientation of the camera, possibly independently of their player character. The relationship between the player controls and the movement of the character is referred to as the *control reference frame* and is discussed in Chapter 2.

The actual physical controller hardware may also affect the choice of camera presentation style. For example, in the case of computer-based role-playing games, access to a mouse and keyboard may offer interface choices that are not as readily available on game consoles. Because of this, computer users often have differing expectations of both their control over the player character and camera positioning than console-based players. An in-depth discussion of controller hardware is beyond the scope of this book, but camera designers should be aware of the relationship between player controls and camera usage.

SCRIPTING

An important aspect for many games is the ability to dynamically respond to game play events or other changes in the game state. Similarly, there are many cases where it is necessary to ensure that the game state changes in a consistent or pre-determined manner depending upon the occurrence of game events. A common example of such a change is in response to player actions, such as entering an area or manipulating an object. An often-used term for this facility is *scripting*, and it is likely derived from the concept of a *movie script*. A movie script is, of course, the document that specifies the sequence of events, cinematography techniques, and dialogue to be depicted in a non-interactive movie. In a similar vein, game scripting can be considered as a mechanism to control or specify the events or behaviors that define the game play experience for the player, which may also include the construction of non-interactive movie sequences. Game scripting is probably more difficult than traditional film script production in many respects, merely because of the interactive nature of the medium. It must allow for a disparate variety of player actions instead of (or sometimes in addition to) a simple, linear experience such as a non-interactive movie.

Scripting is not limited to simply unfolding the game "story" to the player. It may also be used to change the ways in which the player interacts with the game, including (but not limited to) the actual relationship between the physical controller and the player character. An obvious example is the disabling of specific player controls. Because player control is often dependent upon the camera system, this is of relevance to readers of this book. Of greater importance is the ability to change how the game is presented to the player in response to player actions, or specifically to present a satisfactory view of the game within confined or complex environments.

To this end, the camera system will frequently provide facilities to allow designer-specified control of camera motion, positioning, orientation, and other properties at both a game-wide level or within defined areas that specifically override or change camera behaviors. Detailed information about scripting solutions is covered in Chapters 5 and 6.

Scripting of game events or camera behaviors may seemingly imply a textual (or programming-like) interface for the designer, but is certainly not the only solution, as will be seen later. Care should be taken to provide a simple mechanism that is both easily understood by designers and straightforward to use. Scripting systems are often susceptible to *feature creep*; that is, an ever-increasing list of desirable features that greatly extend the development time required for its completion. Additionally, they are sometimes forced to solve complex problems that may be better suited to programming environments and their access to the internal game systems (as well as generally superior debugging capabilities).

■ SUMMARY

In this chapter we have examined an overview of the basic components of a typical real-time application and how a camera system might function within such a context. The sequence governing the actions performed by such an application is known as the update loop and might be considered as a series of discrete steps. The ordering and presence of these steps is variable, sometimes even within different updates of the same application. An example of how these steps may be applied to a video game was outlined earlier in this chapter.

The same principles outlined in this chapter would also apply to other forms of interactive applications although some of the steps may not be present. It is important to note that camera logic typically occurs toward the end of the update loop, after all other game objects have performed their own logic; however, there is often a need for further camera-dependent logic to execute after the camera.

The responsibilities of a camera system were enumerated although it was recognized that the functionality requirements vary according to the nature of the application or the environment in which it executes. A brief discussion of user controls and game event scripting illustrated that camera system logic is interwoven and dependent upon these other important aspects of game play.

Camera fundamentals

This chapter describes the fundamentals of *real-time cameras* including definitions of the basic types of *game camera*, how they compare to *real-world cameras*, and their common properties.

What do we really mean by real-time cameras? After all, the player is simply presented with a view of the world by the game. What could be difficult about that? We need to understand that the control of game cameras is important because it fundamentally defines how the player experiences the game. Consider this: The player only sees the portion of the game world presented to them by the current game camera. If the position or orientation of the camera prevents the player from adequately viewing their character or the direction in which it is moving, or alternatively, if the movement and reorientation of the camera is unstable or jittery, the result will be player dissatisfaction. It is also important to bear in mind the nature of the display medium. We are presenting a limited two- or three-dimensional view of a virtual world by projecting it (literally and figuratively) onto a 2D plane or screen. This has obvious parallels with film and cinematography, even though in our case the view is generated in real time and has usually differing aesthetic requirements (i.e., game play vs. cinematography).

Game cameras have an additional critical impact upon game play as their position or orientation may greatly affect the player's perception of how their character is controlled. When game cameras are implemented effectively, they are unobtrusive, transparent to the player, and an aid to game play.

REAL-WORLD CAMERAS

Real-world cameras and their properties often form the basis upon which *game cameras* are founded. For the purposes of this book, we are mostly interested in presenting continuous motion rather than still photographs, although there are cases where knowledge of such static photographic composition is certainly applicable (e.g., the *rule of thirds*).

Since most viewers are familiar with cinematographic conventions and other real-world camera properties (whether they are consciously aware of it or not), games often strive to reproduce these effects. A selection of properties affecting the view provided by a real-world camera might include:

- Lens type (e.g., anamorphic, zoom, fisheye, etc.)
- Capture method (optical with film stock or digital)
- Film stock (as appropriate, including width of film such as 35mm vs. 70mm, film grain, light sensitivity, etc.)
- Capture rate (typically 24 frames per second for movies, though sometimes as high as 96 frames per second)
- Exposure of film (perhaps over- or underexposed based upon the shutter speed)
- Projection method (e.g., digital image projection vs. traditional film projection)
- Aspect ratio (the ratio of the projection device dimensions, width divided by height)

Representation of these properties within interactive real-time applications has been restricted in the past due to technology limitations including processor performance and rendering capabilities. As graphics and main processor performance increase, more resources may be devoted to simulation of these properties. Non-interactive movie sequences that are generated within the game engine (as opposed to merely replayed from a series of stored images) may have sufficient control over performance requirements to allow some of these effects to be applied.

The advent of *shader languages* and other advanced rendering techniques have led to the simulation of many aspects of real-world cameras. However, the actual physical means by which a real-world camera captures images is quite different from the calculated view of the world generated by a game camera. Pre-rendered computer-generated cinematic sequences such as those found in movies often attempt to re-create the paths of rays of light through the camera lens and their absorption by the film stock (known as *ray tracing*). Rendering of real-time cameras typically uses a mathematical technique where a representation of the game world is projected onto a two-dimensional plane to form its image.

Game cameras may use a simulated model of the physical world to calculate how the atmosphere and reflection or refraction caused by surfaces or barriers affect the path and properties of these light rays, at least in a relatively crude manner. These and other rendering technologies are utilized to generate a view of an artificial world simulating what a human might see. Real-time applications such as games adopt a variety of short cuts and approximations to present a view of the virtual world that may still achieve a high degree of visual fidelity. However, as rendering performance increases it is likely that physical simulation approaches will supersede polygonal representations. The reader is referred to [Pharr04] or [Akenine-Möller02] for more detail concerning these techniques.

Real-time game cameras have a number of advantages not present in real cameras, although some of these are counter to expected camera behavior, as we will see later. Real-world cameras have an established set of conventions regarding their usage that has become accepted over a significant period. These conventions, known as *cinematography,* describe the movement of the camera, the ways the camera subjects should be positioned within its view, and methods of transitioning between seemingly different scenes. Furthermore, divergence from these conventions (whether intentional or not) can be disconcerting for the viewer in subtle ways.

Cinematographic conventions should usually be observed when trying to re-create the appearance and behavior of real-world cameras, specifically when implementing so-called "cinematic" sequences. Within regular game play, it is not always the case, however, that regular cinematography is either appropriate or may even succeed.

With the advent of computer-generated effects within the most mainstream of films, as well as the adoption of digital capture technologies, the difference between game cameras and real-world cameras is rapidly decreasing. Motion tracking data are often used to duplicate real-world camera motion when replicating a scene to insert computer-generated effects seamlessly. Lighting and other scene information is usually captured and may be used to further cement the link between generated and real-world scenes. It is relatively commonplace for entire films to be post-processed to change lighting conditions, remove film stock blemishes, insert digital characters, and so forth. There are instances within televised sports where physical cameras are adopting placement and movement simulating the views seen within video games (e.g., cameras mounted upon inflatable blimps or moving along wires suspended above a football field). Similarly, techniques from real-time applications are being applied to *pre-visualization*; that is, advance planning of real-world camera shots or previewing of generated cinematic sequences before committing to lengthy rendering.

Usage and properties

Chapter 3 discusses basic cinematographic techniques and how they relate to real-time camera usage; for a more thorough understanding, the reader is referred to [Hawkins05], [Arijon91], and related works. Some of the most pertinent aspects of real-world cameras (specifically, movie cameras) include:

- **Lack of interactivity.** Within movies, each scene is always presented in the same manner and cannot be changed by the viewer. This allows scene-specific solutions to disguise the shortcomings of current technology or to further increase suspension of disbelief. It is simply not possible for viewers to manipulate the camera and so they cannot produce views inconsistent with that desired by the film director.

- **Pre-determined camera viewpoints.** There is an absolute control of the aesthetics of camera subject placement, which can be used to elicit an emotional response in the viewer or to ensure that a particular event is observed. Established techniques are implicitly understood by the majority of viewers and can be used to great effect in this regard. The camera may also be placed to fool the viewer into perceiving that an optical illusion is real (e.g., *forced perspective*, as detailed in Chapter 3).

- **Camera lenses.** A variety of camera lenses can be used to enhance cinematographic elements or distort the view of the world, including variable shifting of focus between objects of interest, often referred to as *depth of field*. Note that these effects may also be applied as a post-processing operation (see below in this list).

- **Scene transitions.** Cross fading, wipes, transitions, and other "standard" cinematic effects are often applied when changing between scenes of movies. Since these effects are implemented during the editing phase of filmmaking, they may be tailored to the particular usage or the desired emotional statement (e.g., to emphasize a particular character within a scene). Wipes, for example, are often matched to camera motion such as a horizontal pan. Since many of such effects are now computer generated, the differences between real-world cameras and their interactive equivalents have been greatly reduced (though performance requirements may still preclude some effects from being used in real-time applications).

- **Film exposure.** Motion blur is present in real-world cameras depending on the length of time that each film frame is exposed to light. Since the camera captures the scene during the entire time that its *aperture* is open, the exposure time of the film stock may result in a subject's position changing during the exposure process. This results in a blurred image of the subject according to its direction of motion; this effect tends to emphasize the subject's motion when the film is finally projected.
- **Post-processing effects.** These might include tinting or color modifications to the original footage in addition to established editing techniques (e.g., to apply transitions between scenes). Since such effects are applied before the film is projected, there are few consequences other than, perhaps, the time or effort required to apply them. Some post processing may require that the original film stock be digitally captured.

Movie projection

Movies and games share some commonality in how the final images are displayed to the viewer. In the case of film projection in movie theaters, the physical process of displaying the film frames in succession faces some limitations not present when using digital technology (whether for games or movies stored in digital formats).

With physical film projected onto a screen, the image is formed by projecting a bright light through the film and focused on a flat surface (i.e., the screen) via a lens. Since each frame must be displayed by itself (and in sequence), it is necessary to turn off the light or otherwise prevent the projection while the film is advanced between frames (e.g., by means of a synchronized shutter). If this process occurs slowly, a flickering effect will be viewed, as the eye perceives the blackness as part of the sequence. In practice, it has been found that while an update rate of 24 frames per second is sufficient to simulate motion effectively, a rate of 48 frames per second is necessary to eliminate the potential flickering caused by this display process.

Recent advances in display technology are changing movie projection. With the advent of the capability to store entire movies in digital format at a resolution approximating or exceeding that of film stock, digital projection has become a viable option. Such projection technology shares many common features with the methods used to display video games. Aside from the usual benefits of digital media (e.g., longevity and consistent quality), these projection techniques offer the potential for more exotic three-dimensional effects without requiring viewers to wear special glasses. It also removes the flickering problem inherent in film projection completely (since consecutive frames may be projected instantaneously, often using a *progressive scan display*). Digital film projections often require high resolution and refresh rates since the displayed imagery is physically large. Thus, digital projection results in an improved viewing experience when compared to older film projection technologies. At the time of writing, however, the technology for digital movie projection is expensive and as yet not in common use.

GAME CAMERAS

Game cameras are abstract constructs that define the way in which we present a view of the game world to the player; although they are called cameras, they actually share functionality of both real-world cameras and projectors. As you might expect, they must specify a number of properties regarding the position and orientation of the viewpoint within the game world. More important, the *presentation style* dictates how the game world is projected (or *rendered*) onto the display device. Other rendering properties might include *field of view*, *aspect ratio*, and so forth.

We may also consider the ways in which the camera reacts to player motion and other game play elements, commonly referred to as the *camera type* or *behavior*. The camera behavior influences the determination of the desired position and orientation of the camera in addition to the actual motion and reorientation of the camera within the camera world. These properties are fundamental in specifying how the game world is presented to the player.

Several defining features can be used to differentiate the myriad of camera behaviors available for use in games. The simplest of these is whether game play occurs while the game camera is active; this distinction is made by referring to the camera type as *cinematic* or *interactive*.

Cinematic cameras within games share many characteristics with their real-world counterparts; the most important is that the player or other game objects are typically unable to influence how the camera presents its view of the game world. Behaviors exhibited by a real-world camera are often replicated in the game version. The same rules of cinematography apply with an added bonus; game cameras may move or behave in ways that real-world cameras may not (although this should be handled with care since viewers are often not very familiar with such behaviors). In the same manner, cinematic cameras usually display their scenes in the same way every time they are used; on occasion it may be desired to change elements of the scene according to the game state (such as the presence of characters or their appearance), but typically the composition and other aspects remain constant.

Often ancillary presentation effects are changed when using cinematic cameras, as an additional cue to the player that they no longer have control over their character. Changes are sometimes applied to the aspect ratio of the rendered viewport (compared to that of the display device) to emphasize the non-interactive nature of cinematic cameras.

Interactive cameras' main distinguishing characteristic from cinematic cameras is that they may change their behavior in response to real-time game events, whether dictated by the player's actions or some other element of the game. Interactive cameras have a more difficult task in that the actions performed by the player (or other game objects) are infinitely variable, as are the situations in which they occur. Thus, interactive cameras must compensate for changes in game play to present the most appropriate view of the game world at any given time, which is often a demanding task.

While both interactive and cinematic cameras share many properties, this book is primarily concerned with the design and implementation of *interactive* cameras. To this end, unless specified otherwise all references to cameras are actually interactive ones.

As mentioned, game cameras are fortunate in having a number of features that are difficult or impossible to duplicate with real-world cameras. The most important difference, of course, is that game cameras are inherently interactive and may change dynamically in response to game play situations to present the most appropriate view of the game. Alas, this is also a pitfall in that many of the short cuts or tricks applied in film (such as scale changes for emotional impact) often elude games during interactive sequences.

Some of the game camera specific properties are included in the list below.

- Game cameras duplicate functionality of both real-world cameras and projectors.
- No physical presence is required for a game camera, allowing motion in spaces that would not be possible with real cameras.

This includes transitions to and from the point of view of the player, passing through obstructions, instantaneous repositioning, and so forth.

- Camera behavior or properties may change dynamically in response to the requirements of game play.
- Different projections of the game world onto the display device may be used to present the same world data in unique ways according to game play need or aesthetic requirements.
- Lighting and rendering filters are changeable according to game requirements or designer whims.
- A greater variety of transitions between cameras and scenes are possible.
- Scene rendering can use special effects to enhance or exaggerate elements of the scene in response to game events.

Basic terminology

At this point, it would be useful to determine some basic terminology to describe game cameras and related matters. While we can adopt many terms from cinematography, game cameras encompass some unique characteristics that require new definitions. It is common to hear terms such as *first person camera* and *third person camera* used when describing camera systems, but to what do they really refer? Are they truly as distinct as their names suggest? There have been very few clear guidelines for describing real-time camera systems, and some current terminology is less than descriptive. Here we will establish definitions for basic camera system functionality; further definitions will be found in subsequent chapters and are summarized in the glossary.

Camera system

The term camera system refers to several distinct elements that are combined to allow the game to control how the virtual world is presented to the player. It is a major component of the *game engine* described in Chapter 1. The main components of a camera system are as follows.

- Management of active game cameras and transitions between them
- Application of specific behaviors dictating the positioning, motion, and orientation of cameras
- Control over changing camera behaviors based on game play requirements

- Generation of information used by the graphics engine to render views of the game world
- Control of reference frames used for player control

These topics are covered in detail in later chapters.

Game camera

An abstract representation of a game entity that contains sufficient information to determine the position and orientation of a view of the game world. Game cameras often include properties that dictate how their desired position and orientation within the world should be determined (e.g., a target object to track). In some cases the game camera contains everything that is necessary to construct a view of the game world including field of view and other rendering information; alternatively this information may be held in other structures such as *viewports*.

Presentation style

The method used to project a view of the game world onto the display device, often simply referred to as 2D or 3D camera systems. See the next section Camera Behavior for more details on their characteristics.

Camera behavior

The combination of camera properties (such as the desired position, field of view, movement characteristics, etc.) used to dictate the displayed view of the game world.

First person camera/third person camera

These terms actually refer to different types of *camera behavior*. In some cases, they are synonymous with the *presentation style*. There is often no difference in how these different behaviors might be handled internally by the camera system, other than the position (and possibly orientation) of the camera in relation to the player character. It is also possible that the rendering characteristics will differ. A first person camera typically offers a restricted subset of third person camera functionality, although player perception might suggest otherwise. Figure 2.1 illustrates typical camera positions and the associated views. See the section View Generation for more information on these types of camera behaviors.

Cinematic versus interactive cameras

By definition, games are an interactive medium. Thus, most of our concerns regarding camera design and implementation are concerned

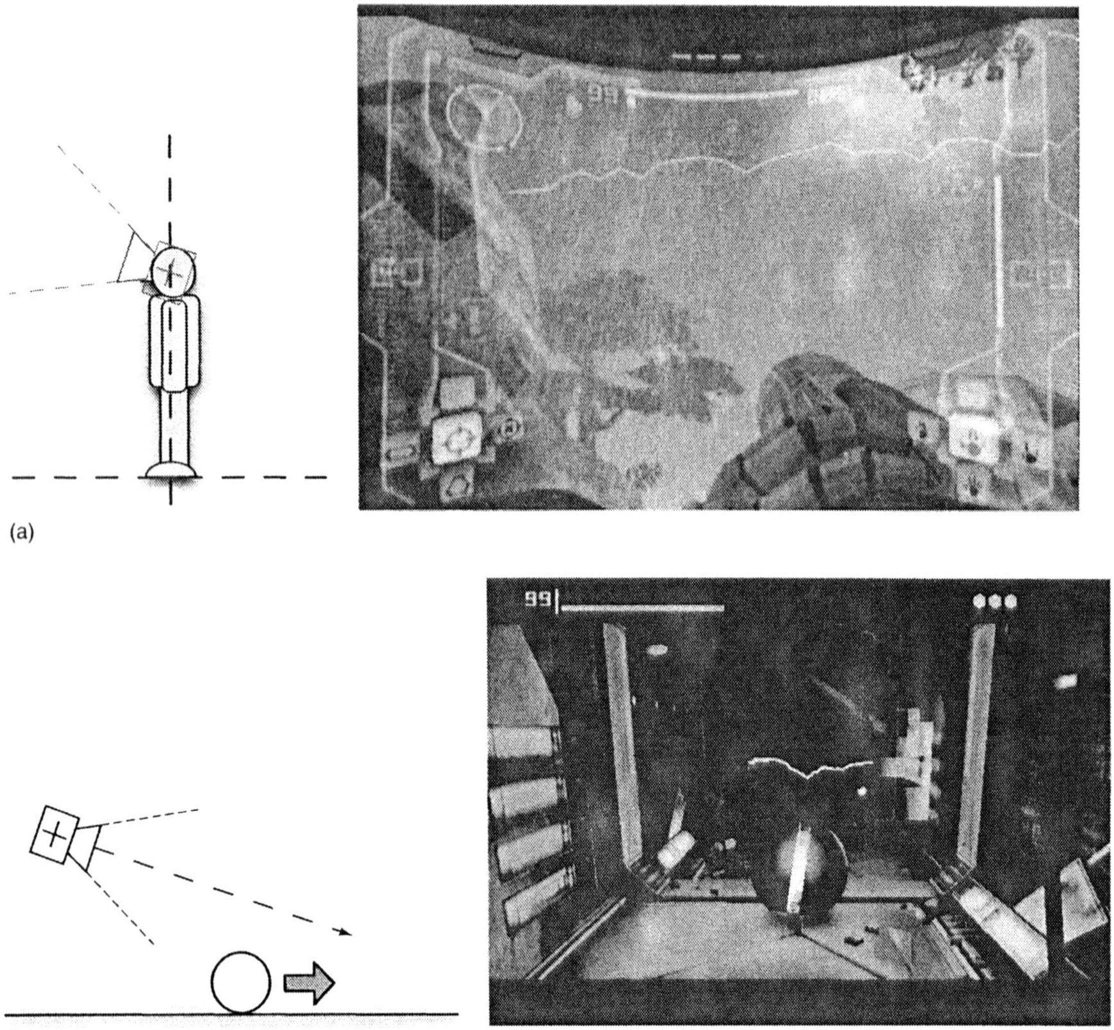

(a)

(b)

■ **FIGURE 2.1** (a) First person camera position and view. (b) Third person camera position and view. Retro Studios Inc. Metroid Prime 2: Echoes. Published by Nintendo, 2004. Nintendo Gamecube.

with interactive cameras, that is, cameras whose behavior varies according to dynamically changing game play situations. Cinematic sequences are certainly found in games, and directly correspond to their real-world equivalents, including the design rules that apply to them.

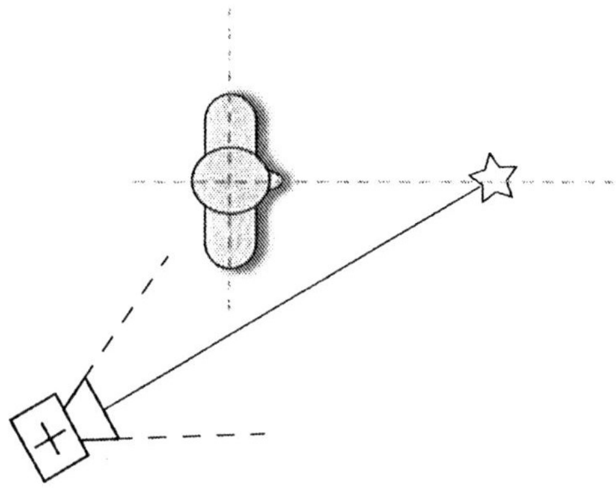

■ **FIGURE 2.2** The look-at position for a third person camera is often distinct from the target object.

Look-at position

The desired orientation of the camera may be defined in several different ways; a frequently used technique is to define a position relative to a target object (i.e., dependent upon the orientation and position of the object) toward which the camera will reorient. As seen in Figure 2.2, in the case of a third person camera, the look-at position can be separate from the target object.

Desired position

The desired position defines a position in world coordinates toward which the camera intends to move. The actual determination of this position is varied and covered in detail in Chapter 7.

Orientation

Orientation is a representation of the current direction of the camera, as specified in world coordinates. It also defines the viewing space of the camera. This includes a representation of the through-the-lens view and the rotation of the view around that direction. Orientation may be specified in many different ways, examples of which are detailed in Chapter 7; it is often considered as three components, as shown in Figure 2.3: *yaw*, *pitch*, and *roll*.

Yaw

The horizontal orientation of the camera typically specified as an angular rotation around the world up-axis.

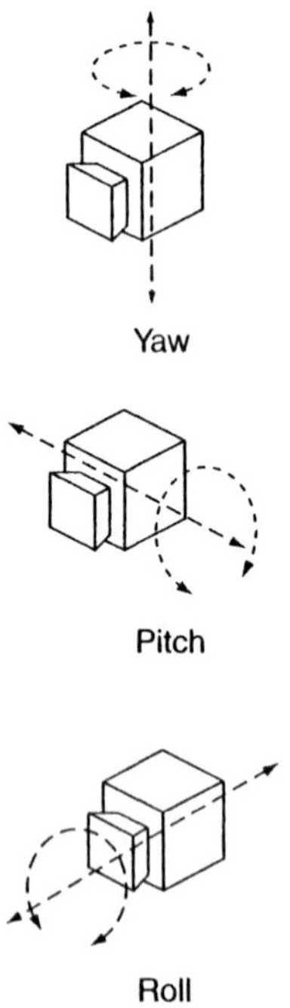

■ FIGURE 2.3 Yaw, pitch, and roll.

Pitch

The vertical orientation of the camera, equivalent to rotation around its right axis and is otherwise known as *tilt*.

Roll

Rotation of the camera around its forward direction is sometimes referred to as *Dutch tilt*.

Desired orientation

The preferred *orientation* of the camera is according to its behavior type; the camera is constantly seeking toward this orientation via *rotation*. The orientation of the camera is sometimes synchronized to its desired orientation; thus, it may not require any rotation to be applied.

Rotation

This is the change in *orientation* of a camera over time, often described as an angular quantity per second.

View frustum

This is a way of defining the portion of the game world viewable by a particular combination of camera and viewport, and is described in more detail later in this chapter.

Viewport

A *viewport* is a game data structure corresponding to a portion of the display device used to show the game world as seen from a specific game camera. Viewports often vary in shape and size, possibly dynamically changing as the game is running. They may overlap other viewports or graphical elements (e.g., a rear-view mirror in a racing game drawn on top of the regular game viewport) and thus require an explicit ordering of rendering. *Viewports* are not necessarily constructed as simple rectangular shapes; they may require additional rendering steps before being output to the render process: for example, a mask applied to composite the viewport within a previously drawn graphical element. Multi-player games implemented on a single display device typically utilize unique viewports for each player (which may vary in size or position according to the number of players, player character size, etc.).

Field of view

Typically, the field of view (or FOV) refers to the angle between the upper and lower limits of the view frustum, thus defining the vertical extent of the projected view of the game world. Alternatively, the FOV may be defined as a horizontal angle (frequently within rendering software used by artists), so care must be taken to ensure that consistency in usage is maintained. Conversions between horizontal and vertical FOV are made by taking into account the *aspect ratio*. Chapter 10 explains a method for converting horizontal FOV into vertical FOV and vice versa.

Aspect ratio

This is the ratio of the horizontal *viewport* size to the vertical viewport size. For regular full-screen viewports on *standard definition televisions* (SDTV), this is usually 1.33 (i.e., a ratio of 4:3). For *widescreen* or *high-definition televisions* (HDTV), this is 1.78 (i.e., 16:9). The aspect ratios used in film projection vary but two of the most common are 1.85 (*CinemaScope*) and 2.35 (also known as *anamorphic*). The aspect ratio is used with the FOV to define the portion of the game world that may be viewed. An extremely detailed explanation of video standards, aspect ratio, and other related matters may be found in [Poynton02].

The aspect ratio of the rendered view of the game world may not always match that of the display device. For example, a widescreen aspect ratio is often adopted to imply a lack of interactivity due to its similarity to film projection formats (regardless of the physical display device's aspect ratio). Figure 2.4a–c shows comparisons of several common aspect ratios and their relationships to standard display devices.

Refresh or frame rate

The *refresh rate* or *frame rate* (sometimes *update rate*) typically measures the number of times per second that the display device is updated by the hardware, though it may also refer to the rate at which game logic is updated. Ideally, this rate is constant regardless of the amount of graphical detail or other processor requirements of the game, but it is dependent upon the game. Usually this updating is synchronized with the physical updating of the display device, even on modern gaming systems that allow game logic to be executed parallel to graphical updating. Some games eschew this synchronization, usually if the graphical update rate exceeds the fixed rate on a regular basis. The consequence of this is an unpleasant ripple or visual "tear" artifact that will be displayed as the display device is updated from the changing video memory.

A consistent frame rate is highly desirable in terms of player control and smooth camera updating. Changes in the frame rate can be very unsettling to players, potentially contributing to motion sickness.

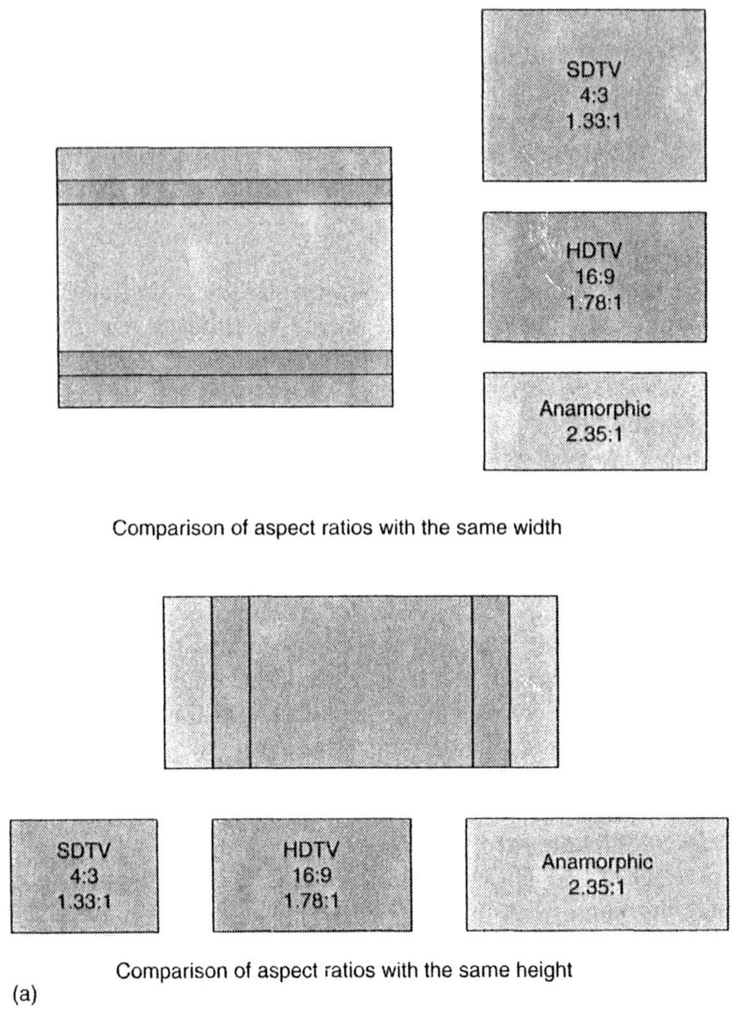

■ **FIGURE 2.4** a–c The relative sizes of common display aspect ratios: SDTV (4:3), HDTV (16:9), CinemaScope (1.85:1), and anamorphic (2.35:1).

Game cameras may be made frame-rate independent by ensuring that changes to camera state are based upon the amount of time elapsed from the previous update, otherwise known as *delta time*.

Safe zone and safe frame

The *safe zone* refers to a region of the display device that borders all four sides; it is possible to have information obscured by the physical border of the display device within this region. Typically, this

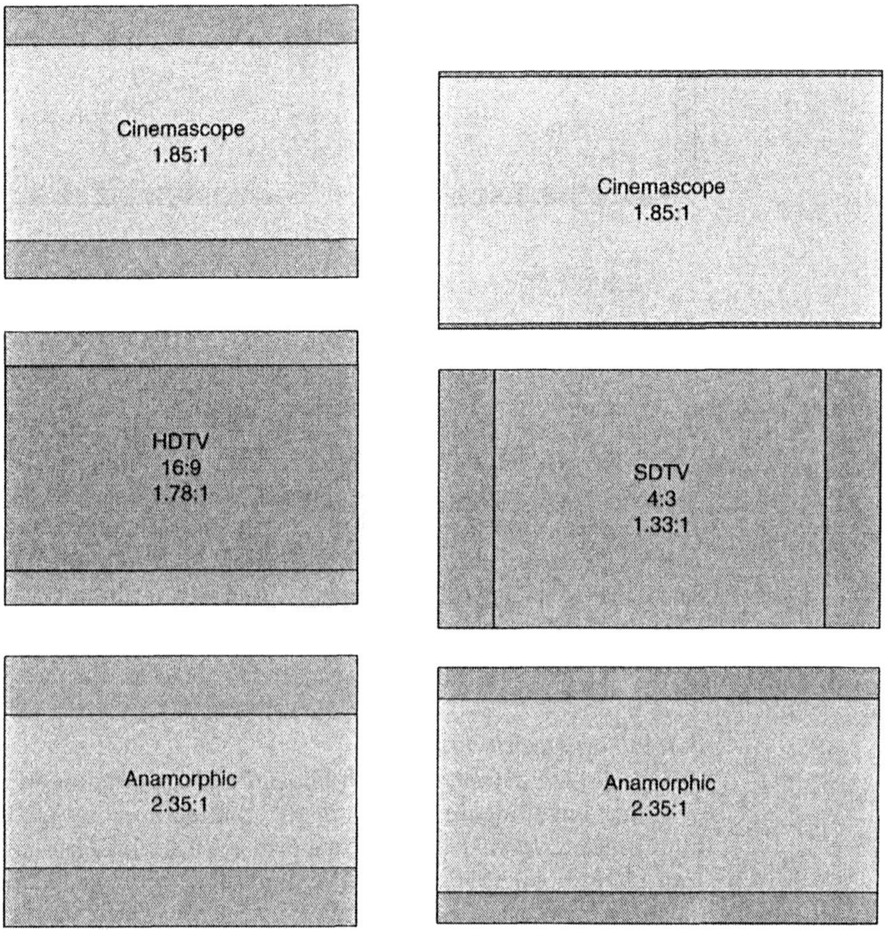

Comparison of aspect ratios within a 4:3 display
(b)

Comparison of aspect ratios within a 16:9 display
(c)

■ **FIGURE 2.4** (Continued)

occurs where the curvature of the display device is reasonably large or the border of the display overlaps the actual screen itself. However, modern displays tend to be flatter and have thinner borders, often avoiding this problem. Nonetheless, since this region remains in the periphery of the viewer's eyesight, it is generally advisable to avoid placing important status information in this region. The size of the region depends upon the physical display resolution. For an SDTV display, thirty-two pixels would be an adequate size. For an HDTV device the safe frame margin should be doubled (in terms of physical

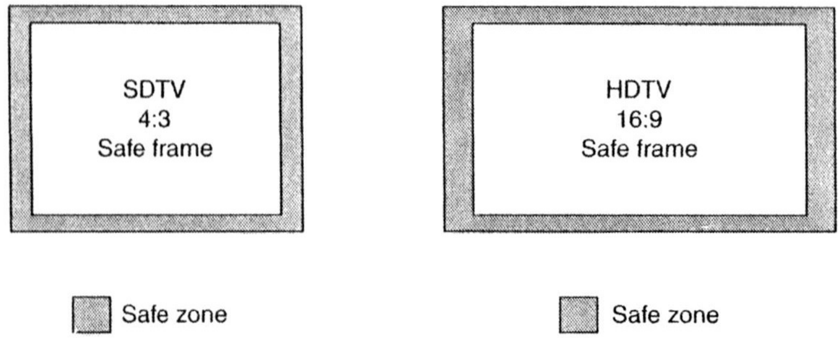

■ **FIGURE 2.5** The safe zone and safe frame for typical SDTV and HDTV display devices.

pixels) to account for the higher resolution. A reasonable rule of thumb here is to leave a margin of approximately 10–15 percent of the display device resolution. The purpose of the safe zone is to ensure that important information is guaranteed to be visible to the player and this size may vary according to the nature of the information displayed. Thus, the area of the display within which important information should be displayed is referred to as the *safe frame*. Figure 2.5 illustrates example safe frames and safe zones.

Refresh and motion blur

Blur due to low refresh rates will hopefully become less of an issue over time, but at the time of writing this continues to be a problem. In this regard, *refresh blur* should be distinguished from *motion blur*. Particularly applicable to older LCD displays, whether handheld or not, *refresh blur* refers to an unwanted effect where the display medium is unable to display the output of the computer fast enough to cope with the required changes. The result is an imprecise appearance that greatly detracts from the desired visual quality of the game. Moreover, this effect applies to the entire display device.

Motion blur, on the other hand, is typically associated with an effect caused by the limitations of film exposure. Fast-moving objects appear to occupy a larger area or leave behind a blurry trail. This is because during the time that the film is exposed via the camera aperture, the object moves far enough to appear in multiple places within the same film frame. An example of motion blur is shown in Figure 2.6.

Sometimes blur can be used to our advantage such that it can hide limitations of the rendering technology. One example is rendering of alternate scan lines within the TV frame. In some cases, the graphics hardware can retain information about the previous scan line as it generates its output, and can thus smooth out some of the artifacts introduced when creating computer graphics. Similar effects are used by hardware "line-doublers," which attempt to upscale video information when using devices with low or standard television resolution compared to HDTV displays. Motion blur is often seen as a beneficial effect since it is an additional cue as to the motion of characters and produces a more movie-like experience. However, current rendering technologies typically require special effort to be expended (with an associated performance cost) to approximate this effect.

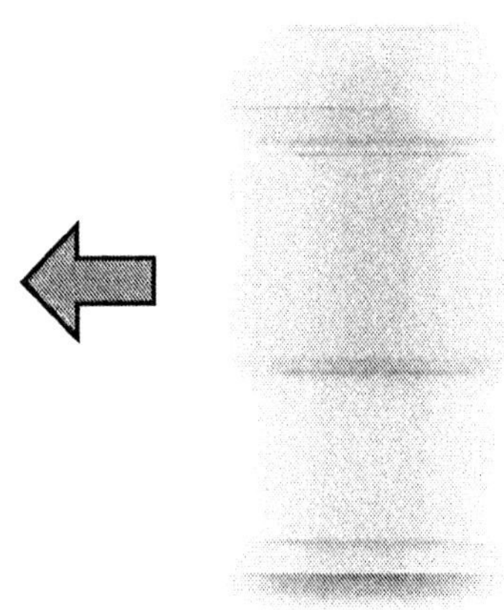

■ FIGURE 2.6 Motion blur occurs when an object moves faster than the exposure time of the film.

Display tearing

Another unwanted artifact, *display tearing*, occurs when the render memory buffer is either copied to the display memory or switched to become the active display buffer during the time that the physical display device is updated. Due to the nature of the artifact, there is a distinct difference between the part of the display showing the newly rendered data and the part of the display that is still showing the previous frame's data. This is greatly dependent upon the manner in which the display device generates its image and thus is not always applicable.

Player character

Given the disparity in representation of the player within different game genres, in this book *player character* refers to a person, vehicle, human, creature, or whatever other object is controlled by the player within the game. The differing characteristics of these alternatives require appropriate camera solutions to be devised. Often the *desired position* and *look-at position* of the camera are derived from the position and/or orientation of the player character in addition to its movement characteristics. In some games, the notion of the player character is implicit; it may not actually appear during game play (e.g., *first person* games).

Target object

The target object is a game object used to dictate the look-at position for the camera; sometimes the camera orientation exactly follows this object though usually there is lag before the camera is able to reorient to the direction facing this object. The actual look-at position may be offset from this object in a variety of ways; these are covered in detail in Chapter 7. In many cases, the target object is the *player character*.

TECHNICAL

In modern game applications, it is unusual to encounter the display tearing effect, as the switch (and copy if so required) between buffers is normally synchronized with the ***vertical blanking*** (VBL) signal. This synchronization occurs during the short period that the display hardware is not reading from display memory. To avoid stalling the graphics or main processor, it is common to switch between multiple memory buffers for rendering purposes. This is known as ***double*** or ***triple buffering*** according to the number of buffers stored. It facilitates immediate switching of the memory used by the display and avoids the tearing artifacts. However, the memory cost can prove prohibitive, and in some limited systems may not even be possible. In those cases, display tearing may be unavoidable, but its effects can be reduced in some limited cases. If the display memory must be physically copied to an output buffer read by the display device, the copying operation itself can be synchronized with the VBL signal. If care is taken, the display device is reading memory behind the copying process (i.e., in parallel) and this avoids the tearing effect.

These techniques are highly dependent upon the display technology used, especially when the rendering memory is not identical to that of the fully displayed resolution. This would occur where interlaced rendering techniques are applied, since they alternate the output of scan lines to both reduce memory or CPU requirements and take advantage of the display characteristics of some display devices (e.g., CRTs).

Interpolation

Briefly, interpolation (or *blending*) refers to a collection of methods for changing camera properties smoothly over time. Usually it is used when changing between differing camera behaviors; most often, it is used to change the camera position or orientation in a smooth manner though it may also be used to control FOV or other property changes. Interpolation is discussed in detail in Chapter 10.

Projection

This is the method used to map a view of the game world onto the display device. Most often, this is achieved via a *perspective transformation*; a method to simulate the stereoscopic view afforded by human eyesight. Figure 2.8a shows a typical perspective projection. *Parallel transformations* are a common alternative in which parallel lines remain parallel when projected; this would include *orthographic*, *axonometric*, and *isometric* projections as detailed in Chapter 4.

Parallax

Originally, this was an astronomical term referring to the visual effect where an object appears to shift position according to the viewing angle. In game terms, it is often used to describe the relative motion of elements of the rendered scene according to their distance from the camera position, such as layers within a 2D side-scrolling game, a fake horizon image, or a *sky box* (i.e., a rendering trick to simulate the display of distant objects without requiring large amounts of geometry).

Transitions

Game camera systems are often required to change between active cameras that are physically separated or exhibit greatly differing behaviors (e.g., movement or orientation properties). The way in which the camera changes between these behaviors is referred to as a *transition* if the properties are significantly different. A clear example would be the change between a first and third person camera.

Transitions normally require special handling to ensure that the change is managed in a smooth and unobtrusive manner. Except for the case of an instantaneous cut, it is preferable to change the camera properties over time in a way that allows regular game play to continue. Some forms of transition may be interrupted by later changes.

Some of the more common transitions include:

- Behavioral changes (e.g., distance or elevation relative to the target object, orientation speed, etc.)
- Interpolation (positional and orientation changes over time; this may include FOV, etc.)
- Presentation style (e.g., first to third person)
- Jump cuts (instantaneous orientation and position changes)
- Wipes (clearing the existing screen data and restoring the new scene view in a graphically interesting manner)
- Fades (fading the existing screen data to a solid color, typically black or white; cross-fading between two different scenes, etc.)

Camera constraints

A common approach to determine the *desired position* or *desired orientation* of a game camera is to use a series of layered *constraints*. The constraints are limits applied to the desired property in an explicit order (e.g., collision constraints are applied after movement has been applied); the sum of these constraints defines the behavior of the camera with respect to the property. Additionally, camera constraints may be applied or removed as necessary according to the game play requirements.

It is often beneficial to consider camera motion and orientation separately.

Motion constraints

Without constraints upon the motion of the game camera, it would be free to pass through geometry, may be left behind by a rapidly moving character, or suffer from any number of other undesirable effects. Clearly, it is necessary to be able to prevent such untoward behavior while determining an appropriate position for the camera to occupy to best facilitate the particulars of the game play specific to this game.

Examples of motion constraints include:

- 2D or 3D distance
- Target character-relative position
- World-relative position
- Path (linear waypoints, spline curves, etc.)
- Implicit surface
- Acceleration limits
- Velocity limits

Motion constraints are discussed in detail in Chapter 10.

Orientation constraints

Orientation constraints are often applied to first person cameras, especially concerning direct player manipulation during *free-look*. Free-look is a general term describing the player's ability to reorient the camera during game play. Constraints applied during free-look include the maximum and minimum pitch of the camera, and possibly the yaw relative to some fixed reference frame. Often yaw motion in the character obviates the need to consider yaw constraints upon the character (since the first person camera is usually associated with the forward view of the character). There are times when the character orientation remains fixed but the view may be controlled by the player relative to the direction of the character in the world.

Third person cameras that feature free-look themselves may be subject to similar constraints; sometimes fixed position cameras that track the player will have constraints to prevent vertical orientations.

Orientation methodologies are covered in detail in Chapter 7. Examples of orientation constraints include:

- Limiting pitch control to avoid disorientation.
- Increasing resistance proportionally (i.e., soft limits vs. hard limits).
- Acceleration restrictions, particularly for small changes.
- Using speed of character to affect orientation changes.
- Limiting orientation speed to reduce motion sickness.
- Look-at position may be constrained to particular positions with respect to the target object, or have its velocity and/or acceleration restricted. Often the calculation of the look-at position varies according to the player character's position, movement speed, or actions.

CAMERA PRESENTATION STYLES

We may consider the presentation of the game world as a major distinguishing characteristic of game cameras, since it will greatly affect the viewer's experience. This *presentation style* is usually restricted to either an orthographic (i.e., two-dimensional) or perspective (three-dimensional) rendering of the game world. Though not entirely accurate, these presentation styles may be referred to as 2D or 3D cameras for our convenience. A hybrid presentation form is also possible, where either the game world or game objects are rendered orthographically (although their actual drawn shapes may suggest a third dimension). This presentation style is referred to here as a *2.5D* camera. Let us examine each of these possible styles:

Orthographic presentation (2D)

A 2D presentation style derives its name from the *projection* used by the rendering process, typically a *parallel orthographic projection*. In an orthographic projection (as seen in Figure 2.7), parallel lines remain parallel after being projected. Even though the graphical representation of the game world and objects within is two-dimensional, camera behavior may still be considered in the same fashion as other "3D" cameras. In this style of presentation, there is still scope for incorporating a sense of depth that might not be initially apparent. Some of the defining characteristics of a 2D camera system are included in the list below.

- *Scrolling* or static two-dimensional background graphics. Sometimes these are layered to provide a sense of depth to the scene. This is especially evident via the use of *parallax effects* as

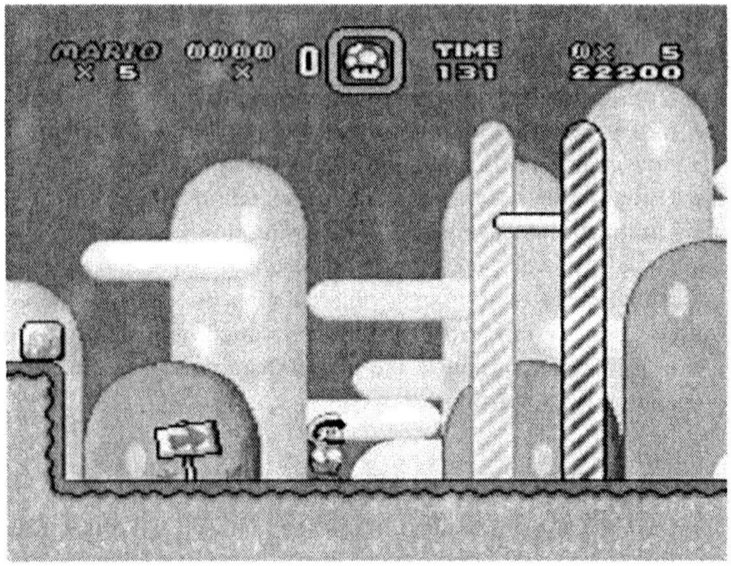

■ **FIGURE 2.7** A typical orthographic camera presentation.
Nintendo. Super Mario World. Published by Nintendo, 1991. Super Nintendo Entertainment System.

described earlier in this chapter. The background may be composed of smaller elements, such as *tiles* (otherwise known as *stamps*, or simply *characters*), which may also be combined to form larger *macro tiles*, and indexed via a *tile map*. Tiles are usually static arrangements of pixels of a standard size, perhaps 16 × 16 pixels.

- Camera motion is equated with redrawing the scene (e.g., either in its entirety or though some method of tracking changes, such as the leading edge of motion), calculated from the new position of the camera relative to the tile map position in the world.
- Zoom effects may be replicated by utilizing hardware scaling (if available) or by changes to the tile map rendering. Additionally, layers may be moved outward beyond the edges of the display, as in traditional cartoons. Zoom effects may also be simulated by movement of layered background objects, as used in traditional cartoon animation; see [Thomas95] for many examples of this usage.
- Rotation of the 2D tile map can prove difficult unless sufficient graphical performance is available. Some early game consoles (e.g., the *Super Nintendo Entertainment System* or SNES) had

hardware capabilities that could displace the tile map in a manner that would simulate rotation or perspective foreshortening (in the case of the SNES this was known as *Mode 7*). Others had the ability to render data in a bit-mapped display buffer that was then automatically converted into a tile map by the hardware (e.g., the SEGA CD game console). At least one piece of additional hardware (the *Super FX* co-processor for the SNES) allowed for individual pixels to be set in software with the hardware automatically converting the data into tile definitions.

Although it may not be immediately obvious, the rendering of a 2D presentation style does in fact require a degree of camera management. The position of the camera dictates the portion of the 2D world that is displayed as well as the relative position of the player character on the display device. If rotation of the worldview is possible, then the rotation of the camera should be used to control this property, ensuring once again that important game play elements remain in view.

TECHNICAL

It should be noted that it is often necessary to use an internal representation of three-dimensional coordinate systems even when the presentation style is itself two-dimensional. One possible example is when a zoom capability is used to simulate vertical displacement of the camera above the tile map. ***Isometric*** presentations are often considered as two-dimensional (they are, of course, parallel projections), yet game objects and the camera often use the vertical component of their coordinates to displace their positions relative to the 2D tile map, adding to the illusion of depth.

Perspective presentation (3D)

The majority of games utilize a presentation style that simulates a three-dimensional view of the game world in a manner somewhat akin to human visual perception. This is achieved by a *perspective projection*, where parallel lines are rendered so that they converge at *vanishing points*. This projection introduces some distortion as points in the world are projected back onto a flat plane corresponding to the position of the eye of the viewer. There is extensive literature regarding the generation of three-dimensional images and the effects of different projection types. The reader is again referred to [Akenine-Möller02], [Foley90], or [Pharr04] for further information. A typical example is shown in Figure 2.8a.

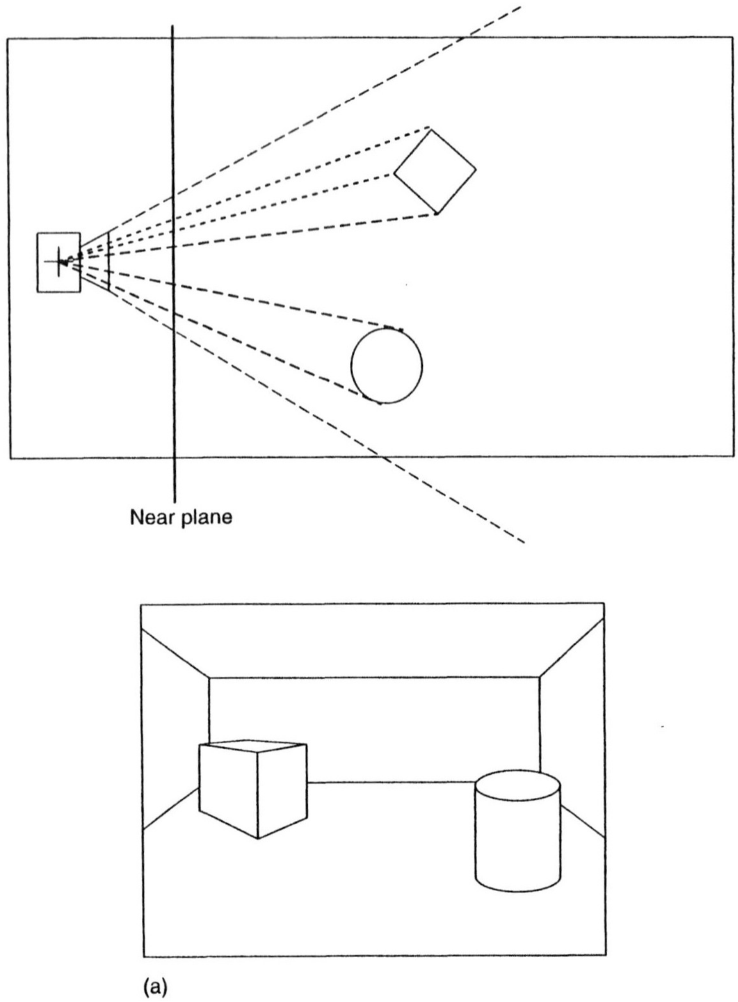

■ FIGURE 2.8 (a) Typical three-dimensional perspective projection of the game world.

Rendering properties of game cameras may be changed to enhance or vary the player's perception of the game world. FOV, for example, can greatly affect the perception of motion through the game world. Altering this value is roughly equivalent to changing a zoom lens on a real-world camera. The FOV literally controls the dimensions of the view frustum and thus the amount of the game world that is rendered. By increasing the FOV, a wider view is rendered, as shown in Figure 2.8b. This technique is often used to emphasize fast motion through the game world, and may be varied over time to simulate

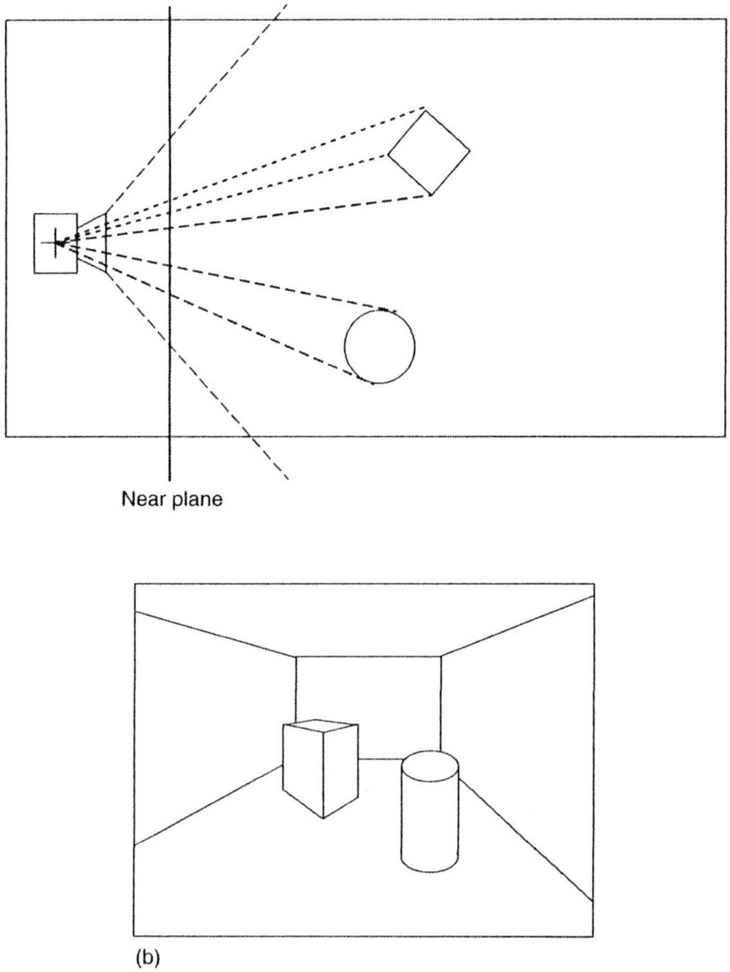

■ **FIGURE 2.8** (b) FOV is one rendering property that may be changed dynamically.

acceleration. Conversely, by reducing the FOV, an effect of zooming closer to elements aligned with the camera view occurs. This latter effect is typically used to simulate the view from a sniper rifle.

Some of the distinguishing characteristics of 3D presentations are as follows.

- May present a view of a 3D environment rendered in a perspective, orthographic, axonometric, or other projection. These terms are discussed in detail in Chapter 4.

- Projected view of the game world changes dynamically with game play.
- Greater realism and player immersion than 2D cameras; the player character appears to be a part of the environment.
- Usually presents a view of the game world in a similar vein to how humans perceive their world.
- Infrequently they may be used to generate stereoscopic displays of the game world (at a significant performance cost), viewed with special glasses.

Hybrid presentation (2.5D)

The difference in presentation style here from a strictly two-dimensional approach is that although the majority of the game is displayed as an orthographic projection there are elements that simulate a three-dimensional view. This may include parts of the background or simply the game objects; several permutations are possible. Camera motion is typically parallel to orthographic projection lines to underscore the pseudo three-dimensional aspects. It should be noted that the mixture of 2D and 3D elements is extremely variable; some games have used 3D backgrounds combined with 2D objects, such as *Paper Mario* [Paper00].

This type of presentation style may still make use of parallax effects to further enhance the sensation of a three-dimensional world. The camera position in this case is usually tightly controlled, and is frequently confined to a pre-determined path or position.

One of the most common parallel projections used to create a pseudo three-dimensional view is *isometric*, a form of *axonometric projection* utilizing world axes that appear to be 30 degrees from the horizontal (see Figure 2.9). This projection gives a pseudo 3D view of the world, typically using pre-rendered background tiles combined with either pre-rendered or dynamically rendered sprites matching the same projection. Isometric projection is often referred to as 2.5D because of this illusion of depth.

Isometric presentation has been used to great effect on target platforms without 3D hardware acceleration, although it does limit the ability of the player to change their view of the world. Typically, this option is not given to the player, although it is possible to present four different directional views given sufficient memory to store the background and sprite definitions for each potential view (if the graphics are rendered in real-time but restricted to an isometric projection then clearly this

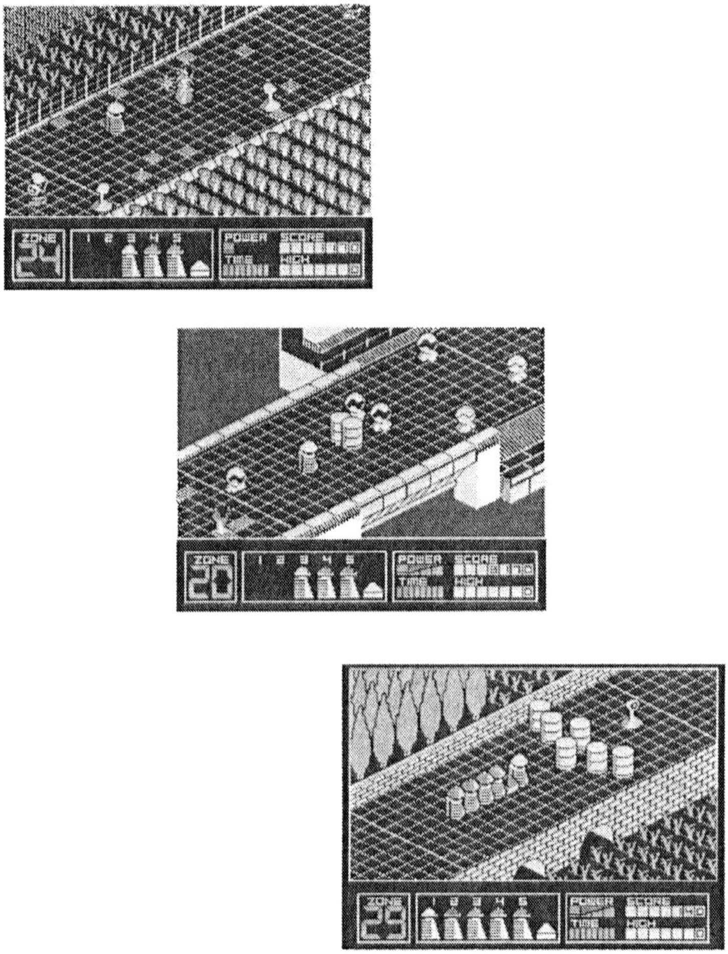

■ **FIGURE 2.9** An isometric 2.5D presentation example.
Vortex Software. Highway Encounter. Published by Vortex Software, 1985. Sinclair ZX Spectrum.

is not a problem). Multiple isometric views may require additional design work to ensure the views are consistent (e.g., if stored as separate tile maps), and that any game play-related tagging of the environment is correct in all views. Other types of parallel projection are discussed in Chapter 4.

CAMERA BEHAVIORS

Regardless of the presentation style, we may consider there to be three main types of game camera behavior. These are commonly referred to as *cinematic*, *first person*, and *third person* cameras. An overview of each type will now be given in addition to a brief discussion of the differences between two additional camera behaviors, namely *reactive* and *predictive* game cameras.

Cinematic cameras

Although open to interpretation, in this book we are going to adopt the convention that a cinematic camera *by definition* is one in which the view of the game world is displayed in a *non-interactive* form. Although the underlying camera may use exactly the same technology as the other types of cameras, the main difference is that the view of the world presented is outside of player control. Note that it is possible to have "in-game" or "real-time" cinematic events that allow for player control, but that these present their own unique problems (e.g., ensuring that the player actually views the desired cinematic events). In addition, it is entirely possible (and often used in the movie industry to varying effect) to have a first person cinematic camera. Cinematic camera sequences are sometimes referred to as *cineractives*, a hybrid term indicating that the sequence is generated in real-time, typically regardless of whether the viewer may interact with the game during the process. Let us examine the two flavors of cinematic camera usage.

Non-interactive "cut" scenes

This is the most straightforward interpretation of a movie-like experience for the player; its name derives from early game technology limitations when it was not easy to provide scene transitions other than simple "cuts." No interaction with the player character or altering of the camera behavior is possible; nor does the action presented vary in any way between successive viewings.

As such, we are able to exploit this property to present information to the player in the most appropriate aesthetic or explanatory way possible, just as it is done in real-world movies. Additionally, we can apply effects to further enhance the presentation that may not be possible during game play because of performance, memory, or other limitations imposed by the real-time nature of game play.

Usually the aspect ratio, viewport size, or other characteristics of the rendering will be altered to emphasize to the player that this is a non-interactive sequence. Filters and sound effects may also be changed to further enhance the differences between this presentation and regular game play.

Cut-scenes, as they are sometimes called, are often used to impart story or game play information that must be guaranteed to be seen by the player at least once. On subsequent viewings, the player is usually allowed to skip the sequence at any point by pressing a button on the controller.

Real-time cinematic sequences

While somewhat akin to the movie-like experience mentioned above, real-time or in-game cinematic sequences are actually pre-defined game events that play out during regular game play that continue regardless of the player's actions. They differ from the non-interactive sequences mainly because there is no guarantee that the player actually sees the event take place, unless the regular game camera is overridden. If camera usage is changed to present the cinematic sequence, care must be taken to ensure that the player character remains visible as well as allowing for control reference changes imparted by dramatic camera motion.

Often these sequences are used to enhance the sensations of a "real world" where events continue to occur regardless of player actions. It is typical that players may not interact with the objects involved in presenting the cinematic sequence to avoid unwanted changes to the scripted events.

First person/point of view

The now "traditional" *first person* (FP) camera usually presents a view of the game world as perceived from the eyes of the protagonist; for this reason it is also sometimes referred to as a *point of view* (POV) camera. A typical example of an FP camera is shown in Figure 2.10. Some of the most notable titles using this presentation include *DOOM* [DOOM93], *Quake* [Quake96], *Halo* [Halo01], *Half-Life* [HalfLife98], and *Metroid Prime* [Metroid02]. It should be noted, however, that the first person presentation was utilized before the advent of modern 3D graphics, although admittedly with typically less graphical finesse (e.g., *3D Monster Maze* [Monster82]).

First person cameras offer the closest experience of the player actually being present in the game world, and can be extremely immersive. Indeed a whole genre of game is associated with this particular camera type, the *first person shooter*, or FPS. Even when other styles of game play are presented using a POV from the player character, they are often grouped into this same classification.

The presence of the player character is mostly hidden in an FP camera, which can actually counter the sense of immersion, although it is possible to add additional visual cues to alleviate this. A common approach is to show a weapon or partial representation of the player character's body, such as an arm, even if the visual positioning of these representations may not be physically accurate. Examples of these techniques may also be seen in Figure 2.10. Other cues might include a player helmet or projection of information in a form representing a heads-up display. Another common approach is to apply a displacement of the rendered view while moving to simulate head-bobbing (although this is easily overdone and may actually make players nauseous), camera shaking in response to game events, and so forth. Similarly, there are audio cues that may be applied especially regarding surround sound positioning of sound effects, reverb, footsteps, and so forth.

Of course, an FP camera may be used in instances where the player is situated within a cockpit or similar location, allowing other visual cues (such as the cockpit environment model or electronic displays) to further emphasize the position of the player within the game world. This approach is common in racing games or flight simulators, even though they are not necessarily thought of as FP cameras.

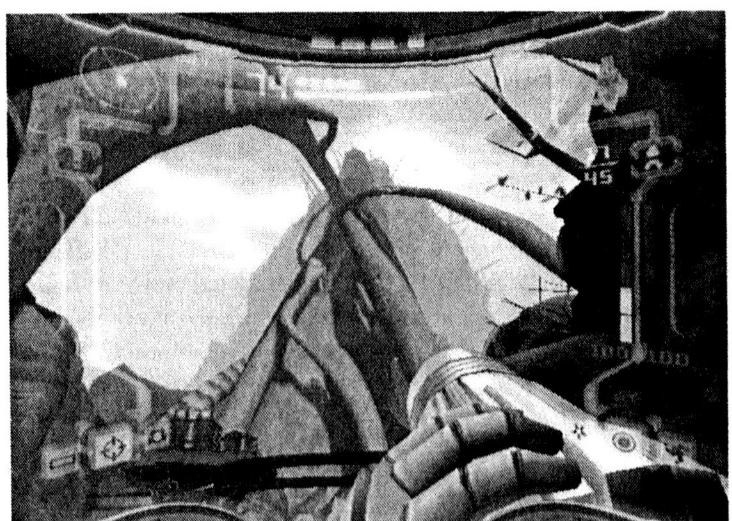

■ **FIGURE 2.10** A typical first person camera view.
Retro Studios Inc. Metroid Prime 2: Echoes. Published by Nintendo, 2004. Nintendo Gamecube.

There are, however, potential problems with FP camera behavior. The view of the game world offered is typically more limited than that of a third person camera; the FOV is often restrictive and it is generally more difficult for the player to understand spatial relationships between the player character position, the camera, and elements of the game environment. This often means that unless the orientation of the camera or player character is altered (either directly by the player or automatically by the game), it can be difficult or impossible for the player to view objects in proximity to the player character. Jumping with precision in particular is often a difficult prospect in many first person games for this very reason.

Direct player control of the orientation of the FP camera may prove complicated if it is allowed to occur while the player character is also moving or performing other actions. This is dependent upon the controller since some physical hardware layouts are more suited to combinations of movement and orientation control. An obvious example of this would be the typical *mouse plus keyboard* control combination used for many PC-based first person games.

When FP cameras are used in vehicle simulators, they are often in conjunction with a variety of selectable third person camera viewpoints. The main view in this case may even be considered a third person view even though it represents the player's viewpoint from piloting the vehicle. One major difference in this case is that roll around the forward axis of the camera is permitted and usually required whereas most FP camera usage in games might prefer to eliminate such roll except under specialized circumstances (such as the player character leaning around a corner).

TECHNICAL

When implementing an FP camera it is advisable to separate the camera from the head of the character, even though its position is dependent upon the former. The reason for this is because there should be some lag in terms of vertical axial motion to dampen the effect of the player walking over small obstructions in the game world. Otherwise, the camera would react to every small bump, just as the player does, which could be jarring and result in discontinuous camera motion. Additionally, it is typically necessary to allow reorientation of the camera independent of the player character orientation to provide either automated pitch control or player-controlled use of *free-look*.

First person games sometimes make use of full-screen (or full-viewport as appropriate) filter effects to change the appearance of the worldview; a typical example is blurring or other graphical distortion used to simulate a view under water. Other effects might include the rendering of objects in screen-relative space such as water running down the exterior of a helmet worn by the player, or the reflection of the player character's face in the helmet glass. These effects may be performed as a post-processing step once the view has been rendered (perhaps prior to rendering a helmet or HUD), or may be combined with rendering changes to simulate object- or view-based properties (e.g., infrared heat signatures).

Third person/detached view

Many 3D rendered games feature a camera where the vantage point is separated from the player character, typically behind and above. This class of camera is commonly referred to as *third person* (TP), since the view of the world is presented from a position external to the representation of the viewer within the game world, namely the *player character*. One of the earliest games adopting this presentation within a 3D rendered environment was *Super Mario 64* [Mario96], now considered a classic implementation of the style. Earlier examples would include classic arcade titles such as *I, Robot* [IRobot83]. However, even the earliest of all video games might be considered as third person despite the fact that the presentation style would likely have been two-dimensional.

While this type of presentation is often not quite as immersive as an FP camera (in part due to the unusual nature of seeing oneself from a distance), it does offer a number of advantages. Although there are many variations on the relative position and orientation of the camera compared to the player character, TP cameras are typically able to show the relationship between the player character and the environment quite clearly, allowing for greater interaction in many cases. Because of this, it is a popular choice for games where the navigation of the environment is an important game play element, such as the *platform* (or *side-scrolling*) genre discussed later in this chapter.

Under such a scheme, it is frequently the case that several alternative positions and orientations are dynamically selectable by the player; this allows the player to decide on their preferred view of the world according to game play requirements. The actual change of camera views may be either instantaneous or interpolated as desired by the designer. Additionally it may be possible for the player to dynamically adjust the distance or angular position of the camera relative to

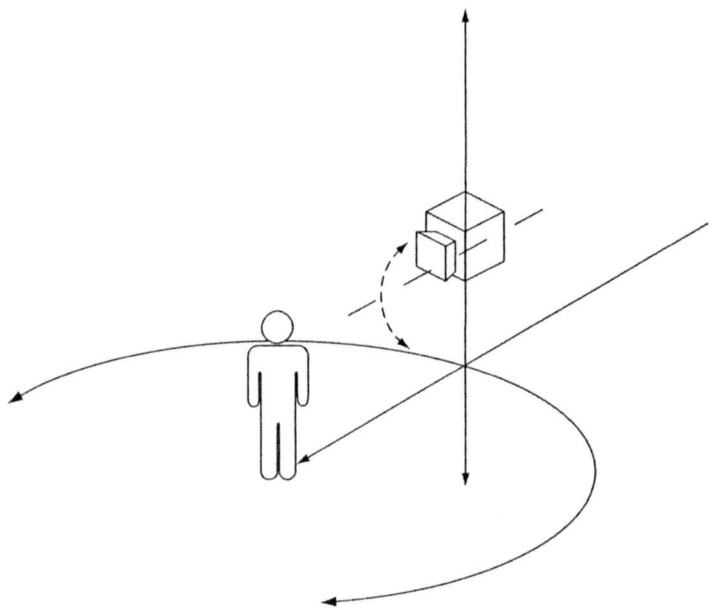

■ **FIGURE 2.11** The player is frequently allowed to dynamically adjust the camera distance, elevation, and possibly orientation.

the direction of motion of the player character, rather than simply switching between pre-defined combinations, as shown in Figure 2.11. This solution is frequently used for character-based situations such as action adventure or role-playing games.

However, there may be game play situations where such control must be disallowed, as it might cause the camera to leave the environment or perhaps reveal game play elements that should be hidden. There are also occasions where it is necessary to ensure that the player view shows specific game elements, and thus camera manipulation must be restricted.

In addition to cameras that are based upon the position and orientation of the player character, there are many other solutions for determining the position of a third person camera. Some typical examples would include stationary cameras or those restricted to motion along pre-determined paths. While it is often preferable to use a single consistent camera approach, there are times when it is more appropriate to present the game play (such as a *boss battle* or other specialized situation) in a specific way that differs from the regular camera presentation. Often this is necessary due to the physical characteristics of an enemy or other game object that requires a different solution to frame it adequately. Alternatively, it might be necessary to restrict camera motion due to a confined environment or other potential collisions with the camera.

As mentioned, there are some difficulties associated with certain types of TP cameras. Two of the main issues are those of *world navigation* and *collision avoidance*. That is, enabling a free form camera to move through a complex (and possibly dynamically changing) environment while avoiding collision with either game objects or the world geometry, as shown in Figure 2.12. Additionally, the camera must be moved into a position to present the game play in a desirable fashion; in great part, this can depend upon the physical layout of the environment, as there may be restrictions upon the possible positions for the camera. These problems are often compounded by the movement characteristics of the player character (such as rapid acceleration or jumping). Such problems may be lessened or avoided by the use of pre-determined camera positions or movement; however, game play requirements often demand a more dynamic solution. These problems are often difficult to resolve and sometimes require changes to the construction of the environment.

A related common problem is that of player character occlusion. Many games allow the player character to move into a position where it is occluded by the environment. Partial or temporary occlusion is certainly allowable, and sometimes even aesthetically pleasing. Total

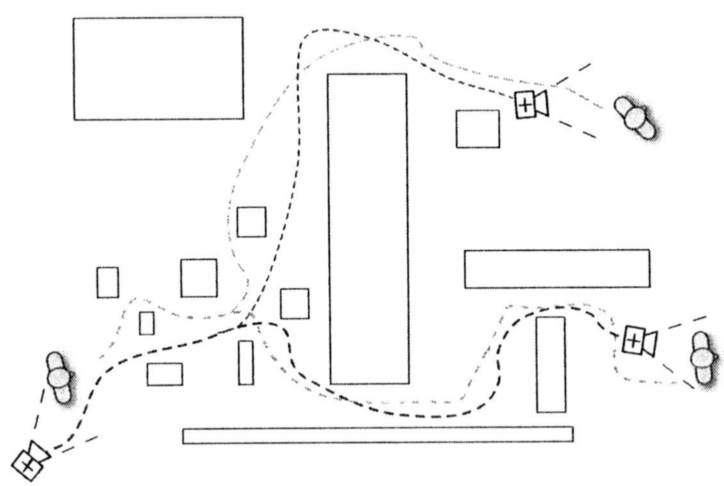

■ **FIGURE 2.12** Navigation through a complex environment may be a demanding task.

occlusion, however, frequently leads to a situation where the player is disoriented, which may be critical if it occurs during a high stress situation such as combat.

An even more significant problem pertains to aiming within TP cameras. Usually this is only an issue because most of the time the player is not looking along the line of sight of their targeting. Visual cues such as 2D or 3D reticules overlaid on top of the world, tracer fire, and the like may assist the player enormously. Adding auto-aiming (requiring no player input), assisted-aiming (some player input but not pixel-accurate aiming), or auto-targeting (or at least some assistance in these regards) can also obviate the need for precise aiming finesse. Further discussion on related player and camera control issues can be found in Chapter 4.

Nonetheless, TP cameras are appealing because they not only show the player's presence (or alter ego) in the game (with ample opportunity for graphical finesse such as animation), but also because they allow for a better understanding of the player's position within the game world. They also allow for camera positioning and movements that are not normally possible with real-world cameras. Third person cameras are attractive because they are able to show exactly what the player needs to do if utilized well. However, if implemented poorly, or with little regard to the dynamically changing nature of interactive game play, they can ruin the player's experience completely.

The choice of a TP camera also entails a commitment to producing adequate animations of the player character for all potential activities. This raises another issue common with this type of presentation, that of the determination of the camera orientation. Often character-based or action adventure games will focus (literally) directly upon the player character itself, or more likely a position slightly vertically above. An indication of this is that the character retains the same screen-relative position regardless of activity. While this is fine when the character is stationary, once the character begins moving (particularly if at high speed), it is more useful to be looking *ahead of the character*, in the direction of motion. This would usually allow the player a much better understanding of the upcoming environment and allow additional time for the player to react to game events (such as enemy fire, etc.). Figure 2.2 shows an example of this look ahead and a more detailed explanation of this phenomenon may be found in Chapter 7.

Third person cameras are the catchall category for the majority of camera types found in games (or cinematic sequences) and therefore feature a variety of positional or orientation behaviors. We may enumerate a number of common examples as seen in the next sections.

Behind the character

The position of the camera is fixed with respect to the character orientation (often above and behind the character to avoid the character obscuring the view of the game world), or may have rotational lag around the vertical axis of the character (Figure 2.13a).

Over the shoulder

The camera is positioned so as to give an over the shoulder view, typically with little or no orientation lag (Figure 2.14). This approach is often used within hybrid first person/third person presentation styles to aid with aiming.

Visible feet

The camera is positioned away from the character such that animation is still clearly visible, and a good view of the surrounding area is possible. This includes the ability to observe the character's feet, which is often important to judge jumping or other character positioning (Figure 2.13b). This camera behaves in a similar manner to the regular "behind the character" camera illustrated in 2.13a.

Far distance

The camera is located far behind the player character; this is greatly dependent upon the environment (since it is usually desirable to avoid occlusion), and is a common solution in vehicle games. The orientation of this camera often lags behind movement of the character to avoid rapid reorientation and to allow the character to be seen as three-dimensional. Figure 2.13b also covers this type of presentation.

Character relative

The camera maintains a position with respect to the character position (often used for replay cameras). Examples include rear or side facing (flight simulator), fender (racing), and so forth, as seen in Figure 2.13c.

Stationary

The camera is positioned at a (usually high) vantage point and is stationary, reorienting to track the player character or other target objects as required (Figure 2.13d).

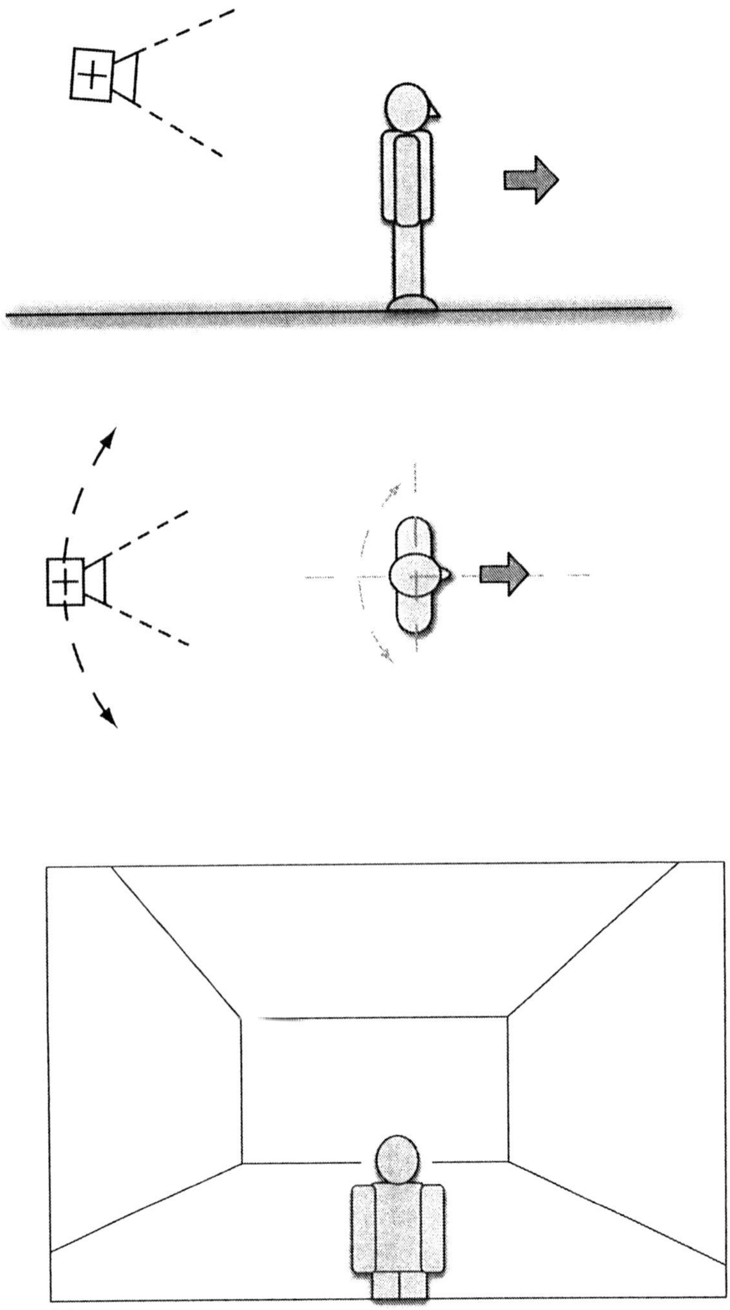

(a)

■ **FIGURE 2.13a** Behind the character.

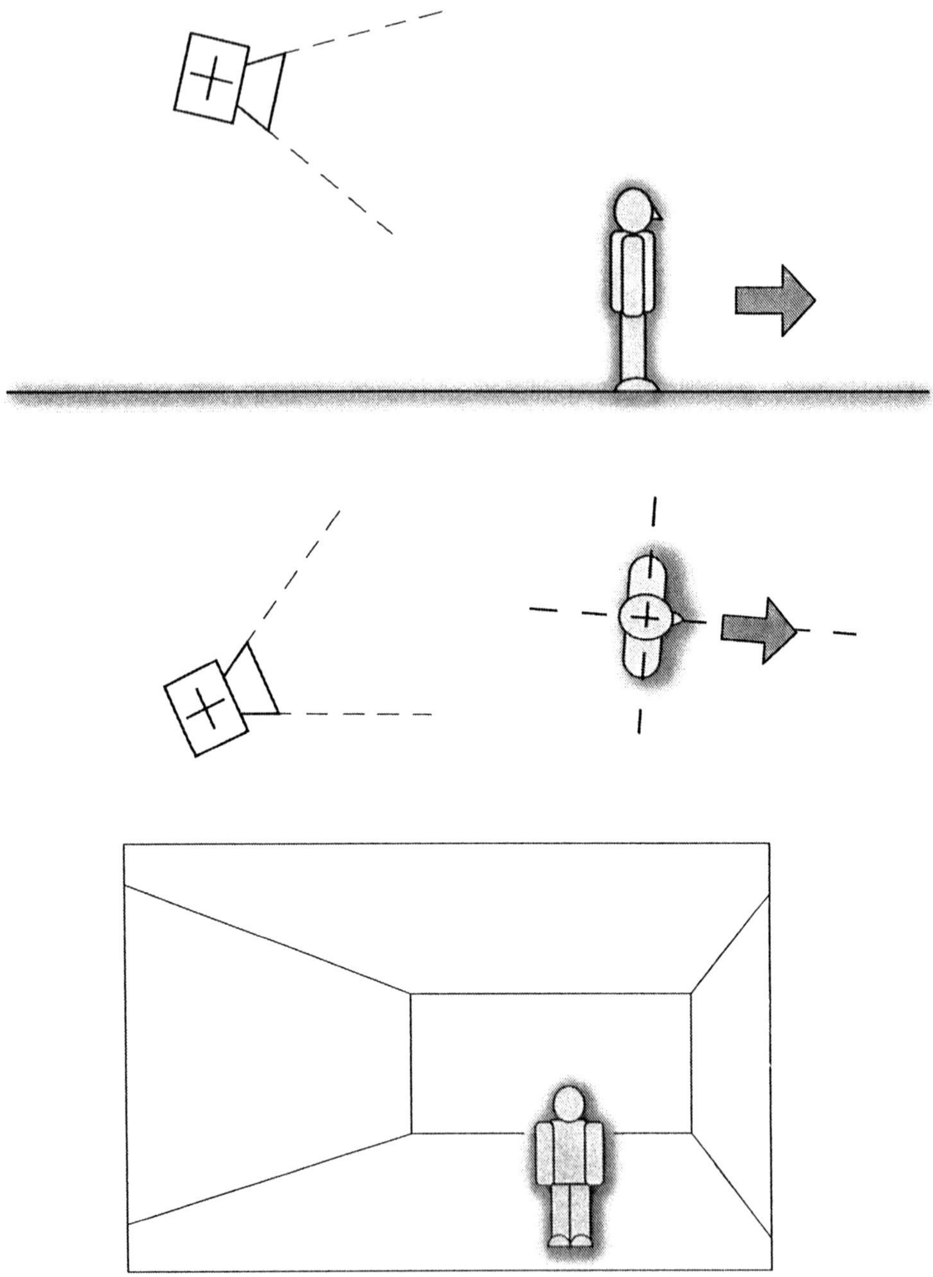

(b)

■ **FIGURE 2.13b** Character feet are visible with a medium distance.

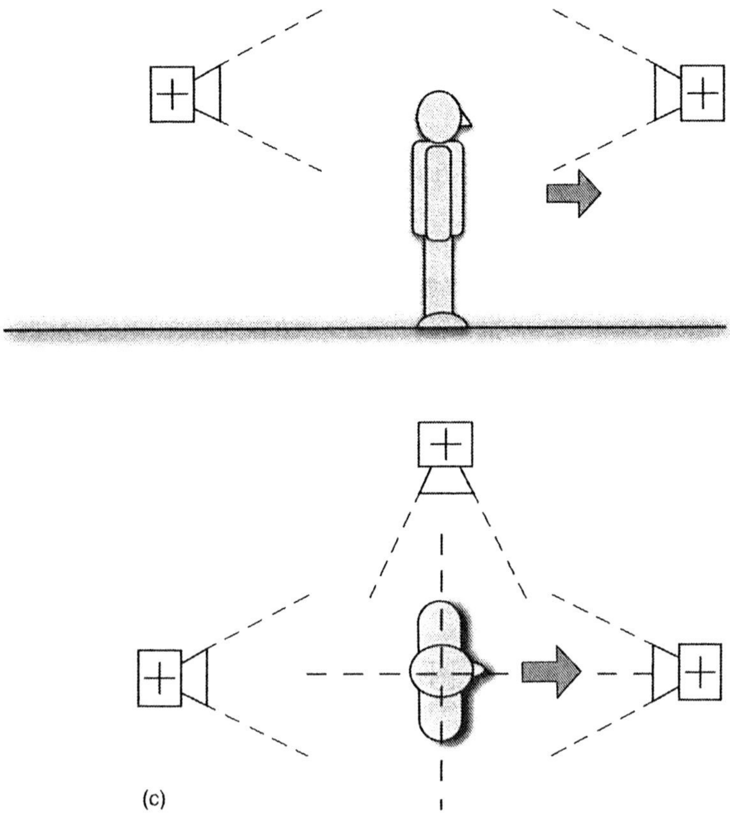

■ **FIGURE 2.13c** Character relative.

Path-based

The camera is constrained to follow a pre-determined path through the environment; the position of the camera along the path is determined by the relative position of the player character to some reference frame, possibly the camera path itself (Figure 2.13e).

One of the benefits of a TP camera is that it allows players an improved understanding of their position and orientation versus an FP camera. However, determination of the position and orientation of the camera to provide a clear view may be challenging within complex environments.

An important consideration of TP cameras is not only the position of the camera relative to the player character, but also the orientation of the camera. Many third person presentations focus the camera directly on the player character; although this may initially seem to be

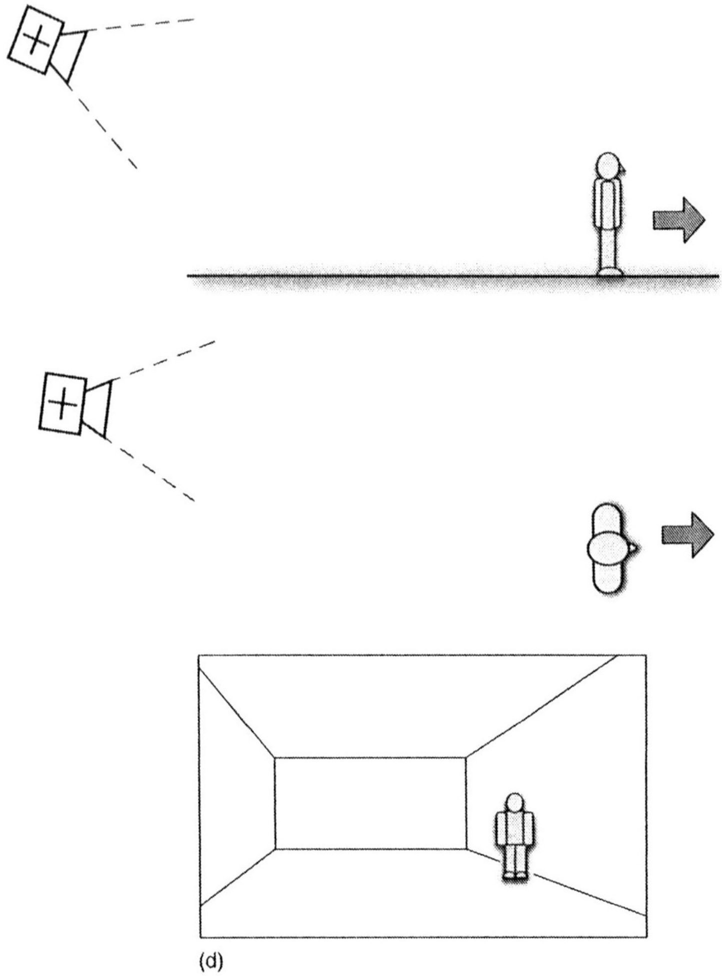

■ **FIGURE 2.13d** Stationary, tracking the player character.

TECHNICAL

The internal representation of FP and TP cameras within the camera system, and how their view of the game is used by the rendering system, are essentially the same, and may often be derived from a common base class. The mathematical transformation matrix (i.e., projection matrix) used to convert coordinates from camera space into screen space would be identical unless there are differences in the FOV (or potentially the near and far clipping planes). In most cases, the only real differences between such presentation styles are the position of the camera with respect to the player character, and changes to player control.

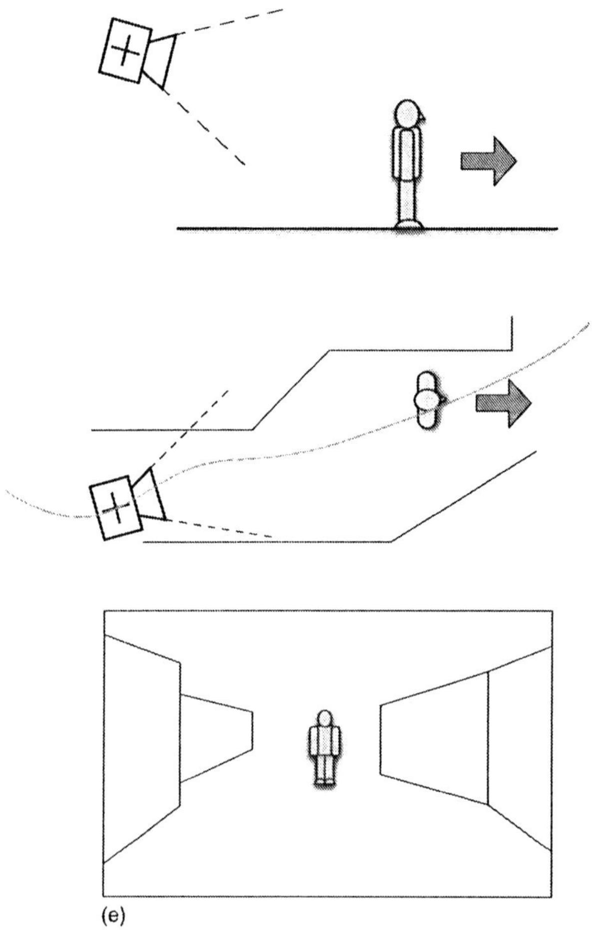

■ **FIGURE 2.13e** Path-constrained.

an appropriate view, it will be shown later that there are good reasons for the camera to look ahead of the player character.

Hybrid FP/TP cameras

Some games attempt to improve the aesthetic qualities of FP cameras by adopting a solution where the player character is viewed from an external position while retaining first person control and orientation determination. Typically, this solution is presented via a camera located close to the shoulder of the protagonist, although the exact position can vary according to game needs. Games that have included this camera approach include *Jet Force Gemini* [JetForce99], *Resident Evil 4* [Resident05], and *Gears of War* [Gears06]. Figure 2.14 shows

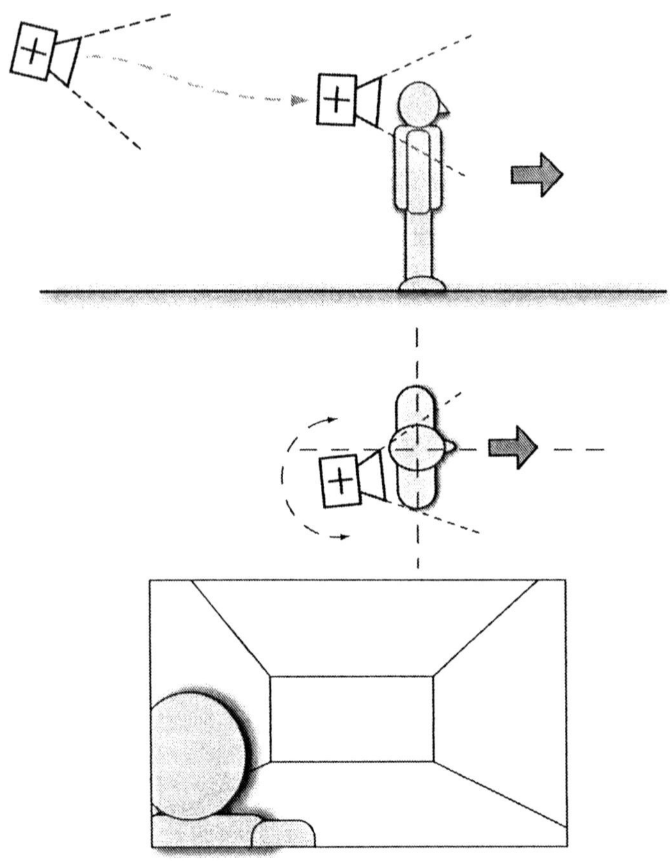

■ FIGURE 2.14 Hybrid FP/TP camera solutions vary their position according to player need.

some typical example positions that may be adopted. Its position may be even be determined by the game play situation. In some games the camera adopts a regular third person position until the player unholsters a weapon or enters an "aiming mode," at which point the camera moves closer to the player character; the viewpoint may also change to allow interaction of the player with elements of the game world (e.g., manipulating a lever in *Metroid Prime 3* [Metroid07], etc.). A similar change in position may also occur for TP cameras when the player backs into collision geometry; the camera may ultimately even move into a FP camera position both as an aid to game play and to avoid geometry interpenetration.

TECHNICAL

With the player so close to the camera, care must be taken to ensure that the player character model does not intersect the near plane of the camera's view frustum to prevent unsightly graphical artifacts. Additionally it is possible that the resolution of the Z-buffer is insufficient to resolve sorting of the player character accurately, which may require an explicit rendering solution (possibly ignoring depth sorting entirely or using an explicitly specified sorting order). Near-plane intersections with world rendering geometry may still prove to be an issue even if the camera remains completely within the collision volume of the player, due to the shape of the viewing frustum. This is typically prevalent at the edges of the screen when the player character is adjacent to render geometry. If it is necessary to move the camera to avoid collisions with geometry (say, as the player backs into a corner), ensure that the direction in which the camera is oriented is adjusted to look at a position ahead of the player character.

Hybrid solutions are an interesting approach to resolving the problems with ranged interactions often found in TP cameras. They also have the benefit of improving player immersion, although to a limited degree since the view is still external to the player character. Camera navigation is less of an issue than with traditional TP cameras, especially if the position of the camera remains within the player collision volume. Rotational lag of the camera position around the player character is still appropriate with hybrid characters, as is orientation lag.

Hybrid cameras that combine elements of FP camera control with TP camera positioning can be useful when game play requirements include long-range weapon aiming using free-look or similar control schemes.

TECHNICAL

In implementation terms, "third person cameras" really reflect the behavior of all camera types; the "first person" cameras mentioned above are in fact a subset of third person cameras with specific constraints pertaining to their position and orientation determination. Construction of the view transformation matrix, visibility calculations, or access to other pertinent camera information is the same regardless of the presentation style. It is quite common for camera system implementations to use first and third person camera classes derived from a common base camera class. More information concerning such implementation issues and alternatives may be found in Chapter 11.

Predictive versus reactive cameras

The majority of game cameras may be described as *reactive*; that is, they react to the current (or past) state of the player character and other game objects regarding position, orientation, or some other property. A *predictive* camera, on the other hand, attempts to analyze the probable actions of the player character or other pertinent game objects and somehow anticipates the best position or orientation to achieve to present the best current and future view of the player and environment. Additionally, both types of cameras attempt to avoid potential problems caused by world geometry obstruction, object collisions, or other future events. This usually entails not only predicting the future position of the player, but possibly other objects/creatures/state information about the world, including that of the camera itself.

Most FP cameras are required to be reactive, since they are very dependent upon the player character, but may still benefit from predictive techniques; one example might be automated changes to the elevation of the camera as the player character traverses inclines, as shown in Chapter 7. Third person cameras, while often implemented as purely reactive, may benefit tremendously from the use of predictive techniques.

It may be argued that only predictive cameras are able to solve difficult camera problems such as navigation through complex environments. However, since player input is inherently random, this approach is extremely dependent upon the kinds of motion that are possible as well as the rate at which the target character can change direction and/or speed. It is also greatly dependent upon the environment in which the player is maneuvering. Analysis of player behavior can help in this regard, but more important is knowledge of the limitations of player movement imposed by its physical characteristics. Let us consider some of the forms that prediction might take.

Character motion prediction

Although highly genre dependent, determination of the future position of the player character can be an extremely useful tool in camera logic. This is primarily of use with a TP camera that needs to navigate through a complex environment. However, these prediction capabilities also have worth in the determination of the best orientation of the camera.

Given sufficient processor power, the full game simulation could be run ahead in time giving a reasonably accurate representation of the future state of the game; however, adopting strategies utilized by networked games (e.g., where latency issues often require prediction of future object positions) may prove more appropriate. Realistically, a simplified calculation (such as one based on the velocity of the target object) will often provide a good approximation of the future target object position. However, this is greatly dependent upon the movement characteristics of the target, especially directional changes and its acceleration properties. Most humanoid characters change direction relatively slowly, and do not accelerate quickly; both of these are beneficial to this calculation. However, players are prone to rapidly changing their intended direction of motion which makes prediction difficult.

Vehicles and other high-speed objects may present more of a problem in this regard. When combined with sufficient damping of the camera's reaction to the changes in the future position (to reduce oscillation due to rapid changes), this prediction will allow the camera movement or orientation to change in anticipation of the player's actions.

[Halper01] describes the benefits of motion prediction, and we can show a simplified example of this. In Figure 2.15, the player is shown

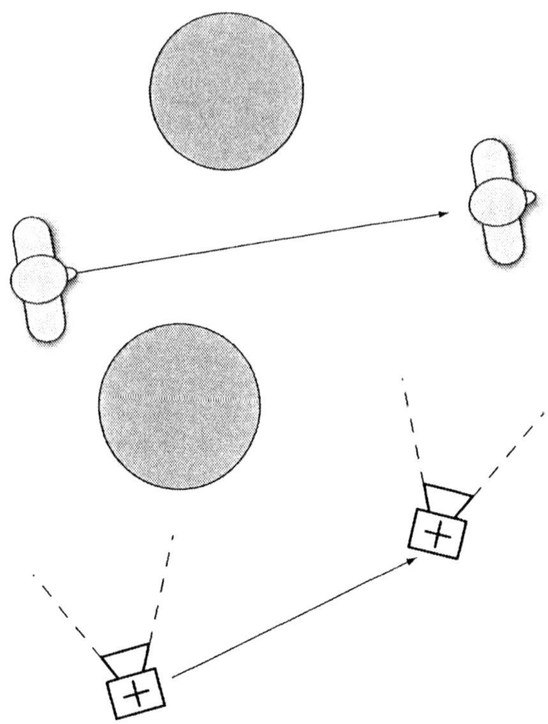

■ **FIGURE 2.15** Predictive cameras are able to navigate more easily than reactive ones.

to be moving in a straight path between two columns. By anticipating the future position of the camera, the camera system is able to navigate to a position avoiding a potential collision ahead of time (rather than simply attempting to close in on the player position). In complex environments, predictive cameras will face additional difficulties when accurately determining future state information and will likely incur higher performance costs.

Camera path prediction

Camera motion is often constrained to remain on a pre-determined path, usually defined in a world-editing tool. However, there are cases where the motion path is formed dynamically in response to game play, such as geometry avoidance. For camera motion on dynamically formed paths, there are some features common to those usually encountered when implementing AI functionality. Indeed, a general TP camera can be considered as an AI agent, with additional aesthetic constraints regarding its motion and orientation. Oftentimes the same underlying technology may be used for the camera as for AI movement or navigation.

Path finding solutions

When dynamically determining a camera path, we can break the problem down into several discrete cases.

- **Global path determination**. Searching through the environment to find a suitable path toward a target position, while maintaining appropriate aesthetic qualities such as distance from environmental elements, and so forth.
- **Local path determination.** For example, game object, ledge, or column avoidance.
- **Target-based searches.** Finding the best position around the target character under various constraints, such as occlusion avoidance, geometry avoidance, and so forth.

Data-driven versus programmatic solutions

As usual, compromises must be made regarding the memory cost of data-driven or preprocessed solutions versus an on-the-fly determination of the best camera position. Additionally, there is most likely a large CPU performance impact with real-time or programmatic solutions.

Orientation prediction

As briefly touched upon above, by predicting the future position of the target object, this can be used to determine a future orientation of the camera. However, if the interpolation toward this "ideal" future orientation begins too early, or if the prediction is too far ahead in time, the resolved new orientation may in fact hinder current game play.

A case in point is angular interpolation. When simply interpolating between two fixed orientations, it is a simple matter to use either linear or spherical linear interpolation to determine a new orientation over time. In this example, the angle between the current orientation and the desired orientation is becoming smaller over time. If the target orientation, the source orientation, or indeed both are changing over time, it is necessary to take additional steps to resolve the interpolation. This is because the angle between the source and target can in fact increase over time irrespective of the interpolation, especially if the angular reorientation speed is low. If the new angle is based upon the proportional amount of the angle between the source and destination, it is possible for the angle between the current camera orientation and the destination to actually increase compared to the previous frame. Alternatively, if the angle is based on a proportion of the original angle between the source and destination, the result, although time-constant, will have discontinuous motion depending on the speed at which the destination angle is changing.

To ensure that the interpolation changes smoothly over time, the key is to ensure that the interpolation is performed as a reverse orientation calculation from the target back toward the source orientation. In this manner, the angle between the two orientations is guaranteed to become smaller as the interpolation progresses.

VIEW GENERATION

Given our basic knowledge of the fundamentals of game cameras, how are they used to generate a view of the game world? A more thorough understanding of this process (otherwise known as the *render pipeline*) may be found in many of the standard computer graphics texts such as [Akenine-Möller02] and [Foley90]. Readers familiar with this process may skip this section; designers may find this informative although an understanding is not required.

View generation may be broken down into a number of discrete stages; depending upon the nature of the graphics hardware available, some of these stages may execute in parallel with regular game logic or within the graphics hardware.

1. Game logic updates the internal state of all active game objects, including determination of position, orientation, animation, or other changes to the representation of the object to be generated.
2. Game cameras have their logic updated to ensure that their position, orientation, and other properties that affect view generation are now current.
3. For each view of the game to be generated (as shown in Figure 2.16):
   a. Determine the position and orientation of the requisite game camera.
   b. Determine the portion of the display device to contain the generated view (often referred to as the *viewport*).
   c. Determine the *view volume* or *frustum* that dictates the portion of the world that is visible from the camera position and orientation.
   d. Given the view frustum, determine which game objects or elements may be trivially rejected (or *culled*) for rendering purposes.
   e. For each game object or world element:
      i. Transform the game model (i.e., the geometric primitives used to construct its shape, such as triangles or quadrilaterals) according to the camera view.
      ii. Apply lighting and shading effects.
      iii. Project the primitives from three dimensions onto a two-dimensional plane.
      iv. Discard (*cull*) the projected primitives that lie outside of the view volume, and *clip* those that intersect.
      v. Draw (or *rasterize*) the primitives.

Note that this list is only representative of the process, which may vary depending upon the specifics of the rendering system (e.g., the capabilities of the graphics hardware available, ray tracing, rasterization, etc.).

Given this overview, let us examine three elements of this process that are directly dependent upon the camera system; namely the *view frustum*, *view transform*, and *projection transform*.

View frustum

A view frustum may be thought of as a pyramid with a rectangular base whose tip has been removed by a plane parallel to that of the

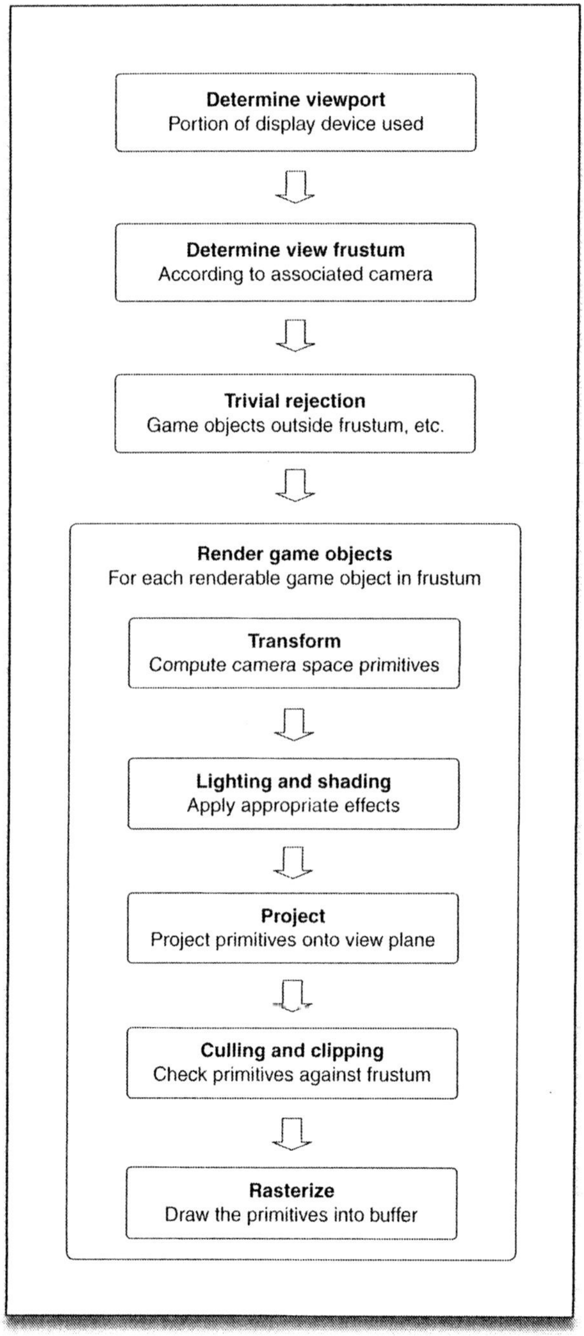

■ **FIGURE 2.16** A simplified render pipeline.

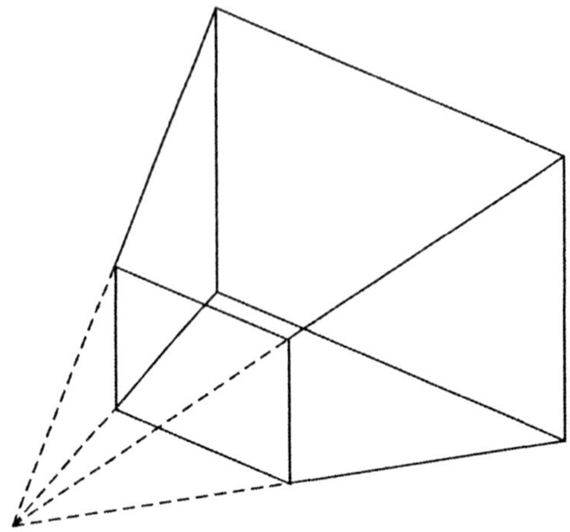

■ **FIGURE 2.17** A rectangular-based frustum formed from a pyramid.

base, as shown in Figure 2.17. Other shapes of frustum are quite possible and may be used to simulate different forms of camera lens. If we consider the view frustum as a pyramid, its tip will be located at the position of the camera. The center line of the frustum extends along the direction dictated by the camera orientation, with the rectangular sides of the frustum rotated around that axis to match the camera roll.

The closest of the two parallel planes of the frustum to the camera position is known as the *near plane*; the furthest away is referred to as the *far plane*. Objects closer than the near plane or further than the far plane are not rendered.

The FOV of the game camera roughly corresponds to how a real-world camera lens affects the amount of the world that is seen. In camera systems the field of view may be specified as a vertical or horizontal angle, and these angles determine the shape of the view frustum as shown in Figure 2.18. Given either of these angles we can calculate the other according to the *aspect ratio* of the displayable view.

View transform

The view transform is a mathematical construct (typically a 4×4 *matrix*) used to take world space coordinates and map them into

TECHNICAL

Since the field of view directly affects the viewable portion of the game world, it is sometimes used as a means to re-create telephoto lens effects. This artificial "zooming" is achieved by reducing the field of view. Conversely, increasing the field of view allows a greater portion of the world to be viewed (with an expected performance cost) but will also cause rendering artifacts (such as the apparent bending of straight lines) as the angle widens.

Additionally, the distance between the near and far planes may greatly influence the precision of depth buffers that are often used to determine the correct ordering of drawn primitives within the scene. As this distance increases, objects further from the camera may be sorted incorrectly or may contain portions that vary their draw order in unexpected ways.

camera space as part of the rendering process outlined above. In game camera systems, the view transform is constructed from the known position and orientation of the camera chosen to generate this view of the game world.

TECHNICAL

It is often the case that the camera position and orientation are already stored in matrix format and may thus be used as-is. Since the camera matrix represents transforming the local camera space into world space, the view transform is actually the inverse of the camera matrix.

However, it is perhaps reasonably common that the view transform is constructed as required using a `LookAt()` function based in world space coordinates (since we may not actually store the camera data in matrix form). This `LookAt` function is a cornerstone of camera mathematics; it constructs a transformation matrix based on a source position, a target position, and a vector specifying the up direction of the world (e.g., to account for roll). Note that this calculation does not generate an actual rendering transformation, it simply reorients the game camera object toward a target. During the preparation for rendering, objects will be brought into camera space before passing to the rendering mechanism. A simplistic implementation of a game camera reorientation function performing a `LookAt` calculation will be found in Chapter 10.

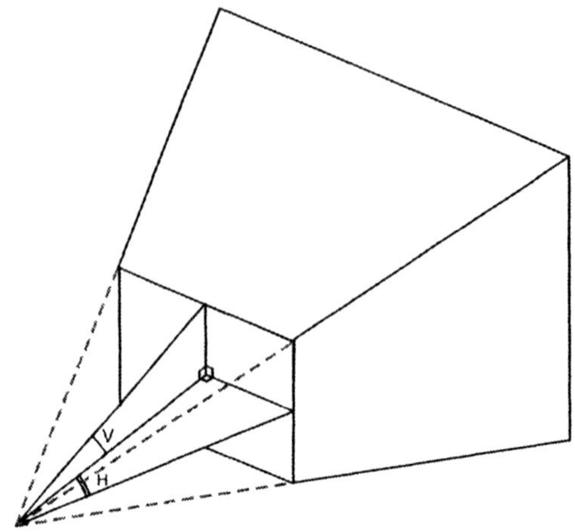

■ **FIGURE 2.18** The horizontal (H*2) and vertical (V*2) field of view angles specify the shape of the view frustum.

Projection transform

The projection transform is another mathematical construct (again, often represented as a 4×4 *matrix*), in this case mapping camera space coordinates into a unit cube. Thus, after this transformation, valid coordinates will be in the range of -1 to $+1$, otherwise known as *normalized device coordinates*. Primitives that intersect with the boundaries of the unit cube are *clipped*, causing new vertices to be generated. These coordinates will be converted into screen space coordinates (e.g., applying the offset of a particular viewport) before passing to the rasterizing stage. There are two main projection methods, *parallel* and *perspective*.

TECHNICAL

Construction of a perspective projection matrix typically requires the following data:

- Field of view (either the vertical or horizontal angle)
- Aspect ratio
- Near plane distance
- Far plane distance

An orthographic parallel projection usually requires a slightly different set of data:

- Near plane distance
- Far plane distance

- View width
- View height

For orthographic parallel projections, since direction of the projection is parallel to the forward direction of the camera local space, only width and height values are required to specify the sides of the view frustum. For a thorough derivation of projection matrices, see any standard computer graphics text such as [Foley90], [Akenine-Möller02], or [VanVerth04].

PLAYER CONTROLS

Control of the *player character*, a cornerstone of game design, is often intimately linked to game camera systems as it is dependent upon the presentation style and behavior chosen. While the topic of player control is beyond the scope of this book, there is one important element worth a brief discussion.

A *control reference frame* refers to a relationship between changes to the controller input and how it affects movement or other aspects of player control. In a typical first person game, the control reference frame typically corresponds directly to the direction in which the player character is facing (we will refer to this as *character-relative*), and is usually restricted to a 2D orientation rotated around the world up-axis. In third person games, the control reference frame is often based on the relative position of the camera and the player character (known as *camera-relative*, as shown in Figure 2.19), or sometimes the view transform of the camera (*screen-relative*). On rare occasions, the character-relative scheme can be used in third person games, although this can cause problems when the character is facing the camera. A lesser used control reference frame is *world-relative*, where the controls are based purely on the world coordinate scheme irrespective of player character or camera position.

A problem encountered by some third person games is an unexpected change to the control reference frame. Most often, this occurs when the camera performs a *jump cut* to a new position, and the new position is on the opposite "side" of the player character from its previous position. For camera- or character-relative control schemes, this will often cause the player's current controller input to force the character to move back toward its previous location. Such a control change is ultimately very confusing and frustrating for the player.

The most important part of the control reference frame is that it should always reflect the *intended action* of the player. Preserving the

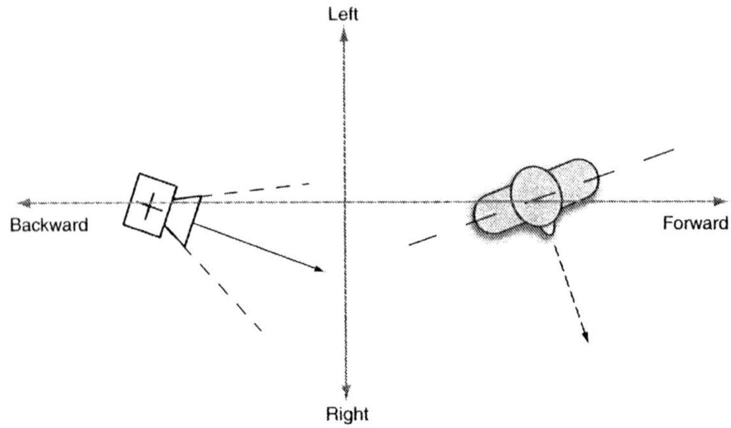

■ **FIGURE 2.19** An example of a camera-relative control reference frame.

intended movement of the character under control reduces the disorientation that many players feel.

■ SUMMARY

In this chapter we have discussed the fundamental concepts behind the use of virtual cameras within games and other real-time applications. In the process we have laid the groundwork for a common vocabulary to describe their behavior and properties. We saw that the choice of presentation style and behaviors to use will greatly influence the player's satisfaction, and this is further explored in Chapter 3. Many games feature multiple combinations of both presentation style and behavior, according to either player choice or game play requirements. Camera designers must choose which of these combinations is appropriate for their particular game, within the constraints of available technology.

Cinematography

Even though this book is primarily concerned with real-time cameras, knowledge of cinematic theory and conventions can prove very useful. This is especially true since camera systems in games often have to deal with cinematic concerns, whether in regular game play or in *cut-scenes* (i.e., non-interactive film-like sequences).

Cinematography has developed into a number of established "rules" concerning scene composition, transitions, lighting, camera movement, and so forth. These same rules are directly applicable to cinematic sequences within games, as long as no game play takes place during them. However, a more interesting question is this: How can we apply these techniques during regular game play? Moreover, is it even appropriate to do so? (One school of thought is that game cinematic cameras should behave exactly as their real-world counterparts, including both realistic physical properties and realistic limitations.) Initial research into this area suggests that it is possible to apply at minimum some of the same aesthetic considerations. However, determination of the appropriate techniques to apply during dynamic game play can be difficult and is greatly dependent upon the game genre and environment.

There are options available for implementing those techniques in games that are not as readily available when doing so for a regular movie. For example, since a game maker is not constrained to a physical camera (or to the exposure properties of film stock for that matter), he or she can freely move the camera in any way imaginable. With the relatively recent advent of *computer graphics* (CG) within mainstream cinema, this distinction is becoming somewhat lessened and will likely eventually disappear. An obvious example of that lessening distinction would be the so-called "bullet-time" effect (as seen in the original *Matrix* film [*The Matrix*, Warner Brothers, 1999]), where the speed of objects within the game world are slowed yet the camera is able to move at a normal rate, thus allowing detail to be observed that would otherwise occur too quickly. Indeed, this technique is easily applied to real-time games where changes to the movement rate of game objects and the camera may be freely manipulated. Increased freedom from the camera's physical constraints will likely lead to discoveries of new cinematic techniques. Further, movie makers are already adopting many digital editing, production, and (most important) display technologies. Game technology itself may be used as an effective visualization tool for filmmakers. We may further expect the advent of effective three-dimensional display technology (i.e., without the restriction of wearing special glasses or headgear) to revolutionize both mainstream cinema and real-time games, and to further reduce the differences between them.

NOMENCLATURE

Cinematography has a rich language used to describe the ways in which camera shots are specified, how the scene is lit, the framing of actors, camera motion, and so forth. Real-time camera systems are developing a similar set of terminology, adopting those terms from cinematography as appropriate. However, some aspects of real-time camera systems use inappropriate or confusing terms. As an example, the generic term "real-time cinematics" (alternatively, *cineractives*) is often used to describe a variety of different situations, both interactive and non-interactive; at best, it is confusing. It also increases difficulties in communications between different disciplines who understand the same term to mean quite different things. Let us examine some of the basic terminology used within non-interactive movies.

Standard cinematography terminology

A full description of cinematography is beyond the scope of this book, and the reader is referred to [Arijon91], [Malkiewicz92], and others for a more thorough understanding. A more direct application of cinematographic techniques specifically toward gaming may be found in both [Hawkins02] and [Hawkins05]. A related subject, the integration of traditional storytelling with game technology, is covered extensively by [Glassner04]. However, a brief review of some of the main cinematographic terms is useful.

Dolly

Dollying refers to motion of the camera across the 2D plane parallel to the horizontal axes of the world. Motion in the direction of the camera orientation is known as *dollying in* if toward a target object, and *dollying out* if away from a target object. Sideways motion of the camera (i.e., relative to its 2D orientation in the world) is known as *crab left* or *crab right* as appropriate. These types of motion are illustrated in Figure 3.1.

Pan

This refers to horizontal rotation of the camera around the world up-axis; in many computer texts it is referred to as *yaw*, and we will adopt the same convention here. It does not define any kind of motion, nor should it be used to refer to other axial rotations. This rotation is shown in Figure 3.2.

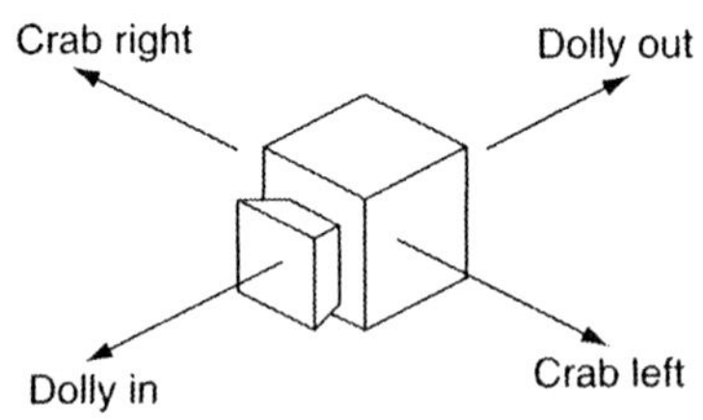

■ **FIGURE 3.1** Dollying motions are restricted to a 2D plane parallel to the ground.

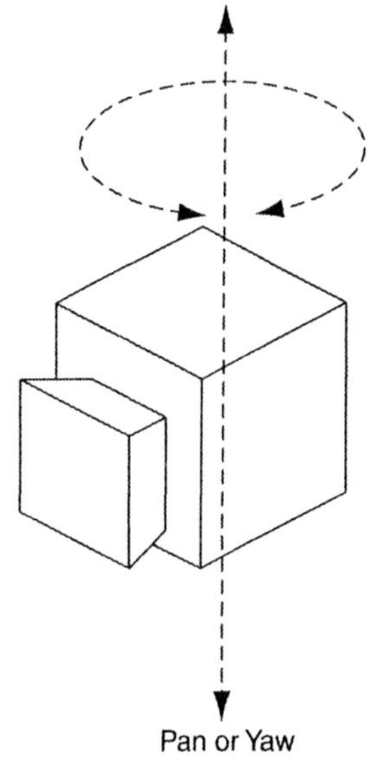

■ **FIGURE 3.2** Panning refers to rotation around the camera up-axis, sometimes known as yaw.

Tilt

Tilt refers to rotation of the camera around its right axis; that is, the vertical orientation of the camera (we will refer to this by the term *pitch*), as shown in Figure 3.3.

Tracking

Tracking refers to motion of the camera relative to another object in a consistent direction; in game camera systems, this is typically the player character, but not necessarily so. The movement of the camera when tracking is usually restricted to a plane parallel to the horizontal ground plane. Many third person cameras within games might be considered as a form of tracking camera. Figure 3.4 shows a camera matching the movement of the player.

Depth of field

Although a real-world camera lens normally focuses on objects at a set distance, due to the size of the camera *aperture* (or *iris*), a small region on either side (i.e., closer or further away than the focal distance)

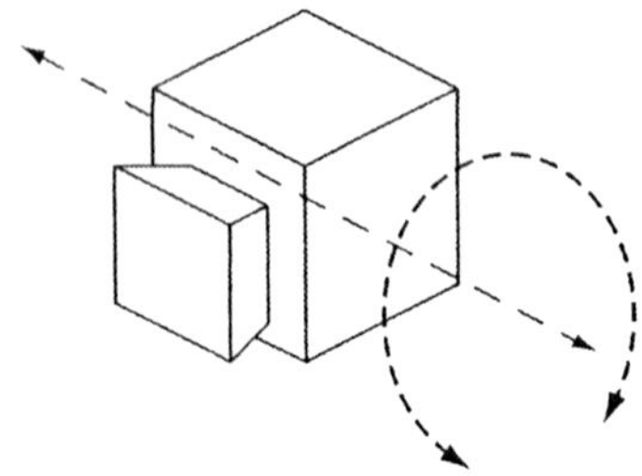

■ **FIGURE 3.3** Tilt is rotation around the camera's right-axis, otherwise known as pitch.

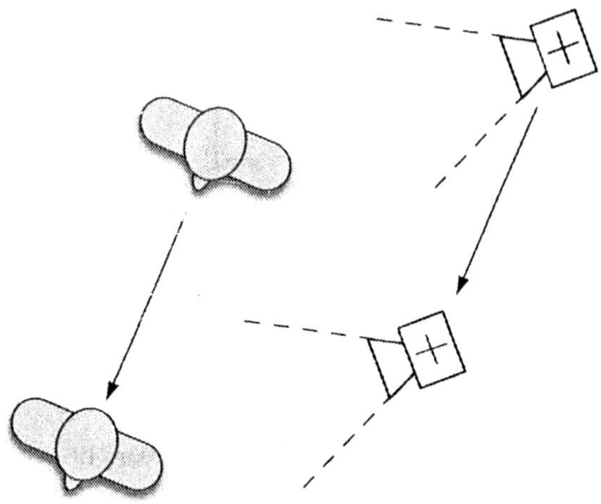

■ **FIGURE 3.4** Tracking refers generally to consistent camera motion, usually relative to another object.

will also be in *focus* (i.e., details will be sharp and clearly distinguishable). This region is known as the *depth of field* (DOF) and does not exist in real-time game cameras unless artificially simulated using rendering effects to blur elements of the scene that are not in focus. DOF is often used to emphasize a particular element of the rendered scene, usually without reorienting the camera, because the object coming into focus will naturally gain the viewer's attention. Changing the focus between characters within a scene is a common cinematographic technique used to shift audience attention (possibly to highlight the reaction of a character to an event or speech made by another character). A simple example of DOF may be seen in Figure 3.5.

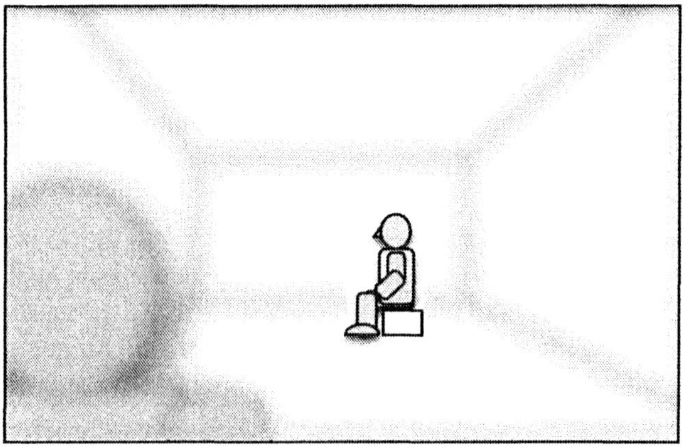

■ **FIGURE 3.5** Depth of field effects are often used to emphasize a particular scene element, and are often dynamically changed to shift the viewer's attention.

For a survey of techniques used to simulate DOF within computer rendering, the reader is referred to [Demers04].

Color fade

During a color fade, the scene is faded out to a solid color, usually black (known as a *fade out*), but not necessarily so. Color fades are often used at the conclusion of a scene, or as a transition between scenes. The nature of the fade can be based on linear color space interpolation, or more "interesting" effects such as intensity or alpha blending. Alternatively, a fade from black to the normal scene is known as a *fade in*.

Lens flare

A lens flare is a generally undesirable visual artifact caused when excessive light enters the camera lens. One typical example occurs when a *pan* causes the camera to briefly look toward a setting sun. The result of a lens flare is that the physical film becomes *fogged* (or *overexposed*). Real-world cameras may also suffer from visual artifacts generated by the silhouette of the camera iris itself, usually manifesting themselves as a series of offset circular colored disks or circles. Many games simulate lens flare effects in an attempt to add a sense of realism to their rendering of a scene. While the goal is laudable, the implementation of lens flare is often misguided. It could be argued that the presence of a lens (or the simulation of such) artificially places a camera within the game scene, thus negating attempts at immersing the player within this artificial environment. For this reason use of lens flare should be restricted to situations where this type of artifact would naturally occur. A related effect used in game software is *bloom*, where the rendered scene is blurred around bright edges to simulate overexposure of the camera.

Cut-away shot

A cut-away shot takes place when a different scene is shown briefly to underscore an element of the original scene. An example might be a *jump cut* (see below) to show the consequence of an action, such as a door opening after a mechanism is operated. This technique is often applied during game play to indicate the results of player actions or to reveal the next objective that must be solved.

Insert shot

This is somewhat similar to a cut-away shot, in that the scene is changed for a brief period. In this case, the new scene is actually a more detailed view of part of the original scene, such as a close-up (e.g., a *head shot*) of an actor to show their reaction to an event.

Jump cut

A *jump cut* is an instantaneous transition to a similarly composed scene compared to the current scene. Although there are similarities between the two scenes, the new scene is in a different location than the original shot; alternatively, it may present the same scene at a different time (e.g., day to night) or different period (season or year, etc.). This type of transition is viewed favorably when it provides a common frame of reference between potentially disparate scenes. On the other hand, it is sometimes avoided because it draws attention to the editing process used for the film.

180 degree rule/line of action

These terms are two different ways of describing an imaginary line between two actors in a sequence. During the scene, the camera should remain on one side of this line; movement across the line will result in the actors appearing to swap positions as seen in Figure 3.6.

Point of view shot

This term refers to a scene as perceived from the *point of view* (POV) of one of the actors, somewhat akin to the ubiquitous *first person* camera used in games. The POV shot is rarely used in movies, but can be effective in games when applied carefully.

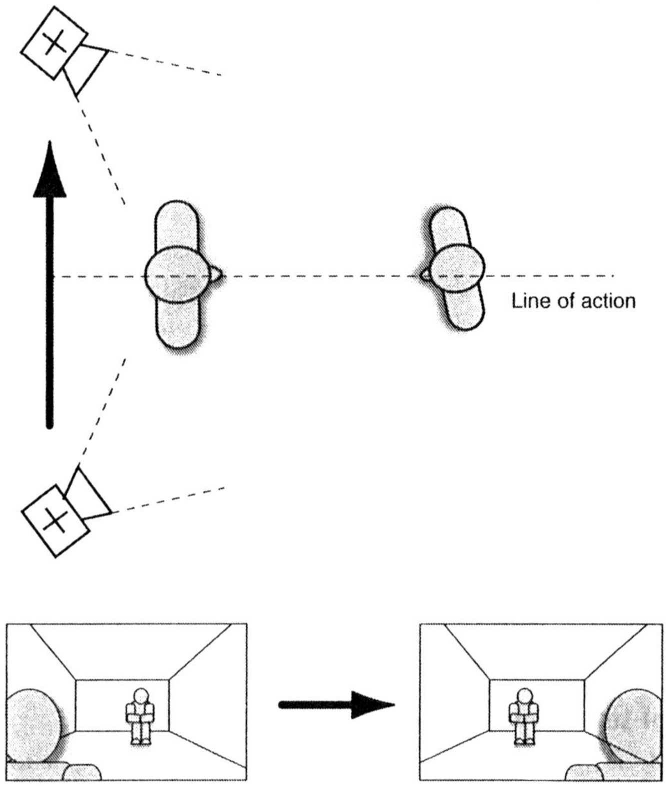

■ **FIGURE 3.6** Line of action.

Crane shot

A crane shot is literally a shot where the camera is attached to a crane to provide a vantage point above the actors. This directly translates into a typical *third person* camera in games, where the camera is mostly situated in a similar position. Vertical motion of the camera is sometimes referred to as *boom*.

Reaction shot

A *reaction shot* precedes a *POV shot* to establish the POV or follows a POV shot to show a character's reaction to an event. Alternatively, a reaction shot is used when an actor is listening to (i.e., reacting to) another actor (possibly off-screen).

Reverse shot

A shot where the direction of the camera is reversed from the previous shot, but still obeys the 180 degree rule.

30 degree rule

When repositioning the camera using an instantaneous jump cut, the difference in camera angle (with the same framing) should be greater than 30 degrees. Smaller movements than this will make the viewer believe that objects in the scene have moved, rather than the camera itself. The jump cut is an exception that exploits this behavior.

Forced perspective

Forced perspective refers to various techniques used to fool the human visual system into believing that the relative sizes or positions of objects is different from their actual values. A common use of this technique is to make miniatures appear to be further away from the camera thus giving the illusion that they are in fact larger than they actually are. Some films have made extensive use of forced perspective to make humanoid characters appear to be different sizes; one notable example is Peter Jackson's version of *The Lord of the Rings* trilogy (Newline Cinema, 2001–2003) in which the actors were often physically displaced to change their relative sizes, yet appeared to be positioned alongside each other in the final film frame.

Real-time cinematography terminology

Much of standard cinematography terminology is applicable to real-time camera systems, at least when describing the same type of non-interactive, passive replaying of pre-recorded movies. Similarly, the terminology developed in Chapters 2 and 4 is applicable to non-interactive cameras; that is, for defining their behaviors or properties such as desired position or motion method. However, one problem often encountered is finding appropriate terminology to describe the use of cinematic techniques in a real-time situation.

There are two main categories of cinematic camera sequences; the distinguishing characteristic is whether the player has the ability to interact with the game during the sequence. Let us examine each case separately.

Movies

The term *movie* here refers explicitly to *non-interactive* sequences. The player cannot change how the information is presented; the sequence is constant and established ahead of time to depict a particular event, in the manner of traditional film. For real-time systems we can further divide this category into two types, according to how the sequence is actually displayed.

- *Pre-rendered movies* are non-interactive sequences that are defined and recorded offline. Playback of the movie is the same every time the movie is shown, just as with regular film sequences. Individual images are stored and replayed in order, typically using compression techniques to reduce the tremendous amount of data required. This type of movie is typically recorded at the same rate at which it will ultimately be displayed to account for differences between international television standards (i.e., NTSC and PAL).
- *Real-time movies* are also non-interactive. Although the actual sequence is usually defined or recorded offline, it is replayed using the game engine to render the elements of the scene. Alternatively, the sequence may combine pre-defined camera behaviors (such as a sequence of stationary cameras) with dynamically generated data, such as the movement of game objects. This form of movie is often used for replaying sequences of game play as a reward for the player, such as those used in racing games.

The data requirements for real-time movies, while potentially large, are much smaller than for completely pre-rendered movies. Additionally, using the game engine allows for dynamic elements to be introduced if required. Examples of this might include positioning (or compositing) the player character within the sequence, applying dynamic effects, changing rendering to reflect state changes of characters (e.g., damage), etc. Thus real-time movies can represent objects in a way that matches the game play experienced by the player resulting in a unique (and more personal) viewing experience.

Mixing non-interactive movies within games is sometimes problematic; while using movies often allows the designer to impart story information in an easily understood manner, they do disrupt regular game play and remove the player from the game. This will reduce or lose any sense of immersion that may have been established by previous game play. The effect may be minimized by careful transitions between regular game play and movies such that the camera movement and other characteristics match at the point of transition. However, even if the changeover is seamless, as soon as players lose their ability to control their character there will be a discontinuity that cannot be overcome. Moreover, the lack of interactivity must be communicated to the player in some manner to avoid confusion (e.g., adopting a different aspect ratio).

An alternative to movies is allowing the interaction between the player and the game to continue during the cinematic sequence, which may take several different forms. A general term for this approach is *interactive cinematics*.

Interactive cinematics/cineractives

Fundamentally, we would normally consider that cinematic sequences and interactive game play are mutually exclusive. This is because cinematic sequences are by definition non-interactive, and as such enjoy the luxury of absolutely controlling the position and orientation of the camera to maximize drama, information, or any other characteristic as required (within, usually, the confines of "accepted" cinematography). Since those normal cinematics degrade or eliminate the player's immersion in the experience, a mix of game play and cinematics is often used, known as *interactive cinematics*.

Interactive cinematics have the ability to dynamically change according to game play requirements, game events, player actions, and other factors as required. Moreover, the sequence is not necessarily viewed in the same manner every time. In many cases, the player is not able to interact directly with the cinematic elements; however, they are often able to control their character in the same manner as regular game play. Sometimes it may be necessary to restrict the player's motion to ensure the elements of the cinematic sequence remain in view (or earshot).

A common example of an interactive cinematic sequence is the depiction of a "boss battle"; that is, combat within a restricted area with a typically formidable enemy signifying the end of a game play sequence. In such situations, it is frequently necessary to present a view that highlights some characteristic of the enemy, a weak point perhaps. Additionally it is usually necessary to dynamically frame the scene such that the player character is visible at the same time as the highlighted element.

This category may be divided into three types.

1. *Pre-defined interactive* sequences are rendered using the game engine in real-time, but the motion and orientation of the camera is defined offline. Usually the camera positioning is chosen such that the viewable play area is adequately covered,

often requiring the camera position to be moved further away than in regular game play. Alternatively, since the game engine is rendering the sequence, camera orientation (in addition to FOV, etc.) may be determined dynamically according to game play requirements.

2. *Real-time interactive* sequences are also rendered by the game engine, but the placement and orientation of the camera is determined dynamically by the requirements of both game play and the cinematic. Usually the game play takes precedence, which can result in the cinematic elements not being visible. Often the environment is designed to restrict player character motion to ensure that the cinematic elements remain in view. An excellent application of this approach was found in *Half-Life 2* [HalfLife04], where the majority of cinematic sequences occur during regular game play, and the first person viewpoint of the player is generally retained during cinematic exposition. A combination of extremely effective facial animation, interaction of non-playable actors with the player character, and carefully scripted game events lead to a very immersive experience.
3. *Pre-rendered interactive* sequences combine pre-rendered imagery with real-time rendered game elements. In this case, the background elements are treated exactly as a non-interactive movie. If the background is generated by a modeling package or game engine, it is possible to store depth buffer information on a per-frame basis, in addition to the regular graphical data. This would allow easier compositing of objects into the 3D background elements. In such a case, the player is restricted to following a pre-determined path, at least as much as is required to use the pre-rendered imagery. Collision or depth information may also be generated from the original source data, potentially adding further realism to the scene.

Interaction by the player during such a sequence can take many different forms. Often it is of a very limited nature, in part to reduce the number of divergent branches required. [Glassner04] covers a number of the alternatives that are available, but some of the more common are as follows:

- Cinematic branching depending upon player choice (e.g., dialogue choices or other interaction with the game character during the cinematic)

- Cinematic branching depending upon player actions during the cinematic (e.g., button presses or other controller usage)
- Modified cinematic sequence depending on previous game events (e.g., a particular character is killed, a certain action is performed, etc.)

It is important to consider whether these techniques would increase player satisfaction with the game. In some genres, this approach could detract from the game by preventing the player from observing important game play elements. Additionally, it is unlikely that a series of heuristics will be able to provide an adequate view of game play under all situations, thus it is important to retain the ability for the player to override camera control if possible. Nonetheless, interaction during cinematic sequences offers another way that games may advance the medium beyond conventional game play and should prove a fertile area for research.

MOVIE CINEMATIC CAMERAS

The most common approach to cinematic cameras is *movie cinematic cameras*, where there is no interactivity involved. These cameras should exhibit certain properties, specifically regarding their motion and orientation.

Camera motion

Movie cameras are not that different from in-game cameras in that smooth (i.e., *frame coherent*) motion is of paramount importance. However, movement of the camera should be minimized during non-interactive sequences. Even though it can be tempting to perform wild camera movement with virtual cameras, this should be used sparingly. Particular attention should be paid to ensuring that motion from a stationary position has gentle acceleration and that when the camera finally stops it should decelerate smoothly. In some cases, abrupt motion may be used to emphasize similar motion of an element in the scene, but generally, it should be avoided. Additionally, rapid camera motion is to be avoided especially as it may give the impression of a jump cut (see the previous section). Some forms of cinematic camera deliberately introduce an element of shakiness to camera motion, such as *cinéma verité*. The intent here is to simulate a handheld camera or to increase the sense of immediacy in the scene as if the viewer were actually present at the location and to lessen or remove the sense of there being a camera present at all. While this goal is perfectly laudable, and may be effective within non-interactive situations such as these, it should be used judiciously within real-time game play as it may interfere with player actions.

Camera orientation

While cinematic cameras also require smooth reorientation of the camera, they can use orientations that may not normally be amenable to good game play or player controls. Since the sequence is non-interactive, these requirements are less important than framing the actors to present the appropriate emotional impact.

Use of roll (rotation around the view direction of the camera) is more acceptable in a purely non-interactive cinematic sequence and can be useful to increase tension or create confusion in a scene. However, uncontrolled or rapid roll of the camera may induce nausea in the viewer; thus, it should be used sparingly and avoided if possible.

DYNAMICALLY GENERATED MOVIES/REPLAY CAMERAS

Many genres of games require or offer the ability to *replay* previous sequences of game play. This may be considered a separate action from simply replaying a pre-rendered movie, or from real-time rendering of a pre-defined cinematic sequence. This approach, often referred to as a *replay camera*, requires game play elements and events to be accurately replicated to re-create the game sequences. This requires the ability to re-create the motion and visual state of any game objects involved in the sequence. This could be achieved by recording the rendering state of every object on every frame, or every couple of frames, using interpolation if that provides an acceptable result. Since that sort of recording can be too memory-intensive, a common alternative is the use of *determinism*. In this method, only the initial game state and player input are stored. Playback substitutes this stored player input and proceeds to run game logic at the same interval at which the input was captured. Since the playback is deterministic, the replay will appear the same as the initially recorded sequence, at a fraction of the memory cost.

In some cases, a replay camera is an exact duplication of the previously presented camera viewpoint; this is the most straightforward form and is often used as a debugging tool when developing camera or other game systems. A similar approach is to adopt the view from a game object, such as a creature or vehicle. Once again, this may be used for debugging purposes as with *Halo 2* [Halo04], where it proved useful to see how AI enemies would change their view to watch for the human player to appear (and verify that they behaved in a believable manner). A more detailed explanation of this particular usage may be found in [Isla05]. Additionally, it may also provide an interesting view for the player. Multi-player and squad-based games often allow *observers* (i.e., non-combatant players) to view the game from the perspective of another player. This also offers a potential learning tool so new players may see how experienced players play the game, or further their understanding of how the AI characters evaluate game play scenarios or implement their tactics.

A different use of replay cameras is to review the recent game play performed by the player. This facility is typically offered in racing games, flight simulation, and occasionally fighting games. Such a system may be considered as a variant upon automated cinematography, depending on the extent to which the camera positioning and orientation is dynamically determined.

There are three main forms of replay cameras: *reproduction*, *scripted*, and *dynamically generated*.

Reproduction cameras/keyframed cameras

A *reproduction* cinematic camera simply adopts a series of stored positions and orientations previously generated at a defined (usually fixed) time interval. This replaying of such stored data is often referred to as *key framing*, and may be considered as a form of animation. Indeed, three-dimensional modeling packages are typically used to generate these key frames in the same manner as other animated objects. This method is popular as it allows artists to work within a familiar environment but naturally requires that game assets are imported into the modeling software.

The exported keyframed camera data may be sampled at the same rate as the game is updated, or potentially at a lower rate and interpolated to match the current game update rate. Reproduction cameras are straightforward to implement, but are reliant upon determinism in the replaying of other non-keyframed game events (e.g., object logic, collision response, etc.).

Scripted cameras

The use of scripted replay cameras may be thought of as a hybrid solution, mixing both interactive and pre-defined elements. The position of the replay camera is typically pre-determined by the game designer in one of several ways.

- **Discrete camera behaviors.** Scripted cameras using discrete behaviors perform jump cuts or interpolations between pre-defined camera positions in a specific order. The conditions for changing camera position may be based on a variety of factors including time within the cinematic sequence, position of the player character (in absolute positional terms or relative to the current camera), and scripted events (e.g., based on elapsed time, an enemy death, a building explosion, etc.). After the jump is performed, the new camera may not remain stationary; each separate camera may have distinct behaviors including tracking, dollying, or other more complex path-based motion.

TECHNICAL

Key framing of camera data requires at a minimum that both the position and the orientation of the camera are stored as well as the time interval between samples; additional information to be stored might include the field of view or other rendering-related data. However, it is entirely possible to reduce the storage requirements. For example, if the sampling rate of the data is constant then clearly it is not necessary to store the time interval between samples. Additionally, the data may be stored as differences between subsequent frames rather than absolute data values. Obviously other standard animation compression techniques may be applied, such as spline curve fitting. However, camera animation is very sensitive to compression artifacts as any change in the camera orientation or position will be reflected in the rendering of the entire display.

- **Path-based motion.** Path-based scripted cameras follow a pre-determined path defined by the game designer. The position of the camera along the path may be based on time, the player, or any other variable. Movement along the path need not be constant; in fact, this is typically not the case. A non-linear mapping of camera position over time allows for gentle acceleration and deceleration of the camera as often used in film. Similarly, a *jump cut* may be performed while moving along a pre-determined path simply by changing the mapping function.

- **Slaved motion.** Scripted cameras that use slaved motion are positioned relative to a specified game object, typically the player character. In some cases, it is desirable to have a selection of camera positions relative to the target object. The camera may automatically switch between these vantage points (say, after a certain amount of time) or be under user control. Obvious examples of this type of replay camera would be a racing game, showing dramatic views from around the vehicle.

Similarly, the orientation (and even field of view) of the scripted cinematic camera may also be determined in a variety of ways.

- **Fixed orientations**. A common situation is to use unchanging orientations, chosen to highlight a particular game event, environmental feature, or to convey an emotional state. Transitions between cameras using fixed orientations can interpolate the orientation over time, or perform a *jump cut* as desired. Chapters 6 and 10 cover orientation and interpolation issues in detail, respectively.
- **Pre-defined orientations**. Rather than simple interpolation of orientations, direct control over the camera axes may be defined using *piecewise Hermite splines* or some other mapping function. Hermite curves lend themselves well to this application as they are easily manipulated by the designer and are used by professional software packages such as *Maya*. This use of spline curves to control camera properties (or animation for that matter) is a common practice in non-interactive movie production.
- **Object tracking**. Object tracking cameras orient themselves based upon the position of the player character, or another game object. This may include prediction of the target object's position over time.
- **Object framing**. Object framing cameras are oriented to ensure that a single object (usually the player character) remains at a particular position relative to the display device. The size of the target object may be altered by varying the position or field of view of the camera. A similar technique adjusts camera properties to ensure several characters remain on-screen, although this may require drastic camera motion in some situations.

Dynamically generated

Dynamic generation of replay cameras is a technique often used within third person games to add greater variety of presentation. Typical examples include viewing of completed racing games, dynamic viewing of player deaths in action-adventure games (sometimes repeatedly, from differing angles), highlighting of special attacks in fighting games, and so forth.

The goal of dynamic generation of replay cameras is to reap the benefits of the large variety of camera movements or positioning possible with real-time rendering, and combine it with known cinematographic knowledge to produce a seemingly endless selection of shots. This ensures that even though the player may view the cinematic sequence repeatedly (as some game events occur many times), a degree of freshness and personalization will maintain player interest.

Dynamically generated replay cameras often use some scripting to assist their choice in positioning. This may encompass restricting the camera position to a specific location or volume.

Death cameras

Another example of dynamically generated cameras is the so-called death camera. When the player character is killed, it is often appropriate (particularly within multi-player games) to illustrate this fact in an interesting and rewarding manner (for the victor, at least). Sometimes this is achieved via a stationary camera that focuses on the player character while an animation or special effect sequence is completed. Other forms may include camera motion around the player character or dramatic camera cuts between varieties of pre-defined or generated positions. Further dramatic effect can be achieved if the previous few seconds of game play are repeated to show the precise moment at which the player character was killed, typically from a variety of camera angles. As with any dynamic camera position generation, care must be taken to ensure that the camera remains within the environment and does not intersect either the environment or other characters. In first person games it is not necessary to cut to a third person view to produce an effective death camera; applying roll and motion to the ground may be used to indicate (or simulate) that the player character has fallen, although more satisfaction may be gained from an external view showing the death of the character in greater detail. Regardless of the specifics, having a variety of sequences available will greatly increase player satisfaction, particularly if the chosen camera sequence reflects the method in which the player was killed.

Respawn cameras

Often when a player character enters or re-enters the game (perhaps after saving progress, or dying during a multi-player game) there is a period in which a non-interactive introductory sequence is shown.

In some cases this may be a pre-defined movie or in-engine cinematic sequence. However, it is sometimes desirable to vary this sequence according to either game play situations or to add visual interest to the game (similar to the death cameras).

Replay camera effects

It is often desirable to endow the replay camera with properties that would indicate or at least suggest to the player that the camera is operated by a simulated human, rather than a computer.

Reorientation changes

One of the most common ways in which this is achieved is by adding lag to the reorientation of the camera. This is typically coupled with overcompensation when reorienting the camera (i.e., going slightly past the desired orientation and then correcting the "error"). Both effects are "less than perfect" reorientations, thus assisting in the illusion of a human-operated camera. Naturally, these effects must be used judiciously: the amount of inaccuracy should be limited and should not be present in every shot. Heuristics based on the speed of motion of the tracked object and distance to the camera may be used to change the amount of overshooting applied. Sometimes deliberate orientation errors are scripted to impart a sense of ineptitude on the skills of the cameraman, or to imply that physical forces are imparted that prevent accurate framing of the target object (e.g., the camera is on the deck of a ship that is on rough or choppy water).

Camera shake

Camera shaking refers to seemingly physical motion imparted to the camera as a result of outside influences such as vehicle motion, vibration caused by explosions or other physical phenomena, or instability in the mechanism holding the camera (e.g., such as a human operator moving over rough terrain). Such slight motion is generally undesirable as it causes visual artifacts and blurring of the captured scene, although on occasion it is sought after to add an element of immediacy to the scene. Camera shaking typically imparts oscillation of the camera position in one or more axes rather than simple displacement; this oscillation is frequently sinusoidal in nature with the amplitude of the sine wave translating the camera and the period determining how quickly it moves.

Camera shaking in a virtual world is typically added explicitly under controlled circumstances; accidental shaking of the camera due to mathematical inaccuracies or movement noise is generally undesirable, as it will certainly distract the player or may actually be perceived as a problem with the camera system. These effects are more noticeable in real-time situations than cinematic sequences due to the interaction with the dynamic player-driven changes of camera position and orientation.

With the advent of modern real-world cameras that are able to counteract the wobbling and shaking effects of a handheld camera, this method of simulating realism in cinematic cameras is becoming somewhat outdated. However, it may still add some dynamic behavior to an otherwise staid scene, even though it has an implicit suggestion that there is actually a physical camera located in the scene. As with all of these effects, camera shake should be used sparingly. It is especially effective when combined with a known game event to use this kind of effect in a meaningful context that may offer additional feedback to the player and thus enhance their experience.

There is one important point to consider when implementing camera shaking. Rather than moving the actual camera within the game world, shake effects are often implemented as a displacement applied during the rendering process. The benefit of this approach is that the camera remains in a valid location, regardless of the magnitude of shaking. Nonetheless, it is still necessary to verify that the shaking motion will not cause the rendering position of the camera to either leave the game environment or cause the view frustum to intersect geometry.

It is interesting to note that camera shaking is typically less effective when viewed from a third person camera. From a first person perspective, it can be an extremely effective visual cue for the player, but from a third person perspective, it may mistakenly suggest there is an improperly implemented camera system. Camera shaking is not restricted to non-interactive sequences; it may also be used in real-time game play to simulate not only explosive effects, but also weapon recoil, reactions to landing hard after a fall or jump, and so forth.

Roll

In regular game play, it is normally undesirable to have rotation of the camera around its forward direction. This rotation is frequently referred to as *bank* when less than 90 degrees or more generally, *roll*. In non-interactive cinematic sequences roll can be an effective mechanism to create a sensation of loss of control. In cinematography, this is known as *Dutch tilt* or *canted angle*, although these typically use a fixed amount of roll. When viewing the game from the cockpit of a vehicle, roll may be implicitly required according to the capabilities of the craft to emphasize motion of that vehicle. From a third person viewpoint, a small amount of roll mimicking that of the vehicle itself can further underscore the sensation of motion. Roll is also used during camera transitions to emphasize motion, especially when combined with other graphical effects such as an iris transition.

Field of view/depth of field

Another method used to introduce a sense of "realism" to cinematic cameras is to simulate less-than-perfect focusing of the camera "lens." This may be achieved by combining field of view changes with depth of field effects to slightly blur the object on which the camera should be focused. This blurring should not be applied all the time; rather, when the camera is due to change its focus from one object to another, allow the field of view values to oscillate briefly around the target values rather than constantly achieving a perfect focus. Alternatively, this effect can be used to blur the extraneous objects in a shot to further draw the player's attention to a specific location.

SCRIPTING

Scripting of cinematic sequences refers to the method by which the camera designer specifies the positioning and orientation of the camera over time. Such scripting is often defined within a proprietary tool such as a *world editor*, particularly when the sequence will be both rendered and updated using the game engine. This gives some greater flexibility and a quicker iterative cycle than using purely pre-rendered sequences not to mention the savings in storage requirements. Additionally it allows in-game sequences to be controlled via game events and to occur while regular game play takes place. It also allows for tracking of actual game objects, which would be useful for dynamically generated sequences. A side benefit is that the aesthetics of the cinematic sequence will match those of the real-time sequences resulting in a more consistent appearance.

An alternative is reading camera and other pertinent information from a modeling package such as *Maya*, even though the game engine itself might be used to render the scene. One of the difficulties with this approach is that it may not be possible to exactly duplicate all functions available within the modeling package (e.g., spline curve evaluation), which can lead to a subtly different sequence than was originally desired. Additionally, the environment used within the game must also exist within the modeling package.

Regardless of the particulars of how scripting is implemented, a camera scripting system often provides methods to control various elements of the cinematic sequence including:

- Camera position and orientation changes over time
- Shot transitions
- Interpolation between cameras
- Field of view changes

A more detailed examination of camera scripting for both interactive and movie sequences may be found in Chapter 6.

One important part of any cinematographic scripting toolset is the ability to quickly iterate and preview the camera work. This inevitably means that the cinematic preview must be built into the toolset, or easily viewed in parallel to changes (perhaps via downloading to a target machine). One of the potential difficulties faced with previewing cinematic sequences is a possible dependency on game logic to control elements of the scene. This further complicates the preview process since the preview tool must effectively include the game engine. For this reason previewing often takes place within the game, rather than the editing program.

Many scripting solutions require explicit control of camera position and orientation in a similar manner to those provided within a modeling package. Some approaches use a scene description language, actually typed by hand. A better solution might be to provide a means to both specify type of shot and position the camera directly. Additionally, the system could provide initial placements based on the shot type, and then allow adjustment of those positions and/or orientations as the preview is shown.

One of the more interesting applications of cinematographic knowledge is to create cinematic sequences based upon game play situations that are inherently dynamic. That is, to blur the boundaries between game play and cinematic sequences in a way that conveys the desired emotional impact (or one that is inherently appropriate for the current game play situation) yet is based upon a dynamically changeable starting or ending condition. A variation upon this theme is to allow designers or artists to specify the intent of the cinematic sequence in general terms, but to use the computer itself to resolve camera placement and motion to achieve these goals. Even though such automation is possible, the results are variable. In great part, they are dependent upon the starting conditions and the intent of the cinematographer. Simpler situations that merely exhibit a particular well-defined game element, such as the death of the player character, are relatively straightforward to solve even in dynamic environments.

Discussions with artists concerning automation of cinematic sequences often result in a very guarded response. The perception is that this process would either replace the artist or reduce his contributions. In reality, the reverse is actually true. This automation process is a tool, and nothing more. It is there to help the artists realize faster, and perhaps offer movement or orientation types that might not have been initially considered. As such, it should be implemented so that it complements and assists handcrafted camera scripting.

There has been active research into partial or fully automated cinematography since at least the early 1980s. Later papers written by [Hornung03] and [Hawkins02] reveal radically different approaches.

EDITING

Editing is the crux of all cinematography, combining aesthetic choices with recognized conventions to produce the final sequence of images seen by the viewer. The basic component of editing is the *shot*, an uninterrupted set of recorded images. Arranging or *splicing* shots together comprises the basic task of editing, which in movie production is typically performed after filming has been completed.

Real-time editing consists of three main elements; *shot selection*, *framing*, and *transitions*.

Shot selection

Shot selection for games typically adopts the same conventions as mainstream cinema regarding the emotional impact produced by a typical shot. The choices of the type of shot are in some ways far more flexible for games in that we are able to generate an infinite variety of camera angles or positions to satisfy any desired shot requirements, whereas film directors are limited to the scenes that were captured to film (which is why scenes are often filmed from multiple viewpoints).

Framing/composition

Standard cinematography has very specific definitions on the placement and orientation of cameras to achieve a particular emotional statement, or to emphasize a particular story element. This placement is typically referred to as a shot and is the basis of all cinematographic techniques. An integral part of shot selection is subject framing. Once a type of shot has been decided upon, achieving that shot demands that the subject matter be framed in a very particular manner. Framing is the application of shot selection according to the rules of cinematography. The same relative position of the camera to its subject(s) can be made to exhibit very different emotional statements depending upon how objects are positioned within the screen frame.

Much of this technique was originally derived from traditional painting techniques and theater staging; indeed, early movies were presented in the same manner as traditional theater, with a stationary camera often with a static orientation. This soon evolved to include presentation of actors from varying distances and directions. This important component of cinematography is referred to as shot composition; that is, the placement of objects within the screen frame. Standard references such as [Arijon91] discuss this topic extensively, but two of the most important "rules" to consider in this regard are the "line of action" (as discussed earlier) and the composition rule known as the rule of thirds. The rule of thirds is a way of dividing the screen such that important elements in the scene are situated so that the results are aesthetically pleasing. Essentially the screen is divided into nine equally sized sections by drawing imaginary lines parallel to the horizontal and vertical screen axes. Important elements should be placed on or close to the intersections of these lines, as shown in Figure 3.7. Alternatively, vertical or horizontal elements may be aligned with one of the lines, creating a more interesting composition than merely placing the object of interest in the center of the screen. Use of this rule in an interactive situation must still take into account the current game play requirements.

Transitions

The transitions referred to here are typically from one scene to another. The rules for transitions are well understood for traditional cinematography, especially regarding placement of characters on the screen. Often a transition will be made to include some common element between the two scenes. Even if the common element is not literally identical, the simple fact that the items are similar is enough to provide a common reference point for the viewer. One typical example is when the main actor remains constant between the two

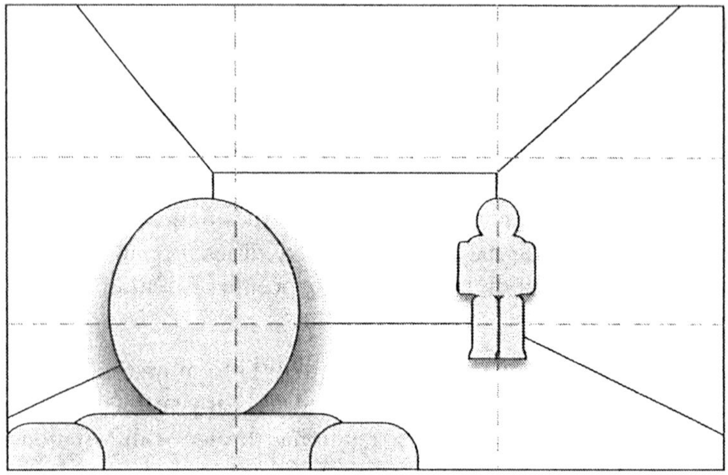

■ FIGURE 3.7 Rule of thirds.

scenes by walking into the camera (obscuring the view completely) then walking away from the camera revealing an entirely different scene. Similar transitions occur when the camera movement direction is maintained during the transition but the scene is changed as the view is obscured by a foreground object (e.g., a tree).

Let us briefly discuss the basic forms of transitions that are commonly used.

Jump cut

One of the simplest of all transitions, the jump cut is an immediate change between one view of the game world and a completely different view of the world. Change in view must be greater than 30 degrees from the previous scene to ensure that the cut is taken as a scene change, rather than simply a jumpy camera.

Everything about the scene can potentially change in a jump cut transition. However, it is established cinematographic technique to retain some common element (e.g., relative positioning or movement of characters) between the two scenes.

Cross fade or dissolve

Probably one of the most desirable transitions, the cross fade is unfortunately computationally expensive. It involves rendering two scenes with an alpha-blend between them, which is a challenge if the game is pushing its performance limits when rendering just one scene.

There is a cheaper form that can be effective, namely to capture one frame of the source scene (normally without any non-world elements such as player score, overlays, etc., that may have been rendered) and then to alpha-blend that captured screen against the newly rendered destination scene. Other effects may be applied to the source scene that was captured, for example, decomposing it into triangles or other 2D polyhedral shapes and then "shattering" the original scene to reveal the new scene, or perhaps wrapping the original scene onto a model, and so forth.

Iris transition

A common transition in animation is the *iris* transition, sweeping from the center of the screen to its edge in concentric circles. This transition may be used to either clear the current screen or reveal a new scene; in fact, it is often used consecutively to clear the screen and refresh it at a different location. Iris transitions are similar to *viewport transitions*, which are explained below.

Wipe(s)

Wipes are methods to either clear the screen to a solid color, or to reveal a new scene. The former is usually given to mean a wipe-to-black, where the screen is cleared by a continuous moving edge of black. This moving edge typically moves in a direction parallel to the edges of the display, either horizontally or vertically. In some cases, a more interesting wipe is achieved by moving diagonally or in a circular manner. Many more possibilities may be achieved using digital compositing to wipe the screen in a non-linear fashion, often thematically based upon an element of the scene (e.g., windshield wipers when looking through a car windshield).

Movies often use these wipe methods combined with a reverse wipe, bringing in a new scene in the same direction of motion as the original wipe. In this way, the new scene is revealed as if it were "behind" the original scene. Sometimes wipes are combined with camera motion (panning) so that the direction of the wipe results in the new scene being revealed ahead of the camera motion. If the wipe is used as a transition between two different scenes, it will also be computationally expensive, as two scenes must be rendered, similar to the dissolve mentioned above. However, not only can one scene be treated as a static scene to save on processor requirements, but the edge of the wipe is typically the only part of the scene that requires pixel manipulation unlike a full-screen dissolve or cross-fade effect.

Viewport transitions

A different form of transition is to change the actual dimensions of the rendered window dynamically. There are examples in movies where the display is temporarily divided, and each separate section shows a different view of the world or characters within it. This division may be instantaneous, but more often the rejoining of the views is performed by a smooth transition; this can be achieved by expanding one view until it fills the full screen, or by animating (interpolating) the size or shape of the window in an interesting manner. The iris transition may be considered as a form of viewport transition.

TOOLS

One of the key elements in constructing cinematic sequences for games is the toolset available to define and control the properties of the cinematic cameras and the transitions between them. Many artists are familiar with standard cinematography techniques and the facilities provided by modeling or animation software packages to generate scenes using those techniques. For completely pre-rendered movie sequences, it is often advisable to remain completely within the scope of these packages. If the scene is to be rendered using the game engine, consideration should be given to either extracting scene information from the modeling package or to providing cinematic scripting support within the tools used to define and control regular game objects.

Still, to provide a seamless transition between regular game play and cinematic sequences in pre-rendered cases it is necessary to limit the polygonal complexity of the pre-rendered scenes, and the components used therein, to match those of the game. This also means limiting the use of special rendering effects that may not be available during regular game play. This particularly applies to lighting effects since real-time games typically cannot support the same type of realism supported by software rendering solutions.

If a movie sequence makes use of the game engine to render its display, or if it is important to include regular game environments or objects in the sequence, it is beneficial to provide functionality within the world-editing tool to support control over cinematic sequences. Some development environments are based on proprietary tools tailored specifically to the needs of real-time games. Others are developed as plug-ins to a particular modeling or animation package. Regardless of the editing environment, it is necessary to provide a common set of functionality for implementing cinematic sequences.

- Position and orientation of the camera over time based on explicit control.
- Position and orientation of the camera based on properties of another game object (e.g., tracking an object or orienting toward an object automatically; moving the camera in response to the motion of another game object).
- Control over the changes between different cameras. This is usually a form of interpolation, in addition to a standard *jump cut*.
- Triggering of game events based on time or camera position (e.g., audio effects, music, particle systems).
- Transitions between different cinematic scenes (using wipes, etc., as mentioned previously).
- Control over the field of view of the cinematic camera based on elapsed time, camera position, or other pertinent factors.
- Control over the orientation of the camera around the forward direction of camera, i.e., *roll*.
- A user-controllable preview of cinematic camera behavior within the level-editing tool as a means to decrease the time spent within the iterative loop. It is required that the view must replicate exactly the motion, orientation, and other camera properties seen in the actual cinematic sequence.
- Additionally for editing or debugging purposes, it is useful to examine the cinematic camera from an external view both within the editing environment and the game.

Typically, these properties are determined by a mapping of elapsed time to the appropriate range of values. While a linear mapping is simple to provide, a more flexible system might offer a piecewise Hermite spline or other cubic polynomial curve to allow greater control over the rate of change of the properties. An example mapping of field of view is illustrated in Figure 3.8.

Previewing of the cinematic sequence is extremely important, as is any facility that improves the iterative cycle. In cross-platform

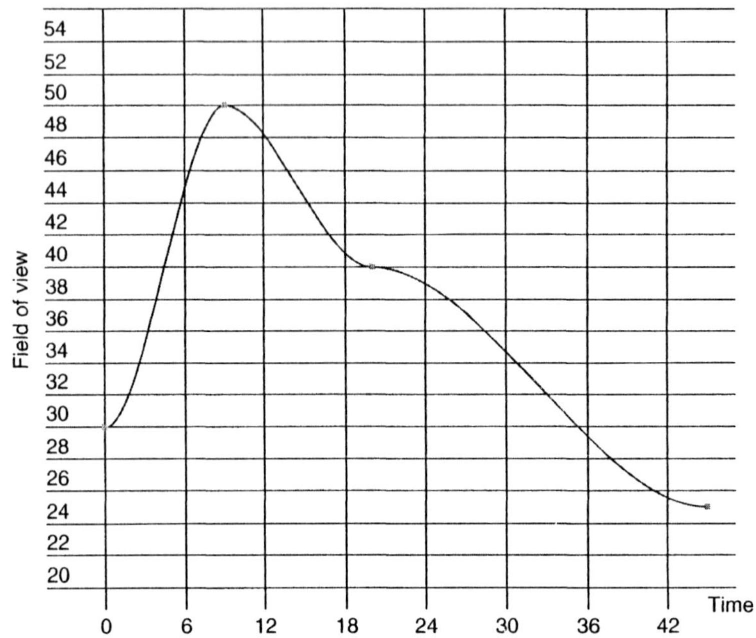

■ **FIGURE 3.8** A piecewise Hermite curve may be used to map camera properties such as field of view according to an elapsed time value.

development it is often not possible to run game logic within the editing tools; this situation requires remote communication with the development system to download changes made within the editing environment. Ideally, these changes may be viewed as they are made, preferably with the ability to dynamically change the time value of the cinematic sequence and to see the effect on camera motion and orientation directly on the development system.

■ SUMMARY

Having a command or understanding of standard cinematography conventions is helpful in several respects. First, it is well understood among practitioners and may be used to bridge communication between game designers and artists who might be unfamiliar with the demands of real-time applications. Second, many of those conventions may be applied to interactive situations, always remembering to take into account the requirements of game play over those of aesthetics. It is also important since it enables creation of video games that impart story or character development in a familiar and easy to understand manner.

Part 2

Design Principles

We notice things that don't work. We don't notice things that do. We notice computers, we don't notice pennies. We notice e-book readers, we don't notice books.

— Douglas Adams, "The Salmon of Doubt."

Given a basic understanding of virtual cameras and how they apply to real-time applications, we should next consider how to determine which types of camera behaviors should be applied to our specific situation. The process of analyzing game play requirements and choosing the appropriate camera solution requires an understanding of the potential options available. Such knowledge also helps in designing new types of camera behaviors or variations upon existing ones. Often simple changes to existing behaviors may provide interesting alternatives. This part of the book supplies the information necessary to make these decisions.

Chapter 4

Camera design

The design of game cameras requires a blend of aesthetic sensibility combined with a thorough understanding of game play requirements. In this chapter, we will examine the basic components utilized within the design of a camera system. This will include the main methods of displaying the game world and how these methods may be applied to particular game genres. Additionally, we will examine why it is necessary to consider the actual camera design process and its requirements as a significant part of the game production cycle.

As outlined in Chapter 2, the manner in which the game world is displayed by the camera system may be referred to as the *presentation style* (or more simply, *presentation*). Game cameras usually adopt only one of these presentation styles, although many games will feature multiple *camera behaviors* even within a single presentation style. A camera behavior may be broadly classified by the position of the camera relative to the representation of the player within the game world, colloquially known as *first person* and *third person*. Camera behaviors (also known as *camera types*) may also encompass a variety of specific camera properties (such as the determination of desired position), yet are often referred to as simply first or third person cameras.

There is nothing to say, of course, that a specific presentation or behavior must be used for a certain genre of game. Experimentation in this regard is certainly encouraged. A completely new perspective (pun intended) can sometimes radically improve the player's perception and enjoyment of a game. The preferred choice of camera behavior during interactive sequences is usually the one that allows the player the best vantage point for whatever kind of game play is currently underway; it should, however, permit player control over the camera if dictated by both the game design and the particulars of the situation.

The behavior of the game camera must also take into account the size and movement properties of the player character, as well as the ways in which the player character interacts with its environment and other game objects (e.g., ranged interactions, close combat, etc.). The choice of camera behavior is sometimes difficult to define, but should be driven by a design philosophy appropriate to the particular game. Some guidelines regarding such philosophies are outlined later in this chapter and Chapters 5 and 6.

We will also examine the possible solutions associated with displaying multiple viewpoints on the same output device such as those found in many multi-player games (and occasionally even within single-player games).

As mentioned earlier, there are two main presentation styles for games, 2D and 3D. Recall that hybrid presentation styles are also possible with either the background or the game objects represented in 2D or 3D. As we will see, each of these styles shares a common set of functionality. In addition, these presentation styles may be considered for both interactive and non-interactive (or *cinematic*) sequences. Let us examine both forms of each style to understand the differences.

INTERACTIVE 2D CAMERA SYSTEMS

While we can think of 2D camera systems in much the same way as 3D camera systems (other than their *orthographic projection*), there are a number of important differences in presentation. This 2D approach to presentation was historically forced on the camera or game designer due to the limited hardware capabilities available (e.g., with early game consoles and handheld or mobile phone devices). However, even given the advent of 3D acceleration hardware (and faster processors in general), there are games utilizing this approach for both stylistic simplicity and innovation. Additionally, many 3D games feature a series of sub-games, and these are often well suited to a simpler 2D presentation.

Early 2D camera systems did not often consider the concept of a camera per se; they simply mapped a position within the game world to the output device (possibly via an intermediary off-screen buffer), although given the orthographic projection this amounts to the same thing. This physical mapping may be applied in a variety of ways. One of the most common techniques used is the *tile map*. Again, while this is usually driven by hardware requirements, it also offers the potential for significant memory savings (or bandwidth reduction for streamed game worlds). Tile maps are typically regularly spaced two-dimensional arrays of *tile index values*. Each index value references a collection of small images (often referred to as *tile definitions, stamps,* or simply *tiles*); these images are pieced together to form a larger mosaic. The display device mapping equates to a window moving across the surface of the tile map, typically aligned with the axes of the map, although not always. Since each element of the tile map is normally stored as an index or hash value (rather than the tile definition), repeated use of the same tile results in significant memory savings.

TECHNICAL

There are variations in how the tiles are stored in memory; it is not necessary, for example, that the tiles are stored individually. Instead a *macro*, or larger scale tile map, may be used to further save memory, at the cost of a slightly more complicated indexing and rendering method. Alternatively, groups of tiles may have their relative coordinate space specified by explicit world coordinates rather than an implicit position defined by their position within a regular tile map. This is particularly efficient when dealing with sparsely occupied tile maps, and presents designers with a greater degree of flexibility, although possibly at the cost of greater complexity in collision detection. Positioning of tile elements in this manner requires a screen buffer into which the tiles are rendered; some hardware configurations only store the tile map thus requiring alignment of the tiles to regular boundaries. It is also possible to use variable sizes for the elements of the tile map, which allows a variety of two-dimensional images to be used together to construct the game world.

Further, tile maps may be considered as a series of layers, usually with a per tile priority value. If tiles may be layered in this manner, then a pseudo three-dimensional effect may be achieved by allowing characters to seemingly move between layers according to the relative priorities of the tile layers and the character. Additionally, tile map layers need not be aligned with each other, thus enabling parallax and other multi-layered scrolling effects by offsetting layers in one or more axes.

Tile maps may also be used in marking regions of the display to update; this is relatively common where tile hardware is unavailable and the main processor must generate the display. Rather than refreshing the entire tile map, sections of the tile map are marked as "dirty" or "requiring update" whenever a change is noted, such as a sprite being drawn. Thus, only the sections marked in such a manner are copied to the display device. This technique was commonplace in early 8-bit computers that had little or no graphical hardware acceleration.

Desirable features

As you might expect, one of the main requirements of a 2D camera system is to ensure that the player character(s) remain on-screen at all times. This can prove problematic in the case of single-screen, single-viewport multi-player games and may result in game play changes to accommodate this requirement.

The feature set for a 2D camera system contains a number of elements that are specific to this presentation style. Mostly they relate to the placement of the camera in relation to the player character or world position; this is usually referred to as *scrolling*, implying that the background is moving relative to the camera. The reality, of course, is that the camera position is moving relative to the background. As with 3D cameras, the determination of the desired position and movement method of the camera dictates the player's perception of how the background elements appear to be "scrolling." In many cases, the amount or direction of the scrolling is dependent upon the movement of the player character; alternatively, the scrolling may be decoupled from character motion and may in fact be continuous or dependent upon game play events (e.g., the scrolling may cease while a "boss-battle" ensues, resuming once the boss has been defeated). Let us briefly examine some of the more common scrolling types:

Continuous

The scrolling of the background is continuous throughout game play, although its speed and direction may vary according to game requirements. Often, the player position has no effect upon the speed or direction of scrolling, although the rate or direction is sometimes varied to ensure the player cannot reach the edges of the screen. In some situations, the scrolling will actually move the player character unless it actively moves against the direction of scrolling. In others, if the player is forced to leave the screen (i.e., if the scrolling motion is faster than that of the player, or if the player is prevented from moving to avoid it because of environmental features), then a player "life" is lost.

In many cases, the player position is constrained in one axis (for two axes, see the following section *Character-relative*). For vertical scrolling games, it was common for the player to have a fixed vertical position relative to the screen, but still be allowed to move horizontally. In general terms, the player character may only be allowed to move perpendicularly to the direction of scrolling, if at all. This limited range of motion is sometimes extended to a bounding box whose sides are parallel and perpendicular to the scrolling direction allowing player motion within its limits.

Character-relative

The camera motion is synchronized to that of the player character (i.e., there is no lag) in one or two axes as required. Use of two axes is typically less desirable as the entire display changes whenever the character is moved; this may result in a jittery display depending upon the movement characteristics of the player character or input noise supplied by the controller. In either situation, the position of the character is constant relative to the display device. Often this is the center of the screen, although with some types of scrolling games, especially when the direction of scrolling is fixed, the character is positioned closer to one edge to allow a larger view of the upcoming environment.

Directional lag

The desired position of the camera is based upon the direction of character motion, and the motion of the camera to the desired position is not instantaneous. Thus, the position of the character is no longer fixed relative to the display device. Care must be taken to ensure the character remains inside the *safe frame* (see Chapter 2); this can be avoided by ensuring the speed of scrolling matches or exceeds the speed of the player character as it moves toward the edges of the screen.

Burst

The desired position of the camera is fixed until the player character reaches a particular position (or distance) relative to the camera. At that point, the camera automatically relocates to a new position over time, during which player control (and often the entire game logic) may be suspended. This produces an effect where the new section of the game world is revealed in one *burst* of motion; as the new section is revealed the screen position of the player character changes, since they must retain their same position within the game world. In many cases the player screen position returns to a standard location, depending upon the scrolling direction.

Screen-relative

The camera motion starts when the player(s) moves close to the edge of the viewable area or some pre-defined boundary within the screen. The motion of the camera continues as long as the character is moving in a direction that would cause them to leave the screen.

The speed of camera motion is tied to that of the player character, thus ensuring that the player character remains in the same relative screen position until the movement direction is changed. When a pre-defined boundary is used it is often restricted to a small portion of the screen area, perhaps only the center 25 percent or so.

Region-based

When the player character crosses a world-relative boundary edge, the camera motion begins. The camera motion continues to the desired position over a period. The desired position remains fixed until an alternate boundary is crossed, where the process is repeated.

View determination

The region of the 2D tile map displayed on the output device is sometimes referred to as the *window* or *viewport*. Early 2D sprite hardware required this window to be aligned with the axes of the tile map. With software-based rendering solutions (and sufficient processor performance), or use of texture rendering hardware acceleration, this requirement is removed. Combined with layering of multiple tile maps it is possible to produce rotating, multi-layered backgrounds with parallax effects.

Even when a 2D presentation style is used, it is not necessarily appropriate that the game camera has its focal point directly on the player character. There are cases where it is important for the position of the camera to be determined independently of the character position. It is still important to consider how the player character is interacting with the environment. If the player character has to aim or otherwise interact over long distances, it is often necessary to look ahead of the player character. Given that the character may be able to reorient quickly, the determination of the camera look-at position becomes more complicated. This is discussed in detail in Chapter 7, although the additional

TECHNICAL

2D camera systems internally share many of the characteristics of their 3D counterparts; indeed the very same system may be used with constraints over one axis of motion. If the camera system is suitably abstracted, the underlying cameras are not aware of whether the projection is orthographic or perspective-based. Thus, the same specifications for viewport handling (interpolation, cross fading, etc.) apply here as well.

caveat for 2D camera systems is that the camera look-at position and desired position are aligned (due to the *orthographic projection*).

In multi-player games within a shared viewport, the position of all of the player characters will typically determine the position of the game camera. For multi-player games, this position often equates to the average or sometimes the center of the bounding box of all player positions. In some cases the position calculation may use weighting values on each player character to determine the desired position, perhaps giving priority to one particular character according to the game play situation (e.g., during a boss battle).

In this situation, there are physical limitations to the player character's motion to consider. If one player character moves into a position that prevents motion toward the other(s) due to the necessity of keeping both players visible, it is possible for neither character to be able to move.

Clearly, this is an undesirable situation with potentially drastic game play consequences. How can this be avoided? The limitation here is that the player characters must remain on-screen; otherwise, it would be difficult if not impossible for a player to control the position of their character. One possible solution is to split the viewport into two distinct sections, one per player. Assuming this split can occur in a way that makes sense to the players, this is usually acceptable. It is even possible to allow player characters to move when off-screen; while this is not an ideal solution, it could be considered preferable to no player movement (sometimes referred to as a *soft-lock*). If the viewport is scalable, an alternative is to move the camera further away from the background plane, i.e., to "zoom out"; this would presumably allow enough motion on the part of the player(s) to resolve the situation, but may not guarantee a further occurrence of the same situation. A more esoteric solution is to teleport one or more of the players to a valid position. This final, drastic, *fail-safe* action should be avoided if possible.

For most 2D camera systems, it is often necessary to restrict the visible viewport to remain within the confines of the tile map; revealing an area outside of the game world is typically undesirable as it breaks the game illusion. Sometimes it is necessary to restrict the position of the viewport relative to the game map to prevent the player from viewing a portion of the game world that has yet to be made accessible (i.e., *unlocked*). This may be achieved, for example, by marking tiles as "un-viewable" and to test for any potentially visible tiles when determining the new camera position.

CINEMATIC 2D CAMERA SYSTEMS

Cinematic 2D camera systems construct their view by compositing two-dimensional images in a layered fashion. An illusion of depth can be achieved by varying the order in which the layers are drawn, and by including transparency or irregular shapes. This presentation style is similar to early cartoon or comic-book techniques; the illusion of depth may be enhanced by the relative motion of these different elements. A typical example of this is a technique used to simulate motion of the camera "into" the scene; this is achieved by moving elements that are closer to the camera outward from the center of the display device (often simply horizontally). Similar effects may even be used with still photographs to create a more interesting slideshow sequence. Here the camera pans across the image while the image is scaled up. An authoritative guide to all aspects of this type of presentation style is [Thomas95].

Typical features provided by a 2D cinematic camera system would include:

- **Viewport panning control.** This refers to the ability to define paths of motion for the viewable window across the world map. Often this path is defined as a series of connected waypoints or a spline path. It is necessary to be able to control the position over time, with motion in a non-linear fashion (to allow for ease-in/out of target positions).
- **Zoom in/out.** Zooming may be facilitated by simulated motion of the camera toward the 2D elements (by scaling the entire viewport or elements within) or by movement of layers within a viewport (see [Thomas95]).
- **Object tracking.** Camera motion need not be defined explicitly as a path or via fixed positions, but could also be defined as a position relative to some target object (usually the player). Even this relative displacement could change over time if so required, and may be constrained by other cinematic requirements.
- **Keep an object within screen bounds or other arbitrary viewport-based constraint.** The camera may move on defined paths or as a displacement from an object, but must also satisfy the constraint of ensuring an object (or specified portion thereof) remains visible at all times.

INTERACTIVE 3D CAMERA SYSTEMS

Interactive 3D camera systems are the most challenging and complex of all camera solutions. Satisfying aesthetic concerns that are married to the dynamically changing requirements of game play is a difficult task at best.

The overriding concern of any interactive camera system is to provide the viewer with a contextually appropriate view of the game world. This means that game play requirements typically override aesthetic concerns; not that aesthetics are to be completely ignored. Additionally the camera system would ideally allow player control over the orientation or position of the camera when appropriate; there are obviously situations where camera manipulation could be problematic (e.g., due to geometry constraints), or contrary to game design requirements (revealing hidden elements or rendering artifacts) and should be disallowed. It is preferable that the player is made aware of when camera manipulation is permissible, through a consistent interface or visual cue.

Interactive 3D camera systems typically have the largest feature set of all. They encompass all of the requirements of cinematic cameras with the added problems posed by an infinitely variable set of player actions. Providing a flexible camera system will allow the designer a better choice of solutions to present their game play to the player. Typical features of such a camera system would include:

- Rendering projection type (e.g., perspective, orthographic, etc.).
- Determination of the camera's desired position (otherwise known as navigation).
- Camera motion characteristics; how the camera moves from its current position to the desired position.
- Determination of the camera's desired orientation.
- Reorientation characteristics of the camera; how the camera changes its orientation from the current direction to the desired orientation.
- Dynamic changes to rendering properties of cameras; examples include the field of view or aspect ratio.
- Ways of interpolating the position or orientation of active cameras.
- Fail-safe handling when the camera is unable to move to a valid position, or is unable to view the player character.
- Multiple viewports rendered on the same display device (also known as *split screen*). In principle, this is irrespective of the projection method and thus should be the same as 2D cameras.

Camera projections transform the game world representation of objects or geometry coordinates into the form to be rendered on the output device. This projection transformation is used by the rendering mechanism (whether software- or hardware-based) to transform world-space coordinates into display device coordinates. In some cases, this transform is only used to calculate screen space positions (e.g., orthographic or isometric projections using pre-defined graphical elements). In most 3D projections, the transform is used to convert vertex coordinates to be used in polygonal (or higher surface) rendering; the actual transformation process is often performed in hardware but the matrix used is supplied by the game.

There are two main types of projection typically used for 3D camera systems, *perspective* and *parallel*.

Perspective projection

This type of projection is most common in 3D games, although it is sometimes simulated in 2D games by use of object scaling or parallax. As an attempt to simulate human stereoscopic vision it works reasonably well. Essentially, the perspective transformation maps world positions by tracing a line back from each position in the world toward a single eye point, with a viewing plane intersecting between the two positions. Thus, parallel lines will converge toward the vanishing point(s), and the size of objects will be reduced as their position moves away from the camera. A full description of this process may be found in any standard computer graphics text such as [Akenine-Möller02] or [Foley90].

Parallel projection

There are several types of parallel projection used in games. Each shares the common property that parallel lines on objects are retained by the viewing transformation (hence their classification). Three main types of parallel projection are often used, and these vary in both the orientation of the camera and the handling of scale along each of the projected axes. They are *orthographic*, *axonometric*, and *oblique*.

Orthographic

Orthographic projections are often used within technical drawings. Typically, three views or *elevations* are used in orthographic projections (top, front, and side); each view is rotated about the center of the object through 90 degrees from the other two, and thus aligned with an axis of the viewed object. Orthographic projections retain parallel lines and each axis has the same scale. Additionally, objects retain their relative scales when projected orthographically regardless of their position relative to the camera.

Orthographic projections are most common in two-dimensional games, since they consist of a projection that is non-perspective and parallel to one of the world axes; this is often preferable for console hardware that is only capable of displaying a tile map. However, orthographic views are often used in 3D games to provide additional information to the player; obvious examples include overhead maps, radar displays, and so forth. The orthographic view may be generated using pre-defined artwork as with many two-dimensional games or can be rendered as such with the appropriate transformation matrix.

Axonometric

A sub-category of orthographic projection is *axonometric projection*, where the projection is not aligned with an axis of the viewed object. The up-axis of the object usually remains vertical in an axonometric projection, even though the other two axes may be skewed according to the flavor of *axonometry* used. There are three types of axonometric projection: *isometric*, *dimetric*, and *trimetric*. The most common of these used in games is isometric.

- **Isometric.** To be strictly accurate, an isometric projection has three equally spaced axes (i.e., 120 degrees between each axis) as well as the same scale along each axis. Additionally, the scale of the receding axes is approximately 80 percent of the vertical axis; this scaling may be determined by projecting lengths along a 45 degree line downward (parallel to the vertical axis) as shown in Figure 4.1a. For ease of calculation, games most often use a 2:1 ratio of the horizontal step size to vertical step size for the side axes, resulting in an angle of approximately 26.56 degrees from the horizontal, rather than 30 degrees. However, since this is an accepted "standard" and close enough to the actual angle (certainly more convenient for calculating screen positions), this is forgivable. Isometric projections can be quite pleasing aesthetically, and it is still possible to actually render polygons in this manner rather than using pre-rendered or drawn 2D elements. Isometric projections may be drawn to show a view either from above or below an object; games would normally adopt a view where the camera is above the terrain. It is possible, of course, to provide four different views of the world (one for each of the cardinal world axis directions), although with pre-rendered graphics this may prove too time-consuming for development

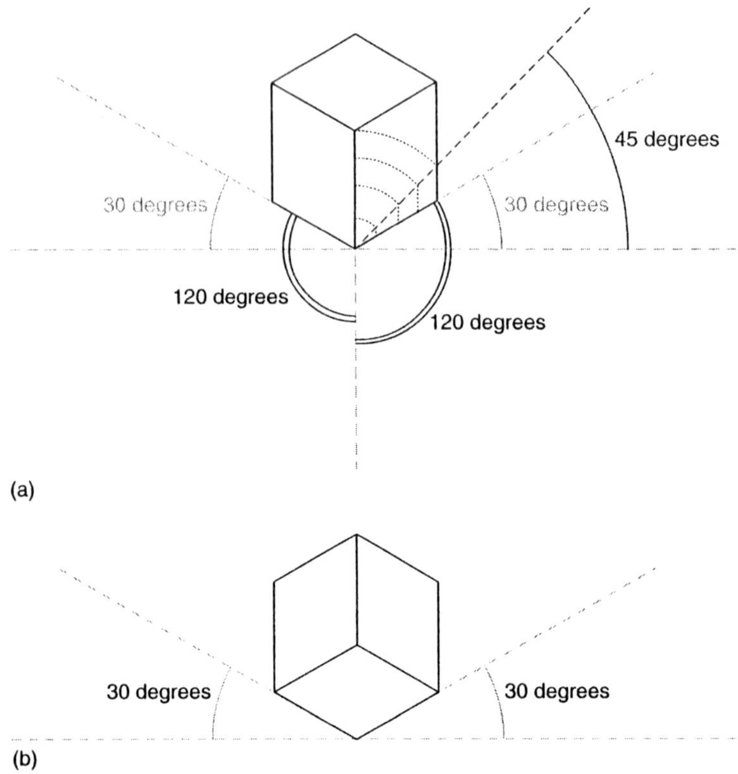

■ **FIGURE 4.1** (a) Isometric projection viewed from above. (b) Isometric projection viewed from below.

and/or require too much storage in the final game. Though it is possible to mirror graphics horizontally to reduce storage requirements, it is usually too obvious to the player (e.g., a character holding a weapon in their right hand would suddenly be holding it in their left when the image was reversed).

- **Dimetric.** *Dimetric projections* have two axes that share the same scale and angle from the third axis, as shown in Figure 4.2. Note that this differs from isometric where the angles between all three axes are equal. Dimetric projections are a good choice for a pictorial view but not as realistic as a *trimetric projection* (see below). This type of approach was used in early illustrations prior to the discovery of perspective projection during the Renaissance.
- **Trimetric.** *Trimetric projections* may have any ratio of angles between the projection axes. Similarly, the scale may vary between axes while retaining parallel lines. Trimetric projections, as seen in

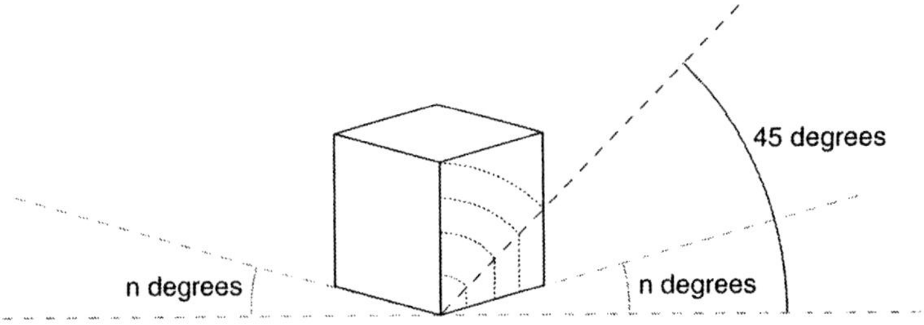

■ **FIGURE 4.2** Dimetric projection.

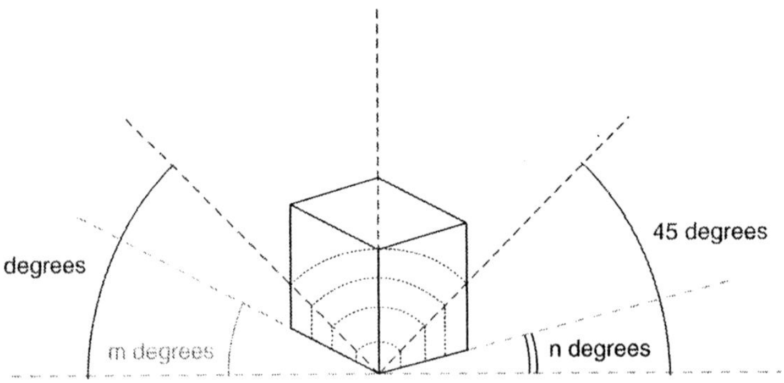

■ **FIGURE 4.3** Trimetric projection.

Figure 4.3, offer a more realistic view of an object than the other parallel projections.

Oblique

Oblique projections are not often used for games, although they can be well suited to tile-based graphical approaches. Oblique projections have two axes that are parallel to the projection plane; the third axis recedes at an angle of 45 or 60 degrees to the horizontal. There are actually two main forms of oblique projection, *cavalier* and *cabinet*, as shown in Figure 4.4. Cavalier projection uses the same scale for all three axes whereas cabinet projection uses a scale of one-half for the receding axis. Oblique projections offer a true view of the front face, that is, a proportionally correct aspect ratio.

CINEMATIC 3D CAMERA SYSTEMS

The main requirement of any cinematic system is to provide the mechanisms that may replicate any traditional cinematographic techniques

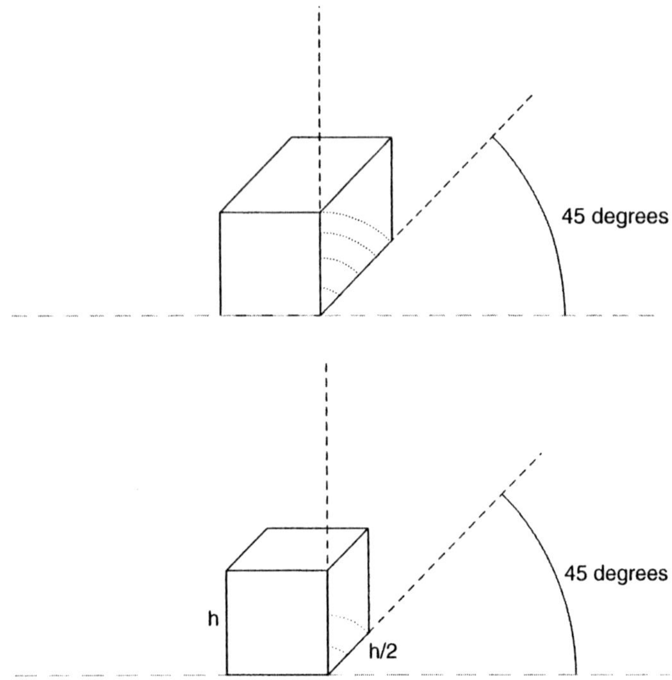

■ FIGURE 4.4 (a) Cavalier oblique projection. (b) Cabinet oblique projection.

required by the designer. The assumption is that the regular game engine will be used to render the cinematic sequence, at least initially. This offers several benefits. In addition, cinematic camera systems have the ability to provide additional functionality not available to "real-world" physical cameras.

When designing 3D cinematic camera systems it is necessary to consider how an artist or designer will create their cinematic sequences. To this end, it is likely that the artist is already familiar with creating cinematic sequences in a high-end modeling package. It would be beneficial, then, to adopt some of the same conventions used in traditional cinematography, and this will help communication with the artists and designers. Here are some useful pointers when developing a 3D cinematic camera system:

- **Duplicate controls and functionality from modeling packages.** If possible, adopt the same methods of control afforded the artist in their modeling package of choice. Sometimes the data can be extracted from the package itself; in other cases, the cinematic sequence will be defined within a proprietary world-editing tool.

The point is to make the artists as productive and comfortable with the camera system as possible. Communicate frequently with the artists to ensure that the camera system is supplying the functionality that they actually need.

- **Develop a common terminology.** Use standard cinematographic terminology wherever possible. The artists will be able to express themselves more clearly if they are able to describe and utilize standard cinematographic devices. If your cinematic camera system allows the artists to compose shots without having to directly control every aspect of the camera motion or orientation, express the shot composition rules in cinematographic terms (e.g., *close-up, head shot, two-shot,* etc.). See Chapter 3 and [Arijon91] for more detail.
- **Consider pre-rendering cinematic sequences.** This can be very beneficial in terms of performance requirements, which tend to be significant when producing dramatic visual effects during cinematic sequences. The sequence may be rendered utilizing special effects not available in the game engine or only using the facilities normally available. It is then stored in a compressed form to be streamed into memory for display as required. As you might expect, the process of rendering and compressing the sequences may be time-consuming; additionally the compressed sequences will require large amounts of storage on the actual game delivery media.

  Alternatively, the sequence may be rendered using the game engine itself; this approach reduces the storage requirements considerably and is likely to improve the iterative development cycle. An additional benefit would be that the cinematic sequences would blend naturally with the rendering style of the game itself, enhancing the overall appearance of the game.
- **Distinguish non-interactive sequences from regular game play.** While it is laudable and even desirable to produce cinematic sequences that are seamless with regular game play, at least in terms of transitions, this presents a potential problem. Namely, we must ensure that players are aware that they can no longer control their character. Visual cues, such as changing the aspect ratio of the viewport, are a common device used to underscore the "cinematic" effect (e.g., to a standard film ratio of 1.85:1). This works fine for SDTV display formats where the change is relatively obvious, but the adoption of HDTV

widescreen display devices lessens the difference in aspect ratios, unless an extreme change is used (e.g., anamorphic at 2.35:1).

- **Allow an early out after viewing scene once.** Generally speaking we should allow viewers to skip a cinematic sequence after the initial viewing has occurred. While a great deal of time and effort will likely have been spent on ensuring the cinematic sequence is worthy of multiple viewings, many players would rather get back into the main game as quickly as possible. This is especially true when the cinematic sequence occurs shortly after the player has restarted a game play sequence (i.e., they would otherwise be forced to view the sequence multiple times in quick succession).

Most cinematic sequences, regardless of the projection used for their display, synchronize object motion, animation, graphical or audio effects, and other events via a single time line. Thus, it would also be desirable to have the facility to alter camera properties over time in an easily understandable method. Typically, this would include motion, orientation, and field of view.

The reader is referred to Chapter 3 for further detail regarding cinematographic techniques, and Chapter 6 for scripting techniques used to produce such cinematic sequences.

2.5D CAMERA SYSTEMS

Hybrid solutions to the presentation of the game world may include blending both 2D and 3D techniques together to produce an altogether unique view of the game world (e.g., *Viewtiful Joe* [Viewtiful03]). While such an approach cannot be considered "realistic," it offers a number of interesting choices and game play advantages. It may also allow non-gamers to become more accustomed to the peculiarities of video game playing; it may surprise some readers that many casual gamers have a difficult time understanding the projection of a three-dimensional world onto a 2D display surface. For these gamers, the visual interface is actually a barrier to their enjoyment. Coupled with camera systems that do not present the game play effectively, it is not surprising that these players do not wish to continue playing. By limiting the presentation of the game world the game designer may allow the player to concentrate on the game play elements themselves, rather than understanding the presentation style. Such a solution is not a panacea, but some 3D games have adopted this approach as a part of their regular game play to assist the player's perception of the game world, especially when the movement of the player character is restricted.

DISPLAY DEVICES

Although camera systems often function without knowledge of the final display device used to illustrate the rendered view of the game world, it may be important to consider its aspect ratio. This is especially important when supporting multiple display formats, for example, both *widescreen* and legacy *full frame* displays. Games executing on personal computers often have to consider different *resolution* capabilities (i.e., the physical number of pixels available) in addition to varying aspect ratios.

Most home video games are designed to support a single display device, typically a monitor or television; portable gaming devices will usually offer a built-in display. Many computer games and arcade machines allow support for multiple output devices. In the former case this is often simply due to the capabilities of the operating system to map application windows across separate displays; there is no guarantee that the displays have the same aspect ratio or even the same native resolution. In the case of arcade games, the displays themselves are a part of the game design. One notable use of multiple display devices is the *Nintendo DS* portable gaming system, where two displays are mounted in a vertical arrangement (although physically separated). Additionally, there are examples of games that split their output between a main display device (such as a television) and that of a portable gaming device, either a separate console (e.g., the *Nintendo Gameboy Advance* connected to a *Nintendo Gamecube*) or even a display built into a controller or memory card (such as the *VMU memory card* plugged into a *SEGA Dreamcast* controller).

Aspect ratio

There are occasions when the aspect ratio of the display does not match the native aspect ratio for the game. In Chapter 2 we briefly discussed four of the most popular aspect ratios, two of which directly correspond to television standards: SDTV (4:3) and HDTV (16:9). Computer monitors frequently offer native widescreen formats that do not correspond to these same standards (e.g., a native resolution of 1920 × 1200 with an aspect ratio of 16:10).

There are several different methods that may be adopted when adapting a game designed for a particular aspect ratio to a different display format. Some of these methods may be adopted without significantly affecting game play; others may affect the visual fidelity of the game. It is often a requirement to support legacy displays that may not be capable of displaying sufficient resolution to discern fine details and these factors should be taken into consideration early in the game design process. Let us examine some of the methods used to adapt the game output to differing display devices.

Resize

If memory and hardware constraints allow, a simple option is to use a render buffer and viewport that match the output resolution and aspect ratio of the display device. Many personal computer games offer a selection of resolutions to account for varying processor performance.

Pan and scan

The technique of *pan and scan* will be familiar to purchasers of DVDs, where a *full frame* (i.e., 4:3 aspect ratio) version of a movie is produced from the original widescreen source material. In this case, a portion of the original material is cropped (i.e., removed) leaving a section with the desired aspect ratio. Unfortunately, this means that approximately 30 percent of the original image is lost. In regular movies this often significantly changes the emotional impact of a scene and may inadvertently remove important information. Clearly care should be taken when adopting this approach. It should be noted, however, that the entire original widescreen format image may be displayed within the 4:3 format display though occupying less physical space and thus subject to lower resolution.

Stretch

Some display devices offer the ability to stretch the generated display to match the aspect ratio of the display. Alternatively, personal computers using windowing operating systems similarly provide methods of stretching windows to user-defined shapes and sizes. In the latter case it is generally preferable to ensure that the allowable aspect ratios are locked into those directly supported by the game to preserve the integrity of the original graphics.

CAMERA DESIGN PROCESS

Camera design is a combination of aesthetic sensibilities tempered by the requirements of game play, and is something that will need to be developed over time. As with most design skills, observation and analysis of existing systems is perhaps one of the most important elements to practice. When playing any new game, intentionally take some time to manipulate the player character in ways that tax (or break) the camera system. Observe how the system handles difficult cases as well as simply noting how it behaves with respect to regular character motion and orientation changes. Determine how your camera system would deal with similar cases.

The significance of camera design as a part of the entire game design cannot be over-emphasized; the player's perception of the game is largely based on the ways in which the game is presented to the player. Thus, it is necessary to consider camera design as a basic building block of game design. This naturally requires that camera design is an important part of the initial design task, and continues to influence game design throughout the development process. It also requires dedicated development resources as with other major game systems. Aside from the tools considerations, dedicated staff are required to design, implement, and refine game camera systems. This includes designers that are capable of defining and controlling camera behavior; an understanding of how camera systems influence game play is a fundamental design skill. Additionally, camera design must occur early in the development process to be effective. An initial pass at camera design will reveal potential game play problems at a time where they can still be changed, and since camera design inherently affects environmental design, changes to the game environment may be implemented before commitments have been made to modeling and texturing. Some guidelines to the design process would be helpful at this point.

Game play and technical requirements

Initially, the game play requirements of the situation should be assessed. This should occur before any firm commitment has been made to the physical layout of the environment, art resources, and so forth. Game play requirements will normally have a higher priority than aesthetic requirements, but they are both bound by the limitations of available technology. In many cases aesthetics overlap with game play in the sense that aspects of game play often rely on a visually pleasing and understandable view of the game world, but this does not mean that cinematography rules may be strictly applied.

Design process overview

Let us examine the practical application of camera design as a part of the development process. What steps are required when approaching camera design and how do they relate to the other aspects of game play design? A top-down solution offers some guidelines as to the functionality required by a potential camera system:

- Examine high-level design goals
- Evaluate player character abilities
- Determine scope of environments
- Define base camera behavior(s)
- Determine area-specific requirements
- Technical evaluation of cameras

Let us examine each of these steps in more detail.

Examine high-level design goals

The first step in any camera design is an understanding of what is required of the camera system. Determine the overall scope of the game and how that impacts camera design on a global scale. What commonality is present in the differing parts of the game? Will a single presentation style be sufficient and what should the style be? Discuss with the game designers their vision for how the game should be presented to the player and which camera presentation style(s) best matches their requirements. Look for existing examples of camera solutions that succeed under similar circumstances and determine what properties are desirable for your particular situation.

Evaluate player character abilities

How the player character moves or interacts with the environment directly influences camera design. Without a thorough understanding of how the player character behaves it is difficult to present the game play in a meaningful manner. A player character that walks upon two feet at a relatively slow pace has different requirements than, for example, a flying vehicle. Moreover, do the player abilities change over time and thus require varying camera solutions? Obvious examples include the player character obtaining new methods of movement through the game world such as new vehicles, more powerful jumping, flying, and so forth.

Determine scope of environments

The game camera must be able to function effectively within the confines of the game environment. Consider the implications of the environmental design upon camera placement and motion. Clearly, a more confined environment such as a dungeon has a larger impact on camera design than canyons or other open environments. Is the player able to pass from one kind of environment into another?

Early prototyping of camera behavior is key to ensuring that the environments satisfy both game play and camera requirements. Once a *game area* (sometimes referred to simply as a "room") is initially constructed, even in its rudimentary form, it should be possible to understand the scope of what will likely be required for the camera. At the very least, major concerns regarding potential geometry complexity and positioning of the camera should be evident. Prospective changes to the geometry or layout of the area are best determined before a commitment has been made by the art staff to fully implement the design for the area.

Define base camera behavior(s)

Once an understanding of the previous three items has been made it should be possible to determine the fundamental desired camera behavior used in the majority of the game. This may be the full extent of the required camera behaviors, except for refinements caused by subsequent game play changes. More likely is that specialized solutions will be required for those situations where finer control over camera positioning or orientation is necessary to highlight a particular game play element.

The base camera behavior should be prototyped as quickly as possible. Since the game play experience is dependent upon the camera presentation, determination of the camera solution is a high-priority item. Nonetheless, it is true that the simplest camera solution generally proves to be the easiest to design.

Determine area-specific requirements

Each area of the game should be analyzed for situations where the default camera behavior is unable to present the game play in a satisfactory manner. For each such region it is necessary to examine the specifics of that area in terms of both the environment and the actual game play elements. An example might be a case where the player's motion is restricted within, say, confined tunnels and we wish to present a view of the tunnels from a distant or elevated position.

We would start by analyzing the particulars of how the player moves, where the camera needs to be positioned during that movement, where enemy AI objects may be placed, and so forth. This should occur before any firm commitment has been made to the physical layout of the environment, art resources, and so forth. Game play requirements such as these will normally have a higher priority than aesthetic requirements, but they are bound by the limitations of available technology. In many cases aesthetics overlap with game play in the sense that many aspects of game play rely on a visually pleasing and understandable view of the game world, but this does not mean that cinematography rules may be applied.

Technical evaluation of cameras

Just as with any other game system, the processor and memory requirements for a camera system must be considered when determining a solution for particular game play scenarios. If a custom camera solution is required for a particular game play situation, the engineering effort required for that solution as well as the technical requirements must also be considered. Often an engineering solution may be avoided by small modifications either to the game play requirements or to the environment. The easiest camera problems to solve are the ones that you do not have, which is another way of saying that you should design problems away whenever possible. Good communication between the three disciplines of programming, design, and art is as important with camera system design and implementation as any other major game system.

Therefore, we need to continually assess the amount of system performance dedicated to the camera system. Running multiple cameras simultaneously will naturally affect this, as will the actual camera types involved. There are four main points to consider regarding technical limitations of the camera system.

Processor usage

Camera systems are often expensive when they have to test or explore the environment. Frequently this entails projecting mathematical rays through the game world (e.g., to determine line of sight), or other spatial analysis; pre-computed solutions typically avoid these costs. Some dynamic systems call for multiple rays to be cast every frame, and this is often an area of optimization through amortization. It may also be possible to limit the testing to ignore certain materials or to have collision geometry that is specific to the camera system and optimized for its testing.

Memory usage

Often camera systems require additional information about the environment to adjust camera behavior, avoid collisions or player occlusion, navigate complex geometry, and so forth. Separate collision data may be too expensive depending on the complexity of the environment and amount of detail required.

Scripting capabilities

How much control can be given to designers to modify camera behavior according to game play requirements? Alternatively, must additional functionality be programmed by hand? Data-driven solutions offer greater flexibility at a potentially higher cost in maintenance and learning curves for the designers. Chapter 6 discusses scripting techniques in detail.

Debugging capabilities

Understanding the reasons behind camera behavior is key to effective control of the camera system. Are we able to expose or reveal internal workings of the camera system in an understandable fashion? Are there methods to manipulate a free-form camera to observe game events outside of the regular camera system? More information on camera debugging may be found in Chapter 11.

Camera design questions

After designing camera systems and behaviors for some time, the process of evaluating the game design can be reasonably standardized. One effective method is to produce a list of questions particular to the requirements of the game design. Consider the following possible questions and customize them so that a full understanding of a particular game play situation has been gained before starting its camera design.

Player abilities and controls

The manner in which the player character is controlled and its abilities within the confines of the game engine have a significant impact on camera design.

- How does the player character move? Does it accelerate slowly? Is the motion constrained to be upon a path or surface? Is the player able to jump or fly?
- Have character motion and abilities been finalized? Changes to either of these components may greatly influence camera requirements.
- Where should the camera be located compared to the character?
- Is it important to retain a position that allows a view from a particular orientation with respect to the character orientation?
- What is important for the player to see?
- Should the camera be focused on the player character or on a point ahead of the character (especially in aiming or long-range weapon games)?

- Is there a part of the character that must be kept visible (e.g., feet in some platform games)?
- Is there some other game object that should be framed rather than the player character?
- Does the orientation of the camera need to vary according to the position of the player or other game play considerations?
- How should the player character be controlled?
- Does the situation demand a different kind of control scheme from regular game play?
- Will this control scheme change according to the game play requirements?

Environmental concerns

No camera system is likely to be able to cope perfectly with the arbitrary complexities of game environments without either pre-determined motion paths or extensive analysis (and storage) of possible camera positions; the camera system has to both dynamically navigate the environment and present a view of the world that satisfies both aesthetic and game play requirements. There will undoubtedly be cases where the physical nature of the environment precludes camera placement to satisfy either (or both) of these conditions. This should obviously be avoided whenever possible and is a good case for prototyping of camera placement and motion before committing to a particular environment. Attempting to find camera solutions after artwork has been completed can lead to both designer frustration and additional work for the artists. Design the environment around game play and camera limitations if possible, anticipating compromises in the process.

Let us enumerate some of the questions that a camera designer should pose when considering how the camera system should function within a particular game environment.

- Within what kind of environment is the character moving? Is the world confined with relatively small spaces or open and able to allow easy positioning or movement of the camera?
- Does the environment influence camera positioning or orientation? For example, the character could be moving through the surface of a water plane, thus requiring the camera to avoid interpenetration of its near plane. A confined, closed space will require a different camera solution compared to free-form flight over a wide open space.

- Does the camera need to be positioned outside of the environment and if so, how will that be presented to the player? How will the camera transition between regular game play and this special case?
- Is the camera required to follow the player through an environment that may dynamically change (e.g., closing doors)? If the camera were prevented from moving, would the player be able to interpenetrate the camera?
- Does the camera need to avoid complex geometry or large game objects?
- Should the camera motion be restricted to a specific path or surface to aid this avoidance?
- Are there changes that can be made to the geometry to simplify camera design or implementation?
- Are there any specific requirements for the camera in this situation, for example, framing of a specific game object in addition to the player character?
- What kind of presentation would work best: first or third person? Does the player character have differing abilities that would demand wildly different camera behaviors?
- How will changes between different camera behaviors occur?
- Can interpolation methods be guaranteed to work given the environment?
- Are different camera solutions required according to how the player enters the area, for example, from different sides of a half-pipe shaped room?
- Is it necessary to have collision geometry that is marked specifically for the camera?
- In general, collision geometry should be chamfered or otherwise angled to allow the camera to move smoothly across surfaces if necessary, assuming that collision geometry is distinct from that of rendering geometry.

Technical concerns

In addition to the more general technical concerns laid out earlier in this chapter, we must consider the capabilities of the existing game engine that pertain to camera usage:

- Are there technical limitations that must be considered when designing camera motion, placement, or orientation? Such limitations may include rendering performance issues, proximity to the game characters or geometry, control reference frame determination, and so forth.

- If the camera is forced to pass through game objects or geometry, can their rendering be altered to make them transparent or otherwise unobtrusive without adversely affecting game play?
- Is it possible for the camera to be prevented from moving to its desired position, and if so, how should this be dealt with?
- Is it necessary to have fail-safes built into the camera system to cope with unexpected situations that normally do not arise in regular game play? Examples might include doors closing between the camera and its intended target, the camera being forced outside of the game environment, interpenetration of the camera and its target, etc.
- Do we wish to allow camera manipulation including repositioning? To what extent will this be allowed?
- Can the camera be positioned such that game objects will be unable to pass through its location or obscure the player character? If not, do we have the ability to control rendering of objects that satisfy either of these conditions?
- Does the environment offer opportunities to occlude the player character that cannot be resolved? Can the environment be changed or constructed so it can be removed as necessary?
- Is it necessary to interpolate or otherwise transition smoothly between different cameras? If so, how will the transitions cope with geometry or objects that might prevent the transition from completing normally? Additionally, how will such interpolation occur between potentially different camera behaviors or properties?

These lists of questions are by no means exhaustive, but they should provide enough information for the initial pass at a potential camera solution. It is advisable to create a document that outlines the capabilities of the camera system and how the game design can work within those constraints. This document will be a useful crib sheet for both level and camera designers to ensure that level construction takes account of technical limitations and the desired aesthetics for the camera solution required by a specific game.

Production pipeline

An important aspect of camera system design is working together with other disciplines in the production of the final data to be used in the game. Several equally important stages define the production pipeline. As a camera system designer, we need to be aware of all of the production stages and to stay involved in all steps of the production pipeline.

Game development is a difficult, expensive, and lengthy process, thus it is necessary for camera system designers to remain vigilant throughout the process regarding the demands placed on their camera system. Constraints upon usage of the camera system should be determined early in the project and enforced with few exceptions. Naturally we cannot anticipate all future camera requirements so we should be prepared to add additional functionality as needed, but we should be wary of implementing significant changes later in the project, as with any major game system. Relatively simple game play changes may have inadvertent consequences on a game-wide scale, and this is certainly true regarding camera systems. Something seemingly innocuous, such as changing the amount of time that a door stays open, can result in cameras being separated from their target object.

Changing fundamental game play requirements late in a project has been the death knell for many games. Good communication between the different disciplines involved in the production of the game is essential to minimize surprises.

Staffing requirements

Once the importance of camera system design and usage has been recognized, it will become apparent that this element of game design will require dedicated resources (for large-scale projects). In practical terms this means that there will need to be at least one person whose major responsibilities will include management of all camera related tasks; the *Camera Designer*, if you will. Not only will their responsibilities include the design of how the game is presented to the player, they will also define and implement the base camera solutions used for the majority of game play situations.

It is usually desirable to have this one person be in charge of the camera system design to provide a single interface and contact point for other disciplines. However, given the complexities of modern game design it may prove necessary to have several individuals (typically game designers) pool their efforts for actual camera scripting and other game camera usage, under the supervision of the aforementioned main camera designer.

It should be noted that camera design requires a particular aesthetic sensibility, both in terms of the presentation of game play but also in how game controls and player perception are affected by camera usage. In fact, these skills may be developed over time and it would be wise to mentor the other designers to increase the overall awareness of camera-related issues. This should also lead to an understanding that camera design must be considered as part of the fundamental game design due to its influence over player satisfaction and enjoyment.

CAMERA DESIGN GUIDELINES

The philosophy of camera design is intimately linked to that of game design. Camera design is a vital component of game design and must be regarded as such. Dedicated resources and development time are required to create a camera system of sufficient quality, but how is this to be determined?

Camera design, like many aspects of game development, is both somewhat subjective and dependent upon the game genre or requirements of game play. Some design choices depend upon the presentation style; others according to the game genre (e.g., sports vs. adventure games, etc.). Nonetheless, it has proven to be the case that there are general guidelines that may apply irrespective of the game genre. Some of these guidelines are dependent upon the presentation style, and some must give way to greater design requirements. Keep an open mind and use judgment as to which works best for the particulars of your game. It is unlikely that a case will be encountered that breaks this set of guidelines, although it can sometimes be necessary to adapt to the specifics of the game play. Care should be taken to ensure this is accomplished in a manner that is meaningful to the player. Some of these guidelines may only pertain to a third person presentation style, and are noted as such.

- **Attempt to keep the player character in view (third person cameras).** Total occlusion by geometry or other game objects (or alternatively, view frustum culling) of the main player character will disorient and confuse the player, yet surprisingly few games pay attention to this essential point. Note that this does not necessarily mean focus on the player character directly, nor does it mean that partial or temporary occlusion is not permissible. The determination of the look-at position of the camera and how this pertains to the player character will be discussed at length later.
- **Prevent the camera passing through (or close to) game objects or physical environmental features.** If the near plane of the camera view frustum intersects render geometry, unwanted visual

artifacts will be produced. These will certainly detract from the graphical quality of the game, and at best seem very unprofessional. This problem is typically easily avoidable; it should be considered as simply unacceptable in modern camera systems. A passable solution to avoid this problem is to apply transparency effects to the geometry in question. By effectively removing the geometry (and indeed actually doing so according to camera proximity), the camera may be allowed to pass through without creating distracting visual artifacts.

- **Do not require the player to manipulate the camera simply to play the game — unless it is a design requirement.** For third person presentations, the camera system should be able to choose the most appropriate solution automatically, even in the most complex of situations. It is permissible to allow the player to control the camera when it is absolutely necessary or desirable to do so, but it should certainly not be required. Many games adopt a laissez-faire attitude to camera manipulation, which is unfortunate given its importance. If camera manipulation is allowed (or specified as part of the game design) then care must be taken to ensure the player cannot position the camera outside of the world geometry or into a position occluding the player character. The range of motion and method of manipulation must be carefully matched to the game design and technical requirements. An obvious exception to this rule would be first person games, where camera manipulation is an important part of regular game play. Even in this case, there are times where the camera orientation may be automatically adjusted to aid the player without overriding player control. Usually this is a subtle assistance to the player in clearly defined situations. Motion up or down steep inclines may induce some vertical pitching of the camera to assist in aiming or navigation of the world.

- **Allow camera manipulation when possible or dictated by game design requirements.** Certain game play situations will disallow camera manipulation, but certainly denying the player this control can often seem restrictive. Naturally, we should strive to present a view that does not require this manipulation, but there are certainly cases where the design would demand the player to examine their environment in detail. It is also true that it can be difficult to judge player intent and camera manipulation allows a greater sense of control and determinism for the player. There can be nothing more frustrating to a player than being prevented from seeing the world in a manner relevant to their current situation or intended action. The problem, however, is that the camera designer should not abdicate this responsibility as a solution. Additionally, restrictions to camera manipulation after such control has been allowed may be confusing and frustrating to the player unless adequately explained.

- **Minimize unintentional camera motion whenever possible.** This is especially true of cinematic sequences, but it is true to say that camera motion should be avoided unless it would either result in the camera being left behind by the player character, or the camera interpenetrating the player character. Slight or unintentional camera motion caused by reactions of the player character to environmental factors (or noise from player controller inputs) should be avoided. Similarly, if camera motion is directly linked to that of the player, it often results in an "unnatural" or "stiff" feeling to the camera.

- **Ensure camera motion is smooth.** Smooth, frame-coherent motion of the camera is necessary to avoid disorienting or distracting the player. Of course smooth motion is normally achieved via velocity damping, which has the adverse effect of allowing the target object to either accelerate away from the camera or worse, overtake and interpenetrate the camera. Nonetheless, smooth camera motion is of great importance and there are techniques available to assist the camera in cases where the player character is subject to rapid acceleration. Low-pass filters can help smooth out irregularities in movement especially when the camera motion is tied directly to that of the player character, where noise from unwanted player input may cause slight motion.

- **Limit the reorientation speed of the camera.** Unless it is under direct player control, rapid or discontinuous reorientation of the camera is disorienting and confusing. Reorientation of the camera causes the entire rendered view of the world to be redrawn; since the direction in which the camera is facing (*through the lens* as it is often called) determines the part of the world to be drawn. By limiting the velocity of this reorientation, this effect can be minimized. In third person cameras, this may be at the cost of losing sight of the target object for a short period. Instantaneous reorientation is permissible when the *cut* is made in an obvious fashion such as in combination with a repositioning of the camera, but only when the new orientation is retained for a sufficient period to allow the player to understand the new situation. Retention of the player *control reference frame* (see Chapter 2) can assist in this regard. Still, instant reorientation should occur infrequently, and preferably not in quick succession. Reorientation to a new desired heading should usually prefer the shortest angular direction.

- **Limited roll should be allowed in most regular game cameras.** Little or no rotation should normally occur around the forward axis of the camera. Again, this is distracting and disorienting during regular game play, but within cinematic sequences, it is certainly permissible. Occasionally roll is used as part of an interpolation sequence to change the player's view of the game world, perhaps as part of a special mode of game play (e.g., climbing a wall and crawling along it). Some games have used this effect to intentionally disorient the player, but it should be used sparingly. Flight simulators and their ilk are an exception to this rule, as they usually present a view of the game world from the point of view of the vehicle. Even so, many people react poorly to extreme roll, so in external vehicle views it may prove wiser to only allow a limited amount of roll to emphasize vehicle banking, etc. There are cases where roll can be used to a limited degree to emphasize differences in game play or to underscore an emotional state of the player character. Clearly, roll is perfectly allowed during cinematic sequences.

- **Do not allow the camera to pass outside the game world.** In the vast majority of cases, the camera is required to remain within the visible geometry of the world to prevent the player from seeing the construction of the game environment and thus destroying the illusion of the game play. There are limited cases where it is necessary to position the camera outside of the main game environment but only when care has been taken to hide construction details from the player.

- **Retain the camera position with respect to the player when instantly moving the camera to a new position (third person cameras).** In other words, try to retain the same control (and visual) reference frame when repositioning the camera. Many games fail to take this into account, which usually results in player frustration as the character moves in unintended directions when the camera is repositioned. This can often result in the demise of the player character, or possibly cause the player character to cross an area boundary forcing data loading or other delays. Retention of player intent is of paramount importance. As with rapid orientation changes, repositioning of the camera in this way should occur infrequently and in reaction to established game play or player motion requirements. It is also permissible to use this when camera motion would be forced through geometry and/or the camera has lost sight of the player for an extended period (say 2 seconds). This case would be known as a *fail-safe*.

- **Do not focus directly on the player character when it is moving.** This pertains to third person cameras that are often made to look directly at the player character, i.e., the position of the player character does not vary in screen space. While this might seem initially to be correct, and it does present the player character well, it is actually undesirable in many cases. Typically, we need to be looking ahead of the character motion to evaluate the position of the character within the environment and to anticipate future actions. However, the rules governing the amount of look ahead are complex and will be covered in Chapter 6.
- **Retain control reference frames after rapid or instantaneous camera motion.** With third person camera systems using a camera-relative control reference frame, instant or rapid camera motion will potentially disorient the player. This often results in unintended player character motion, possibly resulting in the demise of the player character. At best, this is merely frustrating; at worst, it can induce a desire on the player to throw the controller across the room in annoyance. If the control change occurs at the threshold of a game area, it may in fact cause the player character to cross back into the previous area, possibly forcing a load delay and yet another control reference change.
- **Avoid enclosed spaces with complex geometry (third person cameras).** There needs to be sufficient space for the camera to be positioned such that the player character may be viewed in relation to the game play elements within the environment. Small enclosed spaces will require the camera to be moved outside the environment to achieve this. If kept in close proximity to the player character it will likely result in poor framing and frequent loss of line of sight. Environmental construction should take camera framing requirements into consideration from the initial design stages.

■ SUMMARY

In this chapter we have seen the importance of camera design and how it should be considered as a fundamental part of the game design process. For large projects, dedicated resources are required to fully integrate camera design into real-time applications and this must be accounted for early within the production pipeline.

The main types of camera presentation were discussed in addition to the choice of those styles in both real-time and non-interactive sequences. We have seen that 2D presentation styles also require effort in ensuring that the displayed portion of the game world reflects the desires of the game designer while avoiding aesthetic problems.

Camera design is not a trivial process, rather, it is an integral part of the game design that exerts a great influence over user satisfaction. It requires time and planning to be successful and as with all such tasks benefits from additional research and development.

Chapter 5

Camera solutions

Given an understanding of the basic presentation styles and camera behaviors, let us examine some of the more common game genres and discuss the camera solutions most often applied. To reiterate, these camera choices are by no means set in stone; the reader is encouraged to experiment with different camera solutions as part of the ongoing design process.

The definitions of specific game genres are somewhat subjective and certainly open to interpretation; however, it would be useful to have a reference that can be used to help define the required types of camera behavior. Any potential taxonomy of genres presented here would likely be out of date before the publication of this book. However, useful material for such definitions may be garnered from [Salen04], [Wolf02], [Crawford03], and so forth. Naturally, there are several online repositories of game genre definitions, including [Lionheart].

GAME GENRE CAMERA SOLUTIONS

For our purposes, we will enumerate several of the major genre categories that might require different camera solutions. These solutions may subsequently be applied to any game genre as long as they provide the player with an appropriate view of the game play.

First person shooter/adventure

The *first person shooter* (or FPS) game usually presents an immersive view of the game world to the player, particularly since it closely resembles how players experience the real world. Of course many games depicted in this manner are not focused only on combat, even if it may be present. A clear example of this is *Metroid Prime* [Metroid02], which garnered a new moniker, namely the *first person adventure* (FPA). Even though this is one of the most straightforward camera genres to implement, the typical FPS game may involve several subtleties that are not immediately obvious to the casual player. Of course, this is how it should be; the role of the camera system is preferably unnoticed. Let us examine some of the particulars of FPS camera design.

Position determination

Since this view represents the player's position within the game world, the first person camera motion is typically synchronized to that of the player. This is achieved by specifying the camera position as a pre-defined offset relative to the player character's origin, often as a purely vertical displacement relative to the world coordinate axes. Sometimes this position is determined by a locator or other position and orientation markers attached to animation or model data.

Although it might be expected that this position would correspond to the physical location of the player character's eye point (with respect to an external view of the player character model), this is often not the case. There are several reasons for this: first, the vertical position of the camera influences the player's perception of the scale of the world and their sensation of speed when moving through it and second, there may be rendered elements such as a weapon, or part of the player character's arms or hands used to enhance the player's perception of their presence in the game world. These rendered elements are typically of a size (and position) that is appropriate for actual game viewport size (so as not to obscure the player's view of the world), rather than their true physical size in relation to the scale of the game world. Moreover, these elements are often positioned simply to ensure that they are visible. In reality, such elements are rarely seen from eye positions of humans unless the head is tilted.

TECHNICAL

Any disparity between the actual positions of the player weapons (i.e., according to the scale of the character or its rendered model) and their position when viewed in a first person camera may be a problem in multiplayer games. While the projectiles fired from the player's weapon may be issued from a visibly correct position for the player that is firing, if they are viewed from an external camera (such as that of a different player) there may potentially be a large enough gap that is undesirable.

This problem may sometimes be masked by a muzzle flash or similar graphical effect overlaid at the position the projectile is created. Alternatively, it is possible to modify the rendering position of the projectile during the initial moments of its launch (at least in the external view) to lessen or remove the problem. If the projectile is sufficiently fast moving, the problem may be less apparent (depending on whether the projectile is moved before the first time it is rendered).

Another possibility is to select a vertical position for the camera that allows a sufficient view of the ground to better facilitate jumping or other navigation of precipitous situations. Additionally, the vertical pitch of the camera may be automated (e.g., under certain circumstances such as ramps or slopes, or during the downward motion of a jump) to present the best contextually appropriate view.

Orientation determination

Since the first person camera represents a view from the player character's position, it is usually the case that the orientation of the camera is set to present a view similar to that experienced by humans when walking or standing; that is, a level view looking straight ahead in the direction that the character is facing. First person games often require players to explore their environment or to react to attacks from enemies outside of this basic view. Thus, it is usual to allow the player limited control over the orientation of the camera, often independent of the player character's motion. This technique is normally referred to as *free-look*. The forward direction of the player character often defines a reference frame around which the free-look controls will function. If the player is prevented from moving while using free-look, the range of reorientations of the camera form a cone with its apex at the eye position of the player character.

If player motion is allowed during free-look, then horizontal and vertical controls should be considered separately. In both cases, the vertical orientation of the camera is constrained in the same manner as the previous example. In one instance, the horizontal orientation of the camera is synchronized to that of the player character. Thus the free-look controls will turn the player character and no restrictions are necessary other than those normally applied to limit the character's angular rotation speed. In the second instance, the horizontal free-look controls alter the orientation of the camera based upon the orientation of the player character, as if its head and/or torso were turning independently of its legs. Naturally free-look may be used in many instances where a non-humanoid representation is used for the player character, but the analogy is valid.

It should be noted that free-look is not limited to first person cameras; further details of both first and third person camera usage may be found in Chapter 7. Additionally, there are other potential influences to the camera orientation in first person cameras. It is possible, for example, to automate the vertical reorientation of the camera under some circumstances as an aid to the player. One such example would be lowering or raising the camera elevation to assist the player when moving down or up a steep ramp. A similar example would be automatically pitching the camera downward toward the end of a jump so that the landing area is slightly more visible. Naturally, the changes in orientation must typically be smooth and should not prevent the regular use of free-look.

Weapon or arm position

The depiction of the player character in a typical FPS is often limited to a weapon or partial view of the character's arms with the position of the weapon often chosen for aesthetic concerns and visibility.

Discrepancy with external views

In multi-player games the representation of the player as seen by others may not match the position within the world from which the player fires.

Transitions from third person

For games that allow transitions between external views of the character and the regular first person viewpoint it is necessary to ensure that the change occurs seamlessly. A common method is to use a jump cut, particularly if it would be problematic to move the camera through the environment (perhaps due to geometry complexity or distance).

Zoom effects

Many FPS games feature weapons that simulate the effect of a telephoto or zoom lens.

Lack of peripheral vision

The limited horizontal field of view (FOV) in many FPS games can make the player feel claustrophobic as well as restricting their view of enemies and the like. Many FPS games apply this limit for performance reasons but also to reduce the distortion of the game world caused by a wide angle perspective transformation. With the advent of widescreen displays the horizontal FOV must be increased accordingly with potential performance concerns that must be taken into consideration.

Aiming position

While many FPS games use a static position relative to the camera view for shooting purposes, it is sometimes necessary for the player's weapon to track a position within the world. This position is typically determined by the use of an aiming reticule, but may also be based upon game scripting or player mode (e.g., locked-on).

Motion sickness

Many readers are likely to be familiar with the nausea that is often induced when watching an FPS game played by someone else.

Camera shaking

During FPS games it is sometimes necessary to emphasize the results of explosions or other shocks to underscore the player's presence within the virtual environment (e.g., weapon recoil). Typically these involve multiple cues including audio effects but more specifically, movement of the first person camera.

Camera bob

As the player character moves through the environment, FPS games will sometimes add some slight motion to the camera, relative to the player position. This movement is often a pre-defined path or vertical displacement, with a magnitude proportional to the movement speed of the player. Some circumstances will reduce or remove this motion, particularly cases where the motion of the player is not reflective of the character walking or running under his own direction. Occasionally this type of effect is used to imply that the player character is in some way injured. Care must be taken when applying such motion to ensure the camera will not pass through geometry, but more important that the player is not subject to nausea.

Idle wandering

Somewhat akin to a camera bob, some FPS games will apply a random or semi-random reorientation of the camera over time once the player character has come to rest and not received any player input for a reasonable period. This is often combined with animation of the player character's weapon or arms in a manner to suggest that the character is awaiting the player to perform an action.

Scale

Issues of scale are prevalent in FPS games such that viewers may not feel as if their character is moving quickly through the environment even though the actual speed (in relative terms) of the character may be quite high. For example, in *Metroid Prime* [Metroid02], the protagonist is able to move up to 12 meters per second while on foot — fast enough to easily obtain the world 100 meter record! While the placement of the camera in FPS games approximates the position of the protagonist's eyes, it is often the case that this position must be moved vertically away from the "correct" physical location to allow the viewer an improved view of the game world.

TECHNICAL

Given that the position of the camera is calculated as a fixed position relative to the player character, the camera is subject to anything that affects the motion of the player character. This includes any slight or momentary motion to the player induced by player controls or elements of the game environment such as small protuberances or other uneven surfaces. Many games featuring characters that move on the surface of terrain (whether using first or third person cameras) allow the player character to move across such small obstructions as an aid to game play rather than causing the character to be stopped by something that should not really influence their motion. This is typically achieved by allowing the player to be repositioned vertically above the collision point if the amount of motion would be reasonably small. This amount of allowable vertical motion is often called the *step-up threshold*. The vertical movement of the player would be instantaneous and perhaps only last for a fraction of a second before moving back to its original vertical position. Since the camera view is tied to the position of the player, this causes the camera view to move vertically by a small amount resulting in an unwanted visual anomaly or "glitch."

However, this problem may be avoided by incorporating a small amount of damping on vertical motion of the camera (not the player). Essentially, we can limit the vertical movement of the camera so that it remains smooth regardless of how the player character is moving. This damping is only applied while the character is traversing across uneven surfaces in the game world. It may also be used to enhance the sensation of jumping and landing by adding a small amount of lag into the camera's vertical motion. Chapter 10 discusses in detail a method of such damping.

Care must be taken to ensure that the damping is not applied where rapid vertical motion of the player character requires the first person camera to remain fixed relative to the player (e.g., in an elevator). Additionally, the amount of damping should be smaller in first person than third person cameras; we must ensure that the camera stays close to the player characters to allow players to correctly manipulate them. Third person cameras are usually sufficiently far from the player character to allow vertical lag not to affect the player's understanding of their character's position within the game world.

Character/action adventure

The character-based game genre, where the player is depicted by an animated humanoid or similar character (including the action adventure category), encompasses a wide variety of camera solutions. In many cases, we can determine the camera solution according to the player character's abilities. The methods used by the character to traverse the environment, for example, can greatly affect the positioning and orientation of the camera. Broadly speaking we can divide player character abilities into two main properties in this regard, ground-based and flying (or swimming). Vehicle characters, whether flying or ground-based, require a slightly different approach and will be discussed later in this chapter, in the Racing Games and Ground (or Surface) Vehicles sections.

Ground-based characters

A common situation is that the player character walks or runs across the surface of the environment, possibly with the ability to jump above the ground for short periods. Additionally the character may be able to fall off ledges and other raised portions of the environment. A typical camera solution in this case is to locate the camera behind the direction of motion of the character and slightly raised above the height of the character.

As the player character turns, the camera tries to maintain a position behind the direction in which the character is facing by pivoting around the player in a horizontal arc. In some games the camera is tied to this position as if there were a "rod" connecting the camera to the player character, thus causing the camera position to be synchronized with the rotation of the player character. This can be disorienting to the player due to the high angular velocity that is imparted to the camera, and thus the whole rendered scene. An often used solution is to limit the angular velocity of the camera around the player character as well as damping the angular motion as it approaches the desired position (or angular displacement). This angular *lag* in determining the position of the camera has some pleasing aesthetic qualities. First, it reduces the disorientation caused by rapid rotation of the player character (although orientation is a different matter). Second, the camera view will sometimes show views from the sides of the character, further emphasizing the three-dimensional nature of the player character model. Care must be taken to ensure that the lag is not so great it causes the camera to be positioned to change the control reference frame or prevent the player from seeing where the character is moving. This may be achieved by having constraints for the maximum and minimum angular displacement of the camera from the desired horizontal angle. There are many examples of this type of camera behavior in third person games, for example, *Tomb Raider* [Tomb96].

A different approach to determining the camera position is to ignore the orientation of the player character. In this case, only the required distance and elevation are necessary; the direction is the current bearing between the camera and the target object. Since the camera does not rotate to its desired position around the player character, the player character is free to adopt any orientation with respect to the camera. With this type of non-directional camera positioning, the *control reference frame* is usually based upon the positional relationship between the camera and the player character (*camera relative*), rather than the character orientation itself (*character relative*). In this way, the player character is able to rotate or move in circles without forcing the camera to move rapidly through the world to maintain a position behind the player character. Popular examples of this approach include the *Ratchet and Clank* series [Ratchet02], and *Super Mario 64* [Mario96] or *Super Mario Sunshine* [Mario02].

The reaction of the camera to vertical motion of the character should be carefully considered. If the vertical camera motion is directly tied to that of the player character, the resulting motion may be distracting, especially if the player character is traversing uneven geometry. Damping of the vertical motion of the camera, as previously mentioned with first person cameras, can greatly help in reducing unwanted camera motion. However, the vertical motion of the camera cannot be slowed excessively such that the player character leaves the view frustum for an extended period, or that the camera orientation must pitch suddenly to keep the character in view.

Usually the camera is raised above the head of the character and moved away by a distance such that a sufficient amount of the surrounding environment may be seen. There are cases where the camera needs to be positioned below the character. An obvious example would be stealth games where the character may be suspended by the hands.

Flying or swimming characters

Flying characters share sufficient similarities with swimming characters that they may be considered together, although the latter typically move slower. The distinguishing characteristic of this type of motion is the freedom for the player character to move within the environment in ways that may cause difficulty in determining a position for the camera. Both of these cases often benefit from a non-directional camera solution even though they are often approached with a solution that requires the camera to remain behind the direction of motion. Non-directional approaches work well when a swimming character is able to change direction rapidly including moving directly toward the camera itself. Depending on the environment, stationary cameras may work well if the swimming area is contained within a small volume. Flying characters often move faster than swimming ones and may require faster reorientation of the camera in addition to faster motion. In both situations positional or rotational lag can greatly add to the sensation of acceleration of the character. If the flying character is able to roll or bank, the camera may wish to introduce some measure of this to its own orientation. However, a direct relationship between the two may induce motion sickness in some players; it should therefore be used with caution.

Stealth

A popular genre of third person games is that of the stealth or close combat game. These games often use a variant upon the character-based camera style mentioned previously. One of the most important aspects of the camera in these games is to be able to adequately present a view that shows the relationship of the character to other enemies. An additional problem would be the use of ranged weapons, as with other related third person presentations. If precise aiming is required by the game design, a hybrid solution combining elements of both first and third person cameras should be considered, as discussed next.

Alternatively, a modal camera that automatically changes viewpoint according to the player action may work well; here the camera system would react to weapon or item usage. Naturally, it is possible to give players a selection of camera positions or behaviors under their control. The *Splinter Cell* series of games falls into this category of camera presentation. A common feature of similar stealth games is contextual positioning and manipulation of the camera. A typical example occurs when the player character moves close to a wall near an outside corner. As the character approaches the corner, the camera moves into a position (often far from the player character) to allow viewing of the area around the corner from the character without requiring the character to move into an exposed position. Often the player is able to manipulate the orientation (and possibly position) of the camera to a limited degree, thus allowing some limited exploration of the surrounding area while remaining in cover. Sometimes if the player chooses to use his weapon then the character moves to a position clear of the cover and the camera adjusts to allow better aiming. First person games may also offer an option for the camera to move to an external view for cover purposes. This may involve applying a small displacement of its position away from the player character simulating the effect of the character leaning around a corner (this might be combined with a small amount of roll to further emphasize the simulated movement).

Stealth games often feature situations where the player character must move through confined spaces. This may cause problems in positioning the camera to allow a good view of the player character and his surroundings. Indeed, the player character is likely to occupy a relatively large amount of screen space in such a confined space, actually preventing a good view of the game play in many cases. In these situations, it is common to use transparency or alpha-blending rendering effects on the player character to allow the player to see more of the game play. Naturally, this approach may be viewed as somewhat unnatural, at least in terms of the fiction of the game, but it is a reasonably acceptable solution given such positional constraints imposed upon the camera.

Sometimes it is preferable to move the camera to a vantage point actually outside of the regular game world, simply to ensure the player has an unobstructed view of the game play. Care must be taken in such a course of action; such a presentation style must be seen to be intentional and will likely involve additional art production to ensure that inappropriate environmental elements are hidden (e.g., back-facing geometry). It is also suggested that transitions between cameras confined within the environment and external ones should be accompanied by a graphical and/or audio cue to emphasize the deliberate choice of positioning the camera outside the game world. These transitions tend to be best achieved through *jump cuts* (see Chapter 4) rather than interpolation. In fact, a consistent approach for any jump cuts performed during game play would be an additional aid to player reorientation.

An alternative and often used solution is to pre-define the motion of the camera using paths or other direct positioning controls such as implicit surfaces (see Chapter 8 for more details). Stationary cameras are another type of camera that works well, but the transitions between them and regular tracking cameras can prove difficult in such areas unless a *jump cut* is performed. This is mainly because the change in position may affect the player control reference frame and disorient the player considerably.

3D platform

The 3D platform game is a mainstay of third person camera usage. Since it requires a view of the player character and the environment, this presentation style places great demands upon the underlying camera system; this is evident for both camera navigation and orientation. Of course, the techniques outlined here are also suited to other types of third person games, although they are usually dependent upon sufficient space for camera positioning that may not always be available.

There are two main approaches to cameras for 3D platform games with each approach chosen according to how the camera responds to dynamic game play. We may broadly categorize these approaches as *free form* or *pre-determined*. Elements of each approach may be combined to create hybrid behaviors.

Free form

The most popular solution for platform games is to use a free form camera, which responds dynamically to the behavior of the player character. In addition, free form cameras often allow the player to manipulate the camera position (and possibly orientation) with respect to the player character, unless overridden by either game play requirements or other designer specifications. In these cases, the free form camera often uses the same techniques as those available to pre-determined cameras as discussed in the next section. Nonetheless, free form cameras are still reasonably dynamic in their behavior and response to player actions.

The manipulation of a free form camera by the player may take several different forms.

- The camera position may be revolved around the player character, such that the camera inscribes an arc of motion parallel to the horizontal plane of the world.
- The camera position may also be rotated around the player character such that the camera inscribes a vertical arc of motion along the plane formed between the camera position and the player character.

- The distance of the camera from the player character may be altered according to player desire or game play necessity. These changes are often between pre-defined distances and elevations; the transition between defined positions may be an instantaneous cut or interpolated over time as desired. Sometimes the distance is varied according to the velocity of the player character or to emphasize a game play element such as an animated "special move."

Various combinations of the above properties are possible as desired by the game designer. Environmental concerns must be taken into account whenever camera manipulation is allowed to ensure that the camera remains within the world geometry and that the player is not permitted to move the camera to a position where game play is adversely affected (e.g., occlusion of the player character, vertical alignment of the camera orientation, etc.). Similarly, the player should not be allowed to manipulate the camera into a position that completely occludes the player character. Alternatively, the camera may correct itself by quickly moving to a position where the character is not occluded (perhaps once player input has ceased). Altering the orientation of the camera to examine the environment in ways that cause the player character to leave the viewing frustum is only acceptable if performed briefly, to reduce player confusion. If the player is able to manipulate the view completely away from the player character it might be necessary to provide a control to explicitly reorient the camera back to a safe view, or to have the camera reorient automatically once player input has finished.

Pre-determined

The other popular choice of camera position (and quite possibly, orientation) for this game genre is *pre-determined*. Usually the position is specified via *spline paths*, implicit surfaces, stationary waypoints (using interpolation of position and sometimes orientation), or similar techniques. Methods such as these are discussed at length in Chapter 8. The award winning *God of War* [God05] featured significant use of this camera style; *Ico* [Ico01] used pre-determined cameras to portray a cinematic approach with the ability for the player to temporarily free look from side to side (although the self-centering joystick used for this would cause the view to automatically return to the original orientation once released).

Pre-determined cameras, as their name suggests, offer absolute control over camera position and orientation. This can be very effective since it usually offers sufficient control to ensure that game play may be viewed in a meaningful and clear manner. In situations where the player motion is strictly controlled (and this is often the case for the 3D platform genre), pre-determined camera solutions may be tailored specifically to the position of the player within the world. Equally important is that camera collision and other notable problems can be effectively sidestepped; this can be particularly useful because camera navigation is a difficult and processor intensive task. For these and similar reasons, use of pre-determined camera positions can be an attractive route to take.

One down side is that it is not always possible to allow for the myriad of player interactions with such a camera solution. Moreover, changes to the environment may require multiple iterations during development as well as variable paths according to game state changes. Pre-determined cameras rely heavily on an understanding of the exact sequence of game play. Should the player find a way to traverse the environment that was not anticipated, for example, the pre-determined camera may not be able to present the player with a playable view of the game. There is little that can be done at this point, since the camera is restricted to remain within its pre-defined behavior. Adequate testing is necessary to ensure this situation does not arise in regular game play.

A further point to consider is the aesthetic qualities of pre-determined paths. On the one hand, care can be taken to ensure that camera motion, orientation, and positioning are as appropriate as is possible. This should result in perfectly smooth and controlled camera motion, which is certainly desirable. However, given that the view presented to the player will typically be the same, this can lead to a sense that the player has little control over the game. This is hard to quantify: essentially the exact repeatability of camera motion can actually prove to remove a level of interaction. This sensation may be lessened by using motion volumes rather than exact paths, or by allowing some variance on camera acceleration and position. In these cases, the pre-determined nature of the camera is less strict (and thus appears more "organic" or "natural" to the player), but remains controllable.

Role-playing games/massively-multi-player online games

Role-playing games (RPG) and *massively-multi-player online games* (MMOG) share many common features and frequently adopt a third person view of the player character and their environment (*Final Fantasy XI*, *World of*

Warcraft, et al.). Their camera systems may generally be considered as a subset of the character-based genre previously described. Sometimes the camera may use pre-determined paths or have a fixed location (and possibly orientation). The latter method may be useful in reducing processor requirements, as the background elements may be pre-rendered since the camera viewpoint does not change. Similarly, many older RPG games used a 2D presentation with essentially a "pre-rendered" background due to the graphical limitations of the available game hardware. Often the background was composed of smaller elements sometimes referred to as *tile maps* or *stamps* (see the next section Scrolling). These techniques are discussed in the section on orthographic cameras in the section Orthographic Presentation in Chapter 2. MMOGs sometimes utilize a first person camera to provide a more immersive experience, although this may often make interactions with other characters more difficult. Regardless, it is usual to offer the player a selection of third person camera choices in addition to a first person view. This permits the player to decide how large a view of the game world is necessary for their current game play requirements.

The framing requirements of RPGs and MMOGs are usually more involved than most character-based games; however, they may typically demand a view of multiple player- and game-controlled characters simultaneously. Framing of objects is a large topic that incorporates elements of cinematography. Determination of the camera orientation may also require the camera to change position to ensure the appropriate game play elements are viewable. This often requires a commitment on behalf of the artists to produce environments that allow the camera to move sufficiently far away from the game objects to achieve the required framing. This is often achieved by having a camera that is located outside of the game world, especially for orthographic camera presentations.

Some RPGs allow the player full control over camera positioning and orientation, often with the option to reorient and position the camera relative to the main (or active) player character. For multi-player games, there may be the facility to observe the game as viewed by another player.

Scrolling

Scrolling games are often presented using an orthographic view of the game world, whether viewed from the side or above the player character, although a similar style may also be produced via axonometric projections. This type of presentation style is derived from the hardware constraints of early game machines. Such machines were not capable of generating real-time three-dimensional images and had low-performance processors and limited memory. Early game consoles or dedicated arcade machines often even lacked bit-mapped displays. Instead, they featured character or *tile-based* graphics (sometimes referred to as *stamps*), essentially displaying a mosaic (or *tile map*) of small, regular sized images arranged in a two-dimensional grid. An early example of a scrolling background was found in the seminal game *Defender* [Defender80].

For tile-based hardware there would sometimes be a mechanism to layer multiple tile maps on top of each other (using a simple one-bit "transparency" effect); if the different layers are moved at different rates in response to player movement, this can generate a parallax effect and thus a limited sense of depth.

As the game moved its view of the game world horizontally across the tile map, the background graphics would appear to "scroll" in the opposite direction; this became known as a *side-scrolling* game. Usually the position of the camera (in reality, simply the position of the viewport in world coordinate space) is determined by the position of the player character. This relationship may vary according to movement direction, speed of motion, or other properties of the player character. Sometimes the camera is prevented from moving outside of the limits of the tile map or from displaying certain sections of the tile map. Some variations on scrolling games include constant motion by the camera. This motion may be in a single direction (e.g., top right to bottom left as in arcade games such as *Zaxxon* [Zaxxon82] or *Paperboy* [Paperboy84]) or in multiple directions that vary over time (e.g., *Splat!* [Splat83]).

Such constant motion often forces player characters to remain on the screen (if they are able to move faster than the scrolling rate) or ensures that their position remains constant relative to the screen or the direction of scrolling. Further examples of scrolling techniques may be found in Chapter 4 in the Desirable Features section.

A similar variant changed the axis of motion and became *vertical scrollers*. An extension to this type of presentation is the *isometric* game, where the background may also be comprised of tiled elements but the graphics are drawn in a pseudo-isometric projection to simulate a three-dimensional effect. Other pseudo-projections are possible. Movement of the camera is often locked to one of the projected axes of the game world and moves in appropriate pixel step-sizes along that axis. Isometric games were a popular variant as their illusion of depth was considerable given the limited resources of the early machines. More detailed information regarding isometric and other projection types may be found in the Interactive 3D Camera Systems section of Chapter 4.

This scrolling presentation style may be extended to include three-dimensional elements, either game objects or the entire scene itself. The movement of the camera is usually pre-defined and constrained to a path or plane; the camera position and orientation may be carefully controlled to give the best possible view of the game play at any given time. This also allows extra emphasis to be given to particular three-dimensional elements to enhance the sensation of depth.

Movement of the player character in side-scrolling games is typically limited to a plane or path, much as the camera is. Sometimes elements of the background are treated as three-dimensional protrusions. These are to be avoided by the player or may be used to access different regions of the game world (i.e., platforms). These protrusions may be treated as three- or two-dimensional elements according to dynamically changing game play, although conveying these differences in functionality can be a difficult task. Consistency of behavior is a desirable property in this regard.

It is possible to simulate movement across (or "into") the plane formed by the background elements. In two-dimensional games, multiple graphical layers may be used to simulate this direction of motion in a manner somewhat akin to that of traditional two-dimensional animation ([Thomas95] is a comprehensive study on traditional animation techniques).

Sports

Sports games are an extremely popular genre and feature a large variety of environments and game play requirements. Many sports games benefit from a clearly defined and confined environment, and thus may often present a more limited set of camera problems; it is often possible to pre-calculate appropriate solutions in these cases. This is especially true for stadium or indoor sports, although track-based sports (such as skiing or cycling) have much in common with racing games.

When representing the most popular sports, a TV-style presentation can be very desirable. This often pertains to introductory sequences, replaying of important scoring or other events, and so forth. In well-known sports, such as American football and so forth, there are usually well-defined approaches to presenting the game that may be replicated to great effect. Even so, additional camera techniques will be needed to present the sport in the best light for player interaction, and here games benefit from the ability to move virtual cameras freely through the game world.

Stylistically, camera properties often depend on whether a realistic approach is taken with the sport. This often equates to a view similar to those experienced by spectators, although this does not always lend itself well to game play concerns. Presentations that are more realistic may require camera movement, for example, to be restricted to the same methods used for real-world cameras. Non-perfect framing and reorientation can surprisingly add a great deal to the atmosphere or replication of televised coverage, as it mimics the fact that real cameramen sometimes find it difficult to match fast-moving sport events. In non-realistic sports, there is more flexibility to the positioning and motion of the camera.

Camera replay technology, where sequences of game events are replicated to highlight a player's achievements (or failures), can be very important. Rather than viewing the game world from the same perspective as that of the player during these sequences, external views may be pre-defined or automatically generated to show particularly interesting views of the events (e.g., a close-up of the action or a pan around a particular participant), or just to provide visually interesting angles. This process of automation is covered in detail in Chapter 10; one frequently used method is the placing of cameras at fixed locations within the world. This is common within the racing genre, where grandstand views are frequently chosen to show the movement of the cars around the track (in addition to a number of vehicle-relative camera positions). The choice of which camera to use at a particular time and how to transition between them may be varied according to designer intent or chosen automatically by the camera system according to pre-defined criteria (e.g., the position or distance of the target object relative to a camera position).

Given the wide variety of available sports, are there any common approaches to camera presentation that may be applied? This is indeed the case, and this can be shown by first dividing sports games into several distinct groups. The first point to consider is whether the sport is played by a small number of participants (either a single player or one player per side) or is a team sport.

Single-participant sports

Some sports only require a single participant to be controlled or displayed at a given time (e.g., golf). These games do simplify the camera requirements somewhat, even when the player character hits a ball at high speeds. The framing requirements of a single participant per player are typically the simplest since the point of interest is either the player character or a single other object, such as a ball. Once the ball is struck, the camera view typically tracks the position of the ball, perhaps performing a jump cut (or several for that matter) to show the ball arriving at its destination.

Even where there is more than one participant, it may be appropriate to treat the camera solution in this way. This is especially true of situations where the participants do not interact directly, or alternate turns. An example of this is a simulation of track and field sporting events (e.g., jumping events, archery, etc.).

Two- or four-participant sports

A more common situation is for there to be two participants in the sport and many cases feature two pairs of opponents (e.g., tennis). For a single human player, the other three participants are usually controlled by the game, but of course, they may just as easily be controlled by another human. In the latter case, we must be concerned with the potential requirement (and problems) of a split-screen display depending on whether the opponent is playing locally or via a remote network connection. Networked play can treat each individual as if playing a single-player game, at least in terms of camera usage. Split-screen presentation poses its own problems, and will be discussed in the section Split-Screen Techniques.

Team sports

In team sports, the player typically has control of one participant at a given time, but is able to change between different participants as desired. Often this process is automated so that the player is in control of the most appropriate participant. In a soccer game, for example, if the ball is kicked ahead of the current player character, control may be required to switch to another one that is now closer to the ball (or better positioned). The context of changing which participant is controlled is usually specific to a type of sport. Additionally, it is important to ensure that players remain in control of their current participant unless otherwise desired; in other words, control is only changed when it is obvious to the player. One method to achieve this is to assign a specific controller command to switch players. Regardless, it is usually necessary to have an on-screen indication of both the current participant under control and which ones may optionally be controlled. Such indicators must be clear yet not obscure game play; one method of doing this is to change the rendering colors of a participant.

Team sports often have more difficult camera framing situations, especially if the player wishes to pass to a participant currently off-screen. It is not always necessary for a player to see the target participant. On-screen information may relay enough positional information for the player to make such tactical decisions, especially if the passing mechanism is sufficiently automated to assist the completion of the pass. To a degree, these facilities are dictated by the desire of the game designer when determining a balance between simulation and "game."

Irrespective of the number of participants, sports games may be divided into two broad categories: indoor court (or arena-based) sports and those taking place outdoors.

Court and indoor sports

Due to the restrictions of a physical court or arena, indoor sports are often easier to present to a player. One of the main reasons is that camera positions (and orientations) may be completely pre-defined to show the best possible view of the game play under most if not all circumstances. This may require careful construction of the surrounding environmental geometry, including possibly allowing the camera to be placed outside of the environment. The main concern with indoor sports games is showing the game characters adequately rather than dealing with geometry avoidance, so removal or fading of geometry is usually acceptable.

For many indoor sports, it is necessary to present the game play similar to real-world television presentations. This is mostly because the player is likely to be familiar with or expect the same presentation style, and it is probably the best way to present the game play in an understandable fashion such that players can understand the relationship between their player character and other participants. Game cameras, of course, are able to move in ways not available to typical real-world cameras due to their physical constraints, although care should be taken to avoid distracting the player from the game by rapid or confusing camera motion and orientation changes.

Replaying of significant game events should similarly be styled in a manner to which the player is accustomed; once again, the nature of game cameras allows more dramatic motion than would be possible on television (e.g., circling a player as they score a goal). Simultaneous display of several game areas is also possible, either as a player aid or as a presentation effect.

Some of the more common indoor or arena-based sports include:

- **Ball sports (tennis, basketball, squash, racquetball, volleyball, water polo, etc.)**. A significant problem for ball sports is visual tracking of the ball. Television presentations of ball sports frequently use overlaid graphics to highlight the position or motion of a ball; this is easily applied to game cameras.
- **Table sports (pool, billiards, snooker, table tennis, pinball, etc.)** Table sports are often required to provide multiple or player-controlled views of the game play. Determination of angles of motion can be difficult when removed from the view along which the ball may travel, as is common with third person camera presentations. Given the relatively small size of the playing area, it is quite possible to provide a view showing the entire table. Since depth perception can be difficult to gauge for some table sports, assistance to the player is frequently provided by either control simplification (e.g., non-exact placement of a table tennis paddle and simplified shot selection) or indication of the ball trajectory.

Outdoor sports

Outdoor sports offer a wide variety of game play styles and thus may require unique or variable camera solutions. There are three main categories of outdoor sports.

1. **Arena based (tennis, soccer, football, baseball, rugby, etc.)**. These sports are restricted to a specific locale in a similar fashion to indoor sports though often on a larger scale. Similar benefits may be gained from pre-definition of camera motion or orientation. However, a variety of player-controlled camera options may be offered; usually this is necessary since the scale of the arena is such that an encompassing view may be too distant from the players to adequately view the game play.
2. **Free form (golf, skateboarding, skiing, snowboarding, water-based racing, etc.)**. These sports naturally have limitations as to their game play area much as arena-based sports, but the movement or positioning of the participants is much more variable and usually requires a more involved camera solution.

3. **Track based (athletics, racing, cycling, skiing, etc.).** These games can often be straightforward for camera solutions since the positioning and orientation of the camera may be completely pre-determined in many cases. It is still likely that multiple camera positions may be offered to the player, but the environmental navigation is typically much easier to determine in this type of sport.

Abstract sports

Not all sports games present their sport in a realistic manner, nor are all sports games based upon actual real-world sports. Sometimes the game is an exaggeration of an existing sport where the players are able to outperform those of the real world. Examples might include players that jump tremendous heights or hit a ball harder than would be possible. The sport may be based in a unique environment, say underwater or in outer space, that is very different from how the sport is normally played. Alternatively, physical characteristics of the world may have changed (gravity, friction, etc.). Such changes may not greatly influence camera solutions unless the player is expected to view the game world in an unusual manner. An example would be a zero gravity sport where the player's view of the game arena may roll around its forward direction. In many cases, the similarities with real-world sports camera presentation are actually beneficial in making the sport seem more believable.

Racing games

Racing games as a genre encompass a variety of kinds of racing types, but share some common camera and game play design functionality. Typically, player motion is restricted to some form of track, at least in the sense of a pre-defined region with a specified starting point and constraints upon the movement of the player character. Naturally, this can be confined to two- or three-dimensional motion attached to the surface of the track, as typified by automobile racing. However, this also includes flight, sailing, and so forth. As with arena-based games, the camera position and orientation may be pre-computed. Usually the position of the camera is still somewhat variable in racing games; while it is possible to exactly specify the path of the camera using a spline curve, for example, such motion often feels unnatural as it lacks a sensation of being operated by a human. It is possible to relax the reorientation of the camera (perhaps through use of a PID controller as described in Chapter 6) to improve this situation.

An important aspect of racing games is that of the replay camera. Replay cameras provide typically non-interactive viewing of previously recorded game play. Sometimes the viewer is allowed some control over the camera positioning during the replay (in some genres, even total control of camera position and orientation), usually through a series of defined camera positions and/or orientations. For racing games in particular, it is preferred that the style of camera presentation is close to that of TV racing programs.

Racing games usually need to provide the player with information regarding the position of other vehicles relative to the player character, especially when an opponent is about to overtake their vehicle and is not yet visible within the view frustum of the camera. Obviously if the camera is placed sufficiently behind the player character it will be possible for players to discern this for themselves. However, such a camera position would likely mean that the player's own vehicle would be too small to see clearly.

One alternative is to provide additional views to the player. An obvious example of this would be a rear-view mirror or other picture-in-picture rendering of alternate views. A performance-friendlier version is to include a dynamically updating map of the circuit showing the relative positions of all vehicles. This map may be rendered as a two- or three-dimensional image, depending upon the amount of screen space available. Additional cues may be provided in two-dimensional form to alert the player to the proximity of other vehicles, such as icons overlaid on top of the rendered view of the world.

Racing games often offer the ability to turn off or otherwise limit the amount of information displayed to increase the player immersion in the game. Some simulations will only offer information in ways that would normally be available to a driver in the real world, such as gauges.

Racing games must typically decide whether to emphasize *realism* or *accessibility*. This decision affects many aspects of the game, from the movement behavior and characteristics of the vehicles (and their physical reaction to environmental influences such as surface materials) through the control options and rendering of the game world. A non-realistic approach allows greater flexibility in many respects, especially since many players would typically lack the necessary skills required to drive performance vehicles at high speed without considerable practice. This is not to say that realism is not a worthy target; simply that care should be taken in emphasizing the aspects that best suit the game design. Racing games in particular come under scrutiny, as they are reasonably familiar to many players although their expectations may not always match reality. A particularly noteworthy camera solution for racing games was adopted in *Burnout 3* [Burnout04] that managed to combine a very cinematic approach within real-time game play.

TECHNICAL
Field of view effects may be used to increase the sensation of speed and have been used effectively in a number of games. By widening the horizontal field of view, objects will appear to pass quickly by the player. This must be used cautiously, as it will cause distortion of the view if applied too liberally. Additionally, changes to the field of view should be applied relatively slowly, to lessen disorientation of the player. Often changes to the field of view are combined with other screen-space distortion effects. A popular choice is to apply motion-blur to both game objects and the rendered display. In the former case, accumulation buffers or other multiple-pass rendering techniques can be used (see [Akenine-Möller02] and [Foley90]); in the latter post-processing may be performed on the frame buffer, usually before the player craft is rendered. Here the principle is that the player craft remains "in focus" (i.e., assuming that the craft is located at the correct distance from the camera lens as to be in perfect focus) whereas the background elements are blurred according to their relative speed with respect to the player. Depth of field effects may also emphasize the sensation of motion by causing background elements to become more blurred as the speed of the player character increases.

Ground (or surface) vehicles

Ground- or surface-based vehicle games have similarities to character-based games. Vehicle cameras of this type usually prefer to retain a position behind and above the forward direction of the vehicle. The camera motion normally uses lag for both the position and orientation of the camera to provide a more "natural" sensation; this also allows the orientation of the vehicle to vary relative to the camera, emphasizing the three-dimensionality of the vehicle. The positional lag also means that the position of the vehicle will vary on screen. Care must be taken to ensure the vehicle remains at least partly on screen at all times. This is covered in more detail in Chapters 8 and 10.

Additionally, some games may offer camera viewpoints close to the vehicle, positioned and oriented to allow the player to quickly judge the relative positions of other vehicles or game objects. Many vehicle games offer the ability to rotate the camera around the vehicle. While this can be desirable, it may cause control difficulties under character-relative control schemes (as likely used in a ground vehicle game). Most ground-based vehicle games will allow the view to be positioned within a cockpit or similar structure aligned with the direction of motion. To all intents and purposes, this may be considered in the same manner as a traditional first person camera, including the ability to use free-look controls.

If the vehicle is capable of drastic orientation changes, acrobatic feats, or uncontrolled tumbling (such as might be imparted by a collision), then special handling may prove necessary to avoid drastic camera motion in a third person presentation. Part of this solution may involve using the movement direction of the vehicle to dictate the camera position, rather than the orientation of the vehicle itself, as well as applying extra damping when the craft is out of control, etc.

Real-time strategy

Real-time strategy (or RTS) games offer several different ways in which the player must view the game world, from a small-scale view of game objects to higher-level tactical views of multiple game objects, and finally very high-level strategic views of large areas (possibly the entire game world). There might be a tactical display showing a close view of the action, combined with possibly multiple levels of strategic or high-level views of the world. Often RTS games use a fixed orientation for the camera with pre-rendered graphics; this is especially true when an isometric camera is desired, for both clarity and performance reasons (in a similar manner to scrolling games as noted above). With the advent of powerful GPUs, there is less reliance upon a strictly 2D representation of the battlefield, although sometimes the background remains pre-rendered while the vehicles and other game units are rendered three-dimensionally for greater realism as they traverse the environment.

If a free form camera solution is used, it is advisable to provide an interface that allows the player to select between pre-defined views and a player-controlled view.

Flight simulation

Flight simulators are a specific subset of vehicle simulators with their own camera and control requirements. Although it might be expected that players of these games are very familiar with the concepts of flying and the view from a cockpit, the camera requirements typically go beyond providing a view that simulates this particular aspect. External camera views are often provided, and these views usually involve some degree of player manipulation.

One important consideration of camera views for flight simulators is whether the camera should be allowed to roll to match the orientation of the craft. Clearly for viewpoints tied to the cockpit of the craft, the camera must certainly match the world orientation of the craft. However, with external views that are not similarly attached to the craft (or at a very specific offset to be maintained in local craft coordinate space), we do have an option of retaining the same up-axis as that of the world. Many game players are not familiar with the intricacies of actual flight and its effect on their perception of the craft's position and orientation within the world. Moreover, many people do suffer from nausea and other motion sickness effects when playing video games. Often this is a function of the display medium (i.e., a fast-moving 3D world projected onto a static 2D plane with no peripheral motion).

Additionally, when flying a craft through a virtual world, there often need to be visual cues to help the player understand its motion through the world as well as reference planes to determine the orientation of their craft. Casual players may become confused when there is no clear distinction as to which direction is considered "up." Artificial horizons can certainly help in this regard, and may take many forms depending on the particulars of the environment. Space-based games, for example, though not truly "flight" games, often exhibit many of the same properties and require these visual cues. In fact, space-based games, with their lack of any notion of "up" or "down," perhaps require this to an even greater degree.

A further consideration is that of player craft control. For a "true" flight simulator, these controls are typically complex and numerous, especially since they replicate actual real-world control schemes, even if the input mechanisms may be very different. When simplifying these control schemes we also need to consider how "realistic" the flight model will be. Even the most hardcore of flight simulators available in the commercial gaming marketplace do not truly model the flight characteristics of their vehicles to the extent of airflow over the fuselage, although improvements in processor performance make this inevitable.

Regardless, exact simulation does not necessarily equate to fun. In many cases, players expect aircraft to behave differently than the reality of flight, perhaps because for many players their experience of actual flight only comes from films or merely as passengers. Often the belief is that aircrafts behave more like a car than a plane, especially with regard to turning. This perception also brings with it an expectation as to how the plane is viewed. Many players do not cope well with cameras that roll; they expect up to be up and down to be down. The lack of a consistent frame of reference, such as the horizon, can also be confusing to many players.

In some cases, it is better to maintain a consistent camera relationship with the world's up-axis, so that the player can determine up and down, so to speak. True flight simulators cannot take this approach, except for playback techniques.

Realistic flight models

Realistic flight models refer to games where the movement of the craft reflects an attempt to create an accurate (or reasonably accurate) simulation of how the craft would behave under real physical forces. Such games are normally viewed from the craft cockpit, or from a position behind the craft, as portrayed in movie dogfights. Games may offer many different vantage points within the cockpit (e.g., looking over the shoulder, behind, sideways, etc.). Additionally, a selection of external views at differing distances, elevations, and angular positions is usually provided. External camera choices may also include a player-controlled camera moving around the craft as if on the surface of a sphere. If the craft is capable of upside-down flight, then the camera will usually maintain its relative position and orientation to the craft, thus presenting the world upside down.

Non-realistic flight models

Non-realistic flight models would include spacecraft with unusual orientations/freedom of movement, such as flying creatures and so forth. For the most part, the same camera techniques used with realistic flight models may be applied here. Difficulties arise when the craft is able to fly in directions that are counter to the player's perception of the world. Good examples would be consistently flying upside-down or vertically parallel to the world up-axis. The craft or creature may be able to execute maneuvers that would not be physically possible under a more realistic flight model, and may require special camera movements to avoid player disorientation.

Artificial horizon

Many game players are not familiar with the controls of real aircraft, nor are they always able to understand the orientation of their craft (both pitch and banking). Aircraft instrumentation features a device (usually a gyroscope), sometimes referred to as the *artificial horizon* or *attitude indicator*, which informs the pilot of changes to the pitch or banking. Similar instrumentation is required for flight simulators, but other flight models may represent the same information as part of a heads-up display or other on-screen graphics.

Sensation of motion

As many flight games involve the vehicle flying high above the ground terrain, this often results in a discrepancy between the perceived and actual speed of the craft. Without a local reference frame against which movement may be measured, players will feel that their craft is actually moving much slower than it is. Once again, realism does not necessarily result in a good game play experience for the player. The sensation of motion may be improved in a variety of ways. In part, the method chosen depends upon the genre or game setting. Often particle effects such as clouds or contrails may be used to emphasize motion. These effects may be applied to the player craft or separately as models with transparency effects showing the direction of motion. Space flight games will typically use small, non-collidable debris (either models or particle/billboard effects) to provide an additional sensation of motion. Audio cues may also emphasize the movement speed of the craft, from changes in the pitch of the engine sound to *Doppler effects* and non-realistic "swooshes" as objects are passed at high speed. Additionally, field of view effects as mentioned in Chapter 2 are also applicable to flight simulation games.

Adventure

Adventure games are a genre with a rich history and have been presented in many different ways as technology has improved. From the initial text adventures through to full three-dimensional environments, one of their most common elements has been that of player interaction with their environment. Early text adventures, of course, had to rely upon parsing the textual inputs typed by the player or by presenting a menu of choices to the player. A further development was to combine still imagery with text descriptions, although the player was generally unable to interact with the displayed graphics (unless a player action caused a graphical change such as opening or closing a door).

An enduring development that was featured in the later adventure games (those featuring both a graphical display and mouse or other pointing device input handling) was the "point and click" presentation style. These games allowed the player to manipulate the position of a cursor or other indicator around the display device to interact with elements of the game world. These types of adventures often presented an orthographic view of the game world, possibly with some elements of three-dimensionality suggested by scaling the size of two-dimensional game objects as they moved "into" and "out of" the scene. Additionally the camera would move (or *pan*) across the game world to track the player character's position or other cinematic requirements.

Even when hardware acceleration was not available, some notable adventure games (the most well-known of these is probably *Myst* [Myst93]) used pre-rendered graphics to show a highly detailed three-dimensional view of the game world. Even though the player was unable to manipulate the camera orientation, enough detail was provided to form a compelling view of the game world.

With the advent of faster processors and graphical hardware acceleration, there have been forays into three-dimensional adventure games. They have usually been presented from a third person camera, although camera placement often has entailed completely scripted camera movement and orientation.

Adventure games are driven by their story elements; they usually seek to emphasize this by using a very cinematographic approach to the positioning and movement of the camera (especially when interacting with game characters). Since the pace of adventure games is relatively leisurely (due to their preference for puzzles over action elements), camera movement may also take advantage of this to present a very cinematic experience to the player.

Puzzle/party games/board games

Puzzle and party games share some common properties in their presentation style, especially in the case of a split-screen multi-player presentation. Board games often translate well into a video game format and may utilize a variety of presentation styles in common with party games. Similarly, puzzle games are extremely varied in their content, player control, and presentation requirements. For example, the rate of player interaction varies from turn-based to real-time, there may be a single-player or multiple players, and so forth. Many puzzle games do not feature a player character per se, rather the player is manipulating game objects to resolve the puzzle; possibly the most iconic example of this would be the classic *Tetris*. One of the most common approaches (as used by the original version of *Tetris*) is a two-dimensional presentation. In this example, the entire playing area is visible within the bounds of a single screen, even for multiple players. This two-dimensional approach rarely has camera concerns, unless the playing field is larger than the viewable screen area. In this case, it would be necessary to move the camera automatically.

A puzzle game with three-dimensional elements, however, must typically allow some amount of player camera manipulation since given the limitations of current display devices it is likely that the player needs to be able to obtain the best vantage point of the puzzle at any given time. An alternative to moving the camera is to manipulate the object itself. Simulations of physical puzzles (such as a *Rubik's Cube*) often use this method to simplify player controls. This process can be somewhat automated depending on the nature of the puzzle, or assistance may be provided to show the player the next object of interest, or to automatically rotate the object as required. The allowable camera manipulation may take the form of pre-defined camera positions or direct rotation of the camera around an object of interest. Sometimes it may be necessary to provide complete control over both the camera position and orientation.

Some puzzle games use camera manipulation as a part of the puzzle itself. In such cases, the camera must often be moved to facilitate the player's manipulation of a game element. Alternatively, the camera orientation may be used as part of the puzzle interaction. There are some games where the player marks an object in the game by keeping the game camera pointed at it for a period.

Sometimes puzzle games do feature a player character separate from the puzzle elements. Often it is the case that the player character must be moved directly through the game world to change elements of the puzzle or alternatively elements of the game world may be manipulated to move the player character. This approach is often taken with real-world puzzle games where a physical element (effectively the player character) must be moved indirectly by changing the arrangement of puzzle elements (such as a sliding puzzle).

The simplest puzzle games use a statically positioned and oriented camera, where the entire puzzle may be viewed at the same time. An obvious example once again is *Tetris*. Often multi-player puzzle games, especially competitive ones viewed on a single display, will use this approach so that each player may quickly assess the other player's progress.

Frequently camera motion in puzzle games is restricted to remain on a plane parallel to a world axis. In some cases, it may allow repositioning of the camera across a plane.

Fighting/close combat

Fighting games are another popular genre, one that has endured from the early two-dimensional sprite-based arcade and home computer versions through three-dimensionally rendered graphical extravaganzas. These games typically feature only two opponents at a time, usually to simplify character interactions, not to mention reduce performance requirements and to allow detail to be applied to the characters. Having only two opponents also allows some player controls to be implicit in their usage (i.e., attack commands do not need to specify which opponent to attack). There are examples of multiple character fighting games, although it can be difficult for a player to specify which opponent they wish to attack at a given moment.

Often the combat is located within a relatively sparse environment, featuring little interaction between the characters and the world (perhaps an occasional wall or object that may be destroyed). Sometimes the arena may feature a navigation hazard such as a steep ledge, causing any character to fall to their death that might cross it (whether intentional or not). On occasion, there might be non-interactive cinematic sequences triggered during regular game play by events such as breaking through a wall. There are variations upon this theme (e.g., a floating platform on a river), but essentially the environment remains simple. By keeping the environment simple (at least those parts in proximity to the player since background elements may be as complicated as desired if the player is unable to interact with them), processor requirements for collision detection may be reduced. Modern fighting games usually strive for realism in the depiction of the combatants in terms of both their physical appearance and their animation. The processor requirements for *inverse kinematics* and other ways of resolving the interactions of the limbs or weapons of the opponents when they collide can be significant, so simplifying the environment can be of great importance. As game platforms become more powerful, this area of research will be greatly expanded, eventually leading to detailed, believable interactions between player characters and their environment.

Another reason why fighting games often have sparse environments is that this makes camera positioning more straightforward, especially with regard to the framing of the protagonists. To dynamically frame the opponents in an appropriate manner often involves moving the camera away. The larger the distance between the opponents, the further the camera must move away, although widening the field of view may help. Dramatic movement of the game camera is typically undesirable, so having sufficient space around the opponents to position the camera consistently at a distance that permits both characters to be seen, even during extreme movements, can be beneficial. Care must be taken to keep the actual screen size of the characters reasonably large, otherwise animation detail will be lost.

There are alternatives to moving the camera away from the combatants. One solution is to use split-screen or multiple viewports to show the relative positions of the enemies. This need not take the form of physically separated portions of the display. It is possible to use picture-in-picture mini-viewports to display grandstand views. These additional views may be contextual or constantly present. In the latter case, it is perhaps better to split the screen in a clearly understandable way, even though this reduces the amount of screen space available under "normal" conditions. Another use for viewports is to show close-up effects of a blow (perhaps even replays while regular game play is continuing). If presented cleanly, such views can add greatly to player satisfaction.

Fighting games rely heavily upon the presentation of the protagonists, especially as a precursor to the actual battle or upon defeat of one character. In this regard, they make extensive use of cinematographic techniques for framing and moving the camera during non-interactive sequences. In particular, fighting games will often move or orient the camera to emphasize a variety of special movements or attacks performed by the characters as the game progresses. In many cases, these camera movements are elaborate, lengthy, and sometimes only partially interactive. This lack of interactivity allows time for the camera to be positioned in a way that would best highlight the movements without distracting the players from controlling their characters. Since the relative positions of the characters are known during the special movements, the camera position and orientation may be consistent whenever they are performed, assuming sufficient space is available for the camera to move without passing through the environment.

A common technique for emphasizing a particularly proficient move by a character within a fighting game is to replay the action several times in rapid succession. This occurs most often when the action results in the defeat of one of the opponents. While the simplest solution is to strictly replay the sequence exactly as it was first viewed, more interesting and aesthetically pleasing results may be obtained by varying these views. Simple rules of cinematography may be applied to position the camera in a way that is visually interesting as well as dynamic and changing according to the nature of the situation. Since fighting games often take place within large open environments, they are well suited to this type of dynamic cinematography. An alternative solution (and one that is straightforward to implement) is to predetermine a selection of camera moves according to the action causing the defeat of one of the opponents. Certain cases such as an opponent forced out of the combat arena (referred to as a *ring out* in many cases) may require a more dynamic solution to be effective, but this is dependent upon the nature of the environment. One of the best examples of fighting game cameras may be seen in *Soul Calibur* [Soul98].

MULTI-PLAYER CAMERA SOLUTIONS

Multi-player games, regardless of genre, sometimes face difficulties in displaying the game world adequately when more than one player shares the display device. These problems typically stem from the inability to display appropriate views of the game play when individual players are performing actions that are positioned separately, or require unique views of the game world. Networked multi-player games (or physically linked consoles, etc.) typically do not face these problems, as each player is typically utilizing their own individual display. Some gaming devices support multiple display devices that may be utilized for multi-player games, but this is rare outside of dedicated arcade machines.

When presenting a multi-player game on a single display device, there is usually a more limited set of options available to the camera designer. In many cases, these choices are dictated by game genre, since there are game types where each player must have their own display to be able to adequately control their character. However, many third person multi-player game types can actually benefit from a single-screen approach. Cooperative third person games or party-type games often use a single display combined with an environment that prevents character motion beyond the limits of the arena displayed.

Given the limitation of a single display device, how can the game be presented to multiple players? A less frequently used approach is to alternate players; that is, the display is dedicated to a single player at any given time, with each player taking a turn as the active player. This approach works well for party games where there is little game interaction between players or turn-based role-playing games. Curiously, many early arcade games adopted this convention, but this was only possible because each player's game was treated as completely separate.

When multiple players must interact simultaneously on a single display device, there are only two options available: split the screen into multiple sections (one per player) or display a single view of the game world encompassing both players. These options are covered in detail in Chapter 4. Several early examples of single-screen multi-player games are *Super Sprint* [Super86] and *Gauntlet* [Gauntlet85].

Single-player games benefit greatly from the ability to utilize the full extent of the display device to present the game world to the player, even with the ability to present multiple views simultaneously. Multi-player games where a single display device is shared pose a more difficult challenge to the game and camera designers. What are good approaches to take for the different presentation styles outlined earlier in this chapter?

Multi-player games offer a design challenge when determining the method of presenting the game world to several players on the same physical display device. First person games often function best when each player has a separate display since the level of immersion is much greater. Since many first person games utilize network connections between multiple computers or game consoles to support multi-player play, there is often no need to alter the camera system in this situation. However, it is sometimes necessary to allow multiple players simultaneously on a single device regardless of the camera presentation.

Split-screen is a common solution to presenting multi-player games on a single display device. Since each player has a distinct area of the screen dedicated to their view of the game world, they can be treated as separately rendered views.

Multi-player games may take several forms in both 2D and 3D games. Clearly, the simplest case is a single player per display device, which is typically the same format used in a single-player game. Things become more interesting when multiple players must be represented on the same display device. Here are some of the potential options for this situation.

- **Single viewport.** All players share the same region of the display device, typically the entire displayable area. Problems with framing all players arise if the play area is larger than can be displayed by a static, fixed orientation camera.

- **Static multiple viewports.** Each player has his own portion of the display, usually formed by dividing the display vertically or horizontally as required by the number of players. This is a common solution, especially for a first person camera presentation. One of the drawbacks is the limited amount of screen space given to each player, which makes it harder for the player to see their view of the game world. Additionally it requires extra processor performance for traversing the scene hierarchy to determine the visible geometry in each player's viewport.
- **Variable viewports.** An approach taken by some third person camera games is to use a single viewport when players are in proximity to each other, but to change to separate viewports as they move apart. This can be difficult to achieve in practice, but does offer benefits especially for cooperative games. For one, it avoids the framing problems caused when players move in opposite directions. Additionally, when the players are relatively close by there is an improved view of the game world. Of course, care must be taken to ensure that the viewport transitions are smooth. It is also necessary to prevent oscillation between the viewport layouts as player characters move repeatedly back and forth across the boundary distances that would cause such a change.

Additional problems are present in split-screen multi-player games. For games with environments that allow players to move apart, it may become necessary to have sufficient memory to hold two distinct areas of the game present simultaneously. As the players move apart this may also impact the rate at which data may be streamed from a mass storage device, since there may be little common data between the two areas.

Single-screen techniques

There are occasions where a single "full-screen" approach is either preferable or unavoidable for multi-player games; it is usually only feasible for third person cameras since each player must be able to control their character simultaneously. Turn-based games may succeed in using a full-screen approach as long as it is clear which player is currently active.

Fighting games are a genre that typically presents a single view of the game play, regardless of the number of opponents. This can lead to difficulties in choosing an appropriate position for the camera to frame all opponents in a meaningful and clear way. Cooperative games often use a full-screen approach to ensure all players have a clear view of the game play, and often restrict player motion so that they must remain within the boundaries of the viewable region of the world. While this is an artificial concept, it solves most of the problems relating to character framing, with one exception. It is possible, depending on the construction of the environment, that two players may move into positions where neither of them can move. This can only occur if the possible movements of the players would result in their positioning off-screen. This situation may be tested for explicitly as a fail-safe condition (the result is to instantaneously move one player to a "safe" position); a better solution is to prevent the situation from occurring by modifying the game environment accordingly.

Further considerations for multiplayer full-screen games are as follows.

- **Placement of the camera can be difficult to determine.** A common approach is to use the center of all active players as a reference frame for the positioning of the camera. Such an approach works well for non-perspective projections, but even in this case the camera must usually be positioned high enough to provide a view surrounding all players.
- **Non-perspective projection (e.g., *isometric*) cameras.** Since the orientation of an isometric camera is constant, its world space position can be derived according to desired screen-space positioning of the player characters. It is not necessarily the case that the camera position is constantly repositioned as the player characters move. *Motion lag* is discussed in detail in Chapter 6, and often the motion of the camera may be restricted to avoid untoward or jittery motion. Isometric games will frequently base the camera position at a fixed height above the surface to the game world irrespective of player motion (e.g., jumping).
- **Determination of the camera position may result in rapid orientation changes.** This is generally to be avoided and may require that the camera be positioned relatively far away from the player characters. Many fighting games change the position or field of view according to game player actions. For example, when one player character has been temporarily disabled due to damage received, there is often an almost cinematic approach taken to underscore the effect of the blow received by the

character. Such a camera change is permissible as long as the sequence is relatively non-interactive. In cases where there are more than two players, this technique is difficult to apply without detrimental effects on game play.

Split-screen techniques

Multi-player games are relatively commonplace in 2D presentation styles. Typically, they may feature players working cooperatively or more often, competitively. If the extent of the game area can be displayed without moving the camera, the background may be pre-rendered and treated as an unchanging element, significantly saving on CPU or GPU performance. When graphics hardware is available that allows for compositing of different graphical layers (e.g., multiple tile maps), it may not be necessary to refresh the background data.

If the game play area is larger than may be presented in this manner, then we must determine a way to ensure that all player characters remain visible. This is usually ensured by displacing the camera along an axis perpendicular to the game play area, effectively equivalent to a "zooming out" effect. This may be handled dynamically during game play, although this is greatly dependent upon the hardware rendering capabilities of the target platform. Alternatively, the screen size rendering of the world may be fixed, if the characters are sufficiently sized to have enough freedom of motion within the environment presented. With a fixed rendering size, the position of the screen window over the environment must be moved to best accommodate a view of all of the players. Having said that, this may result in almost constant screen motion, which is hardly desirable. A more aesthetically pleasing solution is to prevent movement of the camera position (which is what determines the background rendering, after all) until the player characters move within a threshold distance compared to the physical borders of the screen space projected into the world. With an orthographic projection used in 2D camera systems, this is a simple calculation, even if the viewport has an arbitrary rotation relative to the world coordinate scheme.

If it is necessary to frame the characters in this fashion, there can be cases where one or more players are effectively trapped in a position that will be moved off the screen. For multi-player games, it is necessary to consider whether each character has its own viewport, or if they should share the same full-screen viewport. In the former case, it is relatively straightforward to render each viewport separately.

Here are some other points to consider concerning a split-screen solution:

- The divisions of the screen are normally chosen to provide an equal amount of screen space for each player. This typically equates to a horizontal or vertical separation between their viewports. In some cases, it may be appropriate to give a larger amount of space to one particular player, especially in cooperative games (e.g., one player is piloting a craft, the other operating a gun turret).
- The number of players dictates the screen divisions. If players are able to join an active game in progress, then usually the screen is divided according to the maximum number of available players. It is, of course, possible to maximize the viewports according to the number of currently active players.
- Many games have environments that are too large to keep in memory at all times. Often the game will stream data from an external mass storage device (a CD or DVD drive in most cases, although sometimes a hard drive or even over a network) in anticipation of the traversal of the player through the game world. In this manner, a seamless experience of exploring a large environment may be achieved. In multi-player games where each player may explore the world in different directions, it may prove difficult to stream data fast enough from the external storage. In single-player games, it is possible to arrange the data on the external device to optimize the streaming process. With multiple players, the external drive must likely seek different locations repeatedly, potentially stalling the game play until sufficient data are loaded. One possible solution is to limit the level design such that each player may only explore the same (hopefully sufficiently large) section of the game world. This may be achieved by requiring both players to traverse the world in the same general direction, perhaps by requiring players to work together to open an exit. Care must still be taken to ensure that one player is not left behind.
- When using a split-screen approach it is necessary to reduce the amount of extraneous information overlaid on top of each player view. There are two main reasons for this. First, since each player view is reduced in size, overlays should be reduced or simplified to allow the same relative amount of screen space as in a single-player game. Secondly, the reduction in screen

space also means that a reduced amount of screen resolution is available to display the player's view, thus making it more difficult for a player to discern small details.

- When designing the placement of important player information it is usual to avoid placing data close to the edges of the display device. This border area is often referred to as the *safe zone*; the area within this border is referred to as the *safe frame*, as described in Chapter 2. In addition, it is often possible to reduce the height of the rendered viewport, thus imparting a small performance gain.

According to the division of the screen space, it is likely that there will be cases where the dimensions of the player view will have a different aspect ratio than that of the display device. This may require changes to the view frustum, field of view, or other rendering of the player view to avoid distortion of the world. Wide-angle field of view may lead to a fisheye form of distortion, which is usually undesirable.

Transitioning from full-screen to split-screen

It is indeed possible to transition between split- and single-screen techniques dynamically according to game play requirements. As mentioned above, there can be problems when the game play allows multiple players to move in differing directions within the environment; splitting the game display into multiple sections is a possible solution.

The determination of when to split or re-join the screen is the first consideration. Ensure that there is a buffer of time or physical space before the split/join may be performed in succession.

- Distance exceeded between characters such that one or more characters is about to leave the visible screen area.
- Screen splits into two (horizontally or vertically as required). One important thing to ensure is that the player characters retain their screen-relative positions during the split. This can be orchestrated by careful positioning of the camera during the transition. It is not necessary that the player characters remain in the same place on the screen after the split. The transition may be used to reposition each player character's new view according to game play requirements.
- During the transition, any overlaid elements showing player abilities or scores must be replaced with ones appropriate for the final view size.

- Next, the field of view is interpolated to match the aspect ratio of each new player character view.
- If necessary, the camera position must also be interpolated to a position more appropriate for the new player character view.

Transitioning from split-screen to full-screen

Once the player characters move close enough together to warrant returning to a full-screen display, a transition may begin. Ideally, this transition should start when each character has reached a position where they are close to the actual position on the full screen they will occupy when the screen is re-joined. This will minimize player confusion.

- Player characters move close enough to start transition
- GUI and other overlaid elements are removed until transition is completed
- New camera position adopted that retains current screen positions of each character
- Field of view interpolates to the new value for the full-screen display
- Camera position interpolates to the new desired position determined by the player characters

■ SUMMARY

This chapter has discussed a number of popular game genres and presented common camera solutions used within them. The methods outlined here are by no means definitive, but may be used as guidelines to develop new camera behaviors that may be used with more than one specific genre. The reader is encouraged to continually analyze further examples of game genres and apply this knowledge to combine different approaches in unique ways.

Chapter 6

Camera scripting

A major component of camera system design is the ability to dynamically alter or control the behavior of active cameras or to introduce new camera behaviors. This is often required due to changes in game play (alternatively referred to as *game events*) or changes in player character properties, but sometimes it is simply to emphasize a particular environmental feature, or to ensure that a sequence of game object interactions are viewable. Additionally, it is frequently necessary to instigate non-interactive movie sequences in response to similar game events or player actions. In many cases, it is also necessary to change camera behaviors due to environmental complexities, typically to restrict or explicitly dictate the motion (and possibly orientation) of the camera.

This chapter discusses the requirements and problems of game event management, highlights specific details pertinent to camera systems, and offers some potential implementation approaches.

WHAT IS MEANT BY SCRIPTING?

The general process of defining and controlling object interactions within video games is often generically referred to as *scripting*. This nomenclature is typically adopted because of the analogous concept of a *movie script*. Whereas a movie script defines a sequence of non-interactive actions and the manner in which they are portrayed (in written form or sometimes via graphical storyboards), a *game design script* often does not exist in a textual format, although it may begin in that format. Moreover, although a game design script may indeed describe a series of linear events (and is often used to produce similarly non-interactive sequences), it is frequently concerned with dynamically changing situations. This is especially true when scripting is used to control camera properties that depend upon player actions.

Although we are primarily concerned with the definition and control of *camera scripting*, a general discussion of *game scripting* is useful at this point. It is common in game systems that there is a need to be able to control the timing of game events and communication between game objects. Scripting in this context refers to a technique where such relationships between game objects may be specified.

Scripting often works well for complicated puzzles or mechanisms, although iteration may be relatively slow. Sometimes access to a game object's internal state variables or parameters are exposed by programmers to allow behavioral changes to be made by designers. Care must be taken when using scripting to implement complex game play or object behaviors. Direct programming within the game engine is often the best solution to involved AI behaviors as exhibited by game play situations such as "boss battles." Such explicit programming often provides greater flexibility and easier debugging facilities than scripting solutions. On the other hand, scripting solutions often allow iteration by designers without programmer intervention.

TYPES OF SCRIPTING

As with other game systems, there are many ways in which scripting of game events may be specified. The scripting requirements and methods chosen often depend upon the game genre. For example, action-adventure games will typically require different scripting solutions from, say, a racing game. The former might require many changes to camera behavior for activation and solution of puzzles according to player actions, and so forth. The latter may only require scripting of preferred camera solutions for replay cameras.

Regardless of the genre, it is preferable to develop a scripting system that is adaptable to differing requirements. Two of the most common scripting solutions are *scripting languages* and *event messaging*.

Scripting languages

As the name tends to suggest, scripting languages often involve a textual definition to specify the handling of game events. However, there are alternatives that do not involve editing or maintenance of text files. Some scripting languages are defined via a diagrammatic or graphical interface; typical examples include *finite state machines* (FSM) and *visual programming* components. Let us consider these different approaches.

Text-based scripting languages

These may often be specified in terms of a general-purpose programming language or sometimes as a game- or genre-specific custom language. Text-based scripting languages typically take two main forms, *pre-compiled* or *interpreted*. In the former case, actual machine-executable code is produced and will be linked to the main game program so that individual routines (associated with a particular game event) may be called as necessary. It may be possible to only load these external routines when required, thus generally reducing the memory footprint. In the *interpreted* case, an intermediate form of data is produced (from the original text) that is not directly executable on the target platform. This intermediate form is typically independent of the target platform but must be converted into executable code (hence *interpreted*) as the game is running. This facility may ease conversion of a game from one target platform to another but has a potential performance cost imposed by the interpretation process.

General-purpose programming languages

One of the most common solutions for game event scripting is to use an existing programming language, such as C, C++, Lua, Java, Forth, LISP, etc. This approach offers several advantages.

- Typically, these involve clearly defined languages with available documentation and implementation examples.
- Compilers and debuggers are generally available (caveat: they might not be available for a particular target platform).
- Ultimate flexibility since any desired functionality could be implemented (theoretically), including access to internal functions of the game engine if necessary. However, particulars of the implementation may prevent use of essential components from the game engine such as memory management.
- Interpreted code may be run within a virtual environment preventing the game "scripts" from accessing or changing inappropriate data. This may also ensure that it is impossible to crash the machine via the scripting language.

However, use of traditional programming languages for game scripting may also have some disadvantages.

- May not have a debugger available if the scripting code is running within the game itself; this is most common when using an interpreted system.

- Requires knowledge of programming constructs, which may not be suitable for some game designers. Designers are often not trained in programming and debugging techniques, which may limit their effectiveness in using a full-blown programming language; this does not imply that this is always the case. However, designers' talents are usually best suited to game play concerns rather than implementation issues. It might be preferable for the designer to work closely with a programmer on specifications and iterative development than actual implementation themselves.
- The temptation is often to do too much with the scripting language. This is certainly true where it is possible to construct complicated, nested levels of code (or calling functions outside of the script object). As a rule, scripting should be kept as simple as possible. A good rule of thumb for any scripting language is that the code should fit on one page. Of course, it is also harder to apply such constraints when a general-purpose language is used. Complicated functionality is usually best implemented within the game engine itself, where superior debugging capabilities and access to other engine functionality is available.
- There may not be good control over memory management and garbage collection. This may prove problematic in limited memory game consoles or similar embedded systems.

Custom scripting languages

Custom scripting languages may sometimes be more appropriate than one of the more mainstream programming languages. One of the chief benefits is that a custom language is completely under the control of the engineers and may include facilities that are very specific to the problem domain (even to the point of syntax, specific keywords, or operators). With the advent of advanced language creation and parsing tools, maintaining and expanding custom languages has certainly become more manageable.

One of the earlier uses of custom scripting languages was the *Script Creation Utility for Maniac Mansion* (SCUMM), used for a series of personal computer adventure games from the mid-1980s. This particular language had keywords and constructs that were particular to the movement and placement of "actors" within a film scene, in addition to a number of conventional programming constructs. Indeed, the programs written in SCUMM were even referred to as "scripts." The original intention of SCUMM was to allow designers with little experience in programming to specify and control game events and object interactions (e.g., puzzles, character interactions and movement, etc.) Unfortunately, while it succeeded in many respects, SCUMM suffered from a number of problems relating to custom script languages.

- It was difficult to maintain or expand (including porting to other platforms)
- Often relatively slow due to the interpreted byte-code "instructions"
- Had limited debugging capabilities
- Required custom tools to handle animation, and so forth
- Restricted programming constructs

Many of these problems may be addressed if taken into account when initially designing the language. However, practical game development is a large enough task as it stands, and maintenance of an additional language is better suited, perhaps, to a separate tools department rather than the game team itself. Additionally, SCUMM also illustrated that designers are not always best suited to performing programming tasks, particularly when the language might not support standard programming constructs; a balance must be struck between the language complexity and the problems that are expected to be solved with it. If the problem domain is inappropriate then a more expedient solution is to use a true programming language.

TECHNICAL

A typical custom scripting language might look something like this:

```
MyActor = UseActor("Bob"); // N.B. typeless
TheDoor = UseActor("Door"); // N.B. No error handling?
With MyActor; // refer implicitly to our actor
WalkTo(TheDoor);
TheDoor.Open();
FaceCamera();
CloseUp(); // camera shot definition
Say("Leaving.mp3"); // a resource name would be better
Wait(5);
Exit(TheDoor);
Close(The Door);
StartCinematic("BobLeaves"); // an identifier of some kind
FadeToBlack(2);
```

Note that although seemingly object-oriented, the syntax reads in a way that is closer to English than many typical programming languages. Additionally, the scripting language is typeless and has no need for pointers, eliminating some of the potential problems associated with memory overwrites. The keywords and function calls are usually problem-domain specific and deal with the game objects directly. Camera scripting would likely be a simpler matter still, as it would typically involve activating a new camera type or modifying existing camera properties. For example:

```
Script Trigger.Entered(theActor)
{
if (theActor ==  "Player")
  {
   attachedCamera = GetConnectedCamera();
   if (attachedCamera.Valid())
    StartCamera(attachedCamera);
  }
}
```

This type of activation is simplistic. However, the majority of camera scripting is only concerned with the activation or interpolation between different camera behaviors, although it is certainly possible to be able to change individual properties of behaviors (such as distance from target object). More advanced scripting would involve using cinematographic terminology to specify shots, transitions, and camera properties. An example camera shot script might be:

```
Camera.Script
{
  thePlayer = GetActor("Player");
  HeadShot(thePlayer, 30, 15);
   // camera's angular displacement
  Transition = CameraTransition("CrossFade", 2);
   // i.e. over 2 seconds
  MediumShot(thePlayer, -45, Transition);
   // specifies angle relative to character and
   // the transition type
}
```

Even though such a scripting language may indeed be useful, it is likely that in many cases the artists or designers would prefer to work within an interactive environment that allows for quick iteration. The world editor (perhaps itself a 3D modeling package) may be a good place to implement this type of previewing capability, although dependency upon game logic may preclude this option.

Finite state machines

Finite state machines (or FSMs) are abstract programming constructs often used within the games community (particularly within AI circles) to define the behavior of creatures or other game objects. FSM usage is certainly not restricted to object logic; state management of game systems such as the user interface is often handled in this way.

FSMs consist of several elements: *states, transitions*, and *actions*.

- **States.** Essentially, the behavior of an object may be broken down into a series of discrete *states*, each of which represents an exclusive behavioral condition of the object. For AI objects, typical states might include *combat, patrol, flee*, and so forth. A similar approach may be taken with puzzles or other game constructs (e.g., a door object may have states such as *open, closed, opening*, or *closing*). Game events may cause an object to change its state and typically, the state machine defines both the states and the conditional checks that are required to change the state.
- **Transitions.** Transitions dictate the methods or rules determining when states may be changed. There may be several potential transitions possible to or from any given state; this may then require the ability to specify an ordering in which the transition rules are applied. Therein lives some of the complexity of state machine usage; it can be difficult to track or update all of the potential changes from a myriad of potential states of an object. Transitions occur when a pre-defined condition is met. A typical example is receiving a particular message from an outside object, or changes to a state variable (e.g., a timer reaching zero).
- **Actions.** Actions are functions that are usually called when a state transition occurs. Typical examples would include entry and exit to a state. Actions may also be called on a periodic basis while a state is active (an "Update" function if you will). The conditional test(s) for potential transitions may thus be considered as periodic actions that are performed every update.

State machines are often defined using graphical means, typically within a custom editor that allows the user to view connections between states and to define relationships by simply placing new states and dragging connection markers between them. Existing professional diagram tools such as *Visio* or *OmniGraffle* provide an alternate solution for defining states and transitions, assuming that the state and connection information may be exported in a usable manner (e.g., in a common markup language such as XML). A typical FSM is illustrated in Figure 6.1.

A more advanced form of FSM is the *Hierarchical FSM* in which any of the states may also be considered as a separate FSM in their own right, executing its logic either in parallel to the parent FSM (i.e., allowing the parent to terminate the child FSM) or as a self-contained function.

Visual scripting languages

Visual scripting (or *visual programming*) really refers more to the interface of how the programmer or designer assembles the functional blocks of the script. Often this is implemented via a point and click (or drag) interface. Essentially, the currently allowable programming constructs are displayed (e.g., via buttons or pull-down menus) and are selectable according to their context and usage. For example, if a looping construct is chosen, then only the appropriate iteration operators are selectable. In some cases, pull-down menus are used to choose the programming constructs and optional numeric values or enumerations. In this way, a program may be assembled with a minimal amount of physical typing, ensuring that syntax errors are simply not permissible.

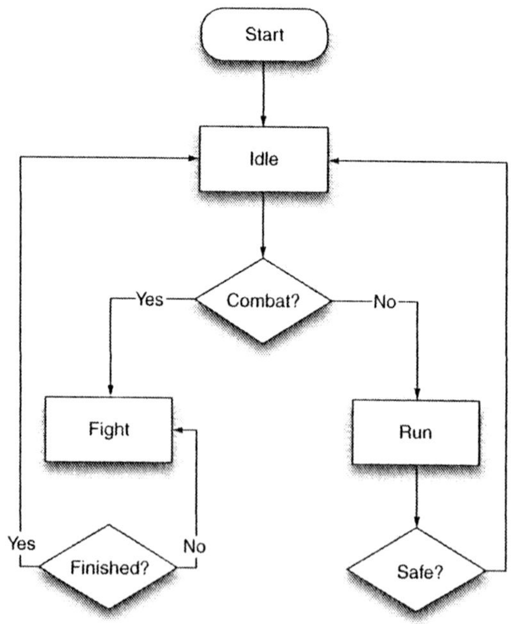

■ **FIGURE 6.1** A simple FSM for a game object.

With such an approach the program may be viewed in a similar vein to standard text editors, except that individual elements (such as keywords) are typically not editable; numeric values may be changed by simply moving the mouse pointer over the value and clicking down. The execution ordering may be changed by simply dragging a program line from its current position; once again, only permissible positions for the line to be moved to are allowed.

Scripting language concerns

Scripting systems can vary considerably in both functionality and complexity. Overblown scripting solutions tend to hinder the development process, especially systems that use interpreted or compiled languages embedded within the main game engine. One of the main reasons for this is the simple lack of debugging capabilities for many embedded scripting solutions. Additionally, the more programming that is allowed within the scripting system, the greater the need for programming knowledge. It also often proves necessary to provide suitable constructs with the ability to link to game engine functions.

It could also be argued that the complexity of object relationships, timing issues, and state management can easily get out of control in such a situation. One can imagine the potential problems that may arise during the QA process, especially with the lack of debugging capabilities.

Nonetheless, some developers have had success using pre-defined programming languages within the game engine such as interpreted C, Lua, or even Python or LISP. Ultimately the benefits of interactive changes have to be balanced against the lack of debugging support. You may find that such a solution works well for you. In many respects, it is better to leave the complexities of such aspects with the main programming language, but for small controlled logical elements, a scripting language may be beneficial; especially with regard to reducing message complexity and improving development iteration. If, however, the scripting for an object exceeds about a single page of code, you should probably consider moving the functionality into the regular game engine, or at least those portions that are the most complicated.

Event messaging

Message-based solutions usually benefit from relatively simple implementation and usage. The basic principle is that game objects are associated together via *connections*. These connections specify two pieces of information. First, there is an *event*. An event is a set of conditions that must be satisfied before notifying a game object of its occurrence.

The second data item is a relationship between the game object acknowledging the event conditions have been met, and another object that requires notification of this event. This relationship takes the form of a *message*; that is, packaged data to be *delivered* to the connected object, as shown in Figure 6.2. Connections that only specify a relationship between objects are known as *links*.

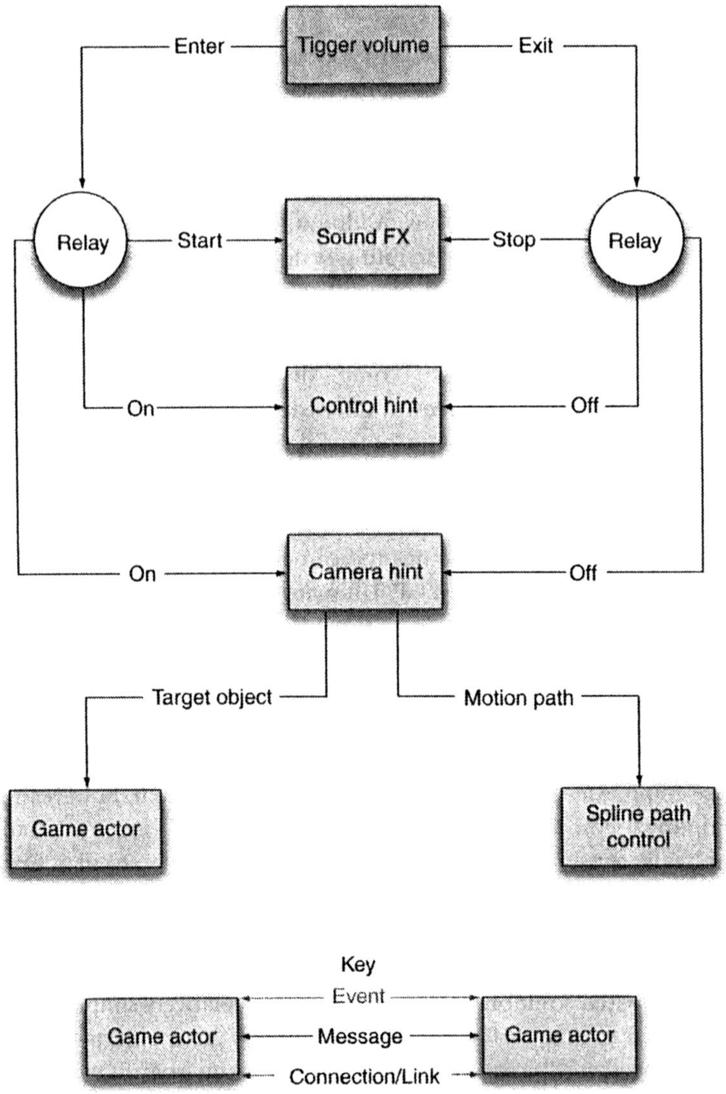

■ **FIGURE 6.2** Examples of events, messages, and links.

A typical example of an event conditional is a *trigger volume*; that is, a pre-defined volume within the game world (such as an axis-aligned bounding box, a cylinder, etc.) that reacts to the entry and exit of the player character or other game objects. The exact meaning of entry or exit of the volume can vary. For example, we might treat entry as any intersection between the collision volume of the player character (which could itself be a simplified axis-aligned bounding box for these purposes) and that of the "trigger" volume. Alternatively, we may wish to only treat entry as occurring when the player is completely enclosed within the volume. However, intersection tests often have lower CPU requirements than enclosure tests, depending on the complexity of the geometry of the collision volumes. It is also unusual to require such fine control over changes in camera behavior.

Exit from the trigger volume occurs when the player was already considered inside the volume and no longer has an intersection of its collision volume. The trigger volume therefore needs to maintain state so that it can update a list of which game objects are currently within the volume, which have entered or exited the volume, and so forth. To avoid situations where a player is entering and exiting the same trigger volume repeatedly, it is often desirable to use two volumes whose edges are positioned apart to prevent this occurrence. In this case, entry to one volume initiates the camera behavior changes, whereas exit of the other volume deactivates the same camera behavior. Figure 6.3 illustrates an example arrangement of trigger volumes.

Some possible position-based event conditions include:

- Entry or exit of characters within volumes (e.g., axis-aligned or arbitrarily oriented boxes or cylinders, spheres, etc.)
- Crossing of plane surfaces (such as moving through a doorway, or below a water plane)
- Proximity to an object while maintaining line of sight

Positional information is not the only possible event trigger; messages may be sent according to state changes upon an object (such as destruction), although camera systems most often respond to the position of the player character for interactive sequences.

These event conditions can now be used to send messages to the camera system regarding the activation (or deactivation) of camera overrides. The same mechanism can naturally be used for a variety of game events, and a generic solution is easy to implement.

Once we have decided to override the camera behavior, it quickly becomes clear that we may well have multiple overrides competing to control the camera behavior, which require a method to order the overrides according to their relative priorities.

The delivered message often changes the state of the target object; a common usage is to initiate a specific action performed by a game

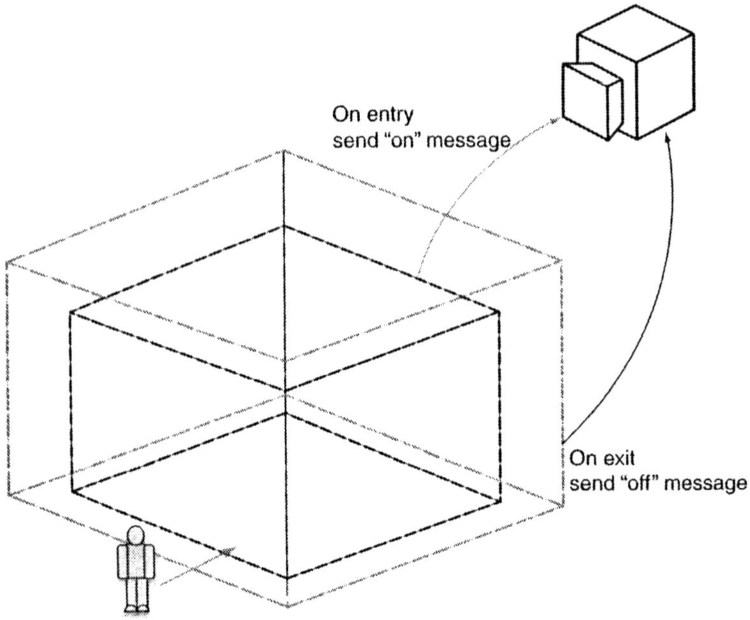

■ **FIGURE 6.3** Trigger volumes used to initiate event messages according to player entry or exit.

TECHNICAL

It is often useful for the object receiving the message to have knowledge of the object sending the message in addition to the original object that caused the game event to occur. This latter object, sometimes referred to as the *originator*, is particularly useful in multi-player situations where multiple objects of the same type (such as a player character) may cause multiple script messages to be sent simultaneously. An obvious example would be changes to the camera behavior altered by a player character entering a trigger volume. Clearly, it is necessary to ensure that the camera manager associated with the correct player (and only that camera manager) receives appropriate notification of the event.

object (e.g., opening or closing a door). Other typical uses might include starting an object moving along a path, activation or deactivation of game objects, and so forth. Note that messages do not have to originate from a script object per se, as they can be generated by code or other forms of scripting.

Event messaging normally requires a method of defining the relationship between various game objects and is often included as part of the base functionality of the game editor. However, since the number of connections can become large, methods of filtering the display of connections are often necessary.

Typical events that might cause messages to be sent include:

- Level startup
- Object loading
- Game is paused
- Volume entered or exited
- Player character is damaged
- Object reaches the end of a motion path
- Object state changes, for example "received damage," "destroyed," etc.

Typical messages sent by game events might include:

- *Start* (alternatively *On*) — cause the object to start its logic
- *Stop* (similarly *Off*) — similarly, cause the object to stop its logic
- *Activate object* — consider the object for rendering, logic, etc.
- *Delete object* — remove the object and its resources from the game
- *Perform action* — perform a specific action on the object
- *Query state* — to see if a previous action is completed, react to a specific state, etc.

TECHNICAL

The actual implementation of messaging is engine specific, as might be expected. One solution is to use inherited member functions; alternatively, game objects could register their handler function with a message manager of some kind. It is often necessary to abstract parameter passing, as many message "types" require differing parameters.

Delivery of script messages may be immediate, deferred to the end of the current update loop, or otherwise grouped according to logic ordering. If deferred, message handling should typically occur before camera logic is processed since the active camera properties may be changed by the messages.

Hybrid scripting solutions

Of course, it is quite possible to combine message sending with scripted languages. Indeed many game engines take this approach as it provides simple messaging for the more straightforward notification tasks. In such a situation the scripting language is able to generate messages to be sent to specific game objects as may be required. Indeed, messaging also provides a method for game objects to communicate back to the scripting system. One common method is for the scripting language to be implemented as specialized script objects whose *Think* logic (see Chapter 1) executes its associated script. Script objects may thus be controlled in the same manner as regular game objects with regard to their activation and so forth.

SCRIPT OBJECTS

Script objects are game objects usually placed by designers within the game world to create both game play and non-interactive sequences. Script objects may define objects with logic and knowledge of relationships to other game objects, or they may simply define objects that add ambience to a scene. Often these objects may be considered as a hierarchy of properties and behaviors and are well suited to object-oriented programming techniques such as *inheritance* where child objects take the properties and behaviors of their parents and may subsequently override or change them as necessary. Figure 6.4 shows an example hierarchy of objects that allows for varying complexity and functionality. Alternatively, game objects may be constructed from a series of *components*, allowing a selection of properties or behaviors to be combined to form new functionality. Regardless of the implementation, the game or camera designer requires methods to define or alter these properties and behaviors dynamically as the game progresses. The sections on *hints* below expand upon this idea.

Object relationships

It is often necessary to define relationships between game objects that do not rely on game events. Such relationships are often referred to as *links* or *connections*. The link itself is usually the only data required to define the relationship; however, a link may be unidirectional or bidirectional in nature. Unidirectional links may be used to define relationships where one object determines its logic based on another,

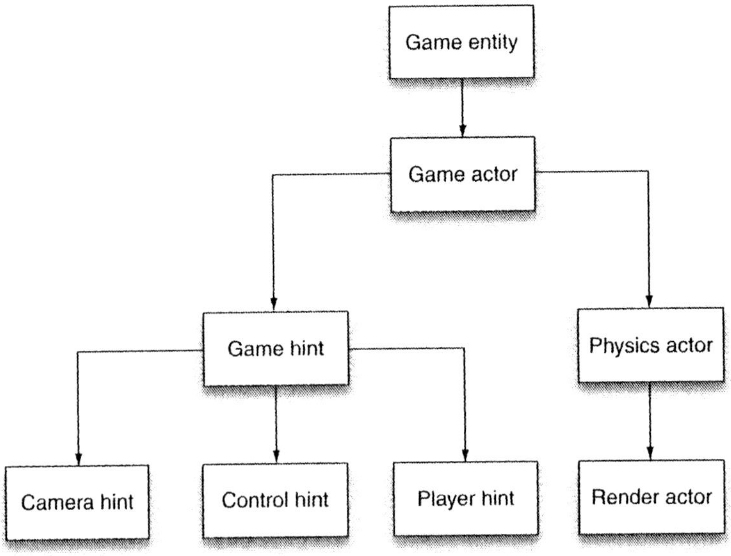

■ **FIGURE 6.4** An example hierarchy of object properties.

or they may be used to define a specific ordering to logic or rendering functionality between objects. Bidirectional links are sometimes used to simplify inter-object communication by allowing two objects to communicate directly.

TECHNICAL

Ordering of object logic is often necessary to ensure that objects dependent upon on the state of other objects are updated after that object's logic has executed. This may be achieved by use of a *directed acyclic graph* (DAG). Such a graph may be produced by traversing a series of unidirectional links between objects. Similarly, this technique is useful to resolve problems with the rendering of objects, particularly if the objects are coincident or feature rendering effects that would defeat hardware sorting according to depth buffer values.

Links are generally static (i.e., they do not change during the game) and are typically used when a script object requires access to external data that is better encapsulated within its own object. For example, a camera that is constrained to move along a path must be somehow connected to the path data defining its possible motion. Links are frequently used during object initialization so that at run-time it will not be necessary to interrogate other script objects for information. However, there are cases where a run-time relationship is necessary. A typical camera example of such a relationship is that of a *camera target* object. This link defines the game object used as an orientation target for the connected camera hint. Similar objects may be used to define the control points of a movement path, and so forth. Figure 6.2 shows examples of states, messages, and links.

Scriptable game hints

Game hints are script objects that provide one possible type of run-time mechanism by which designers can override player properties, game controls, or camera properties according to a variety of events. This allows tight control over specific game play features according to player position, game events, cinematic sequences, and so forth. A full discussion of scripting systems for games is too large a topic for this book, but some of the more useful camera-related script objects are *camera hints, player hints,* and *control hints*. Each of these will be discussed in turn, as well as a *Sequenced Events Manager* object that allows easier synchronization of disparate game events.

Camera hints

Camera hints are scripting mechanisms that allow designers to temporarily override or alter existing camera behavior within a specific area of the game. They are literally "hints" or clues given to the camera system to overcome its limitations, deal with complex environments, or to ensure specific behaviors that match game play requirements. These can take the form of simple modifications to the base camera behavior (e.g., the distance between the camera and the target character, its position relative to the player, etc.) or can completely change the behavior of the camera (such as from a free form motion to a fixed path or position). Changes to the behavior of the camera can be triggered in a variety of ways, from the physical location of a game object (e.g., the player character) through timers and other event-based mechanisms.

A full discussion of game scripting is beyond the scope of this book, however, a mechanism is certainly needed to start and stop camera hints. Additionally, it is entirely possible that there will be several competing camera hints active simultaneously. Therefore, some prioritization control method is necessary, which also requires that a list of currently active camera hints be maintained. It is also likely that the ordering of messages that are sent to activate or deactivate camera hints is arbitrary, which might require messages to be queued and processed at the end of the current frame. Another potential problem area is if game hint objects are removed from memory or unloaded while still considered active. Similarly, they may become activated before the player is within that specific game area.

Camera properties that may be overridden by camera hints include:

- Type of camera behavior (stationary, path-based, etc.)
- Position and orientation (e.g., for stationary cameras)
- Desired positional offset relative to target
- Look-at offset/target selection method
- Movement speed
- Field of view

Some of these properties are such that their values could be altered dynamically in response to game objects' behavior. One of the most common of these is the player position. It is often desirable to change the camera behavior according to the position of the player relative to a reference frame within the environment. For example, if the player character is scaling a mountain, we may wish the position or orientation of the camera to vary according to how high the player has climbed (perhaps to give a more panoramic view at certain elevations).

One useful reference frame is to define a path within the game world. This path may be a simple linear one (i.e., between two specified game objects) or more involved based on a spline curve or other shape. We can then use the player position relative to this reference frame to produce a normalized value (between 0 and 1). A typical example is shown in Figures 6.5a and b. This normalized value may then be mapped into a range of values for the particular camera property in question, for example, the Z coordinate. The mapping function may be of any type, although a very flexible method is to use a *2D control spline* (e.g., a *piecewise Hermite curve*) that maps this normalized value into a particular camera property. While it is not necessary to use a normalized value as the input to the control spline, it can be more convenient when the input value may change magnitude (e.g., if the spline path is altered). The use of a mapping function such as this is helpful in many aspects of camera systems, but it may sometimes be easier to understand the relationship between the input and output values if a non-normalized value is used.

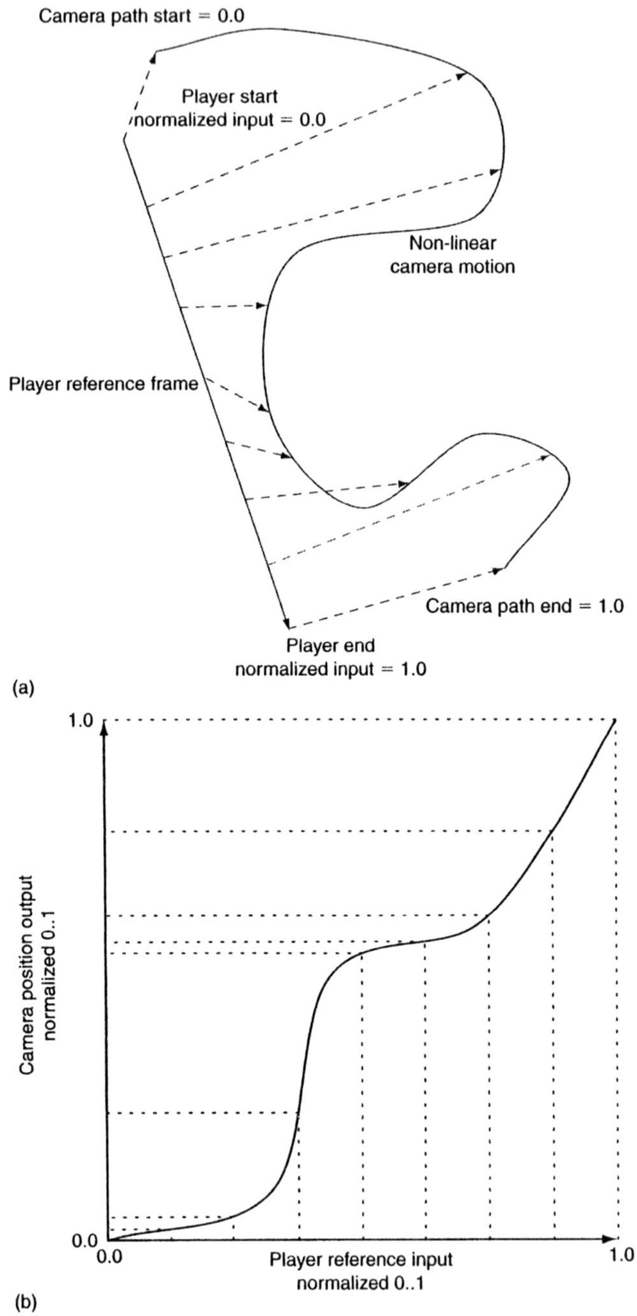

■ **FIGURE 6.5** (a) The player position relative to a reference frame can be considered as a normalized value, between 0 and 1. (b) The normalized value from (a) is used to map into a Hermite spline producing a new camera property, such as position along a path.

Player hints

Not only is it often necessary to override camera behavior due to environmental complexity or game play requirements, but these situations also demand changes to the behavior or control of the player character. In a similar fashion to camera hints, we also need *player hints* to temporarily change aspects of the player control or other characteristics of player character behavior.

Here is an example list of properties that may be overridden or specified by a player hint.

- **Prevent motion of the player.** Often this could be all motion methods or restricted to a particular kind of motion (such as no jumping). This is normally only used when contextually appropriate, and should be indicated to the player in some manner when not immediately obvious.
- **Relocate player position.** On occasion, it is necessary to reposition the player character (e.g., to correct alignment with an environmental element, or to restart the player after a cinematic sequence or at the start of a new level).
- **Change player movement characteristics.** Frequently it is necessary to override some characteristic of player motion (acceleration, maximum velocity, gravity, etc.) due to environmental changes (such as submersion in water).
- **Flags to indicate special kinds of game play.** Player hints provide a mechanism to notify the game engine of special game play situations (such as the player becoming submerged in water, boss encounters, etc.).

Just as with camera hints, player hints may be activated and deactivated in any manner of ways, and may be even dependent upon the state of the player for their activation. In some cases player hints might be used to change the actual state of the player character, for example, causing a weapon to be holstered.

Control hints

In a similar vein to player hints, *control hints* are scripted objects that can be used to override, disable, or remap player controls dynamically. As such, they are often derived from a generic "game hint" class, which will handle all aspects of their prioritization, activation, and deactivation, etc. Depending on the particulars of their implementation, control hints may be combined to override multiple controls as required. Examples of their usage are included in the list below.

- **Disable specific controls or sets of player controls.** Rather than specifying the particular controller buttons to disable, a better solution is to disable player control *commands* that are mapped to specific controller buttons (or combinations, sequences, gestures, etc.). Thus, if the control mapping changes at some future date, the control hint is still valid. It may also prove useful to have pre-defined sets of controls to disable, such as all movement controls, all firing controls, etc.
- **Specify the control reference frame, and the time to interpolate to that new reference frame.** This is particularly useful in third person games where we need to ensure that player controls are consistent regardless of the camera position relative to the player character. These control hints are often used in conjunction with camera hints that instantly cut to a position where the control reference frame would be changed significantly. Changing the control reference frame should always be performed in a manner that ensures player intent is maintained. Always allow the player to understand the relationship between their controls and how their character is moved.

Control hints are activated or deactivated in the same manner as other game hints, for the most part, although it is sometimes necessary to generate them from code (e.g., if an AI object needs to temporarily disable certain player controls). In addition, they are often deactivated in other ways. One of the simplest ways is a timer mechanism where the control hint deactivates automatically after a defined period has elapsed; naturally, timers may be used with other types of game hints and they are more common with player control-related scripting (e.g., disabling player control for a fixed period of time). A more dynamic and malleable method of hint deactivation is to allow the control changes to be "broken" if the player presses particular combinations of buttons. Such combinations often include sequences of buttons, rapid pressing and releasing of buttons (either by count or frequency of presses), and so forth. A palette of such choices is usually offered as a property of the control hint object, and is re-definable by the game designer.

Sequenced events manager

It is common to find that a number of game events need to be triggered in a specific order at defined time intervals. Additionally, it is also sometimes necessary to trigger multiple game events within the same game update, but in a specific ordering. A *sequenced events manager* script object is one solution that allows messages to be defined via a time line interface; that is, object messages are ordered according to the time interval at which they occur from the point at which the sequence object receives its initial activation. This makes it easy to change message ordering and allows an overview of events. It is useful to allow the same event to be triggered multiple times within the same time line.

Sequenced event managers are commonly used within movie sequences as they allow a unified solution to the triggering of disparate events, as well as the ability to easily change the ordering of events.

TECHNICAL

A generic hint manager and prioritization class can be written to handle several kinds of hints — the only real difference is a hint type specific comparison function for the prioritization of multiple hints, and the code to override or restore hint properties. It should be noted that a decision needs to made about restoring properties. While it is entirely possible to restore the previous set of properties that (may) have been set by another hint, this can lead to confusion as to what properties are currently set, as well as leading to a difficult, if not practically impossible test cycle. Instead, it is recommended that a standard set of default values are restored whenever the active hint becomes empty. If the list is not empty then the currently highest priority hint's properties should be adopted. This mechanism is straightforward to implement and easily understandable. It also removes a great deal of complexity about the current hint properties.

In many scripting systems, it is not always possible to control the order in which script messages are delivered. Hence, a currently active camera hint may be deactivated in the same update loop as a new camera hint is activated. If the new hint has a lower priority than the active hint but sends its message first, it will not become active until the following frame. To resolve such potential dependencies, accumulate all the activation and deactivation events until all script messages have been sent. It is then a simple matter of processing all the deactivation events followed by the activation events to ensure correct handling of multiple messages within the same frame of game play. It is even quite simple to find pairs of on/off messages for the same camera hint and eliminate those messages directly.

CAMERA SCRIPTING

What elements of camera systems need to be scripted or modified by scripting? The extent that camera properties may be changed by scripting is dependent upon the situation in which the camera is used. Interactive cameras typically offer direct control over camera properties whereas non-interactive sequences are often limited to basic functionality such as position, orientation, and field of view.

Camera scripting methods

There are two main methods in which camera scripting is used to alter camera functionality: *pre-defined* and *dynamic*.

Pre-defined camera scripting

It is usual that camera systems provide a palette of pre-defined camera behaviors for the designer to adapt to their own needs. Such a palette may be constructed easily if the world editor (or equivalent tool) allows macro objects; that is, combinations of pre-defined game objects. In the case of scripting languages, these pre-defined choices may be implemented as libraries or other implicitly included script objects.

Dynamic camera scripting

This type of camera scripting is used where only specific properties of the camera need to be adjusted on a temporary basis. Rather than defining an entirely new camera type, it may be desirable to only adjust those properties as required, regardless of the other camera functionality that might be active. Such an approach limits the properties that may be adjusted, as they must not affect gross level functionality. In fact, the benefits of easier scripting may not outweigh the complexities introduced by the permutations of hint combinations. Additionally, it may be unclear as to which factors are influencing camera behavior if the scripting is not exclusively applied.

Camera control

The main usage of scripting with respect to camera systems is in its ability to temporarily customize the current camera behavior according to game play or cinematic requirements. Since it is difficult (to say the least) to develop a camera system that can anticipate all of the requirements of the player and the designer, it is usual to want to override the behavior of the camera when specific situations are encountered during game play. A good example would be the use of fixed position cameras in confined spaces, or to explicitly show the player a particular clue as to how to solve a puzzle.

Camera scripting is used in both interactive situations and non-interactive movie sequences. It should also be noted that camera scripting is frequently used regardless of the chosen presentation style.

Third person scripting

Possibly the most frequently used form of camera scripting is for third person cameras. There are many game play situations where it is necessary to specifically control aspects of third person camera behavior to present the game to the player in a meaningful manner. Camera scripting for third person cameras may involve changing the entire behavior of the camera or simply one particular aspect. To simplify the scripting process, major behavior changes are often implemented as specific pre-defined script objects. The camera system will then generate the appropriate run-time game objects required for this behavior (e.g., a path-based camera). For minor alterations to generic camera properties, we may wish to consider using separate script objects that are managed independently of the major behavioral scripting. These script objects (*generic camera hints*, if you will) only change the basic camera properties that are common to all camera behaviors. These would include field of view, focal length (if used), filter or rendering effects, fog distance, distance or elevation from the player character (e.g., if only one type of camera is used), and so forth. On the other hand, this may complicate scripting by adding additional objects as well as requiring the designer to track multiple sets of camera objects.

First person scripting

Upon initial consideration, it might seem that there are few situations (if any) where it is necessary to exert control over the camera when using a first person presentation style. However, there are cases where such control is both appropriate and assists the player. Here are some example situations where automatic control over the camera orientation may be helpful.

- **Traversing up or down ramps or other significantly sloped surfaces.** As the player faces and moves in a direction parallel to the axis of the ramp, it can be useful to automatically change the "rest" elevation of the camera. This assists the player by providing a view closer to the direction of motion, even though the character itself may remain vertically aligned. The amount of pitch to apply is typically varied according to the position of the player character relative to the slope as shown in Figure 6.6. Note that as the player character reorients toward a direction perpendicular to the slope axis, the amount of pitching should be reduced. Additionally, the sign of the pitch angle of the camera should match the direction of the player character relative to the slope; i.e., if the player character orientation is aligned toward the downhill direction of the slope, then obviously the camera should be pitched below the horizontal plane and vice versa. *Metroid Prime* [Metroid02] used this approach since the player was unable to use *free-look* while moving. Thus it became difficult to aim walking up or down inclines until this technique was applied. Note that since this only defines the base elevation of the camera it is still applicable in situations where the player is able to change their view during movement.

- **Jumping.** Traditionally jumping has been problematic when using a first person presentation. One of the reasons has been the inability of the player to easily judge the position of the player character relative to environmental features such as chasms or other low-level obstacles. Many games allow some limited movement of the player character during a jump. Sometimes this is limited to a small amount of sideways motion (strafing), but it may also be possible to change the overall length of the jump. In such cases, it would be helpful if the player could be given a better view of their destination point. One method is to gradually pitch the camera downward

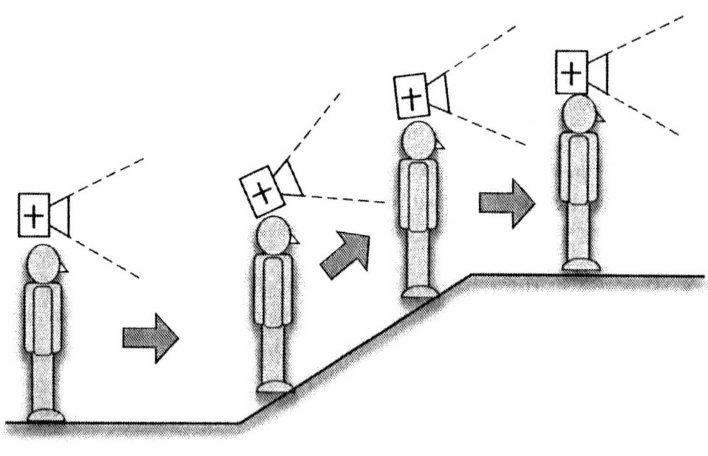

■ **FIGURE 6.6** Automatic pitching of the first person camera according to the player position.

as the player descends, as illustrated in Figure 6.7. Note that the amount of pitching should be limited and may be overridden by the player at any time. Once the player has landed (or possibly slightly before), the camera should gradually revert to the default elevation. This approach was taken in *Metroid Prime* [Metroid02].

- **View locking.** There are times when it is necessary to completely override the orientation of the first person camera. One such situation is when the facility of "*lock-on*" is provided. This ability allows the player to change their movement method to a semi-automated circle strafing, relative to another game object or position. Sideways movement controls now result in an arc of motion around the "lock" position. During this type of motion, it is frequently preferable that the camera orientation automatically tracks the lock position. In many cases it is unnecessary to lock both the yaw and pitch of the camera, although it should be noted that in a first person view it is often the case that the player's 2D orientation matches that of the camera, so this must also be applied when locking the camera

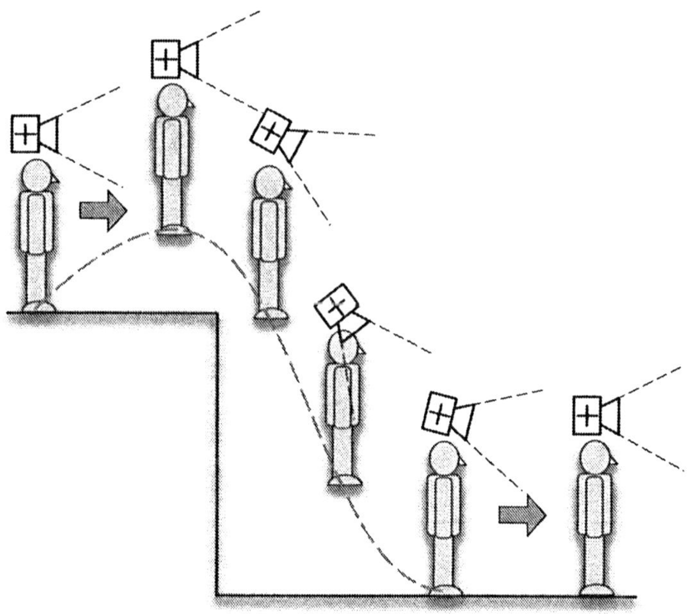

■ **FIGURE 6.7** Automatic camera pitch during player jumping.

orientation in this manner. Thus, the player may be able to use "free-look" to aim while still moving relative to the locked-onto game object. Figure 6.8 shows the effect of lock-on with respect to a first person camera.

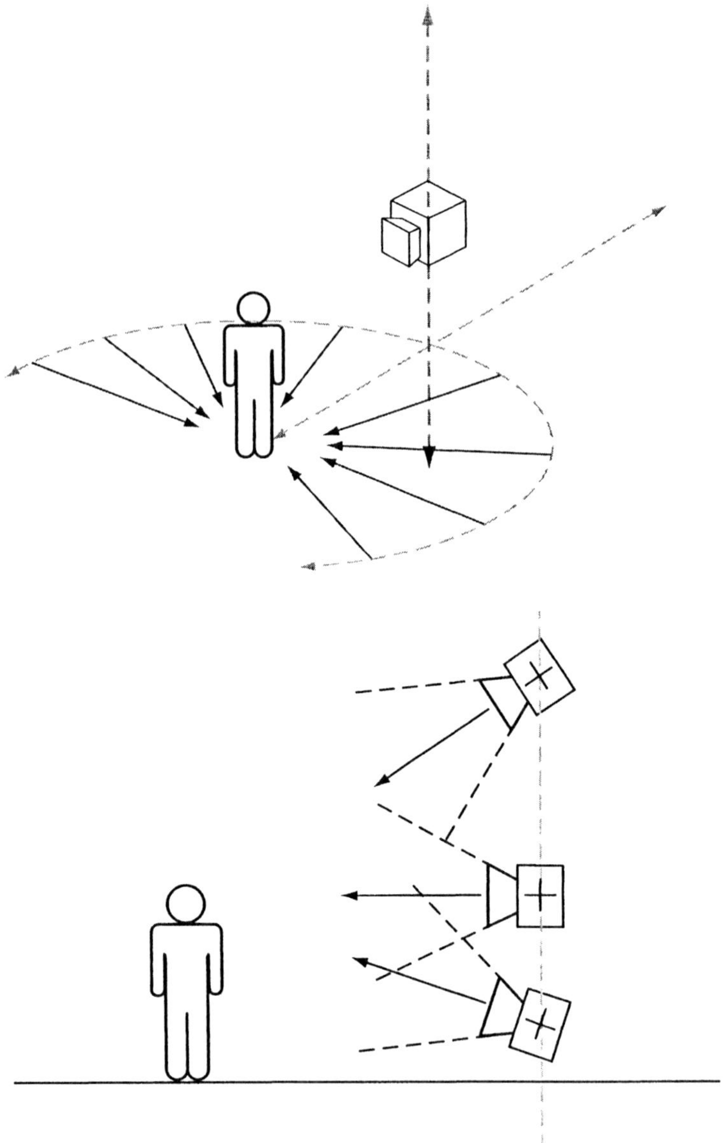

■ **FIGURE 6.8** View locking may be restricted to only the camera yaw if so desired, allowing "free-look" to be used by the player.

Non-interactive movie scripting

Another major use of camera scripting is to control non-interactive movie sequences. Such sequences typically have simpler scripting requirements than interactive ones, mainly due to the consistency of the presentation. Without wishing to oversimplify, game movie scripting is often achieved by simply moving and reorienting the camera over time, similar to real-world cinematography. Any property of the camera affecting the rendering of the scene may also be controlled via camera scripting, such as field of view or depth of field effects (i.e., focal length).

Cinematic sequences of this nature typically use a separate script object from regular in-game camera hints. The majority of cinematic camera motion may be derived in a similar manner to in-game camera motion except that it is more common to use elapsed time as the determining input value for motion control splines and so forth. Cuts between cameras are usually achieved by simply starting a new cinematic camera script object.

Rules of thumb

Regardless of the scripting methodology, some practical rules of thumb may be adopted to assist camera scripting.

Apply Occam's Razor

That is, use the simplest scripting solution possible. When considering the choices between complex camera behaviors (that may be very flexible but difficult to implement and define) and simpler but possibly less flexible solutions, consider that game play is very malleable and simpler solutions are typically easier and quicker to adjust should it be required. Additionally, when revisiting existing scripting that was defined earlier in the project, simpler solutions are often easy to adapt to changing game play or are certainly more easily replaced. One further consideration: try to keep camera motion as simple as possible. The more complex the motion, the more likely it is that the player may become disoriented (since such motion may require significant orientation changes).

Allow for different ways that the camera event may be triggered

Simply entering a *trigger volume* may not be sufficient; the player mode may change the camera scripting requirements or whether the camera should change at all. The relative position (or movement direction) of the player character compared to the trigger may also be used to change the chosen camera hint. For example, Figure 6.9 shows two camera hints both connected to the same trigger volume. Each camera hint represents a stationary camera that tracks the player. In such an example the camera hint that best matches the view orientation of the existing camera when the player enters the trigger volume would be chosen.

Allow previewing of camera motion and orientation

Whenever possible, the camera designer should be able to preview potential camera scripting, either within the game scripting environment or within the game. This is especially important when defining the transitions between active cameras (e.g., interpolation), often these may only be tested within the game engine.

Assess camera scripting requirements early in the design process

Ideally, this should occur before final game artwork is committed, or possibly, before it has been applied. Some game development companies develop simplified versions of all game rooms to establish game play requirements before proceeding to a form that is artistically correct. By determining the camera requirements at this early stage, there

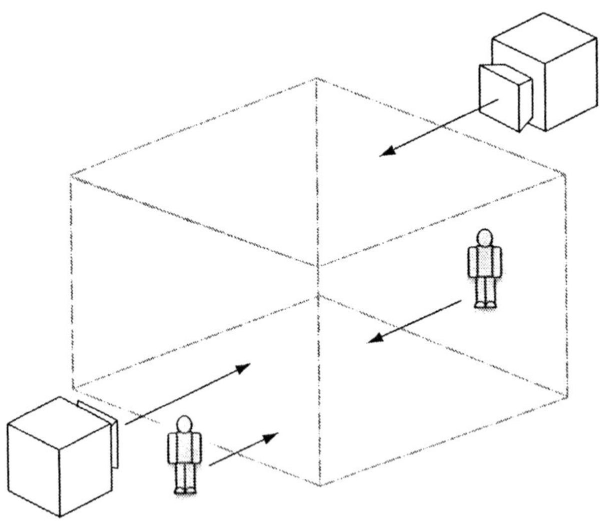

■ **FIGURE 6.9** Two camera hints linked to the same trigger and chosen based on the previous camera positional relationship.

may be an opportunity to change the environment to better suit the camera system.

Make the scripting development cycle as efficient as possible

Camera scripting in general, and cinematic sequence scripting in particular, is a highly iterative process. It is important to make the tools as efficient as possible with respect to the development cycle of making changes and the ability to see them *in situ* on the target platform. Improving and expanding preview capabilities within the game world editor (or generally on the development machine) can help tremendously in this regard.

Mimic the behaviors of the tools used by artists where possible

If possible, do not require your artists (and possibly designers) to learn multiple ways of moving through the 3D environment within the game tools set. Of course, many people are able to switch between differing modeling packages or editors and be able to function efficiently. However, having a unified interface and familiarity in working methods will reap great benefits in productivity. This includes standardizing the use of terminology. In many cases, the development environment is implemented using plug-in capabilities of a modeling package, thus ensuring artist familiarity and possibly easing some of the more onerous tool development tasks.

Allow for game play changes

In many games there can be significant changes to the environment according to changes in the game state (e.g., a door is locked that was previously open). Thus the camera scripting solutions must allow for these changes either in the original scripting or by having different scripting solutions triggered by appropriate game events. Additional advice on camera system design may be found in Chapter 4.

SCRIPTING TOOLS

Camera scripting is greatly dependent upon the toolset used to define and place camera scripting within the game world. Additional tools are necessary for converting the scripting into a format used by the game engine, possibly involving a compilation stage. Once a camera script is running in the game engine, it will be necessary to analyze the scripting to ensure that it is functioning as desired. Let us briefly examine the main tools necessary for camera scripting.

World editor support

The world editor is one of the main tools used when developing video games. Sometimes the world editor is able to preview the entirety of the game logic, but often this is not the case, especially when the target platform is different from the development system. The world editor may be a proprietary solution, a middleware software package tailored directly to game development, or a modification to an existing 3D art package such as *Maya* or *3ds Max*. Ideally, plug-in software would be written to allow a way to preview some, if not all, camera functionality within the editor. Additionally it would be preferable to be able to quickly download information to the target platform for review within the actual game environment.

Clearly, the world editor must allow the placement and manipulation of script objects in addition to mechanisms for specifying message passing, state transitions, event triggering, and other object-to-object relationships. It should also be possible to edit properties of individual script objects and to group script objects and their relationships into collections (or macros) that may easily replicate common game functionality. Editing of scripting languages may not be offered within the world editor, but it should be possible to define their usage.

Communication between target platform and development PC

It is often essential to be able to communicate game state information as a part of the debugging and development process. This is assuming that the target platform is physically separate from the development environment. When developing games for PCs the target machine is often the development machine (even in this situation it may be beneficial to use a networked PC as the target platform). Sometimes this communication is implemented via a simple parallel interface, other times via a local area network. Regardless of the actual mechanism, the ability to interrogate the state of game objects as their logic is executing is extremely beneficial. Additionally, information concerning the active hints and their properties is invaluable.

Message/event logging

A useful debugging technique is to retain a list of all game events that occurred and any messages that were sent because of the event.

It would be helpful if the update loop counter or elapsed time of the event were recorded so that the events may be reviewed in the order in which they occurred. Ideally this event log would be stored on the host development machine so that it might be reviewed at leisure. The event log may be captured in a binary format to save memory if required, but to be of most use it should be expanded into a human readable form once exported from the game; even a simple comma-separated format may be utilized to allow easy importation into a spreadsheet or similar program.

Object properties debugging

An extremely useful tool is the ability to examine the properties of game objects while the game is executing. Clearly this facility is available to programmers who have access to a true program debugger, but this is typically not available to other members of the development team. Ideally it would be possible to interrogate the game from within the game world editor. One such example would allow the editor to pause execution while browsing through the active game objects. Often this type of debugging facility is built into the game executable, allowing properties to be displayed on the target platform display device. However, this approach may be problematic due to limitations of the display device, memory constraints, or similar restrictions.

Replay

Possibly one of the greatest debugging facilities is the ability to replay a portion of the game in a deterministic manner. A poor-man's version of this has been used by QA departments for many years: the VCR. It is *de rigueur* for most QA departments to record all game play testing — if your QA department is not doing this then you might want to find out why. Videotapes (or even hard disc/DVD recorders) are cheap and easy to use; they are an invaluable tool in demonstrating incorrect behavior or those difficult to reproduce bugs. Video recording is best combined with debugging output showing relevant internal game state information.

Actual game replay may be achieved by capturing controller input during game play and then using that data to replace regular controller input. This assumes that the base state of the game at the point at which the capturing started may be reliably reproduced. This includes ensuring that non-deterministic aspects such as random-number generation (usually pseudo random number generation, but necessary nonetheless) is also replicated. Unfortunately there are some factors (such as network traffic or latency) that may not be replicated in this manner, but for most debugging purposes deterministic reproduction of game state is extremely beneficial.

Console window

A further general debugging technique is to provide a method of printing text messages on the target platform display device as well as remotely on the development host (if distinct from the target platform). This may be achieved through an actual script object (thus allowing designers to debug their own logic) or through code where internal state information from the game engine may be revealed.

To prevent the text output from becoming overwhelming, it is useful to have the ability to specify what text messages should be shown. Often this is achieved through internal debugging variables specific to the type of information displayed. These debugging variables are sometimes set via in-game menus (a *debug menu*, if you will) or alternatively though an *input console window* on the development machine. The latter means allows the development team to send commands to the game engine while it is running; this can be a very powerful technique. Commands may be defined to change object state, alter debugging information, enable alternative control configurations, and much more. It may be used to interrogate specific game objects as to their current state, and to even change their properties as their logic is executed.

SCRIPT DEBUGGING

Camera script debugging is concerned with understanding the logic utilized by the scripting system to activate or change camera behavior as the game is executing. As such, it shares many of the same techniques used when debugging other game systems. However, since the users of the scripting system typically have more restricted access to the state of the target machine, it is often necessary to supply additional information showing the internal state of the scripting system.

Some of the common methods used in game script debugging (outside of using a program debugger) include:

- **Script statement execution/filtering.** For any given game script (or other subset of currently active script objects determined by a desired filtering mechanism) show a history of each actual statement that was executed, in lieu of an actual full debugger.

This may be difficult to implement when using compiled languages since this represents a large amount of the functionality of a genuine debugger.

- **Debug message logging.** Script objects are able to generate debugging text messages that reveal aspects of their internal states. These messages are echoed to a separate display, transmitted to the host development machine, displayed as an overlay on top of the main graphical output of the game, or otherwise stored for later retrieval.
- **Message filtering.** Inter-object communication is tracked and displayed via the debug message logging mechanism outlined above. Facilities are often provided to filter the type of messages that are displayed, to ease analysis, and reduce the potentially overwhelming amount of information that might be generated. Typically, filters allow restriction of messages according to source or destination object type, message type, and so forth.
- **Object state.** Individual object types are often able to report internal state information specific to their behaviors. Such reporting is often very informative as to how their logic is being evaluated, in lieu of a true debugger of course. Camera hints may show their orientation and position within the game world, potential movement limits, and so forth. Camera specific debugging techniques are detailed in Chapter 11.
- **FSM state changes.** For objects that use finite state machines, it can be extremely useful to display both the current state used by an object in addition to the results of the conditional tests used to determine state transitions. Internal variables pertinent to state changes (such as timers) may also be exposed in this manner. While this information could be displayed in a textual format (e.g., via a console debugging window), it would be preferable if the game could communicate to the original editing program used to define the FSM itself. This latter technique allows a more direct correlation between the current state of an object and its position within the FSM.
- **Animation state and event management.** Many games utilize blending or interpolation between animations, thus it is useful to track the current animation state and which animations are being combined. Some animation systems allow game events to be triggered at specific times during an animation (e.g., audio

effects cued off foot placement). Tracking these events may be handled by a more generic message logging scheme as noted above or specifically within the animation system.

■ SUMMARY

In this chapter, we have examined a number of potential solutions for controlling camera behavior according to events triggered during game play or non-interactive sequences. Although many methodologies are possible, a form of scripting is often used to define these relationships. Game objects are typically used to define new types of camera behavior that are initiated by the chosen scripting solution. Care must be taken to ensure the chosen scripting methodology is well suited to the types of usage required by the game and that it provides sufficient debugging capabilities.

Part 3

Camera Engineering

The only legitimate use of a computer is to play games.
— Eugene Jarvis, Arcade Game Designer and Programmer
(*Defender, Robotron*, Smash TV...)

Once a thorough understanding of the design requirements of real-time cameras is understood, we may progress to discussing implementation issues. This part of the book details the individual properties of game cameras and discusses their internal design, functionality, and implementation.

Chapter 7

Position and orientation

There are two main components of camera placement within the game world, namely *position* and *orientation*. The preferred position of the camera, referred to here as the *desired position*, defines the location within the game world from which a view may be generated; it is typically specified to satisfy an aesthetic or game play requirement and may well change dynamically. Related to this is the determination of how the camera may reach its desired position, including any physical considerations or constraints that may be required (e.g., the requirement to avoid passing through environmental features or other game objects). We may refer to this as *navigation*. Navigation and the actual *motion* of the camera from its current position toward the desired position will be covered in Chapters 8 and 9, respectively.

The second component of camera placement, *orientation*, defines the direction in which the camera is facing within the game world (possibly with rotation or *roll* about that direction). It may also be considered as two related elements. The first of these is the *desired orientation*, a corollary to the desired position and once again dependent upon aesthetic and game play changes. The second element is the method used to *reorient* the camera toward its desired orientation. Both of these elements will be discussed in this chapter.

COORDINATE SCHEMES

The camera properties of position and orientation specify the most basic information required for all types of game camera, whether used for interactive or cinematic purposes and irrespective of the presentation style. In many cases, these camera properties are specified as relative to a common frame of reference used by all game objects. This is normally referred to as the *world space* or *world coordinate system*. Individual game objects may also specify coordinates relative to their own position and orientation, i.e., in *local* or *object space*; this is typically used for determining the position of the vertices that form the three-dimensional representation (or *model*) of the game object.

Each type of coordinate system consists of three axes, set at right angles to each other, extending from a common point of intersection known as the origin. The name given to each axis often varies between different game engines or between modeling software packages. It is important that artists, designers, and programmers have a common understanding of the axes used in each discipline. Naturally, it would be desirable for these to be consistent if possible to avoid unnecessary confusion.

Let us examine the most common coordinate systems used within camera systems.

World space

World space coordinates are the most frequently used coordinate scheme within games; the coordinate values specify an absolute position within the game world. The rendering process takes coordinates from world space into camera space (see the next section) and then finally into two-dimensional screen space.

Camera (or eye) space

When referring to camera space, this is a coordinate representation where the camera is located at the origin of the coordinate system. Thus, the forward direction of the camera (i.e., extending away from the camera position) typically corresponds to one of the coordinate axes. Depending on the "handedness" of the coordinate scheme, this is usually either the Y- or Z-axis.

Screen space

Calculations performed in screen space are essentially camera space coordinates transformed by the projection matrix used to render the view. It is common for screen space coordinates to have their origin placed in the middle of the output device; in such a case the X and Y coordinates would extend outward in the range of minus one to plus one (the negative values extending to the left and up on the screen appropriately). The Z coordinate would signify positions into or out of the screen, once again normally in the range minus one to plus one. Note that the bounds of the screen space coordinate system correspond to the projected limits of the view frustum, and may thus represent a volume with non-parallel sides (e.g., in the case of a perspective view transformation).

Local (or character) space

This specifies a coordinate system where the player character (or other game object) is centered at the origin and the coordinate axes match that of the character.

Object relative

In this coordinate system, the camera is centered at the origin, and the coordinate axes are based upon the relative position of an object to the camera. Naturally, this scheme changes dynamically as both the camera and the object move, and the camera orientation may not be aligned with the forward axis. This scheme is often used when calculating a *control reference frame* (see Chapter 4 for more detail).

These different types of coordinate systems are applied to specify camera properties that may then be used to determine the actual camera position or orientation. For example, it may be desirable to define the *desired position* relative to the direction in which the player character is facing (in other words, character space). In such an example, an offset value would be transformed from the local space of the character into world coordinates before determining the motion to be imparted to the camera.

DESIRED POSITION

When we consider camera motion, the first important aspect is the final destination of the camera. This is usually called the *desired position* of the camera, or sometimes, the *target position* (although this latter term is often confused with determination of the orientation of the camera toward a specific position within the game world). How the camera is positioned, along with its orientation, defines both the camera and how we view the world. Poor positioning or motion of the camera may cause the player to feel frustrated and unwilling to continue playing the game.

An important consideration in moving the camera is maintaining an appropriate distance from, and orientation toward, the player character or target position. Sometimes these positional goals can directly conflict with the desire for smooth motion, particularly when the target position (however it is derived) is able to move faster than the camera. Equally important for third person cameras is the deter-mination of a position that allows for an unobstructed view of the player character and the surrounding environment in a meaningful manner.

This determination varies according to the presentation style, so let us consider first and third person cameras separately.

First person camera positioning

In most cases of first person cameras, the desired position is usually fixed to that of the eye position of the player. That is, a position in the game world approximating how the player character would view the environment (but not necessarily the actual position of the head of the character — as discussed earlier). To avoid untoward vertical motion while the player character is maneuvering over terrain disturbances, it may prove necessary to apply a small amount of damping in that axis.

This position (relative to the player character) typically remains constant, even if the orientation of the view is under player control (also known as *free-look*). However, it may also be true that the ability to free-look around the player position corresponds to an actual motion of the camera relative to the character rather than simply a reorientation. An example of this would be when trying to simulate a hierarchical bone structure including a neck and torso. This case would allow a greater range of motion when using free-look during regular character motion than simply rotating the camera orientation.

In hybrid first/third person cameras, the position of the camera is usually external to the player character but often moves closer to the player character (possibly to the traditional first person camera position) to allow a better view for aiming or free-look purposes (or when the character backs up against a wall, etc.). Once the free-look or combat is completed, the camera retracts to a following position once more. In addition, with either first or third person cameras it is often necessary to smooth out slight motions imparted by the player character traversing uneven terrain, colliding with the environment or other game objects, and so forth.

Although rare, some games incorporate sequences where the position (and often orientation) of the first person camera is not under direct player control. This type of approach relieves the player of the need to navigate through complex environments and allows a very cinematic presentation, even though this lack of control may cause the player to feel less immersed in the environment. It is frequently used for games that only involve aiming or other limited interaction. An example of this "camera on rails" technique is *Panzer Dragoon* [Panzer95], or arcade games such as the *Virtua Cop* [Virtua94] series.

Third person camera positioning

As described in Chapter 2, third person cameras (by definition) occupy a location external to the player character. In many third person situations, it is necessary for the camera position to be based upon the direction of the player character, typically behind and above to provide an elevated view unobstructed by the character. Additionally, many third person games require special camera behavior within complex environments or during specific game play situations to present the best view of the current game play. We may consider three main types of camera positioning: *automated*, *player control*, and *hybrid*.

Automated

Some games take complete control over the positioning (and often orientation) of the camera, denying the player the ability to manipulate the camera. Sometimes this is necessary to ensure the camera remains within the game world, but usually the goal is to relieve the player of the requirement or drudgery of camera manipulation simply to play the game. The downside, of course, is that this may feel restrictive and care must be taken to ensure that the chosen camera positioning allows for all game play eventualities.

Player control

Third person games often allow some degree of player control over the desired camera position. Usually there are restrictions to the amount of control, either in terms of allowing a pre-defined selection of camera alternatives (e.g., driving or racing games) or simply in the physical displacement allowed. Some games, notably the massively multi-player online games (MMOG) genre, in many cases, actually apply no restrictions to player camera control, cheerfully allowing the player to manipulate the camera through or even outside the game environment. This degree of control is not encouraged; at the very minimum the player should not be able to move or reorient the camera in such a way as to present an inappropriate view of the game world. Certainly the camera should be constrained to remain within the environment (there are some limited exceptions to this, see Chapter 4). Loss of line of sight from the camera to the player character is often an issue with direct player control over camera positioning. One solution is simply not to allow the camera to be moved into such a situation.

Hybrid

A common solution is to automate most of the camera position determination yet still allow some limited player control. One obvious example is where the player is able to rotate the camera position around the player to provide a view of the surrounding area, usually with the camera repositioning itself once the manipulation has ceased.

DESIRED POSITION DETERMINATION METHODS

We will now examine some of the most common methods used to determine the desired position for the camera. The choice of which method to use is typically controlled through the use of game object scripting methodologies such as *camera hints* (see Chapter 6 for more details). The choice may be automated according to player actions if required (e.g., when the player character performs a pre-defined sequence of animations to climb over an obstacle, or when the character is climbing a ladder). The desired position is also dependent upon the player state; first person cameras by definition require a desired position approximating the eyes of the player character, whereas third person cameras typically dictate a position removed from the player character. While the methods listed cover the vast majority of situations, hybrid approaches can prove appropriate depending on the desired camera behavior that would best illustrate the current game play.

In many ways, the desired position dictates the type of camera motion behavior; it can be used as a distinguishing feature of the camera. It is worth noting at this point that determination of the desired position, and movement toward it, should be considered separately from orientation determination; this distinction is useful even though the latter is often dependent upon the former. For the most part this section is concerned with *third person cameras* whose desired position is usually distinct from that of the player character and is dependent upon the current game play situation. First person cameras can be considered to use a *slaved* desired position (see the section Slaved/Tracking), albeit with the horizontal position locked to that of the player character and thus only variable in the vertical world axis. One successful method to implement the determination of the desired position is by considering a constraint-based system. Successive constraints may in fact be layered to achieve the best position for a particular set of game play requirements. Example constraints might include elevation, relative angular offset with respect to the character orientation, distance, and more.

Arguably, the desired position need not be moved directly to the new position as determined by the character orientation or other influences. It is actually preferred in most cases to govern the speed at which the desired position moves according to a spring or other velocity-based damping constraint, thus introducing lag into the movement of the desired position. In this way, we update both the preferred position and the actual desired position separately. Remember that the desired position only dictates where the camera would *prefer* to be positioned, not the current position of the camera. The camera should not be tied directly to the desired position unless care is taken to ensure that the determination of the desired position includes damping or filtering to remove undesirable "jitter" caused by slight character motion (whether player induced or not). Direct motion of the camera to a position fixed relative to a moving target usually results in an "unnatural" feeling since any movement of the target immediately affects the entire view of the game world, regardless of damping effects that may be applied.

There are a variety of ways in which we can dictate the desired position of the camera. These are game genre specific, but there can be many occasions where it is useful to change the desired position contextually within a single game. Let us examine some of the most common forms of determination.

Stationary

It should come as no surprise that the simplest form of motion to deal with is that of no motion whatsoever! There are two main flavors of stationary cameras: *fixed position* and *dynamic fixed position*. Note that "stationary" cameras can be slaved to other objects and thus actually move through the world! Therefore, what we really mean is that the camera *imparts no motion on itself*.

Fixed position

A *fixed position* camera is, of course, stationary yet the camera is free to reorient to face its look-at position as required. There may be limits on the ranges of reorientation (horizontal and vertical), angular speed, and so forth as described in Chapter 11. Often this kind of camera is used in particularly confined areas of the game world, where camera motion would be confusing or disorienting. Alternatively, it can be used when there simply is not enough space to place the camera at a position that can adequately observe the character, or where the collision geometry would be too confining for smooth camera motion. Sometimes a fixed position is chosen for dramatic or other aesthetic considerations, perhaps to emphasize a particular environmental feature or to prevent viewing of incomplete geometry.

One of the drawbacks for this kind of camera is that the target character can potentially move so far away from the camera it makes it difficult for players to see what they are doing, or even have the character occluded by the environment. Additionally, it is entirely possible that the player character moves into a position either vertically above or below the camera, a problem not restricted to just stationary cameras. When this happens, the orientation of the camera can undergo rapid changes (also known as *vertical twist*), particularly rolling around its forward vector, leading to player disorientation. In addition, a camera-relative *control reference frame* becomes meaningless in this situation, adding further to player confusion. This situation should be avoided wherever possible (see Chapter 10 for further details).

There is yet another potential problem relating to the control reference frame. Third person games tend to have camera- or screen-relative controls. For screen-relative controls, stationary cameras do not present a problem because the view itself dictates the control meaning. Character-relative controls can become an issue for all third person cameras but more so for fixed position cameras. This amounts to what is sometimes called the "radio-controlled vehicle" problem. Essentially, as the character turns to face the camera position (i.e., the forward vector of the character becomes opposed and parallel to the vector between the camera and the character), the control reference frame becomes inverted from what the player might expect. Pushing the stick to the left results in a screen-relative motion to the right, and vice versa — counter to what might be expected. In camera systems where the character is not allowed to face the camera (due to repositioning of the camera "behind" the player character), the problem is avoided.

Control reference frames, and possible solutions for this particular problem are discussed in more detail in Chapter 4.

Dynamic fixed position

Dynamic fixed position cameras are essentially stationary cameras where the initial placement of the camera is not defined by a static position in the game world. Rather, its position is determined by some external source, the most common of which is the current position of whatever other camera is currently active. This equates to the new camera being "dropped" into the game world at the instant that it becomes active. Some flight games allow this facility to allow the player to position an external camera view in some appropriate position as required (e.g., *Star Wars: Shadows of the Empire* [Star96]). Other variants would determine a position suitable to frame the target object(s) in a particular orientation, screen size, and so forth. In these cases, there will be a transition between the current camera and the newly positioned camera, often a form of interpolation but frequently simply a *jump cut*.

One potential use for such a camera is when the player character jumps off a high cliff, so the camera remains stationary but tracks the player as they fall, possibly repositioning once more when the character is about to, or has landed, on the ground.

If it is desired that the current camera is simply replaced by a stationary one, then clearly the new camera must adopt both the position and orientation of the active camera. This can lead to a rather abrupt stop, depending on the velocity of the camera at the point of change; it may be more desirable to bring the camera to a halt over a short period to ease the transition. It may also be necessary to use orientation interpolation to allow for differences between the previous and new camera.

Slaved/tracking

Slaved (or *tracking*) cameras are moved in concert with some controlling object in the game world, which may or may not be the player character. The camera may be locked to a position relative to the master object or the controlling object may simply dictate the desirable position for the camera to achieve, according to its requirements.

Slaved cameras are actually one of the most common kinds of third person camera. Many games feature a camera whose position is dependent upon the position of the player character. It is also possible for a slaved camera to inherit its orientation as well as position from the "master" object. In this case, the camera simply inherits a fixed position with respect to the player character, normally corresponding to the "eye" of the player. This is commonly referred to, as explained earlier, as a *first person* camera. The orientation of the camera will often be synchronized to that of the player character except under specific circumstances where it may be controlled directly by the player. This manipulation, known as *free looking*, is usually relative to the base orientation of the player character and is covered in detail in Chapter 11.

The *eye position*, since derived from a character-relative position, may prove subject to small vertical variations in the ground as the character traverses across the environment. In such cases, some vertical damping of the eye position motion over time is necessary. A simple low-pass filter is normally sufficient to keep the motion smooth. Keep in mind that there are cases where this damping should not be imparted, for example, when the player character is moved by an external force such as an elevator or moving platform (but not collisions). Additionally, if the player character is able to pass through or move close to the surface of a rendered polygon mesh (e.g., a fluid simulation or fluid plane), then the camera position has to be managed to avoid interpenetration of that mesh with the near plane of the view frustum. One solution is to hold the vertical position of the camera until the character is completely clear (or submerged). At that point, the regular damping of the vertical component may be applied to bring the camera to the correct position. Note that there will be a discontinuous movement of the camera in this case, but this is the lesser evil compared to clipping visible polygon edges of the surface into the near plane of the view frustum.

It is important to note that all of the position determination methods described in this section (e.g., path, surface constrained, etc.) may be treated as slaved cameras; that is, the base position used for their determination may itself be slaved to another object. This technique is very powerful as it allows designers to manipulate camera solutions to match dynamic game play requirements. One typical example (used in games such as *Metroid Prime* and its sequels) is to rotate entire camera solutions to match the changing nature of objects used within rotating puzzles.

The relative position (or *offset*) of the camera while slaved may be specified in a number of different ways. Let us examine some of the most common forms.

World-relative offset

The desired position for the camera is defined as an offset in world coordinates from the master object, irrespective of that object's orientation. This is most useful for characters without an obvious forward direction or for situations where it is important to keep the camera in the same relative position to the character.

TECHNICAL

This offset is very straightforward since no rotation needs to be applied:

```
Vec3 desiredPosition = GetTargetObject()->
  GetPosition() + mOffset;
```

The assumption here is that the target object returns a position to base the offset upon; in some cases the target object may use an animated model to derive this position but often it is more desirable to use the origin of the target object to avoid unnecessary camera motion. Sometimes the center of the collision bounding volume may be used, although care should be taken in case the animation of the object might cause this position to fluctuate.

World-relative angular offset

Similarly, a *world-relative angular offset* can be specified as up to three angular quantities (based on the world axes, not character orientation) as well as a *distance*. Typically, only two angles are defined, *pitch* and *yaw*. The distance in this case forms the hypotenuse of the triangle formed by the other two. It is also typical that rotational lag may be used to slow the reorientation of the camera around its target to the determined desired position. World angular cameras are not common, but a typical example might be that the camera is looking down upon the character from an elevated position such as in a pinball simulator. The angular quantities may vary according to player position or some other outside influence. One simple example would be to change the vertical elevation as the character reaches the limits of the playing area.

TECHNICAL

For this offset, we are going to assume that the yaw angle is in the range (0..2*pi radians) and treated as a clockwise rotation around the world up-axis (here the Z-axis). The pitch angle will be in the range (0..pi/2 radians):

```
Vec3 offset(0.0f, cosf(pitch) * distance, sinf(pitch)
  * distance);
// construct a rotation matrix around the world up-axis
Mat3 rotation = Mat3::ZRotation(yaw);
mOffset = rotation * offset;
Vec3 desiredPosition = GetTargetObject()->
  GetPosition() + mOffset;
```

World object relative

World object relative cameras determine their position according to the physical relationship between the master object and a separate position or object in the world. The offset to apply is transformed from this new local coordinate space back into world coordinate space before being applied. This type of offset allows the camera to position itself in such a way that the player character is between the camera and an arbitrary position in world space.

TECHNICAL

Here we construct a new frame of reference based on the relative position of the target object and a separate position (here denoted by the member variable `mWorldPosition`). The camera offset is applied relative to the target object in this new coordinate space.

```
Mat3 rotation = Mat3::LookAt(GetTargetObject()->
  GetPosition().DropZ(), mWorldPosition.DropZ());
// note that the reference frame is often 2D, but is
// not required to be
mOffset = rotation * offset;
Vec3 desiredPosition = GetTargetObject()->
  GetPosition() + mOffset;
```

Local offset

Local offsets are derived in a similar way to world relative offsets, except that the offset is transformed into the *local space* of the camera hint or other controlling script object before application. No other object is required to specify the coordinate space. Note that this is not the orientation of the player character (see the section Character-relative Offset). If the controlling object is reoriented then the local offset needs to be updated accordingly.

TECHNICAL

Here we construct a new frame of reference based on the orientation of the script object. The camera offset is applied relative to the target object in this new coordinate space.

```
Mat3 rotation = mScriptObject-> GetMatrix();
mOffset = rotation * offset;
Vec3 desiredPosition = GetTargetObject()->
  GetPosition() + mOffset;
```

Local angular offset

Once again, the offset is specified in angular terms, in the same manner as *world angular* above. The angular offsets are specified in the local space of the controlling script object or otherwise defined reference frame. Similarly, a distance away from the target object must be specified.

TECHNICAL

For this offset, we are going to assume that the yaw angle is in the range (0..2*pi radians) and treated as a clockwise rotation around the world up-axis (here the Z-axis). The pitch angle will also be in the range (0..pi/2 radians):

```
Vec3 offset(0.0f, cosf(pitch) * distance, sinf(pitch)
   * distance);
Mat3 rotation = mScriptObject->GetMatrix();
mOffset = rotation * offset;
Vec3 desiredPosition = GetTargetObject()->
   GetPosition() + mOffset;
```

Character-relative offset

The desired position is defined in *local space* according to the orientation of the player character (or other target object for that matter). That is, the offset is transformed by the character orientation matrix to resolve the real-world position. This is probably one of the most common approaches to third person cameras, and is usually referred to as a *chase camera* (since the camera seems to be "chasing" behind the target object). Mostly the offset is only applied as a 2D transformation (i.e., on the plane parallel to the horizontal world axes), according to the rotation of the character's forward vector around the world up-axis. Roll is infrequently applied, and pitch is rarely used in the transformation. Character-relative offsets are a subset of *local offsets*, as you might expect.

Character-relative angular offset

Once again, the offset is relative to the player character orientation, except this time the offset is described by up to three angular rotations, as well as a distance. The ordering in which the angular offsets are applied is important, since they are non-commutative.

In calculating the desired position, it is usual to impart an acceleration or deceleration to the angular speed in each axis as required. This supplies a degree of "lag" in the angular motion that is in fact quite desirable. First, angular lag around the vertical axis of the character adds to the aesthetic qualities of perceiving the character as a truly three-dimensional object, and secondly it helps to prevent a "rod-like" feeling. However, this needs to be combined with a look-at position that is not restricted to the character to gain the most effective results.

Often properties of a character-relative offset camera will be combined with those of a character-relative angular camera such that the vertical position and distance (along the hypotenuse) are dictated as scalar values with the desired yaw around the vertical axis kept as an implicit value of zero. Character-relative angular offset cameras are a subset of *local angular offset* cameras, as previously described.

Object-relative offset

This offset type is also referred to as a *non-directional* camera as it does not take into account the orientation of the target object. Typically, this offset is defined only in terms of *elevation* (either angular or vertical displacement) from the target object and distance. The vector from the target object toward the current camera position defines the coordinate space used to calculate the desired position. Often this is a 2D calculation (i.e., across the horizontal plane), with the vertical component defined by the previously mentioned *elevation*.

Object-relative offsets are actually akin to *character-relative* offsets, without any consideration given to the orientation of the target object. This kind of offset is most applicable when the target object either does not have an obvious "forward" orientation and/or is able to dramatically change movement direction. Should the character turn to face the camera, no difference in the offset calculation is noted. This allows the camera to remain stable irrespective of drastic character reorientation or motion.

Some games use non-directional cameras but allow the player to quickly reposition the camera behind the direction in which the character is facing, usually via a controller button press. Alternatively, they may allow the camera to reorient more slowly as a button is held down. These are useful properties that the player can exploit when manipulating the camera to a desirable position (assuming such a position is possible), since there is no implicit repositioning of the camera other than according to distance and elevation. Even without player intervention, non-directional cameras will naturally follow behind a moving character with the benefit of not reacting to drastic character reorientation.

For characters without an obvious direction in which they are facing (e.g., a ball, as in the *Metroid Prime* series), the movement direction of the character may be used to determine the "forward" direction when repositioning this type of camera. To avoid noise from small or unintended motion affecting the calculation, a high-pass filter or threshold value may be used when determining the motion direction. Player intent should feature prominently when automatically repositioning the camera.

Some of the most successful 3D platform games have used variants upon this type of offset, often varying the distance or changing the behavior slightly as game play requirements demand.

TECHNICAL

This type of offset is effectively the same as world object relative. We construct a new frame of reference based on the relative position of the camera to the target object. The camera offset is applied relative to the target object in this new coordinate space. Because the camera position is used to determine the reference frame, it only makes sense to specify the offset in terms of distance and elevation.

```
Mat3 rotation = Mat3::LookAt(GetPosition().DropZ(),
   GetTargetObject()->GetPosition().DropZ(),
   mWorldPosition);
// N.B. only elevation (here pitch) and distance are
// required
Vec3 offset(0.0f, cosf(pitch) * distance, sinf(pitch)
   * distance);
mOffset = rotation * offset;
Vec3 desiredPosition = GetTargetObject()->
   GetPosition() + mOffset;
```

Path

The desired position of the camera may be constrained to a pre-defined path within the game world, chosen to avoid geometry or to illustrate a particular style of game play. The path shape may be circular, derived from a cubic spline defined by game objects, a linearly connected series of waypoints, determined by an equation (e.g., an ellipse or parabola), or any other pre-defined shape. Motion along the path may be controlled by a number of methods including projection of the player position or linear time (i.e., a position according to a total amount of time needed to traverse the entire path).

Alternatively, a mapping function could be used to take values from one domain (such as time, or player position relative to some reference frame such as a different spline) into a position along the path. Sometimes the path is generated dynamically according to the current game state, for example, to transition between two different cameras (such as a first and third person camera).

Note that the camera is not necessarily fixed to the path; it may simply be used to dictate the desired position for the camera (think of a carrot being dangled in front of the camera, if you will). In such a case, the camera is quite able to cut corners (since it typically closes on the desired position by the most direct route) and this must be taken into account to ensure geometry avoidance. Similarly, the path may represent a cylindrical volume allowing the camera to move up to a set radius away from the path.

Usually the connections between a series of game objects (referred to here as *control points*) are used to form a directed graph; a consecutive ordering that may later be used to determine the position of the camera according to time or some other parameter. Most often, there are only single connections between the control points. It is possible to have branching paths, but this can add to the complexity of determining the camera position considerably. Choice of path to follow in this situation can be resolved using search techniques normally applied to AI path finding with additional aesthetic constraints to ensure an appropriate framing or distance from the target character. It is usual, though, to have more direct control over how the camera moves along its path, so determination of path choices is more likely to be based on time or target object position rather than other criteria.

As the camera progresses along the path, it can be useful to trigger events based on the camera position.

TECHNICAL

Typically, these events would be initiated when the camera reaches or passes through a control point, although this determination is often made in terms of time (or length) along the path rather than physical proximity to a control point. This is because the curve may not actually pass through the control points, as we will see in the next sections. Care must be taken when the motion of the camera is non-linear in nature. For example, if the position of the camera is parameterized according to time, but length is used to determine if a control point is crossed, it is potentially possible for the camera to cross a control point within one update yet not be recognized as such. This may occur when the time mapping causes the camera position to move across the control point and back during the time interval since the last update. Another way to think of this is that the update intervals are discrete but the motion is (theoretically) continuous. This problem may be avoided by solving the path for each of the control points as time values rather than lengths; i.e., calculating the time values where each control point is crossed (regardless of the direction of motion along the path). Thus, as the current time value crosses a time solution (or multiple ones) for a control point we can react accordingly. In practice, this information can be pre-calculated during initialization of the path data.

While it is usual for the path to be static in terms of its shape, the position or orientation of the path is not necessarily so. Paths are often slaved to other game objects, which may be translated or rotated to maintain a reference frame. This is very typical for rotating puzzles where the camera motion is required to be consistent with an element of the puzzle regardless of its orientation within the world. An additional benefit is a reduction in the amount of special case camera scripting that may be required. Naturally, the range of orientations or positions of the path must be taken into consideration when defining its placement within the environment.

Path types

Within the scope of path-based camera motion, there are a variety of ways to represent the shape of the curve forming the motion path for the camera. Some of the path types described here are only subtly different, but they each offer unique properties that should be used to determine their applicability. For simplicity, it is assumed that the path type is the same throughout all segments of the path, even though they are evaluated on a piecewise basis. It is sometimes useful to combine different types of curvature within the same path, although this may complicate the evaluation of the camera position somewhat. The curve types that can be used to change the shape of the path will be discussed in detail in Chapter 10, but here is a brief overview.

Linear

Probably the simplest form of path is that of a series of linearly connected control points, i.e., straight lines. A number of these connected points can easily form a path, which may optionally be looped by connecting the last and first waypoints. One problem with this approach will be the potential discontinuity in motion as the camera passes through each waypoint. Even though the segments are formed from straight lines, the evaluation of the position of the camera within the segment need not be based on a linear computation. Discontinuities of motion are only of significance if the camera does not come to a stop at a given control point.

Circular/elliptical/spiral

These three types of simplistic paths have similar basic requirements, namely a center and radius. Additionally it may be preferable to include the ability to orient the path in a non-axis aligned fashion, thus requiring a normalized vector representing the up-vector of the plane upon which the circular path is inscribed. A simple way is to use the orientation of a script object to define the motion plane. Circular paths are mathematically simpler and thus less processor intensive than using *splines* (see the next section). They can easily be extended to include elliptical paths by specifying major and minor axes rather than a single radius value. Naturally, such a path may easily be restricted to a specific angular arc rather than a full circle or ellipse. Circular paths may be approximated by using cubic splines, although it is harder to control their curvature or radius than through conic functions. Circular arcs may also be made into spiral shapes by simply varying the radius according to an external factor (e.g., player position). A cylinder or cone of motion may be produced by varying the Z coordinate of the camera according to an outside factor (such as matching the player Z coordinate). This is the basis of the *spindle camera*, as discussed later in the section Axis Rotational/Spindle.

TECHNICAL

A two-dimensional circular or elliptical path may be derived from the same basic equation governing an ellipse, namely:

```
X = a * cos(theta);  // a is the semi-major axis
Y = b * sin(theta);  // b is the semi-minor axis
Where 0 <= theta <= 2*pi, and assuming the ellipse is
  centered at the origin
```

Given this equation, we can vary the *major* and *minor axes* (i.e., the constants a and b above) or the value of `theta` over time to produce a variety of elliptical path motion. For example, if a has the same value as b, the inscribed path will be circular; varying the value of `theta` over time allows the camera to move back and forth in a circular arc. Similarly, the value of `theta` could be changed in relation to the position of the player relative to a reference frame. An obvious example is to use the angle between a vector linking the player to the center of the motion arc and a given world axis (i.e., relative to the movement of the player around the motion spindle). The camera could be ensured to remain at a fixed angular displacement away from the player by making the `theta` quantity equal to the player angle plus a fixed constant. This elliptical motion path may obviously be rotated to match any desired orientation within the game world and need not be constrained to the horizontal XY plane.

Spline

Splines are a form of curved path whose properties and shape are dictated by placing a series of *control points* (sometimes called *knots* or *keys*). The relative position of the control points typically defines the shape and spatial limits of the curve, although sometimes the orientation of the control points is used to specify the limits of the spline curvature (there may be additional properties within each control point depending upon the type of curve). There are a number of varieties of splines, each of which exhibit different properties as to how the control points affect their curvature, and whether the curve passes through the control points. Using the same control points for each spline, radically different curvature is possible according to the spline type. More information regarding spline curves and their evaluation may be found in Chapter 10.

Extruded path

Path-based camera motion is not required to derive all three of the positional coordinates from the actual path. One coordinate (or two for that matter) may be either derived from another game object directly, or based on the position of a game object (typically the player character) relative to a reference point. As an example, it is sometimes useful to determine the vertical position of the camera from the vertical position of the player, yet have the camera position restricted to a 2D path through the world to avoid geometry. In this case, the spline curve can be thought of as an extruded surface, parallel to the world up-axis. Obviously, this can be generalized into an arbitrarily oriented extruded spline and is covered in the section on surface constrained cameras. Similarly, the path may be used to determine the vertical position of the camera and not its position on the horizontal plane. Many such variations are possible and this type of camera is often useful where only simple motion constraints are required. This type of extrusion may be applied to any of the previously discussed path shape types.

Path position determination

Once the shape and position of the path have been defined, there needs to be a method of determining the desired position for the camera along the path. This may be calculated in many different ways and the choice of method is dependent upon the context in which the path motion is used. Examples of determination methods include:

- **Non-interactive situations.** Movie sequences most often simply use a time value to determine the position of the camera along the path; there is a direct mapping between the amount of time elapsed and the position of the camera along the spline. Often the relationship is that the camera moves along the entire path in a set amount of time. A more flexible approach is to allow the position to be determined in a non-linear method; in other words the mapping of time to position is governed by a designer-specified relationship (e.g., a two-dimensional spline curve; see the next Technical section).

- **The position of the player character relative to another object.** For example, the radius of the player position compared to a separate game object or position. Other comparisons may be used such as relative Z coordinate.

- **Player position relative to a defined path.** The path may be different from the one used to define the camera motion. In many cases, the "relative position path" is simply a straight line, as this provides a simple reference frame. However, it may be useful to have a path that mimics the possible player character motion, particularly when the player is constrained to moving within confined spaces such as tunnels even if the camera is moving along a different path. The player position is typically converted into a normalized value (i.e., in the range 0 to 1), which represents its relative position along this other "relative position" path. This value may then act as an input to a *mapping function* (see the next Technical section) resulting in a new normalized position along the actual camera motion path. Often this mapping function is represented as a two-dimensional graph where the input value (normalized player position) is shown as one axis, and the output value (normalized camera motion path position) is the other axis. The shape of this graph may be implicit (i.e., based upon a specific formula such as a parabolic curve) or explicitly specified using a piecewise Hermite curve. Finally, the normalized position along the motion path is converted back into a real game world coordinate.

- **A specified distance away from the closest position on the path to the player.** Measured along the path; if desired this distance may specify which "side" of the player position is desired with respect to one end of the path. The distance is calculated along the path. Finding the closest position may be problematic if the path has a large amount of curvature (e.g., a "U-shaped" curve), since there may be multiple possible solutions. Determination of the initial position of the camera (i.e., which "side" of the position of the player character, if you will) is typically explicitly specified via the camera scripting system, and often as a reference to the ordering in which the control points are connected (i.e., the start would be the first of the linked control points). Such a scheme is often used when the camera is moving within a confined environment such as a tunnel where it is easily possible for the target object to either outpace or interpenetrate the camera. In this case, it is necessary to ensure that the camera remains at least a pre-defined distance away from the closest position of the target object on the camera motion path. However, care must be taken to ensure smooth motion of the camera regardless of this constraint. Sudden acceleration or discontinuous motion of the target object should not result in discontinuous motion of the camera on the path.

TECHNICAL

So how is the desired position determined in practical terms? Regardless of the determination method, path-based motion presents a number of common elements and problems. To calculate a position on the path, it is necessary to evaluate the function defining the path for any given segment, and for any relative position within that segment. Often this evaluation is based on a normalized position within a segment. However, a normalized input to the evaluation function does not necessarily result in an equivalent position.

To be able to calculate an arbitrary position we first need to be able to determine the total length of the path. In addition to calculating the entire length, the length at each of the control points should be stored to facilitate quicker determination of the required segment.

Splines. A brute force approach can be sufficient in many cases to calculate the length of the spline, especially if performed when the data are exported from the game tools. This method is naturally an approximation:

```
float length(0.0f);
for (int i = 0; i < controlPoints.Size();  ++i)
{
   Vec3 pathPosition = EvaluateSegment(i, 0.0f);
     // start of i'th segment
   controlPoints[i].mLength = length;
     // save length at this control point
   for (int j = 1; j <= kMaxSegmentSlices; ++j)
     // includes next control point
{
     Vec3 newPosition = EvaluateSegment(i,
       j/kMaxSegmentSlices);
     Vec3 delta = newPosition - pathPosition;
       length += delta.Magnitude();
     // add the "length" of this slice
       pathPosition = newPosition;
}
} // length now holds approximate total length
```

A faster and generally more accurate solution is possible if the length of each segment may be calculated using numerical methods. An excellent solution is presented in [VanVerth04] for finding the length of an arbitrary arc of a cubic polynomial curve (using Gaussian Quadrature), as often used in spline curves. Once we are able to calculate the arc length of a segment, it is simply a matter of iterating through all of the segments of the path to find the total length.

These methods may be computationally intensive but are usually performed offline, or possibly at load time. If the control points can change their position during execution of the game, then the processor cost of recalculating the spline length may be amortized across multiple frames as necessary; although altering the length will cause other artifacts such as invalidating the current camera position on the spline (which in turn could cause an instantaneous and usually undesirable camera movement). Depending on the type of spline, there may also be changes to the curvature itself, also invalidating the current camera position. In these cases the position of the camera could be interpolated over a short period, which may also allow the changes to the curve to end and thus minimize any potential oscillation in the desired position of the camera. There are mathematical methods for adding points to an existing spline without affecting the curvature, for example [Farin02].

Once the total length of the path and the lengths corresponding to the control points are known (note that the control points may not lie on the path), it is possible to calculate both the segment index and the relative position within a segment for any given length value. The evaluation of the path types are covered in detail in Chapter 10, but it should be noted that it is important to be able to find a position on the path at any specified length. A mapping function may then be used to convert time or any other desired quantity into a position on the path.

Mapping functions. The representation of the camera position on a path depends upon the context in which the camera is used. For those cameras using time as the determining factor, this is relatively straightforward. A linear mapping of time to length along the spline is the easiest solution, where the total time to traverse the path may be used to determine the relative distance of the camera along the path. Of course, this linear mapping will not allow the camera to reverse its direction or stop momentarily (at least, not unless the camera is simply not updated). In this case the camera is said to exhibit constant velocity. Moreover, there would be no acceleration or deceleration of the camera motion, leading to both an abrupt (and discontinuous) start and end. Such behavior is typically undesirable, and may be avoided by specifying acceleration and deceleration times (either explicitly per usage or implicitly as a standardized value). It is unusual for such a simplistic solution to provide enough control over the camera position for most in-game or even non-interactive sequences.

An improvement is to explicitly specify a relationship between time and position via a mapping function. This is a mechanism to define a position on the path for any given time value (or other appropriate property). Note that the evaluated positions do not have to be continuous, although that is generally preferable (other than jump cuts). The function itself may take any form, often a simple parametric function such as `sine()`. `Bump` and `Ease` functions are commonly used because their derivatives are zero at the beginning and end, equating to corresponding smooth acceleration and deceleration of the camera motion.

A more flexible approach is to use piecewise two-dimensional spline curves (often Hermite curves), in a similar manner to animation software. The user defines the curve via control points (or keys) and usually tangents into and out of each control point. The positions of two adjacent control points, along with the out-tangent of the first and the in-tangent of the second, are sufficient to define a cubic polynomial such as a Hermite curve. Using spline curves provides an easily editable mechanism to define camera motion, including the ability to move the camera in either direction along the path, or to hold it at a position for a period. Additionally, this use of spline curves as an explicit mapping function may be extended to many other aspects of camera properties including orientation, field of view, and so forth.

More on mapping functions. As suggested earlier, time is not the only type of input value for the mapping functions used to determine the desired position of the camera. In practice, elapsed time is of most use in non-interactive sequences. Given that many path cameras are used where the environment restricts camera positioning, it is mostly true that their position determination is most likely to be based on the position of the player character. This is particularly true when we consider that players are usually able to freely move through the environment, including retracing their steps. In such a situation, we still require the position of the camera to be consistent and smooth. One solution to this problem is to base the determination of the camera position on its motion path according to the position of the player character relative to its own "motion path." Even though the player is not restricted to moving along this path, we can determine the position of the closest point on this path to the player. The shape of this "player path" need not match the direct motion of the player, although this is often useful. It is simpler in many cases to use a straight line as the reference frame for determining the relative position of the player. Regardless of the shape of the player path, if we can determine the position of the player in terms of its relative position along the path, we can then use this relative value as the input to our camera position mapping function. Thus, we can vary the position of the camera on its motion path according to the position of the player character in any manner that is appropriate. This functionality is extremely powerful since it allows designers absolute camera position control based on arbitrary player motion through the world. Additionally we can extend this theory to adjust other camera properties according to camera position. A good example is the field of view; using this method we can effectively "zoom-in" on players when they reach particular sections of the environment, perhaps to showcase a particular game play element such as a door. The possibilities are limitless.

Closest point on path. As mentioned earlier, it is often necessary to determine the position on a path closest to a world-relative position (such as the origin of the player character). For linear paths this is a straightforward operation.

Path-based motion

The method in which the path is defined can vary considerably, and some of the most common types will be discussed next. Nonetheless, one of the major considerations here is that the camera will not consider collisions with the environment while it moves along this path, unless specifically required. Consequently, a fixed path camera can reduce processor requirements while ensuring absolute control over the position of the camera with respect to the player character. Path cameras are especially useful in confined or overly complex environments since the position of the camera can be assured. By moving along a defined path the camera designer can be certain of providing the player with the best possible view of the action at any time. However, some flexibility is sacrificed and depending on how motion along the path is handled, a sense of "stiffness" can sometimes be imparted.

A secondary part of path motion is that of the camera velocity. Is the velocity constant, or is acceleration and deceleration involved? Linear, constant speed is easy to implement but results in an undesirable effect of sudden initial motion as well as an instantaneous stop, both of which can be jarring to the viewer. When there are only two waypoints in use, it can be a simple matter to damp the velocity of the camera as it approaches either end of the path. With more than two waypoints, this would result in the camera slowing to a halt at each waypoint, which is probably not desirable. Here is where it would be more prudent to keep track of the camera speed and allow an acceleration and deceleration to occur as the camera approaches its destination rather than a particular waypoint. Naturally, this technique is just as applicable to a path with only two waypoints.

Another approach is to treat the connected waypoints as a simplistic Bézier curve — this would allow a smooth transition but the path would no longer pass through all the waypoints.

In all cases, it is necessary to find a way to determine the best position on the path for the camera. This can depend upon several game play related factors. For example, it is often desirable for the camera to track relative to the player position to ensure the camera cannot be overtaken by the player (e.g., within a confined tunnel). Or it may be required that the camera allows some motion of the player toward or away from the camera but there are defined limits beyond which the camera will directly match the speed of the player character.

Matching player coordinates

Each axis may be tied to that of the player character position, to produce a 2D spline, if required. This is somewhat akin to a surface camera, but the locking of coordinates to that of the player makes it axis-aligned.

Closest point on path

Determining the closest point on a path to a particular world space position can prove problematic. First, there may actually be multiple solutions depending upon the nature of the path. Second, should other criteria apply when selecting the "closest" position? In some cases *line of sight* is an important consideration; in others the distance from the current position to the possible solutions either in world space or along the path is important. If the player may cross the physical path then the camera must be offset along the path away from the closest point or else interpenetration will occur.

Surface constrained

There are occasions where environmental complexity precludes the use of either a simple path or it is preferred that the camera position is constrained in two axes of motion but should move in the third axis to match the player position. In other cases it is necessary for the camera motion to adapt to complex geometry in ways that would be hard to specify unless a physical shape matching the geometry was used.

In these cases, the camera may be constrained to remain on an *implicit surface*, most often at a position projected from the player onto the surface. The surface itself could be a simple flat plane, a sphere, cylinder, or some parametrically generated surface. Alternatively, rather than defining the camera position, the surface may be used as a limiter on the movement of the camera, preventing its motion through the plane (in whatever orientation the plane resides). In the latter case, the surface acts as an additional constraint applied on top of whatever other position determination method is chosen.

The size and orientation of the surface may be static or variable as required. Similarly, the position of the surface may be static (e.g., due to world geometry requirements) or could be slaved to another game object, as could the orientation of the surface for that matter. This can be useful where there is complex geometry that moves or rotates yet we want the camera surface to match the geometry at all times. A typical example is a complex puzzle that revolves around a point in space as the puzzle is solved. In this case, it is desired that the surface camera maintains an orientation with respect to the puzzle, and so is rotated with the puzzle itself.

One very cool thing that can be applied to surface cameras (as with others for that matter), is to base properties of the surface constraints upon an interpolated value. For example, with a cylinder surface, we could vary the radius of the cylinder according to the Z coordinate of the player in cylinder space, thus creating a cone. The possibilities of this kind of interpolation are numerous. Changing the Z offset of the camera relative to the player radius is another example.

Another consideration is that the types of interpolation can be variable. The most obvious method would be linear interpolation between defined min/max values over a defined min/max range. By setting suitable values, the interpolation can be reasonably flexible. A better approach is to implement a parametric curve, ideally with defined keys (such as the one used in *Maya* for animation). In this manner, absolute non-linear control of any camera property can be easily controlled, allowing complex camera movement in a simple and easy to edit manner.

Surface offsets

Depending on the type of surface, there are several ways to specify an offset to determine the camera position relative to the player position. First, the offset can be applied in surface-space relative to the position of the player projected onto the surface with the final position constrained to remain within the bounds of the surface. Second, the offset can be applied in surface-space, but relative to the player position before projection onto the surface. Third, the offset can be applied in world space before projection onto the surface.

Surface types

There are a wide variety of choices of surface type to which the camera may be constrained. In fact, the surface does not need to be one that is programmatically generated; it could easily be based on collision geometry or other environmental representations, perhaps using surface normal information to determine the exact position by projecting a target object position onto the surface.

Here are some suggestions for surface types to use with different types of camera constraint:

- **Sphere.** Sphere constrained cameras are particularly easy to implement, and can be very useful. However, they do face some unusual problems. Sphere surfaces are very susceptible to gimbal lock and other singularities if the camera is allowed to pass through axis-aligned locations (e.g., the north and south poles).
- **Plane.** Any (infinite) plane can be defined by a world position and a normal to the plane. In practical terms, we probably

would like to limit motion across the plane to a particular width and height, centered on the world position of the defining script object (although this might be slaved to another object). The normal can have any orientation and we use it to project the position of the target character onto the plane. This projection then defines the desired position of the camera. We can add an offset to this position in either *plane* (i.e., *local*) *space* or some other reference space. Alternatively, the source position could be offset (in world or object space) before projection onto the plane.

- **Cylinder.** Another simple primitive to provide as a surface constraint is that of a simple, oriented cylinder. This can be defined using only a center point, a normal (the major axis of the cylinder), a height, and a radius. Alternatively, the cylinder could be elliptical, which would require defining a major and minor axis rather than simply a radius. The spline cylinder type below describes another way to vary the cylinder radius.
- **Cone.** In this case, the conical surface is usually considered as a cone with the tip removed to avoid the singularity issues common with reaching the apex of the cone. This cone may be treated in the same manner as a cylinder, except that the radius of the cone is interpolated according to the height of the cone, target object's Z coordinate (e.g., in the local cylinder coordinate space), or some other input value.
- **Extruded spline plane.** We may expand upon the basic plane surface mentioned above by taking a two-dimensional spline (perhaps also a piecewise Hermite curve) and extruding a surface from it. Such a surface allows the camera to easily avoid geometry protrusions. With regard to determining the camera position, if a normalized input value may be produced (perhaps according to the target object's position relative to a reference frame) all that is required is to evaluate the Hermite curve to produce a height value above the plane surface.
- **Spline cylinder.** In a similar way, we may create a non-uniform cylindrical surface by wrapping a spline plane around a cylinder. A simple way to envision this is that the input value to a Hermite curve (or other mapping function, for that matter) corresponds to an angular offset around the axis of the cylinder. The output value from the mapping function is the radius of the cylinder at that angular offset. This type of surface produces camera positioning akin to a simplified form of the

spindle camera behavior discussed later in this chapter in the Axis Rotational/Spindle section. It may also be considered as a form of *cam* where the rotation of the camera about the cylinder axis produces a variable radius from the axis.

Volume constrained

In a similar manner to surface constrained cameras, we can restrict the position of the camera such that it maintains a position within a given volume. The type of volume is immaterial, but common polyhedral shapes are often preferred for their simplicity. The determination of the desired position is not affected by the volume; rather the positional constraint is applied once the camera attempts to move to the desired position. Depending upon the desired effect, it may be plausible for the camera motion to cut across corners or otherwise impassible sections of the volume, as long as the newly determined position occupies a valid position within the volume. For example, cylindrical surface constraints may be converted into volume constraints by simply evaluating the surface position and treating it as a maximum (or minimum) radius value of the camera without requiring the camera to be fixed at that position.

TECHNICAL

Typically, collision detection is not required to ensure the camera stays within a volume if the shape can be represented by a simple equation or otherwise bounds checked. For example, cylindrical volumes (especially if axis-aligned) simply require a radius check and an axial length determination, if we assume that the camera is a simple point in space:

```
Vec3 direction = currentPosition -
  cylinder.GetPosition();
direction.SetZ(0.0f);
  // this is for a vertical axis-aligned cylinder
// In other orientations we would use the local
// space of the cylinder
float radius = direction.Magnitude();
if (radius > kMaxRadius)
  radius = kMaxRadius;
direction = direction.AsNormalized() * radius;
Vec3 newPosition = cylinder.GetPosition();
newPosition += direction; // i.e. a 2D offset really
newPosition.SetZ(currentPosition.GetZ());
  // assumes vertical alignment
```

Framing

This method maintains a position (and possibly size) of the target character on-screen, often regardless of character orientation within the world; it can also be used to frame multiple characters simultaneously and to ensure they remain at least partially visible or within particular limits on the display device.

Additionally the relative orientation and vertical displacement can be specified. Alternatively, the position of the camera can be specified in cinematographic terms (close-up, head shot, medium shot, etc.). In these cases, the orientation of the character to the camera may also be specified (e.g., a profile shot). Cinematography rules concerning framing and positioning of cameras are well established, and provide fertile ground for this kind of camera solution (see [Arijon91]).

Framing of objects can be achieved in several ways. First, the screen size of an object may be maintained by moving the camera through the world. Naturally, this assumes that there is space for the camera to move relative to the target object. Second, the size may be maintained by changing the field of view to effectively use a "zoom" effect. Third, the rendered view of the world may be scaled to retain the required size of an object. This latter option is generally undesirable as it may introduce graphical artifacts. In practice, it is usual to combine camera motion and field of view changes. Aesthetically a choice of whether the framing must be perfect at all times should be made. There are situations in games where it is required to view the target character at a specific size simply to be able to play the game, but there are many cases where the camera is repositioned during a non-interactive sequence (such as a recoil effect from the player character being hit). During this time, the player character may partially extend outside of the viewing frustum but this is not necessarily problematic. Often it is more important for players to understand the spatial relationship between their character and the environment or other game objects. In the case of multiple players, there can be additional framing requirements as covered in the next section.

TECHNICAL

To retain screen size of an object, we have to determine what screen size of the object is required. If we can assume that the camera is free to move to any position to achieve this effect, navigation through the environment may be ignored, and we need only be concerned with the distance and orientation of the camera. However, there will still need to be constraints placed upon the desired position of the camera. The determination of the desired position relative to the target object may limit the available choices for maintaining a particular screen size for the object.

There are several alternatives to determining the rendered size of a game object. One method is to render the object to an off-screen buffer using the same view matrix as the current camera. This rendering need only be of depth information, since we are interested in the silhouette of the object rather than its graphical details. The buffer may then be parsed to determine the extents of the object, with the caveat that these extents change as the relative orientation of the object changes with respect to the camera orientation. In fact, these changes are frequently ignored because they would cause the camera to move extensively. An alternative solution, then, is to use fixed dimensions for the target object in world space. These dimensions may be chosen by hand or calculated offline as the maximum extents of the object determined by applying all possible animations. Such extents sometimes correspond to the bounding box of the collision volume for the object.

Once the extents of the object have been determined, we need to determine the distance of the camera required to satisfy a particular screen size of the object. It is usual to only consider one axis, often the vertical axis, when determining this distance. Again, applying this limitation reduces the variability of the final camera position. By inverting the transformation matrix used to construct the view we can reverse calculate the position of the camera.

A simpler solution, however, is to define the desired size purely in terms of the distance of the camera from the target object. For example, the above calculation is not necessary if the object in question is currently rendered at the desired size, as it is only necessary to retain the relative position of the camera. Bear in mind that if the motion of the camera is tied to that of the game object, it will certainly retain the same screen size (apart from profile variations as mentioned previously) but the motion will typically feel unnatural.

Object-framing relative

This method of position determination takes into account not only the screen size of an object, but also its relative position to another object or target position. In this way, both objects are kept visible and within a range of screen sizes. Depending on the motion of the target object(s), this can result in dramatic camera motion. As such, it is usual to allow the camera motion to be reduced by ensuring that the camera is sufficiently distanced from the target objects so that most of the framing results from orientation changes. Additionally, field of view changes can be used to ensure correct framing, if used with care. Dramatic changes in field of view are disorienting (particularly when changed dynamically), and may generate rendering artifacts such as the "flexing" of vertical lines according to the perspective view transformation. In 2D games, the camera is often kept at a fixed distance from the background plane, so only repositioning of the camera parallel to that plane is possible. Hybrid 2D/3D cameras can be treated as 3D cameras in this regard.

Object framing can have additional constraints placed upon it to satisfy aesthetic qualities rather than simply ensuring that the objects are completely within the rendering limits of the view frustum. For example, it may not be necessary or even desirable to encompass the entirety of a creature if the relative scale of the two objects differs greatly. In such cases, the smaller character may take precedence, as long as the relationship between two objects is understandable. In all cases, game play concerns must come first, most important of which is ensuring that the player character is visible and can be seen in relation to the objects or environment with which they are interacting.

Potential framing requirements

There are a variety of methods that may be used to determine the most appropriate orientation and position of the camera. These will naturally vary according to game play demands, object properties (e.g., relative sizes), and environmental concerns. Some of the most common determinants are as follows.

- Object screen size
- Multiple objects must be kept on screen (either fully on-screen or specific points on the objects themselves)
- Distance between objects
- Relative position to other objects
- Relative position to the screen (not rendered size)
- Orientation with respect to the camera (i.e., maintaining a particular silhouette)
- Distance aiming/ranged weapons

Axis rotational/spindle

Axis rotational cameras are somewhat complicated to describe, although extremely flexible. The basic principle is that the camera rotates around an axis (or *spindle*) in the world. It is also able to move parallel to this axis, forming a cylindrical volume of possible camera positions. The axis is often parallel to the up-axis of the world but not necessarily restricted as such. There are constraints placed upon the radius of the camera around the spindle as well as the distance along the spindle, normally relative to the position and orientation of the defining script object placed in the world. By moving the position and/or orientation of the spindle axis in real time, some very interesting effects are possible. Determination of the desired position to move the camera to under these constraints can be very flexible if carefully designed.

Spindle cameras are ideally suited to situations where the player must navigate around a stationary object, or is confined to a cylindrical (or similar) volume. The desired position for a spindle camera to seek is normally based upon the relative position of the player to the spindle. If we project a line from the spindle outward through the player position (at right angles to the spindle), this forms a vector that can be used as a reference frame for determining the desired camera position. In most cases, the desired position is aligned with the player along this vector, but at a greater radius. Indeed this is often the desired behavior when the player motion is around a central stationary object.

However, given such a reference frame, there are varieties of factors that can be specified for calculating the desired position, for example:

- Angular offset relative to the reference vector or the axis origin
- Axial offset relative to the current player position or the axis origin
- Radial offset relative to the spindle axis or current player radius

Additionally, we can also alter the orientation of the camera to meet a wide variety of game play requirements.

- Look at the spindle axis along a projected vector from the current camera position.
- Look away from the spindle along a projected vector that passes through the camera position as above.
- Apply an angular offset either toward or away from the spindle relative to the target object.

The real power of axis rotational cameras is derived from using the player position relative to this reference frame (or the spindle axis) to alter these different camera properties. If we consider any property of the camera as a range of interpolated values (possibly a constant), a unique mapping function can then be used to convert the player position into that range of values. A specific example might help to explain this.

The radius of the player position relative to the spindle axis is the input to a mapping function. This particular mapping function determines the vertical displacement of the camera relative to the player. With a linear mapping, we can have the camera move higher as the player moves closer to the radius and vice versa.

Moreover, the mapping function is not limited to being linear in nature. Great flexibility can be had from using a piecewise Hermite spline, for example, to map an interpolant to a camera property. This would require some method to edit or define the mapping spline curve. This methodology is akin to the process used with 3D animation software, where time is the interpolant, mapping to rotation angles or translation values.

Once there is a generalized mechanism to define the mapping function, we can apply this with a variety of interpolated values, such as:

- The distance of the target object (i.e., its radius) from the spindle axis, normally calculated in local coordinate space.
- Player axial distance from the spindle origin (i.e., the relative height along the spindle axis).
- Player position as an angular quantity within the local space of the spindle axis. This can be an absolute angle in a clockwise or anti-clockwise direction, a relative angle from 0 to 180 degrees, or other permutations.
- Player position relative to an external reference frame, for example, a spline path.
- Player orientation with respect to the reference vector, or spindle origin orientation.

As we can see, the number of permutations from even such a small set of properties as these is enormous. With such flexibility comes a measure of complexity, but it is well worth the effort. A single spindle camera can duplicate complicated motions in direct response to player actions, and may be particularly effective in complex environments or when the player encounters large opponents (aka "boss battles").

COMMON POSITION PROBLEMS

Given the variety of position determination methods, there will arise situations in which the chosen position is inappropriate or it is not possible to find a reasonable position for the camera. Here are some common examples.

- The desired position is coincident with a game object (such as the player character), or sufficiently close that the character's geometry would interpenetrate the camera *near plane*.
- The desired position is too close to the limits of the geometry enclosing the environment allowing an undesirable view of the outside area.
- The distance of the desired position is too far from the target object to allow the player an appropriate view of game play.
- Geometry or game objects prevent an unobscured view of the target object.

Some of these problems may be avoided by relaxing or altering the constraints applied within the determination algorithm; for example, changing the elevation of the desired position with respect to the target object. Alternatively, previous positions of the camera may be used as possible solutions, assuming they meet the appropriate criteria (e.g., not intersecting game objects). Chapter 8 discusses the problem of *occlusion* in greater detail.

ORIENTATION

In this section, we will look at the various methods available for specifying and controlling camera *orientation*. As one of the two main components of all game cameras, orientation determination greatly influences the player's experience with a game. Poor usage in this regard can often result in a game that is unplayable, or at best, irritating to the player. This observation has been noted in many game reviews.

Not only is the desired orientation itself crucial in player satisfaction, so is the manner in which the camera reorients itself. In this chapter, different orientation representations will be examined, followed by the determination of the desired orientation. We will then discuss the actual reorientation motion of the camera (referred to here as *rotation*), and finally examine common problems encountered with camera orientation.

If we recall from Chapter 2, there are three main components to define the orientation of a camera within the game world. Although various terms can be used to describe these components, we will use the following conventions.

- **Yaw (or pan).** This is the rotation of the camera around the up-axis of the world, and it defines the forward heading of the camera. This forward heading is sometimes referred to as the *through the lens* view, as it parallels the notion of a real camera.
- **Pitch (or tilt).** The rotation of the camera around its "right" (or "left") axis, amounting to changes in the vertical orientation of the camera with respect to the forward heading of the camera.
- **Roll (or bank).** This refers to rotation around the forward heading (i.e., through the lens) of the camera. As such, it is not usually applied to most in-game cameras except for certain types of vehicle simulators where the camera rolls to maintain a consistent orientation relative to the orientation of the vehicle (the rotation speed of the camera may be slower than that of the vehicle). It is sometimes used within cinematic sequences as an additional emphasis to exaggerate high-speed motion of the camera, or to create an emotional response, for example. *Banking* normally refers to an amount of roll less than 90 degrees, and is typically used in situations where the camera motion is restricted to a path or attached to a vehicle with limited freedom of motion. In the latter case, the camera typically adopts a damped direction of roll in keeping with the movement or roll of the vehicle to which it is attached. For cinematic sequences, roll is sometimes referred to as *Dutch tilt* or *Dutch angle*.
- **Look-at position.** This is the position in *world space* of the desired focal point of the camera; that is, the camera orientation should align itself to point directly at this position.
- **Look-at offset.** This is an alternative method of defining the look-at position. In this case, the position is a displacement from the player character, but calculated in *character space*; that is, relative to the direction in which the character is facing (optionally the movement direction of the character).
- **View direction.** This corresponds to the forward vector of the camera, that is, the "point of view" or "through the lens" direction of the camera. It is equivalent to a unit forward vector (according to the world coordinate scheme) multiplied by the

transformation matrix constructed from the yaw, pitch, and roll properties noted above.

TECHNICAL

Reorientation of game cameras typically involves using vector and linear algebra to construct rotation matrices, test for vector coincidence, and so forth. A full description of such techniques may be found in [VanVerth04] and others. Some of the more common mathematical functions used in camera systems are discussed in Chapter 9. A typical example of the latter would be a function to construct a transformation matrix whose translation and forward vector are specified by supplying a source and destination position within the game world. The normalized vector joining the two positions forms the forward vector of the new matrix, with the right and up-vectors constructed from this (ensuring that the up-vector points in the same direction as the world up-vector). Such a function is often referred to as a `LookAt()` function since it is typically used to reorient a game object toward another object or position in the game world (literally, such that it is looking at the other object).

Orientation representations

Camera orientation refers, of course, to the forward direction along which the camera is facing in the game world, otherwise known as the *through-the-lens* or *view direction*. This is usually combined with a rotation around that direction, defining the "up" and "right" axes of the camera. This rotation is referred to as *roll*. In many cases, the camera right-axis remains parallel to the horizontal world coordinate plane, thus eliminating roll and orienting the camera with a view mirroring the standard world coordinate scheme.

In this book, positive rotation values will refer to a clockwise rotation direction, negative values will represent an anti-clockwise rotation, with the axes of rotation pointing outward from the object (and viewed in that direction). The order in which these components are applied is of great significance since they are *non-commutative*. This means that if the same rotations are applied but in a different order, the resultant orientation will vary considerably. Detailed explanations of both coordinate systems and transformation matrix construction may be found in [VanVerth04], [Eberly03], and [Foley90].

Several equivalent representations can be used to specify the orientation of a camera, and their appropriateness varies with the task. These include *Euler angles*, *transformation matrices*, *axis angles*, and *quaternions*. Each representation has its benefits and drawbacks and it can be convenient to change between representations according to the task. *Quaternions*, for example, are extremely well suited to orientation interpolations.

Let us examine each of these briefly.

Euler angles

Conceptually easy to understand, *Euler angles* hold the rotation amount around each of the rotation axes as separate values (often in world coordinate space, but not necessarily so). Typically, these angular quantities are stored as *degrees* or *radians*, and the order in which they are applied has a dramatic effect on the final orientation. The order in which they are applied should match the ordering used by other game systems. For example, applying a pitch of 45 degrees followed by a roll of 45 degrees and finally a yaw of 45 degrees results in a very different orientation simply by swapping the order of the last two operations.

Euler angles can be combined into a single rotation around an axis. Applying additional rotations to an Euler angle representation can lead to problems when axes of rotation become coplanar. This typically occurs when the forward vector of the rotation matrix is aligned with the up-vector of the world, for example. Such a situation leads to unexpected rotations and is sometimes referred to as *gimbal lock*; it is discussed in detail in [Hanson05]. Similarly, interpolation between two different Euler angle rotations may also encounter this situation. The use of a quaternion representation will eliminate the problem.

Transformation matrices

Another popular orientation representation is simply to hold the camera orientation as a 3×3 or similar transformation matrix, although it is typically convenient to include a translation component in addition to rotation or scale. We can apply subsequent transformations by concatenating rotation matrix multiplications to rotate in a desired manner. Once again, the order of applying rotations is important, and non-commutative. If the translation is held in the same matrix, it must be extracted before applying rotations and restored afterwards.

The actual format of the matrix can vary, for example, row major or column major. Rotations can be applied in local or world space; the former requiring the translation to be removed from the matrix while the rotation is performed.

Successive applications of rotation matrices, however, can lead to instability in the floating-point representation of the transform such that the vector components may no longer be at right angles. To avoid this, the matrix should be orthonormalized on a regular basis. Additional tests on the validity of the current camera matrix should also be performed per frame.

Axis angles

An axis-angle pair defines a unit vector in world coordinate space, with a rotation around that axis. The direction of rotation (i.e., clockwise or anti-clockwise around the vector) is normally dependent upon the coordinate system adopted within the game engine. The rotation amount is normally held in radians.

Quaternions

Quaternions are a very convenient form to use when dealing with interpolation between orientations, or reorientation around an arbitrary axis. Quaternions may be used as a different and considerably more complex mathematical representation of a direction and a rotation around that direction than the axis-angle pair previously mentioned. One desirable property is that it is possible to interpolate smoothly between quaternions with less of the singularity issue than found with Euler angles. Care must be taken to ensure that source and destination vectors are not parallel (either coincident or divergent) before performing interpolation between them.

Quaternions are extensively covered in [Hanson05]. The original paper suggesting their use in computer graphics was [Shoemake85], and they are discussed in many other mathematical texts such as [VanVerth04].

DESIRED ORIENTATION DETERMINATION

Having established several methods of representing the camera orientation, we are now concerned with determining the actually desired orientation. This is, as you might expect, greatly dependent upon game play requirements and to a degree, aesthetic concerns. However, there are some common characteristics to the determination of the desired camera orientation, especially in the case of third person cameras. First person cameras normally have their desired orientation automatically specified by the orientation of the player character, or directly by the player controls in the case of free-look. Even so, there are still cases where the orientation is variable such as automated pitching of the camera as the player jumps. Let us consider some of the main methods used to determine the camera orientation.

Constant orientation

Perhaps the most straightforward way of specifying the camera orientation, *constant orientation* implies, of course, that the orientation does not change. This kind of camera is prevalent in games where the background environment has been pre-rendered to reduce real-time processor requirements. Thus the camera orientation is constant, but there is no restriction upon the movement or orientation changes in rendered objects (other than, perhaps, a desire to ensure they remain within the view frustum).

Examples of constant orientation cameras would include the early adventure games and some of the "survival-horror" game genre. Constant orientation cameras are not necessarily stationary within the world, although this is often the case. They may be slaved to other objects or move of their own accord in response to player character motion. For example, the player character is situated within a maze and constant orientation cameras provide a way to limit the player's view of the maze.

When the player character is moving quickly within a confined space, constant orientation cameras can provide a good stable view of the environment without disorienting the player due to drastic camera orientation changes (often prevalent if the camera were tracking the player character). Bear in mind that since the orientation is fixed, rapid player character motion could result in momentary loss of line of sight.

A minor variation on constant orientation cameras is *constant elevation* cameras. Here only the pitch of the camera is constrained either via game scripting or alternatively, under player control. The latter mechanism is sometimes offered in first person presentations where a constant elevation is often useful to ensure the player is able to aim freely while maintaining a stable view of high or low objects. Note that the camera is still able to utilize yaw rotation as required.

In the same manner as dynamic fixed position cameras, *dynamic constant orientation* cameras (otherwise known as *snapshot* or *frozen* cameras) simply adopt the same position and orientation of whatever camera is active at the time of their initialization. Thus, they literally provide a snapshot of the game and can be useful in situations where player control is suspended due to some game event. No interpolation is needed on this type of camera, nor is any update logic necessary unless a subsequent field of view change is required.

Typical usages of this camera type would include:

- Player controlled remote cameras
- Dynamic positioning of replay cameras
- Dynamic positioning of cameras for non-interactive game play sequences, for example, a boss creature grabs the player character, shakes it, then throws it aside. The camera view remains stationary to both emphasize the non-interactive sequence as well as avoiding rapid camera reorientation that would be caused by tracking the player character.

Of course, this snapshot feature need not be used only for cameras with constant orientation. Some forms of interpolation may be considered in a similar vein where the original camera orientation is held for a period before starting the interpolation to the new orientation.

Tracking a target object or position

One of the main uses of game cameras is to track a target object or position. That is, the camera attempts to align its orientation such that a particular object or world coordinate maintains a fixed position (or possibly screen size) with respect to the final viewing plane of the camera. We refer to this position (in world space) as the *look-at position.* In some cases the camera orientation will be locked to the target object (or to a specific position relative to the target object), resulting in the target object appearing in the same relative position within the viewport or output device. In most other cases, the camera orientation lags behind that of the look-at position. By *lag,* we are referring to the time taken for the camera orientation to match the ideal orientation that would be formed by a line joining the camera position to that of the look-at position.

The manner in which the camera reaches this ideal orientation depends on the speed of movement of the target object and the reorientation speed of the camera. It is possible that the camera does not actually reach the desired orientation. Tracking of a target object occurs in both first person and third person camera schemes, although it is more common in the latter.

As mentioned in the previous section, while the camera may track an object horizontally it might be desirable to limit or hold the vertical pitch of the camera at a specified angle. This is especially useful when the movement of the target object is erratic or subject to rapid vertical changes within a confined space.

Look-at offset

In third person games, the focal point of the main camera is usually positioned close to the player character, but this may certainly change according to current game play requirements. We refer to the physical displacement of the desired *look-at position* from the player's position as the *look-at offset*. This is a convenient representation of the focal point as the player is most often interested in their character's interaction with the environment and would normally desire viewing the world surrounding their character during regular game play.

Many third person cameras use a constant look-at offset, so that the look-at position is located at a fixed position relative to the player character. Often this is the origin of the player character, or vertically above this position. While this gives a consistent view of the character, in many cases it is a detriment to game play. In most third person games, it is actually more important to see *ahead* of the character's movement to judge the relationship between the character and other game elements. In terms of long-range weapons and aiming, it is even more important to look where the player's weapons will hit rather than looking at the character.

The difficulty with using a constant look-at position, especially one that is positioned ahead of the player character's motion, is that this position will oscillate about the vertical axis of the character every time the character changes direction.

Even with orientation lag, this could cause an unpleasant amount of orientation change for each slight reorientation of the character. This effect may be minimized by using a spring or other damping mechanism to move the look-at position from its current position to the newly derived position over time. It can also be helpful to apply a high-pass filter to remove noise generated by small character motions. Combined with regular orientation lag this is usually sufficient to resolve oscillation of the look-at position.

While the camera is continuing to track its desired look-at position, its right vector should remain parallel to the horizontal coordinate plane to avoid roll.

The look-at position should not necessarily be tied directly to the player character. In most cases, we should scale the offset according to the velocity of the player character to allow players to see further ahead of their character. The amount of offset to use (which is calculated in character space) can also be varied according to the game play situation. However, simply scaling the offset according to player speed will result in rapid camera reorientation whenever the player's motion is interrupted, and would be quite disconcerting to the player. Moreover, when the player character is able to change directions quickly, the camera would track these changes exactly, leading to quick full scene movement or jitter at a disorienting rate of change.

To solve this problem, we can calculate a desired look-at position according to player speed (plus other requirements). The current look-at position is moved toward the desired position over time by using a *proportional controller*, *PID controller*, or *spring* to damp the motion. Additionally, applying *digital filters* to the look-at position motion (or for that matter, the desired position of the camera itself) will reduce sensitivity to slight or unintentional motion of the target object. These methods are covered in detail later in this chapter as well as in Chapter 10.

Locked look-at position

First person cameras can also have their orientation determined by a "lock-on" mechanism; that is, the player would be reoriented over time to match a 2D or 3D heading toward an object or point in space. Once the orientations match, the player character would normally be synchronized to that heading as it changes. Since the first person camera adopts the same heading as the player (at least in 2D terms), the camera will also need to be reoriented vertically over time to match the heading to the desired look-at position. In this situation, the look-at position may be located at a position offset from the root of the target object, especially in the case of boss battles where there may in fact be several possible lock-on positions relative to the object.

Target object position prediction

One of the elements in ensuring that the camera is oriented correctly is anticipating the motion of the target object. If performed correctly, this can allow the player to see upcoming parts of the game world and to understand the relationship of the player character to it.

Accurate prediction of future object position is often an involved task, as evidenced by many standard AI texts, since it greatly depends on the movement characteristics of the target object (not to mention its internal logic). For camera purposes it is not usually necessary to accurately predict the future position of the target object, instead we may use the intent of the character motion to determine how the camera orientation or position may be affected.

As an example, in third person cameras, it is often desirable to orient the camera such that it faces a direction ahead of the target object. This is often achieved by simply calculating a look-at position that is a fixed distance and elevation along the motion direction of the character. The downside to this is that rapid orientation changes of the character cause dramatic motion of the look-at position. This is usually not desirable. The effect can be mollified in several ways. First, we can damp the motion of the look-at position from its current position to the desired position. Second, we can also vary the desired distance ahead of the character according to the velocity of the character. The faster the character is moving, the further we look ahead of the character (although it is often necessary to ensure that the character remains at least partially on-screen).

By moving the look-at position of the camera ahead of its target object, the rendered position of the target object relative to the screen will change accordingly. There is a balance to be struck between looking ahead and ensuring that the player character remains visible. While it is generally okay to have the player character momentarily off-screen, it should not be possible for the player to move in a fashion such that the player character *remains* off-screen.

Object position prediction is also important for determining the motion and navigation of the camera, as discussed in Chapters 8 and 9.

Object framing

Presenting a view of the game in a meaningful manner according to the context of the current activity is a difficult and complicated task. Even so, it is the cornerstone of camera system design. In many games, little thought is placed on how the camera should focus its attention, yet it defines how much or where the player can see within the game world.

In third person games it is often more important to be looking ahead of the player character, rather than directly at them. In other cases, it is important to ensure that a different character or position within the world stays visible, yet we still need to be able to see the player character as well as understand the relationship between the two objects.

A good example would be the fighting game genre. Here both players (or more, potentially) wish to see their character remain on-screen. Clearly, if the distance between the characters increases, then the camera must pull back from the characters and/or increase the *field of view*. Frequently changing the FOV is not usually that desirable, as it will stretch the view of the world in an unrealistic manner, as well as potentially introducing frame rate problems, since more of the world will be visible for rendering.

Determination of look-at position

It can be difficult to calculate the extents of characters on-screen without resorting to rendering tricks. Essentially, we are calculating the bounds of the character in screen space, and then finding a suitable position to ensure all characters are sufficiently visible. There are other ad-hoc solutions to reduce the performance costs of this approach. Simplest is a calculation of the bounding box for the character, and then transforming the eight coordinates into screen space (e.g., by a perspective transformation). This would approximate the shape of the object silhouette, although only crudely. A more controllable solution might be to tag parts of the objects with locators such that their positions signify parts of the object that must be kept within the screen bounds. In this way, we can dynamically change the focal point of the camera according to game play requirements. This latter solution can work especially well in games featuring the "traditional" boss fight, as this often requires framing of the player character against a larger than screen-size opponent.

Aesthetics versus game play

Cinematographic techniques are often referred to when attempting dynamic framing of screen objects, as evidenced by some of the movie tie-in games that attempt to retain a cinematic "feel." However, such techniques are often counter to good game play theory; they concentrate on framing the characters rather than positioning the camera to continue to allow interactive actions to work effectively. Environmental restrictions often make themselves felt most strongly when the camera system is attempting to frame action sequences, especially when there are several antagonists all requiring visibility. Films have the benefit of choreographing the camera motion and placement of actors to maximize our understanding of the action (or to emphasize an emotional state), a luxury not usually present when dealing with an interactive medium. However, a good understanding of cinematography is certainly a useful skill when designing and implementing camera systems, even outside of cinematic sequences. There are some limited cases where cinematic techniques may be applied during game play itself. Chapter 4 discusses cinematography in relation to real-time and non-interactive camera systems.

Replay cameras

Since replay cameras are inherently non-interactive, this is clearly a situation where automated framing of characters is entirely possible. Replay cameras typically show player actions from a variety of viewpoints, usually chosen to present an aesthetically pleasing view of the action. In the case of some game genres, such as sports or racing, replay cameras are an inherent part of the game design. These game genres normally take place in very clearly defined environments (such as stadiums or race tracks), which eases the replay camera's task considerably since the designer can place cameras explicitly. Other genres may also take advantage of this technique, although sometimes a greater variety of camera angles are desired, occasionally selectable by the player. To create camera viewpoints dynamically it is necessary to define a set of rules regarding position of the camera relative to its target(s).

Field of view

One common solution used to frame characters is to alter the field of view of the camera. In some ways, this is akin to changing the focal length of the lens of a real-world camera. However, increasing the field of view only allows for a limited "zoom" effect because the perspective transformation distorts the view to such an extent as to become undesirable.

Nonetheless, subtle changes to the field of view, combined with repositioning of the camera, can aid framing to a large degree. Sudden changes to the field of view, outside of a cut transition, should generally be avoided. Interpolation of field of view values over time can be effective, though, if they are combined with a *dolly* motion. This can produce an effect where the character in view remains a constant screen size while the background becomes larger or smaller as dictated by the direction of the camera motion. This effect is often used in films (known as a *dolly zoom*) to emphasize a character's reaction to an event (most famously by director Alfred Hitchcock in the movie *Vertigo*), and can be useful in that regard, but may be distracting in regular game play.

Idle wandering

A subtle effect sometimes used in first person games (and occasionally in third person games) is a semi-random camera reorientation while the player character is idle (i.e., no input is being received from the controlling player). This loosely corresponds to slight head motion in the player character, and is normally used to both create some minor visual interest when the player character has been stationary for some time, and to lessen the possibility of screen burn-in caused by a static image. The movement of the view must be smooth, and is usually formed by sinusoidal calculations or a spline path with generated control points. Typically the player character must remain on-screen during the idle, and the return to in-game camera control should be swift and smooth.

Automated orientation control

There are a number of cases where it is necessary or preferable that some aspects of camera orientation are controlled or adjusted by the game without direct player intervention. Usually this is done to assist players by removing their need to control the camera while interacting with game elements. In some cases, this reorientation is not merely restricted to the camera, but also the player character. Examples include the following.

Automated control over camera pitch when the player is jumping

Usually this is applied toward the end of a jump so that the player may have an improved view of the landing point (first person cameras especially). In such a situation the game will pitch downward until the player lands at which point it starts to gradually level out, that is, return to the default or "rest" orientation. The process of tilting the camera downward can actually start as the player character begins its upward motion, if the extent of the jump is known. Otherwise, it is probably best to wait until the character motion has reached its peak before beginning the downward pitch. It is usual for the reorientation to be performed in as smooth a manner as possible.

Automated pitch control when traversing environmental features

This is applied to present a view facing up or down a ramp, staircase, or other incline as appropriate, so that players have a better view of what they are moving toward. It can be applied in first or third person cameras. This only changes the "rest" orientation of the camera, but the player is able to free-look around that orientation. If the player turns onto the ramp then the view returns to a direction parallel to the horizontal plane as the character's orientation approaches 90 degrees relative to the slope of the ramp. As the player continues to turn, the view then pitches up or down until the player's orientation is parallel to the ramp once more. The amount of pitch to apply is often different according to whether the player is walking up or down the ramp. Additionally, the maximum amount of pitch may vary according to the player position relative to the ramp itself; that is, to smooth the transition from regular camera.

A similar situation arises as the player approaches a hole, or cliff-side, where it is required that the camera is automatically tilted to afford a view of the drop. As the player approaches the edge, the amount of pitch applied increases. However, as the player turns away from the edge, the amount of pitch should decrease proportionally.

Automated pitch control during combat or interactions

There are often cases during game play (particularly in first person presentations) that the player is required to interact in some manner with an object that remains outside of the view frustum without direct camera manipulation by the player. While it is often easy for the player to perform this operation manually, such manipulation might be a distraction for the player and difficult to control while performing other actions (e.g., combat). Thus, there are occasions where the camera may be pitched automatically (particularly upward) and this is often combined with player reorientation (see the next section). An alternative situation occurs when the player is directly interacting with a game object (perhaps some machinery or device), often with the main game suspended (to prevent other object interaction from occurring). A typical example would be *Metroid Prime 3* [Metroid07], where the player character (in first person presentation) interacts with a variety of game objects that require the game engine to reposition the player in addition to controlling the absolute orientation of the game camera.

Automatic reorientation of the player or a camera toward a target position

This may be a one-time effect instigated by the player or scripting, or may indeed be a constant effect applied while the character is "locked" onto an opponent. In the former case, it is often applied to ensure that the player witnesses a game event, or is oriented toward a particular game object that must be manipulated. This is most often true when the player orientation is synchronized to the horizontal view orientation. In the latter case, the camera will reorient toward the target object quickly (although damped to allow for a smooth start and end to the reorientation), and then remain constantly locked to the target object until the "lock" is broken. This type of constant reorientation may prove useful in situations where the player is unable to utilize a control scheme that allows for circle-strafing, as discussed earlier.

Repositioning and reorientation of the camera to face the same direction as the player character

For third person cameras this action is usually instigated by the player via a control command (it does not necessarily require the control to be held). For first person cameras it may be also be caused by the release of the free-look control. In the former case, the camera moves around the player character (usually) in a circular arc until positioned behind the character's direction of motion. During this motion, the camera reorients to face the look-at position as usual so that by the end of the physical motion, the camera orientation now matches the player character movement direction. It may also be necessary for the camera to avoid surrounding environmental features during the motion. This may be achieved by reducing the radius (when moving in an arc) or perhaps by instantly moving the camera to its desired position.

Transitions from first to third person cameras

In games where it is possible to change viewpoint from a first to third person camera, the actual transition is normally automated regarding motion and orientation. Typically, this is performed over a short period, but must still be smooth. Since third person cameras tend to be elevated compared to the player character, the orientation of the camera will usually change from horizontal to pitched downward. A linear interpolation between these orientations may not ensure that the player character remains framed well during the transition. A further consideration is that as the camera moves away from the first person position, it is necessary to prevent rendering of the player character until the camera has moved sufficiently away to prevent interpenetration artifacts. Often the player character model will be faded in over time to alleviate these problems (once beyond the camera near plane).

Transitions from third to first person cameras

When transitioning out of a third person camera and into a first person view, it is typical that the camera will move in a path so that the final orientation of the camera matches that of the expected first person camera. This may require a sweeping motion with a large angular reorientation. This can be avoided by using a cut transition or by reorienting the character to face the current direction from the camera position to the character position. In the latter case, the camera may simply move in a straight line while reorienting to face the direction of motion; at the same time the player character is also reorienting to the same direction. If the player character orientation is changing during the transition, then the motion path of the camera must change in the same manner; this will impart additional rotational changes to the camera orientation and care must be taken to ensure this does not disorient the player.

These are only a selection of cases where orientation control may be determined outside of player control. The important thing to remember is that it should be done only as assistance to the player. If the player feels that they have to struggle to position or reorient the camera to achieve a game play goal, then the camera system has failed.

REORIENTATION METHODS

Once we have determined the desired orientation of the camera, there needs to be a way to reorient the camera in a smooth yet timely fashion. These would seem to be (and in fact often are) conflicting requirements. Part of the solution is implicitly entangled with the determination of the desired look-at position, the other in the speed that the camera is allowed to reorient itself. Changes to the orientation of the camera over time are referred to as *rotation*. Rotation may be applied in a number of different ways, often dependent upon the orientation representation used. It is possible to represent the same rotation in several equivalent ways. For example, Euler angles, quaternions, and transformation matrices allow for similar rotations but have differing properties that may make them more or less desirable.

Applying rotations

The simplest way to apply a new rotation is to set the orientation directly, thus causing an instantaneous change in the camera. This method is used when we are explicitly controlling the camera orientation, as is often the case with cinematic sequences. In most game play situations, however, we wish to modify the camera orientation smoothly over time, thus only applying small changes at each step.

Let us examine some of the different rotation methods regardless of representation.

Constant angular velocity

A common solution is to apply a constant rate of change to the orientation of the camera, normally expressed as an angle per second rate and scaled according to the time elapsed since the last update. While simple to implement, this type of orientation change is likely to be discontinuous at both the start and end of its application, resulting in a somewhat jarring change to the player's view of the world.

Acceleration and deceleration

As an alternative to constant velocity, we may instead apply successive acceleration or deceleration to the camera's rotational velocity. This allows for a smooth start and end to the rotation, although it may cause the camera to overshoot a desired orientation if the deceleration is unable to reduce the velocity quickly enough. This type of acceleration control is sometimes used with the player turning in first person games, even though in such a situation it is likely that the deceleration rate is higher than the acceleration to prevent or minimize overshooting.

Angular velocity damping

Just as it is necessary to damp the velocity of the camera to produce a smooth start and end to its motion, it is also necessary to apply similar damping techniques to the reorientation of the camera. Sudden initial angular rotation or an abrupt end to the rotation is distracting to the viewer. A proportional damping scheme can be effective in this regard. Unless it is desired that the camera reorientation take a specific amount of time, this usually gives better results than simply applying a constant angular velocity. Essentially, the velocity of the orientation change is reduced in relation to the difference in current orientation from the desired orientation. A more general classification of such smoothing and damping functions is described in Chapter 10.

Free-look damping

Another case of where it is important to damp camera reorientation is that of the classic "free-look" camera. We can use *bump* and other *ease functions* to prevent camera reorientation due to controller noise and/or unintentional input from the player, but still allow smooth movement when required.

The bump function should be applied to the delta between the current and desired angle, so that a large delta still imparts fast motion until the delta becomes small enough to be affected by the bump. Another approach is to limit the acceleration of the camera orientation with damping applied proportionally to the magnitude of the angle between the current and the desired orientation.

Twist reduction

As a camera moves vertically above its target, it reaches a mathematical singularity. For an instant, regular mathematics breaks down, yaw becomes roll, and the camera will suddenly reorient to an unexpected direction. Even before the vertical axis is reached, the camera may need to reorient through 180 degrees to track an object that passes above or below the camera position. This sudden *twist* is disorienting to the player, as is any rapid reorientation that is not controlled by the players. Twist can be reduced by limiting the amount of roll around the forward vector of the camera on a per frame basis. As you pass over the singularity, the camera will then roll around to its new orientation. This only applies in cameras where we need to maintain an up-vector pointing in the same direction as the world up-vector. If the camera is allowed to be "upside down" then the singularity will not occur. Many flight simulator games allow for "downward" pointing up-vectors on the camera by successively applying delta transforms to the current camera transform. In this case, it is typically necessary to *orthonormalize* the transform regularly to avoid accumulation of floating point precision errors causing the transform to become unstable (i.e., non-normalized).

Reorientation lag

It is often less desirable to have a camera that has its orientation locked to that of a target object. In most cases, it is preferable to introduce some delay into the reorientation of the camera (referred to here as *reorientation lag* or simply *lag*), although the motion of the camera's reorientation should typically be smooth (i.e., maintain good frame coherency). By introducing lag, we impart a more natural "feel" to the camera, but it must be balanced with the need to keep the target character on screen as much as is possible.

Orientation lag directly corresponds to changing the position of the player character in screen space. Many games do not have any lag on the reorientation. This has two effects: first, the camera is normally set to look directly at the character, even though this prevents the player from seeing ahead of the character's motion; and second, the camera orientation becomes very dependent upon the motion of the character. Any sudden direction change or non-player imparted motion (such as a collision) will now affect the entire screen, greatly magnifying the most minor of disturbances to the player. This is undesirable at best and downright annoying for the most part.

To reduce or eliminate these effects it is necessary to filter the look-at position so that small movement has no effect and to damp its motion toward the desired position.

When interpolating the current orientation to the desired one, lag can be introduced by limiting the angular rotation allowed per frame. A quaternion look-at function that preserves the up-vector of the camera is most useful here as it provides the most direct rotational change. Additionally, we can damp the angular velocity proportionally to the angle between the current and desired orientations. Alternatively, lag may also be introduced by using springs or feedback controllers, as shown in the next section.

Offsets

One aspect of third person cameras that is often neglected is the relationship between the look-at position and the target object. Often camera designers focus their attention directly on the player character. By looking directly at the character (or vertically above them), we get a good view of the character and its animations (greatly appreciated by the animators no doubt) but unfortunately we miss seeing where the player is going in the world. This can be a large problem, particularly in games that involve aiming or other ranged interactions with the world.

Aiming in third person games is notoriously difficult. The main reason for this is the simple fact that the player is not able to easily determine the direction in which the shots will travel, since the viewpoint is unlikely to be along the direction in which the projectile will travel. If the projectiles have unlimited ammunition, then the actual stream of projectiles can help determine the aiming to use by effectively providing *tracers*. Without a stream of projectiles, it would be necessary to project the target position into screen space to render a targeting reticule, as is often the case with flight simulators. There are additional visual cues that can be used to assist the player in this regard. Highlighting of enemies in addition to HUD elements can be effective. If the player is able to "lock-on" to the target object (i.e., use an object-relative control scheme), then free aiming becomes less of an issue (although shot latency can still prove to be a problem).

Smoothing and damping

The most straightforward approach to smoothing camera orientation is to limit the angular velocity of the camera proportionally to the angle between the current and desired orientations.

This can be a simple curve using trigonometric functions such as:

```
Real32 const kDampingAngle(30.0f *
  gkRadiansPerDegree);
Real32 angle = acosf(CVector3f::
  Dot(currentOrientation, desiredOrientation));
Real32 const kDampingFactor = Cmath::Limit(angle /
  kDampingAngle, 1.0f); // linearly proportional
Real32 angularLimit = angularSpeed * deltaTime *
  kDampingFactor;
CQuaternion newOrientation = CQuaternion::
  LookAt(currentOrientation, desiredOrientation,
  angularLimit);
```

Another way to control the amount of damping applied is to use *bump* or *ease* functions. These are typically curve functions to convert numbers in the range zero to one back into the same range in a non-linear fashion. Examples of bump or ease functions are discussed in Chapter 11 as well as [Glassner02].

This is especially important in a first person camera during "free-look," but it is important whenever the camera is to be reoriented. Keep in mind that we have two contradictory requirements: smooth continuous motion and retaining an appropriate view of the character.

Springs and PID controllers

It is quite possible to control the reorientation of the camera by use of either springs or feedback controllers such as PID controllers. For reorientation purposes, we are attempting to reduce the angle between our current orientation and the desired orientation in a smooth manner. To reach our destination angle smoothly, it is important that the controller does not oscillate around the target angle. Springs and feedback controllers are prone to this behavior unless they are *critically damped*. In practice, tuning the characteristics of the controller to achieve this behavior can be time-consuming but very worthwhile. There are occasions where it is actually desirable to have a small amount of oscillation. Replay cameras and simulating a handheld camera are times where perfect orientation of the camera is not always desirable. Even in these cases the amount of oscillation should be minimized; it may be preferable to overshoot once or twice and not actually reorient to the target at all.

Look-at position interpolation

A different approach of controlling camera reorientation is through manipulation of the camera look-at position. It is often important to retain a view of the target object during camera behavioral changes. While interpolation between source and destination cameras can sometimes achieve this goal, frequently the camera will look away from its target for part if not most of the interpolation process. It can even result in the player character entirely leaving the view frustum. This can be somewhat distracting since it will eventually re-center on the original target when the interpolation concludes. It can be preferable, then, to base the camera orientation directly (or indirectly) on the actual desired look-at position, rather than seeking to the current destination camera orientation. At first glance, these two methods might appear to be the same. To a degree, they are, except that interpolation of the look-at position ensures that the camera retains a view that is usually seeking toward the final orientation, regardless of interpolation rate or changes in camera behavior.

FREE-LOOK

Free-look is a common term that refers to player-controlled manipulation of the camera orientation. Typically used in first person games, it can also prove useful in third person cameras. This manipulation typically alters the original orientation of the camera relative to a defined reference frame. There can be differences between how free-look is handled between first and third person cameras.

First person free-look

Free-look is sometimes limited to changes purely in the vertical camera orientation, with horizontal changes performed by rotating the player character in the same manner as their regular movement controls.

The *free-look* ability presents some potential player control issues. Depending upon the game design, and possibly the controller hardware configuration, it may be undesirable to allow control over the camera orientation while the player character is in motion. Many first person camera systems allow free-look during motion to enable a player motion technique called *circle strafing*. This technique is described in Chapter 10. Essentially, it is a method where a player may perform movement in a circular arc around an arbitrary position in space (usually to assist aiming or world navigation).

It is also worth noting that the orientation control may be limited to purely vertical motion (with the horizontal orientation locked to that of the player character), but sometimes it is required that full control over the camera orientation be allowed, possibly independent of player motion.

With free-look manipulation of the camera orientation, there need to be constraints as to the maximum vertical angle achievable, since we need to prevent *gimbal lock* and other untoward effects as the camera orientation becomes parallel to the world up-axis. Similarly, in first person games constraints may also be placed on horizontal rotation of the camera orientation, relative to the forward direction of the player character. These constraints would be the equivalent of limiting the rotation of the character's torso or upper body relative to the direction of the lower body. Naturally, some player character types do not require this limitation, for example, first person views from a vehicle cockpit. Additionally, such constraints are unnecessary if the free-look control actually turns the player character, which is the case in many first person games.

In the case of first person cameras, this reference frame is usually the forward 2D direction in which the player character body is facing. There are times in which this base (or "rest") orientation may be altered either by the player or according to game play or designer scripting overrides (see the next section). In the case where the horizontal orientation of players and their view are synchronized, free-look equates to turning the player character. However, it is possible (and even desirable in limited cases) to separate the view orientation from that of the character. This separation allows for motion in a direction different from the horizontal camera orientation. With this independent motion, it is often necessary to reorient the player view back toward the physical motion direction whenever the free-look controls are released, at least in the case of novice players. More experienced players may be able to understand disparity in the relationship between their motion and their view orientation.

For vehicle simulation, this behavior is reasonably commonplace, although it is often achieved through distinct camera orientations chosen through player commands rather than simply free-look; for example, it is certainly feasible to use free-look to reorient a gun turret. Typically, in vehicle games of this nature, the player is no longer controlling motion of the vehicle when operating a turret or similar device.

Third person free-look

In the case of third person cameras, free-look manipulation need not be restricted to just orientation changes. Often the position of the camera is altered, usually with the camera effectively moving across the surface of a sphere. This sphere is centered on the regular look-at position of the camera, or alternatively at a position vertically above the player character.

In such a scheme, it is preferred that the camera motion avoids interpenetration with geometry and that the camera has a limited range of vertical rotation around the character. This may require reducing the radius of the sphere of camera motion until clear of the obstruction. It may also be necessary to ensure that the camera may not be moved into a position that occludes the player character.

It would often be necessary to adopt a player-character relative control scheme (or alternatively, some other non-camera space scheme) to ensure that changes to the camera would not affect the player *control reference frame.*

There are, of course, other alternatives for third person camera manipulation. Some games require the player to be able to plan their course of action ahead of time and may thus allow the camera to be moved either relative to the player character or within controlled limits such as along a pre-defined path. In addition to this motion, the player may be able to reorient the camera. It is often required that such reorientation, however, must retain the player character within the camera view frustum. One method by which this is achieved is to allow a cone of reorientation around that of the desired look-at direction, typically with a spring to reorient the camera back to the desired direction once the camera controls are released (see the next section).

Player motion

It must also be considered whether players should be allowed to move their character at the same time as manipulating the camera. While this is usually possible (depending upon the controller layout), it may prove difficult for the player. There are also cases where the game design requires the player to be stationary to emphasize that the player is performing a different action.

Free-look orientation determination

Irrespective of the type of camera, the determination of the free-look orientation usually takes one of two forms: *self-centering* or *non-centering*.

Self-centering free-look

In this scheme, movement of an analog stick or other input device causes the desired orientation of the camera to move in direct relation to input motion. Typically, the range of stick values is mapped into an orientation angle relative to the underlying character orientation (or more specifically the "rest" orientation). Alternatively, the stick values are mapped into a camera orientation velocity, and this velocity is applied to the current camera orientation. In either case, release of the stick causes the camera orientation to seek back to its original "rest" orientation. With the former mapping, this is implicit in the actual position of the analog stick. With the latter, the camera system would detect that no input has been applied, and return to the original (rest) orientation over time. It may be desirable to have the speed at which the camera returns back to the rest orientation faster than the free-look speed, although it should still result in smooth reorientation with damping applied as necessary.

Non-centering free-look

Non-centering free-look schemes do not specify an absolute orientation for the camera. Rather, the input values are mapped to either an angular velocity or angular acceleration to apply to the camera orientation. Release of the stick or input value causes no further orientation change to be applied. Thus, the camera retains the current orientation and does not return to the default rest orientation. Depending on the sensitivity of the input device, there may be some residual motion applied as the stick returns to its neutral position. This unintentional orientation change may lead to some player dissatisfaction as it may cause difficulties in accurate aiming. These effects may be minimized in several ways. One method is to apply a non-linear mapping of the input values to orientation velocity, with heavy damping toward the neutral input position. Alternatively, the acceleration of the camera orientation may be damped but care must be taken so as not to make the orientation too sluggish.

In the case where the camera does not re-center itself, we can no longer easily apply orientation changes according to game play. For example, in many first person games the camera will automatically pitch up or down in a number of game play situations or under designer control. One such situation would be staircases, where it can be helpful to the player for the rest orientation of the camera to pitch upward as the player walks up the stairs and vice versa. This is normally achieved by tagging the surface or explicit scripting. Either way, once the player is able to free-look and the view is not centered upon release, we have to respect the player's choice of orientation, even if it would be more beneficial to apply an automatic pitch correction. It is possible to apply the pitch when no player pitch changes have been imparted, or when they have not been applied for a given amount of time. The difficulty is in determining *player intent*; sometimes this can be understood from the context of the current game play situation (e.g., combat), but it is more problematic to ensure that such automatic camera manipulation is not obtrusive.

Common orientation problems

When applying camera reorientations, it is entirely possible to create situations where undesirable rotations are imparted or other untoward changes to the camera direction occur.

Let us examine some of the common problems.

Gimbal lock

Gimbal lock is an obscure term referring to problems that occur with gyroscopic devices that are designed to maintain a reference frame regardless of how a vehicle (say, a spacecraft) is rotating. When the rotation of the vehicle causes the gyroscope to lose its reference frame (and thus return invalid orientation information), it is called gimbal lock. For our purposes, gimbal lock can occur when the camera's forward orientation becomes aligned with the world up-axis. When this occurs, rotation calculations of the camera can break down causing seemingly random (and instantaneous) orientation changes. This problem can be resolved in a number of ways. One method is preventing the camera forward direction from becoming parallel to the up-axis. Alternatively, use of quaternion mathematics to construct the camera transformation matrix can help. If it is desired that the camera retain an orientation aligned with the world up-axis, this can be handled by explicitly controlling the rotation around that axis to avoid problems with the look-at calculation causing random rotations. It is usually look-at calculations that reconstruct the camera transformation that will fail if they are constrained to retaining a positive up-vector.

Vertical twist

A similar situation to gimbal lock can be found in third person cameras and is known as *vertical twist*. This occurs as the forward vector of the camera is reasonably close to parallel with the up-axis of the world, say within 10 degrees or so. It is also a requirement that the camera up-vector is required to have a vertical component that is positive. Even if the camera orientation is not perfectly aligned with the world up-axis, should the player character be able to move faster than the camera (e.g., or if the camera is stationary) it might be possible for the player character to move underneath (or above) the camera. This will cause the camera to reorient rapidly around the world up-axis. If the camera cannot be prevented from such extreme orientations, steps must be taken to limit the amount of roll (i.e., motion of the up and right vectors) allowed per frame/update. This situation is actually relatively common, and is often used during cinematic sequences, or when a third person camera is backed into a corner. Limiting the amount of *twist*, or rotation around the world up-axis, is a reasonably robust solution.

Rapid reorientation of the camera is usually highly undesirable, as it will lead to nausea and disorientation in the player. It should be avoided if possible, by limiting the reorientation speed of the camera, or by judicious use of camera cuts. An alternative solution is to freeze the camera orientation until the player has moved to a position sufficiently away from the 2D position of the camera. After that point the reorientation speed should still be limited to avoid further disorientation. Care must be taken when freezing the camera orientation as the player character may easily move into a position that may not be visible.

Roll

Roll (i.e., rotation around the forward direction of the camera) is usually something that is best relegated to cinematic sequences, unless explicitly required by the game design. Roll is not a natural way in which humans perceive their world, and for many people it can be extremely distracting. When roll is applied, especially when the angular velocity of the roll is more than a few degrees per second, the results are quite nauseating. However, there are limited examples as to when roll can be beneficial, or even required.

First, flight simulators and their ilk often present a view of the world from that of the vehicle cockpit, and so roll becomes necessary to reproduce the effect that the vehicle is rolling. Indeed, the term roll is an aviation term for that very motion. Even so, some players can find this motion distracting, especially in an external view to the craft.

Second, it can be used during a fly-through sequence. When simulating the motion of a plane or other flying vehicle/character, it is sometimes desirable that the camera should "bank" as the character turns. This means that the character should roll around its forward vector, thus simulating forces that apply to flying vehicles, and so forth. In fact, often the camera will purposely slide to one side to further underscore this behavior. The determination of the amount of roll to apply can be specified within the path data or solved programmatically based on the curvature of the path and constraints as to the maximum amount of roll to be applied. Since this is an aesthetic quality more than anything, it is a little hard to quantify the amount of roll to apply.

A different approach is that some games actually use roll to *intentionally* disorient the player. This must be done carefully and applied infrequently, or the player will not physically be able to continue playing due to nausea.

As mentioned before roll is sometimes used in cinematic sequences to imply or emphasize flying motions, or sometimes to frame a scene to provoke a reaction from the viewer.

Orientation noise

Depending on the reorientation methods used, the camera orientation may react to small stimuli or player motion causing an oscillation or variance in the forward direction of the camera. Small amounts of orientation change, especially if not frame-coherent, will be a distraction to the player. Use of a high-pass filter to remove unwanted orientation changes can reduce or eliminate this problem.

Rapid orientation changes

When dealing with player characters that are able to move quickly, or change direction instantly, there are often times when the camera is forced to reorient rapidly. Similarly, if the player character is able to move above or below the camera, this will also cause rapid reorientation of the camera (see the previous section Vertical Twist). Regardless, rapid orientation changes are confusing to players as they struggle to understand the relationship between their character and the camera. The exception to this would be the case where the player has consciously caused the orientation change. An example would be changing viewpoint from, say, an interior cockpit view to an external view of a plane. Such camera cuts are acceptable, especially if the new camera reference frame is similar to that of the previous one. The more problematic cases are where the camera reorientation is not achieved via a cut. In these cases, the camera is changing its orientation by a relatively large amount per frame, causing a discontinuous sequence of images to be rendered. It is this discontinuity, much as with camera motion, that causes the player distress.

Frustum culling of the player character

The main goal of camera orientation is to frame the game events in a contextually appropriate manner; that is, present the best possible view of the game world for the particulars of the current game play situation. Clearly, aesthetics do play a part in how the framing is determined, but for in-game cameras, this is not the main concern. Note that aesthetic considerations are not limited to cinematography "rules," and in fact are genre dependent. Framing of the player character must come foremost in a third person camera system. However, this does not necessarily mean that the character should be centered on the display device. Frequently it is preferable to *view a position ahead and above the player character*. Even when the character does not use ranged weapons, it can be more helpful to the player to see upcoming parts of the environment. The impact of shifting the orientation of the camera away from the character must be tempered by the requirements of keeping the character within the view frustum. If the player character is outside of the screen then this will confuse the player and usually cause control reference frame problems. However, as the orientation of the camera looks away from the players, their position on the screen will vary, effectively pushing the players in the opposite direction to which they are moving. By establishing a safe zone, or angular limit of the player character from the center of the screen, the camera may be locked into the relative orientation from the player character. This would prevent the character from disappearing off the screen, but may introduce artifacts if the player's speed varies sufficiently to cause the camera to remain close to the angular limit. Use of timers to increase the camera reorientation speed may be sufficient to alleviate this. In many cases, the moving screen position of the player character (particularly in vehicle games such as racing or flight simulation) emphasizes the three-dimensionality of the character and adds a further element of visual interest to the scene.

■ SUMMARY

In this chapter we have seen the importance of how the game camera is positioned and oriented within the game world. A variety of methods used to determine both of these properties have been discussed. The choice of which methods to apply forms a large part of the camera design process. It bears noting once again that there is no single solution to this determination for a given game play situation. Indeed, several methods may be required to work in conjunction to present an acceptable view under changing conditions. The reader is encouraged to try different approaches to the determination of both the position and orientation of the camera since these form the crux of any camera system.

Chapter 8

Navigation and occlusion

Third person cameras are often used within complex or restrictive virtual environments. They are usually required to maneuver through these environments without becoming obstructed or having to pass through rendering geometry or other game objects. Additionally, they must continue to present an appropriate view of the player character or other target objects as dictated by dynamically changing game play elements. There may be other game play requirements that specify particular camera properties pertinent to the player's situation, such as retaining a set distance or framing position. Managing such possibly conflicting demands can be an extremely difficult task even under the best of circumstances.

Pre-computed or pre-defined movement paths can certainly help the camera's movement, but they may present the player with a limited view (as originally defined by the camera designer). It is generally more desirable to react to the current game situation rather than a limited subset as predicted by the designer, although the former is sometimes a valid aesthetic choice if for no other reason than the predictability of the game view. This is particularly true if the game play and camera positioning have been crafted to match each other. Dynamic determination of how the camera should reach its desired position is referred to here as *navigation*.

By its nature, this chapter is reasonably technical in nature, although it is likely of interest to designers wishing to understand some of the technology used to assist a game camera navigating through complex environments. Thus, it may also prove useful in furthering an understanding of how to construct environments that avoid these problems.

This chapter is also concerned with another related aspect of camera systems, namely *occlusion*. This topic relates to the problem of the determination of camera positioning and movement to avoid the target object being hidden (i.e., *occluded*) by environmental features or other game objects. Designers will likely find the discussion of how to resolve occlusion of interest; moreover, they will learn how it may be avoided altogether.

A related subject to occlusion is *line-of-sight determination*. Although this is often used as merely part of the occlusion testing, it may also be used as part of a suite of *fail-safe* conditions. Fail-safes are a way to ensure that the camera consistently has valid properties, such as being confined within the game world or maintaining an unobstructed view of the target object. Once a fail-safe condition is triggered, drastic action is often required to immediately correct the problem. Examples of this are given later in this chapter.

THE CAMERA AS AN AI GAME OBJECT

In many ways, the problems presented by camera navigation have parallels within the domain of *artificial intelligence* (AI). As suggested earlier, the camera may be thought of as an AI character, at the very least in terms of the determination of its position and orientation within the game world. The camera may be able to move more freely than many types of AI characters, however, since it is typically floating rather than being constrained to moving on surfaces or under the influence of a physical simulation. This freedom of movement is one of the benefits of a virtual camera system when compared to real-world cameras.

Yet, even though the camera may determine its path finding in a similar way to that used by AI characters, there are usually additional constraints concerning (for the most part) aesthetic issues such as target object framing, target object distance, and render geometry avoidance.

There are many interesting areas of AI navigation research, such as robotics, that may be applied to cameras. In particular, research toward autonomous methods of movement determination is highly relevant if we desire to have camera motion that is responsive to dynamic game events. The references at the end of this book contain several pertinent examples such as [Borenstein90].

Since there are a large variety of environmental types, we will assume here that the camera is constrained to remain within a *closed* environment consisting of a collision surface representation such as a polygonal mesh, with additional independent game objects. Here *closed* means that the representation of the environment forms a contiguous surface that constrains all usual game objects (even so, there may still be cases where it is necessary for the camera to be positioned outside of the environment). The collision surface may be considered as a separate entity to that of the rendered world (although they may in fact be the same), with additional information regarding surface materials stored on a per face or sub-surface basis. It is also assumed that mechanisms exist within the game engine to cast rays through the environment returning results as to collision points and the materials found at that point. Additionally there may be a need to filter the types of materials that are eligible for detection in any particular ray cast (e.g., some surfaces may allow the camera to pass but not regular game objects). Optimization and organization of collision data is not discussed in this book, but the reader is referred to [VandenBergen04] and [Ericson05] for more information about collision system design and implementation. Additionally, Chapter 9 describes some of the main methods used in camera collision detection and avoidance.

Predictive cameras (as described in Chapter 2) typically have better navigation results than *reactive* cameras, as they are more likely to anticipate changes to the environment that would occlude the player character. Naturally, this comes at additional performance cost.

NAVIGATION TECHNIQUES

Fundamental to all navigation methods are the ways in which the camera may request environmental data regarding potential obstructions or paths of motion. The nature of the game environment, its data representation, and facilities offered by the game engine will greatly influence the choice of navigation techniques. We may consider there to be two general classifications: *dynamic* and *pre-defined*.

Dynamic navigation techniques

Dynamic navigation refers to techniques that do not rely on predefined information to position or move the camera. Instead, they question the game world to determine how the camera should be positioned on a per-frame basis. Since this can be computationally expensive, a number of techniques may be required to amortize the processor cost.

An important consideration when using dynamic solutions is that it is difficult to account for the myriad of positions and actions that may be performed by the player. This means that it is difficult to test all the permutations as well as to be certain that no special case exists that might be problematic for the chosen navigation solution. Let us examine some of the more common dynamic navigation methods.

Ray casting

One of the simplest and most common navigation methods is that of the *ray cast*, a mathematical projection of a straight line through the virtual environment. By using trigonometry it may be determined if the line would intersect with either the *collision geometry* corresponding to the environment or that of an object within it. As might be expected, this can be computationally intensive especially given the complexity of many environments. An important goal when implementing camera systems is to limit the amount of such testing whenever possible. Amortization of ray casting is entirely possible and can be quite effective in reducing the processor requirements at a cost of limiting the amount of information available to use for navigation. Fortunately, navigation does not require a per-frame updating of such information as its decisions are normally longer lasting and may take more time to evaluate than collision or other immediate concerns. Similarly, reducing the set of data to be compared against (e.g., using spatial partitioning or material filtering) is also recommended.

Ray casts can often provide extremely pertinent information for camera systems, for example, collision prediction and player character occlusion. Furthermore, ray casts may be combined together to produce a more detailed view of possible obstructions. On the other hand, since ray casting normally involves (by definition) projection of a 3D line through the game world, it is entirely possible for the ray to pass through small openings and thus not register a collision. Normally this problem is reduced by simply increasing the number and positioning of the ray casts to cover a larger area, although care must be taken given the potential performance costs. It may also be avoided by having a separate collision mesh that only pertains to camera movement and would thus not include such small openings.

An alternative solution is to use ray-casting *hysteresis*, that is, statistical information of the ray cast results gathered over multiple updates. From this history, it is possible to generate a probability graph of likely ray collisions and to reduce the actual amount of ray casts per update. The probability graph is then used to determine the influence applied to camera motion. For example, according to the position of the ray cast relative to the camera, we can deduce that lateral or vertical motion of the camera is probably necessary to avoid a *future* collision if the ray is prevented from reaching its target.

The results of the ray casts can then be used to dictate potential camera motion in a variety of ways. First, a weight or influence factor for each ray cast can be applied depending on the success of the ray cast. Thus, rays not reaching the target cause the camera to move in a direction away from their position.

An alternate method often used is to cast rays from the target object back toward the camera. The results of these ray casts are utilized in a similar manner. If a ray is cut short then once again it influences the movement of the camera. The degree of influence is often based on the proximity of the collision point to the origin of the ray cast, or sometimes simply a pre-defined weighting factor depending on the particular ray cast direction.

One of the problems with ray casting is that the determination of whether the ray intersects with the environment (or indeed, other game objects) is often computationally expensive. Additionally, it is often necessary to apply property information to the collision surfaces. This information may be used to determine if a collision or ray intersection is actually valid. It is common that the game camera may ignore a significant portion of the environment if these filters are set appropriately. This is typically performed by a simple masking operation of desirable properties against the set of properties applied to the surface.

TECHNICAL

A typical implementation of simple ray casts would use a fixed arrangement of source positions around the proposed position of the camera, with the rays extending toward the target object. Care must be taken to ensure the arrangement does not intersect with world geometry. Often the ray positions are arranged in a grid or other symmetric shape. Each ray is given an influence factor that may be applied horizontally, vertically, or both. If the ray cast fails to reach the future position of the target object, the influence is applied to the desired camera position. The influence may even be calculated according to its position relative to the target.

```
For all ray casts
    If ray cast successful
        No influence applied
    If ray cast fails
```

> Scale influence factor by distance of ray cast collision from target
> Add influence to desired camera position
> End
>
> Once the total influence has been calculated, the camera will move toward the desired position plus this influence. Note that the influence may be calculated differently in each axis, if so desired.

Volume projection

Rather than simple rays, this technique projects a volume through the world from the camera position toward its target position. This volume is typically an extruded sphere (sometimes referred to as a *capsule*); for simplicity and performance, it may be either rectangular or cylindrical. Performance improvements can be gained by simulating the volume using several ray casts around the perimeter of the volume. As with other collision determination techniques it is important to filter out any unimportant objects or geometry from the potential collision set. Bounds checking of axis-aligned bounding boxes or similar techniques may be applied to initially cull objects.

Volume projection is often used to determine if the camera would fit within confined spaces, or when determining a new potential position relative to an object (e.g., after a *jump cut*). It may also be used to ensure that camera motion is valid by projecting a motion volume from the current position to the desired position.

Sphere/cylinder collisions

The camera is often considered a sphere for collision purposes. This is partly because sphere collisions are relatively straightforward, but perhaps also because spheres are likely to slide along collision surfaces. The radius of the collision sphere should be slightly larger than the distance of the view frustum's near plane from the camera, thus preventing interpenetration of the camera with render geometry. This is only true, however, if the collision geometry of objects or the environment extend beyond that of the render geometry. Note that this distance is also dependent upon the horizontal field of view. Ideally, the collision volume encompasses all four vertices of the frustum at the near plane.

Alternatively, the camera collision volume may be considered as a simple vertical axis-aligned cylinder. In environments where the camera will not move close to horizontal surfaces such as floors or ceilings, this approximation should provide equal functionality to a sphere at a reduced performance cost. The same caveats apply regarding the near-plane distance, and vertical collision must take into account the elevation of the camera, which might change how geometry would interpenetrate the near plane.

In the case of first person cameras, no collision volume or testing may actually be necessary since the camera should be completely contained within the collision bounds of the player character (it would also be somewhat disconcerting if the camera was prevented from moving and the player was not). However, it is still necessary to ensure the collision bounds of the player are larger than the near-plane distance to avoid the same manner of rendering artifacts as those prevalent in third person cameras. Interpenetration of the near plane is still possible if there are game elements (such as game AI objects) that do not test for collision against the player, or that have render geometry protruding from their collision volume.

Dynamic path finding

Real-time or *dynamic* path finding has obvious similarities to solutions used for AI object navigation of the game world. However, path finding for cameras is more stringent than AI path finding — aesthetic constraints play a large part. The underlying idea is that pre-computed information is available that defines the volumes of space available for motion through the world. The data structure used to represent these volumes can vary but usually includes methods to traverse the volumes through connectivity information (which may also be directional in nature). Traditional search algorithms such as *A** or *Dijkstra's Algorithm* (as described in many AI or computer science text books) may be used to determine the most efficient path through the volumes, given weighting values that dictate the desirability of a particular path. The desirability determination for camera motion is likely to be quite different from that of an AI object, however.

Once a path has been generated, the camera will follow the path until it reaches the desired position or the movement is interrupted by a new request. Usually this occurs when the path is recomputed on a regular basis, to account for player motion or environmental changes and so forth. Often the path searching occurs at two levels. The high-level solution determines the overall motion of the camera between volumes, combined with a low level solution to avoid game objects, proximity to collision geometry, and so forth. The difference between this solution and ones used for AI is that the latter tend to deal with longer paths of motion along surfaces (though sometimes flying or jumping), whereas cameras are normally relatively close to their target positions. In the case of cameras, the path information is used more for collision avoidance rather than a complete motion path. Longer motion paths such as those used during non-interactive cinematic sequences are most often pre-defined and do not require any type of navigation logic to be applied.

Dynamic path generation

Path generation differs from the path finding previously mentioned because the shape and length of the new path is not determined according to pre-determined information built into the game world. Rather, information about the game world is dynamically determined according to the current situation and used to generate the most appropriate path when required. Moreover, it is likely that this path will change over time, although this may cause unwanted camera movements. Dynamic paths are typically used in situations where standard navigation is unable to determine an appropriate movement.

Another technique for dynamic path generation is to use information garnered from the motion of the player character. In many situations, a history of player movement data may be used to derive a potential movement path for the camera. If it is known that the player has passed through a confined space (e.g., a doorway), the camera may clearly follow the same path. However, such a path would likely present a very different view of the player than normally seen. Therefore, it may be necessary to generate a volume around the player movement points to find the potential limits of valid camera motion (e.g., as an extruded cylindrical volume). This volume would be used to present a view in keeping with the expected displacement of the camera from the player character.

Visibility and rendering solutions

With the advent of hardware-assisted rendering, a new variety of solutions became available for determination of the desired camera position. We start with the assumption that the final position for the camera will be somewhere relative to the target object, and that the desired position should have an unobstructed view of the target object. Next, we add constraints for the distance and elevation of the desired position relative to the target object. This produces a cylindrical band of potential positions around the target object. Further constraints can be layered on top of these requirements, such as only allowing a certain angular displacement relative to the target object.

Given all these constraints, we now have a small subset of potential positions to be tested for viability. If we were to render the world from each of these potential positions such that the camera was oriented toward the target object, it would result in scenes that may or may not show the target object according to occluding geometry or game objects. If, instead, we render these views so that the target object is drawn in an easily distinguishable (and unique) color, the rendered screen buffer may be analyzed to determine if the target object was occluded. If the object is sufficiently non-occluded, then we can consider the rendered camera position as a viable position. Other hardware-accelerated techniques may be used to determine the occlusion of the target object from each of the potential positions, including depth buffer analysis.

By exploiting the parallel nature of the graphics hardware, the cost of this determination may be significantly amortized. There are, however, some caveats to this approach. First, the setup for rendering the scene from each potential position may be prohibitive. Second, although rendering via hardware is fast, it is certainly not free. The GPU and CPU cost may be reduced by techniques such as rendering the scene flat-shaded (i.e., no lighting), changing the view frustum to restrict the scene to only the area around the target object (including far clip plane distance), and reducing the resolution of the rendered scene.

Once we have determined which of our original potential camera positions is the most preferred, we can then calculate a path or other movement method to take the camera from its current position to the desired position. Although this technique works well in determining the position, it does not take into account geometry intervening between the current position and the desired position. Additional constraints may be applied to avoid these problems. A practical implementation of these techniques may be found in [Halper01].

Colliders

Colliders are a variant upon the standard ray casting techniques as previously mentioned. The principle here is that the positions from which the ray casts are made are variable. Each of these positions is enclosed within a small collision volume (typically a sphere or approximated to this by another ray cast). These position objects are referred to as colliders, since they are constrained to stay within the environment. Usually the colliders will be arranged in a particular pattern around the camera, such as a circle or semi-circle. The colliders are constantly attempting to regain their desired positions relative to the camera's ideal position as the camera moves through the environment.

The arrangement of the colliders influences how the camera will react to the environment. Each collider casts a ray toward the look-at position of the camera, or alternatively some other pre-defined point relative to the player character. The result of the ray cast is used to offset the desired position of the camera motion. The amount of influence exerted by a collider may be based on a number of factors:

- The physical distance of the collider from the camera possibly calculated in local camera space and applied in the same manner.
- A pre-defined influence factor per collider determined according to the position of a particular collider within the entire group.
- The distance from each collider to the point at which its ray cast struck geometry.
- The acceleration or velocity of the player character, possibly only in one axis depending on desired behavior (e.g., change elevation according to player speed).

Some combination of the above factors may be applied to some or all colliders. Often there are several groups of colliders, each influenced by different factors. The ways in which the influence is applied also varies, possibly using a weighted average or a centroid calculation. Some experimentation will be required according to the types of environment encountered in a particular game.

Differing arrangements of these colliders may be used according to the type of behavior required for the environment. Circular or semi-circular arrangements are common, as are horizontal ones. The arrangement may vary according to changes in the player character, most commonly velocity.

Colliders and other ray casting techniques are susceptible to "noise" produced by ray casts that collide with incidental environmental features that should not adversely affect camera motion. Some knowledge of the environment may be used to filter out results that should not influence camera motion. Tagging of surface properties may also be used to ignore or apply a reduced influence on the camera position determination. Alternatively, surfaces may be tagged to act as motion constraints or to otherwise prevent the camera from approaching. The arrangement of the colliders and the amount of influence each applies may require changing according to the environment properties (e.g., confined spaces, vertical columns, etc.) or game play mode (e.g., to match changing movement characteristics of the player character).

TECHNICAL

Since the arrangement of colliders may vary considerably, here is only an outline of the algorithm used to determine their influence upon the desired camera position:

```
stl::vector<Vec3> influence;
  // might be useful as a class
for (int i = 0; i < colliders.size(); ++i)
{
 influence.push_back(colliders[i].offset *
   colliders[i].GetWeighting());
  // the weighting depends on line of sight and/or
  // other factors such as the relative collider
  // position
}
// will need to get an average or similar
return GetCentroid(influence);
```

The arrangement of colliders will change the calculation method used to determine the average amount of influence to apply. A centroid calculation works well if the colliders are constrained to a plane, but however the final influence is calculated, it must also be applied in the same space as the collider's offsets.

Pre-defined navigation techniques

Many of the problems associated with camera collision can be avoided by pre-computation of potential camera movement or by using pre-defined assistance based on knowledge of the environment (whether defined explicitly by the camera designer or otherwise automatically pre-calculated). Camera navigation pre-computation may take many forms, usually at a cost of both memory overhead and time to compute the allowable camera positions, although the latter is not generally as important. Pre-computation typically has an advantage in lower processor overhead during run-time. Assistance for navigation is often in the form of game script objects placed by designers and therefore tailored to the specific requirements of both game play and environmental concerns. Chapter 6 discusses scripting and its application to camera motion and positioning; however, it is possible to derive navigation assistance information from other game objects than those specifically designed to control camera behavior.

There are a variety of ways in which both types of information may be used to assist camera navigation and collision avoidance. Many of these schemes share common ground with AI or robotic research techniques, and the bibliography outlines some of the relevant papers.

Some of the more common solutions are as follows.

Pre-defined paths

The most common solution for pre-computation is to literally store entire motion paths. Several games have used this effectively since it also allows complete control over camera position (and possibly orientation), irrespective or directly according to player action. Nevertheless, path motion can be somewhat restrictive and could potentially result in the player experiencing a sensation of lack of control. Conversely, the ability to directly specify the position of the camera is a boon when dealing with motion through a complex environment, especially if the determination of the position can be varied according to player position or action. A full description of path-based camera motion may be found starting with the section Path in Chapter 7.

Path motion behaviors

Although the camera may be constrained by using a path to completely define its motion, the interpretation of how the spline actually constrains the motion offers several alternatives.

- **Constrained path camera.** A *constrained path camera* is one that moves precisely along a defined path within the game world. The camera is typically not allowed to leave this path under any circumstance, unless the path is no longer active. This is one of the most typical uses of path cameras, so the camera position may be absolutely controlled to avoid collision or interpenetration with environmental features, and so forth. Non-interactive movies are often driven by this type of camera (as well as stationary or slaved position cameras).
- **Follow path camera.** In many cases, the motion of a camera on a constrained path may not appear as "organic" or "natural" as required by the game designers, even though the motion along the path may be smooth. However, we may still wish to restrict camera motion in some fashion. A *follow path camera* provides a mechanism to both restrict camera motion yet allow some variance. In this case, the path only dictates a desired position — how the camera reaches that desired position can be defined in a number of different ways — i.e., the camera is not locked

directly to the path. This may be likened to a "carrot" being dangled in front of the camera. The camera will seek to the location defined by the current evaluation of the path, but is allowed to move in a direct line toward that position (note that this same technique may be applied regardless of the position determination method). Alternatively, we can use rules to control the distance away from the desired path that the camera is allowed to move; for example, the path now becomes a tube (typically cylindrical) although the cross section may not be circular (e.g., ellipsoidal or rectangular). Indeed, information about the shape of the *path volume* may be contained within the knots themselves to allow for variance of camera motion along the path (including the radius of the tube). Another approach is to use a parametric curve with the input parameter as the position of the camera along the path. These methods allow local control over the camera without having multiple paths. When restricting the motion of the camera away from the follow path, it is normally best not to use "hard" constraints as this will likely lead to unwanted motion artifacts. A *damped spring* or *attractor/repulsor* may be used to provide a more analog response to the distance restriction.

Pre-defined volumes

Camera motion may also be restricted such that the camera is confined by the extents of a pre-defined volume. The actual definition of the volume is somewhat variable. It may consist of a simple convex shape such as a sphere, cylinder, ellipsoid, or cube. Alternatively it may be derived from a complex collision mesh, much as would other game entities. Complex shapes, of course, make navigation a more difficult proposition. The desired position within the volume may be defined in a number of different ways. Clearly, we can use the same techniques as mentioned earlier in this chapter regarding player character-relative positions with the additional constraint of remaining within the volume. This approach is applicable to most of the dynamic determination methods, so that the pre-defined volume constraint is applied after the initial determination has been made. It is typically easier to use fixed dimension volumes, but these could be varied according to game play requirements; for example, the position of the player relative to a reference frame. In the same manner as path behaviors, directly constraining the camera position may lead to non-continuous motion and often benefits from the use of forces or damped springs to keep the camera within the volume.

Attractors/repulsors

Effective navigation assistance may be obtained by using *attractors* or *repulsors*, where the camera is literally attracted to (or repulsed from) pre-defined positions, regions, or other game objects. Often these positions are defined explicitly using script objects that are placed by the camera designer. Alternatively, offline analysis can be made of the environment to determine automatic placement; in practice this can be a difficult prospect without explicit rules governing their usage.

Both attractors and repulsors function by applying *forces* to the camera depending on the proximity (and possibly orientation) of the player or camera. Note that these forces may not be implemented as part of the physical simulation (even if such a facility is available); rather they may simply influence the determination of the desired position or act as hard constraints during the actual camera motion.

The use of proximity as part of the calculation of forces suggests that the attractor or repulsor is spherical in nature, but this is not necessarily appropriate. Cylindrical shapes are frequently the most useful, often with their major axis aligned to the world up-vector. Simplistic shapes are common because of the relatively low cost in the calculation of the proximity of game objects, and thus the forces required. Spheres, cylinders, and planes are common choices.

One specific example that is often problematic for cameras is navigation through doorways, particularly if the character moves quickly. Other than the problems of ensuring that the door does not physically close either between the camera and its target or on top of the camera, doorways are frequently a problem because they are often confined spaces and there are many opportunities for the player character to move in ways that may cause the camera to be left behind. Vertical doorways are the most common case encountered, where the door is aligned with the up-axis of the game world. Horizontal doorways have additional challenges especially regarding camera orientation due to the potential for *gimbal lock*. Additional problems occur when external events may cause the door to close rapidly, leaving the camera behind the closed door (or worse, interpenetrating the door geometry). To cope with such situations it is generally preferable that the door is held open while the camera is on the opposite side compared to the player, but this is not always possible. Thus, it is often necessary to implement a *fail-safe* to ensure that the camera is never left on the wrong side of a closed door.

If the camera system is able to track the proximity of the camera to doorways or otherwise be informed of how the camera is positioned and oriented relative to the doorway (e.g., by means of a trigger volume), an axis-based attractor may be used to help guide the camera motion through the doorway. A proportional attractor can apply forces to the camera dependent upon the camera position relative to the axis of desired motion through the doorway. Care must be taken to ensure that these forces do not impart oscillation and that they are only applied when appropriate.

Considering the general case once again, the direction in which forces are applied by attractors or repulsors is also variable. Common usage would have the forces acting in relation to the physical shape of the attractor or repulsors; for example, a spherical attractor would pull objects toward its origin. They can be based on a world-relative orientation; a cylindrical repulsor may determine its force from the player character's proximity to the central axis of the cylinder yet apply the repulsion force based on a fixed world orientation.

Attractors and repulsors are sometimes attached to (or form part of) other game objects. Thus, they may vary in their position and effects.

As with any force-based solution, care must be taken to ensure that such objects only apply their forces when appropriate. [Stout04] discusses this in detail. Ensuring that forces do not adversely influence the camera is the most difficult part of their usage. Cameras do differ somewhat from AI objects in this determination however, since there are additional aesthetic considerations to consider (such as the requirement to ensure smooth motion whenever possible). Thus if the camera incidentally moves past an attractor, it is not necessarily appropriate that it should be influenced. If the camera were moving away from the attractor, for example, we would not wish to apply any forces.

By careful choice of the attractor positions, camera motion can be made to avoid geometry or pass through confined environments without the necessity for complicated hand-scripted camera solutions. Indeed, the attractor or repulsors can be combined with regular game objects (such as doors) to assist camera motion without any additional scripting support.

Flow fields

Flow fields are sparse arrays of vectors (i.e., directions), normally spaced apart in a grid across a 2D plane or within a 3D volume. The spacing of the vectors is not necessarily uniform. As the camera (or other object) passes through the flow field, vectors that are close to the camera affect its motion by applying a force in the direction of their orientation. The strength of force may be dependent upon the distance of the camera from the plane or some other factor. The name derives from the fact that the array of vectors is akin to a stream or other moving body of water that flows around objects. By adjusting the direction of the vectors, we can ensure that the camera will move around obstacles in much the same manner. Thus, it is important to ensure that the direction of the vectors will not cause situations to arise where the camera remains stationary as competing vectors cancel out their influence, or prevent the camera from clearing obstacles. The use of flow fields is usually applied as an additional influence on camera motion, rather than the sole factor. In addition, it is necessary to determine when the additional influence should be applied. For example, the vectors could be uni- or bi-directional. If the camera is able to navigate through the flow field in different directions relative to the flow field vector directions, the influence might only be applied when the camera motion is parallel to the direction of the vector. Additionally, the amount of influence may also be proportional to the velocity of the camera.

Influence maps

Influence maps are another sparse array, similar to flow fields in some regards. However, the mapping of the camera position from the influence map is normally based upon the position of the target object relative to the influence map rather than the camera itself. Each position on the influence map corresponds to a different position in space for the camera to occupy. The desired position derived from the influence map is used as an interpolant so that the motion of the camera from its current position will be smooth. In some ways, spline motion can be considered a one-dimensional variant of the influence map. In this case, the target object position relative to the spline maps back to a position that the camera should occupy on the same (or a different) spline. Influence maps may be explicitly positioned or generated offline from collision or visibility information.

Potential fields

Derived from research into robot navigation, potential fields are a promising approach to dynamic camera navigation and collision avoidance. While this is an advanced topic beyond the scope of this book, a brief overview might be helpful. Potential fields are based on the principle of *electrostatic forces;* that is, forces whose effect on objects is proportional to the distance of the object from the force applier. Essentially, these forces are applied to the active camera to prevent its approach toward collision or render geometry. Additionally these force components are added to the motion of the camera, aiding navigation through confined spaces and often avoiding many of the problems caused when the camera might be in collision with geometry. The forces may be defined explicitly as points or plane surfaces and thus placed within the environment by designers in a similar manner to *attractors* and *repulsors* as previously mentioned. Alternatively, their position and orientation may also be automatically generated as part of the cooking of world data.

Similarly, the collision geometry may be used to generate forces. However, the complex nature of collision geometry would likely make determination of the forces closest to the camera computationally expensive. One possible solution is to generate an *implicit surface* that approximates the collision geometry in a smooth and continuous manner and facilitates rapid determination of the closest positions to the camera. See [Bloomenthal97] for an introduction to implicit surfaces.

Robotics research has explored these techniques with mixed results (e.g., see [Koren91]). There are some notable limitations regarding the complexity of the environments, especially regarding dead-ends. There may also be oscillation problems when the forces are applied from opposite directions simultaneously (e.g., in a narrow corridor). Refer to [Stout04] for more information on the practical application of potential fields within games. An alternative and very promising solution is offered in [Borenstein90], using *vector field histograms* (VFH). Briefly, VFHs store information regarding the distance of obstacles from the object determined by infrared or other sensors. These sensors are typically mounted either at fixed angular offsets or rotate around a central point, effectively casting rays into the environment. The distance information returned at each angular offset may then be analyzed over time. A histogram of known obstacles is thus constructed, providing sufficient information to determine potential collisions.

OCCLUSION

This section is concerned with *occlusion* of the player character, and its effect on game play. Occlusion occurs when players are prevented from viewing their characters due to environmental or other game features placed between the character and the camera. By definition, occlusion is only a concern with third person camera systems since camera motion cannot resolve player character occlusion in two-dimensional presentations.

In third person cameras, occlusion can be a difficult problem to resolve, requiring a variety of solutions depending upon the game genre, environment, or game play situation. This may even require use of a *jump cut* to move the camera to a more amenable position and orientation. This section includes both reasons why occlusion should generally be avoided (and when it is acceptable), and suggestions on how it can be resolved or even anticipated.

Occlusion testing is greatly dependent upon the facilities offered by the collision system. As we shall see, typical occlusion testing requires the ability to cast rays or volumes through the game world to test either line of sight or to determine the viability of a new camera position.

What is considered occlusion?

The definition of occlusion can be construed in a number of different ways, and is dependent upon the nature of the player character. Our definition would specify that the player is unable to adequately view their player character in a way that allows sufficient control over the positioning, movement, or similar interactions of the character with other game play elements. This is typically due to environmental geometry or other game objects positioned between the active camera and the character. The amount of the character that must be visible to ensure sufficient player control is greatly dependent upon its distance from the camera, as well as the physical nature of the player character (e.g., size and silhouette profile). Occlusion becomes a significant problem when manipulating the position and orientation of the player character in environments requiring finesse over its motion (e.g., where the character may fall from a great height, etc.).

Why and when does occlusion matter?

A quick look at any number of games utilizing a third person camera will reveal that many seem to be unconcerned with maintaining a consistent and unobscured view of the player character. *This is a fundamental mistake.* Occlusion of the main player character forces the player to manipulate the camera and/or player character simply to obtain a view that allows sufficient control. In some cases it may not be possible to achieve this, causing a large amount of frustration in the player. Since some games do not allow free camera control, or actively fight against the player camera control (by design or otherwise), occlusion of the main character often directly impacts game play in a very negative fashion. Additionally, if the player is directly controlling the camera, it can prove difficult or impossible to perform other actions with their character particularly if multiple physical buttons or controls are necessary. Worse still, some control configurations require modal controls to manipulate the camera position or orientation, thus forcing players to interact with the game in a way that may be counter to their desires.

Some compromises can be made in this regard, but only under careful consideration. Partial occlusion of the character is usually acceptable, especially when the character is either sufficiently large upon the screen or the amount of occlusion is small. Total occlusion, on the other hand, is usually unacceptable. The further away the character is from the camera, the more important it is to retain an unobstructed view of the character. However, it should be noted that even total occlusion is sometimes acceptable, if it only occurs for brief periods. In fact, such brief occlusion may actually increase the sense of immersion for the player. This is because it emphasizes the fact that the player character is a part of the environment and may thus be (temporarily) obscured. An example would be the player passing behind a vertical column or pillar to quickly emerge on the other side. Of course, if the character remains behind the pillar, the sense of immersion can quickly be overshadowed by the player's frustration.

Occlusion determination

Now that we have a definition of occlusion, how do we test for this situation? As noted in earlier chapters, ray casts are an obvious solution for generating line of sight or occlusion information, but it must be taken into consideration that the use of ray casting is often computationally expensive. Given the relative speed of motion of most characters, occlusion testing need not be performed in every game update cycle. The cost of determining line of sight is easily amortized over several frames, especially if *hysteresis* is maintained. A threshold value weighted according to the number of consecutive frames of occlusion is one possible methodology for deciding when the object has been sufficiently occluded. The weighting may be based on temporal or positional properties of the ray casts. Weighting techniques such as this are also used for determining camera navigation through the environment. Failure of the ray casts to reach their target is indicative of an obstruction that should be avoided by the camera. The relative position of the ray cast can be used to determine which avoidance motion to perform.

Ray casting

In the case of humanoid or similarly shaped creatures, we can usually use three positions, each of which should be checked for visibility: head, torso, and feet. If all three no longer have direct line of sight to the camera, then the character can be considered occluded. Of course, more extensive testing can be performed (such as Z-buffer or frame buffer analysis), and modern rendering hardware will often report information as to the number of pixels that have been drawn. These data clearly show whether any portion of the model for the character was visible, which could be used as a metric for occlusion purposes.

Because of the typical complexity of environmental geometry and player characters, a single ray cast is normally not sufficient when it comes to occlusion testing. It is usually not important that full occlusion of the character occurs; rather that enough of the character (or specific parts of the character such as their feet) is hidden to make it difficult to position or orient the character as required for game play. In that regard, specific portions of the character may be more significant for this determination. It is of paramount importance that the character is visible in some way. Total occlusion is to be avoided at all costs. With an animated humanoid it is best to use line of sight positions that are relatively close to the rest pose of the character; that is they should not be animated with the extremities of the character joint motion.

In *Metroid Prime* [Metroid02], the player character in the third person view is actually a sphere rather than a humanoid figure. In this particular example, the line of sight calculation actually involves checking three positions on the sphere — the center, the top, and the bottom (in terms of the up-axis of the world coordinate space). All three positions must fail the line of sight test (for a period of time) for the character to be considered occluded. This is an example of a case where total occlusion is required before drastic action should be taken by the camera system; partial occlusion remains acceptable (if not usually desirable) as long as the player is able to understand both the relationship between their character, the environment, and the control reference frame.

Partial occlusion may be used as an indication to the camera system that it should react more rapidly or in a modified manner. This is particularly true when the nature of the partial occlusion reveals how it may be resolved. For example, if only the head of a humanoid figure is occluded this would suggest that the camera should be lowered.

Volume casting

Geometry complexity can sometimes cause ray-casting methods to return false solutions to potential camera positions. An alternative is to project a volume through the game world. Clearly, this is a more expensive proposition in terms of processor performance, and its usage should be restricted if possible. Fail-safe conditions normally result in a camera cut, and thus a discontinuous camera motion. Volume casting is often used when repositioning the camera to an entirely new position. A typical example is after instantaneous motion of the player character; a jump cut is typically performed to place a third person camera in a position behind the direction of motion of the player character. Thus, it is necessary to ensure that the new camera position remains within the confines of the game environment and the player character is not occluded. Since ray casts are prone to failure in this regard, volume casting is a more appropriate method. Of course, if the new position of the player character was pre-defined, then the initial camera position may be similarly specified, avoiding a complex series of testing.

While ray casting is relatively intensive in its processor requirements, volume casting is much more intensive. For this reason the camera is often considered a spherical object during volume casting.

Rendering techniques

Another way to test for occlusion is to use rendering capabilities of the target platform to provide information regarding the visibility of the player character or target object. This may be achieved in many different ways, and is becoming increasingly popular thanks to the advent of rendering hardware. Let us briefly discuss a couple of the most common solutions.

- **Flat-shading using identifiers as color values.** One method is similar to that used when calculating world visibility data sets; that is the potential visible portion of the game world from any given game location. The object to be tested for occlusion is rendered using flat shading and an identifying color. Environmental geometry is rendered in a different color to allow the pixels of the object to be distinguishable. The display buffer is then parsed to see if pixels belonging to the object were drawn. The amount of pixels drawn belonging to the object, or their distribution, may be used to determine the extent of occlusion.

- **Z-buffer (depth buffer) analysis.** If the rendering system allows access to the frame buffers as generated by rendering the current scene, it might be possible to extract Z-buffer information regarding a particular game object, such as the target character. Silhouette information may extracted by a comparison of the Z-buffer from before and after the object was drawn. To reduce the computation cost, a smaller region of the buffer may be analyzed using information regarding the render bounds of the object.

- **Rendering hardware occlusion queries.** Some rendering hardware or software APIs provide means to automatically determine if a rendering primitive or model was unable to be rendered due to depth buffer comparisons, as discussed in [Sekulic04]. That information would indicate if the object was completely occluded or possibly the proportional amount of pixels that failed the depth buffer comparison.

Occlusion prediction methodologies

One of the best solutions to the problem of occlusion is to anticipate the situation before it occurs. This can be somewhat tricky in practice as it greatly depends upon the actions of the player. It is unlikely that the entire simulation can be run ahead in time to anticipate the future state of the game, but prediction of the player position or other target object(s) is indeed somewhat plausible.

This anticipation of future behavior (or position) exemplifies a *predictive* camera, as opposed to one that uses the current (and previous) state of the target object, namely a *reactive* camera. Predictive cameras are more desirable since they are typically better at anticipating camera navigation. However, this prediction can be difficult to achieve in practice, depending upon the nature of the target object. Extrapolation of the previous object motion in many cases is sufficient to determine a future position of the target object. This technique is often applied within the realm of AI routines, especially those concerned with predicting object positions for target leading purposes.

Predicting the look-at position

If the target object is moved by physics simulation, then there should be enough information regarding the object's motion properties to extrapolate a purely linear movement. However, objects rarely move purely in straight lines. Player objects in particular will typically move relative to other objects (i.e., "lock-on" or "circle-strafing"), along constrained paths, or in any number of different ways. Maintaining a history of previous object motion properties can help in this regard as the continued movement of the target object may often be extrapolated from recent motion. Specific knowledge of the game environment will sometimes help determine future positions of the target object, particularly when the movement is constrained (e.g., the character is forced to move in a pre-defined direction).

Often the predicted position is not used as-is. Rather, a portion of difference between the current and future position is applied. One method used to determine this amount is the speed of the target object compared to some threshold value.

LINE OF SIGHT

Occlusion and *line of sight* (LOS) are not necessarily the same, but are tightly related. The exact meaning of "line of sight" is extremely variable, depending on the physical nature of the target object and the complexities of the game world geometry. We may often think of LOS as determining if a single ray cast from the camera can reach the target object without hitting any static (and possibly dynamic) environmental geometry. Game objects are often included in the test for occlusion, but may cause spurious camera motion since the player character is frequently interacting and moving among them. Some types of player character would require multiple ray casts, possibly depending on the state of the character, and this information is often used to determine character occlusion, as noted previously. Line of sight tests are common in AI functions as a relatively inexpensive test for determining potential target objects, and so forth. In such cases the usage of ray casts may be amortized over many game updates, since AI logic rarely needs to update at a high frequency.

Line of sight calculations are often performed as part of the collision detection process. This is particularly true for cameras as they are often used to determine if an object would leave the game environment, or if a door has closed between the player character and the camera.

When determining LOS, it is sometimes necessary to change the avoidance behavior of the camera according to the cause of obstruction. To resolve the LOS the camera might teleport or move differently according to whether dynamic game objects or static world geometry were the cause of the occlusion.

Although it may seem somewhat straightforward, the definition of line of sight can vary considerably depending on the game genre and specifics of both the character and the environment.

The most basic way to determine LOS is whether a simple ray cast from the camera position to the target object can be made without intersecting with world geometry (static or dynamic), other objects, and so forth. This gives an approximate answer, and in many cases, this may actually be sufficient. However, it will soon become apparent that a ray cast may not be a sufficient test when the target object is an animated character, as the extents of the character will vary considerably according to the current animation. Even a simple case of a character that is a sphere (*Metroid Prime*) may require several ray casts to truly determine LOS. The earlier section on occlusion discusses several of the available options that may be used for LOS testing.

Resolving line of sight problems

It is possible for the camera to be unable to move quickly enough to maintain LOS to the player character. This can happen when the collision volume of the camera is trapped in geometry. Many camera systems do not even use collision volumes for this reason. Naturally they still try to avoid leaving the environment or interpenetrating geometry whenever possible. Given that loss of LOS is a problem to be solved, what options are available? Let us examine some of the possibilities, each of which has varying aesthetic qualities.

Prevention

As with many things, prevention is certainly better than a cure. With absolute control over camera position via a pre-defined path or position, we can certainly ensure that occlusion does not occur, or is limited to partial occlusion within acceptable limits. With a more dynamic camera solution, there are other possibilities. Certainly, it is important that the camera is *predictive* regarding the position of its target object; this greatly influences the navigation of the camera through the game environment.

Graphical changes

In some cases it may be acceptable to allow occlusion to occur without having the camera react to the situation. One of the benefits of this approach is, of course, that the camera moves and reacts in the same manner as it would in other aspects of the game. Such continuity is welcome, but how would players control their character when it is occluded? The answer, of course, is to ensure that the character may still be viewed even when behind geometry or other game elements. There are a number of graphical approaches that may be adopted to assist the player. First, the obscuring geometry may be removed or have its rendering altered (e.g., transparency) to allow a view of the player character. Second, the player character may be rendered on top of the obscuring geometry, typically using a different approach such as a silhouette or an outline. *Super Mario Sunshine* [Mario02] is an example of the latter approach. This game also utilized additional graphical elements to illustrate that the character was behind geometry (e.g., fading out screen elements outside of a circular region around the character). A further approach is to indicate the position of the player character via other graphical elements (such as a *heads-up display*), particle systems, and so forth. It is often important, however, that the orientation of the character be discernable in addition to the position. Since third person viewpoints are an unusual experience because viewers are literally seeing themselves in the game, additional visual cues may be added without seeming inherently intrusive.

Finding a desirable position

Determination of a desirable position for the camera is dependent upon both the game genre and the standard properties of the camera. When attempting to find a position, it is usually necessary to employ a mechanism that evaluates a number of possibilities and ranks them according to both aesthetic and game play qualities. Naturally, we cannot choose a position that is outside of the regular game rendering geometry, nor can we choose a position that is also occluded from the character.

A common technique is to systematically move the prospective position as if it were rotating around the vertical axis formed by the world up-axis at the position of the player character. The radius of the camera positions may be fixed or changed, as may the elevation of the camera relative to the player character. A different approach would be to use visibility octree information, where a potentially visible set might yield similar positions. Once a position has been found, the camera is typically relocated immediately; this is usually referred to as *teleportation*.

Teleportation/jump cut

Instantaneous repositioning (*teleportation*) of the camera is a common method used to resolve LOS problems. The new position of the camera may be determined in a number of different ways, and care should be taken that the new position is both appropriate and understandable by the player. In cinematography, instantaneous motion and reorientation is referred to as a *jump cut*. One of the important established rules for camera cuts is the *30 degree rule*, as described in [Hawkins05] and [Arijon91]). The 30 degree rule essentially states that any cinematic cut must ensure that the difference in position and orientation of the camera after the cut be greater than 30 degrees; this difference ensures that the viewer perceives the change as deliberate rather than simply due to a "jumpy" camera. This rule does not apply when a cut results in a movement along the view direction of the previous camera, whether the movement is toward or away from the target object, although it is still necessary to ensure that the player understands the change. One way to underscore scene changes in general is the use of visual cues such as a "flash" or "brightness" effect. If these effects are synchronized with the scene change, the player understands that something significant has occurred.

One of the most obvious solutions is to move the camera along the current LOS vector (possibly in 2D terms so as to retain the same Z position in the world) until it reaches a position where the new LOS is now valid. This test is most easily achieved by casting a ray through the world from the target object back toward the current camera position. Once a collision position for this ray has been determined, a new position is generated on the same ray. The new camera position will be along the same ray (vector), but at a sufficient distance away from the collision point such that the camera near plane or collision volume (if it has one) will not be in a collision state.

Retaining control orientation

When finding the desirable position, it is important to retain the same *control reference frame* for the player if possible. The reason is that drastic repositioning of the camera is temporarily disorienting for the player so it is necessary to keep as many things constant as possible. The net result of changing the response of the character to the currently held controls is at best frustrating and at worst may cause the player to move their character into a potentially fatal situation. This problem was discussed in detail in Chapter 2.

Path generation

Another possible solution is to programmatically generate a motion path for the camera to follow until the occlusion is resolved. Since there are usually a myriad of permutations regarding the relative positions of the camera and player, combined with the complexities of the environment, this can prove to be a difficult task. Not only must the generated path avoid collisions (or interpenetration of the near plane) with the environment and other objects, but it must also satisfy a number of aesthetic constraints. Let us briefly examine some of the possibilities of using a generated path.

Follow character movement

Theoretically, we can use the recent motion path of the player character to determine a path that the camera may take. Clearly, the path must be (at least to a degree) legitimate for the player to move there, although there is no guarantee of a suitable camera position that would typically be positioned above and behind the player character. This technique requires some kind of round-robin storage of player positions over time. New points should only be added once a pre-determined movement distance threshold has been crossed from the last stored point. Once we have a record of the player movements, we can certainly determine situations to move the camera along this path. However, the position of the points is unlikely to be an aesthetically pleasing solution as it stands, especially regarding proximity to surfaces. It is possible to use ray casts or other exploratory tests from each of the player position "breadcrumbs" to find a more aesthetically pleasing path (e.g., doing vertical checks against collision geometry and thus judging render geometry proximity). This may not be entirely necessary if the stored positions were sufficiently raised from the surface yet within the player character collision volume (and thus they should be reasonably valid). If such a path is to be used to determine the camera motion, it is likely that the spacing of the breadcrumbs would be too great to use as-is without causing discontinuous motion. Alternatively, simple linear interpolation may be used within the stored positions to ensure a reasonably smooth motion path (although it will be subject to rapid direction changes). A further improvement is to use the stored positions as control points for spline path generation.

Ledge avoidance

One particularly difficult example of player occlusion is that of *ledges*. A ledge, for these purposes, is a section of world geometry that extends such that it is possible for a character to move from standing on top or above the ledge to a position underneath or below the ledge that would occlude itself from the game camera. A similar situation arises from a *cliff top*.

These situations typically arise when the player is able to move considerably quicker than the camera, and is able to get into a position where the camera is unable to reach its desired location without passing through the environment, or must move in such a way as to pass past the character and (possibly) perform a 180 degree rotation.

Most camera systems cannot deal well with the situation and will remain trapped above the ledge. Often their solution is to rely upon LOS fail-safes to resolve the problem, instantaneously moving the camera to a non-occluded position and often changing the control reference frame in the process. A more desirable solution would include anticipation of the occlusion combined with continuous gentle motion of the camera to a more amenable position while changing the control reference frame as little as possible.

The first step in resolving this situation is to be able to detect its occurrence. While it is possible to script camera solutions for all such situations, a more generalized approach would be beneficial. Here are some alternatives to resolve this situation.

- **Pre-define scripting solutions for all ledge situations.** This is expensive in terms of production time, since it requires designers to specify and control camera behaviors throughout the game. Game play requirements may negate the use of pre-determined camera solutions as well.
- **Use pre-defined solutions for difficult to resolve cases, especially in confined spaces.** Stationary cameras or spline paths may be used to ensure that the camera is able to move or position itself as required. By limiting the amount of custom solutions this solution becomes more feasible.
- **Teleport the camera to a new position if LOS fails due to the "ground" being between the camera and its target.** Determination of the "ground" is easier if the environmental surfaces are tagged by the type of material they represent, although this may also be achieved by the direction of the surface normal. Use of surface normal is not normally sufficient as a test; for that matter, even surface tagging has limitations. Additional tests involving the height of the player character from the ground beneath it will help resolve any questionable situations.
- **Use player movement hysteresis to provide an approximate path taken by the player character or target object.** This path may be used to generate a different path to be followed by the camera until it is able to retain a LOS to the target object. Generation of the camera path may be difficult given that the

player character is likely to continue moving (in a variety of directions), and that the surrounding geometry is variable. However, given the motion of the player it is possible to derive a cylinder of viable positions for the camera to move within; although this is no guarantee of an aesthetically pleasing result.

- **Interrogate the surrounding geometry to dynamically choose a path based on the last position at which the player was visible to the camera.** This position does give the camera system information about the approximate edge of the ledge or cliff that can be used to determine the clearance necessary for the camera path. Keep in mind that with path generation it is necessary to ensure that the camera does not pass close enough to geometry such that the near plane would intersect and cause rendering artifacts. Additionally, we wish to avoid orienting the camera vertically, and wish to reduce the amount of twist (i.e., rapid reorientation around the world up-axis) during the camera motion.

Vertical column avoidance

Vertical columns (or *pillars*) present a similar problem to ledge avoidance previously mentioned in that they are physical obstacles to be avoided by the camera. They can be particularly troublesome if encountered in large numbers within a confined space. Not only will the player character be frequently occluded, but also navigation through the columns (without collisions) is a difficult problem to solve. One difference about columns is that it can be desirable to allow the player character to be occluded *if* it is only for a moment as they pass behind a column. In such a situation, an aesthetically pleasing effect can happen if the character moves around the column and then comes into view without the camera having reacted adversely. There is a delicate balance between camera reaction to any occlusion and situations where the player character is only temporarily occluded. Predictive cameras will typically resolve this problem, as the future position of the character will be used to determine occlusion.

Pre-computed solutions

Pre-computation of camera solutions is attractive in several ways, one of which is the determinism of the camera motion and orientation. Pre-determined paths for camera motion are handcrafted solutions that are tested to ensure the player remains sufficiently visible in all possible positions. Creation of these paths is a time-consuming process. Instead of pre-defining entire paths, valid positions for the camera can be specified offline with the intent to interpolate motion between them at run-time. In a similar vein to linear paths, the camera is constrained to remain in positions that have been determined to give a clear view of the player character or game play elements. As described in Chapter 9, these positions may be treated as volumes (typically cylinders or spheres) to allow more flexibility over the camera position.

Avoiding loss of LOS

If it is not possible to prevent true loss of LOS (perhaps due to environmental complexities or game play requirements), we can compensate for this by attempting to avoid the situation entirely.

Instant movement

Move the camera instantaneously to a new position where LOS is available. When choosing the new position, care should be taken to try to retain the same control reference frame to minimize player confusion. This type of instant reorientation is normally undesirable but is sometimes preferable to total occlusion.

Fade out the obscuring geometry or objects

A popular choice, but it is dependent upon the ability to alpha-blend the environment or game objects. Usually the faded object remains partially visible, which may lead to rendering artifacts. The aesthetic problem is that any illusion of the game world is shattered by this "gamey" solution. Objects do not normally become transparent in our everyday experiences. Although this solution satisfies our game play concerns, it will remind players that they are not really within the game world. It is also necessary to ensure that the underlying world geometry beneath or behind the faded objects must be closed by solid faces.

Do not render obscuring geometry or objects at all

A simple solution for the occlusion is not rendering the obscuring object. However, not only would it seem unnatural that a part of the game world instantly disappears, but additionally it is necessary to ensure that the object would not rapidly change between being rendered and not being rendered if the player character moves back and forth behind the occluding object. The same is true of fading geometry. A simple timer set when the player occlusion state changes may be used to prevent both these problems where the current state of the object is not changed until the time has elapsed.

Render a graphical representation regardless of occlusion

This solution involves rendering a silhouette or other form of representation to show the target object overlaid on top of the obscuring geometry. If the player character is occluded, we can overlay a two-dimensional representation of the player character to indicate its relative position within the world. Unfortunately, this solution is also aesthetically unpleasing since it removes players from their immersion within the game world. Occasionally this type of rendering will fit the fiction of a particular game; for example, spy or stealth games could illustrate X-ray technology or fantasy games might simulate magical effects of seeing through walls.

Visibility pre-computation

In many games, it is common to have data structures that are used to optimize rendering of the game world, or alternatively to allow navigation of the game world by AI controlled objects. Since these data structures often contain information regarding partitioning of the world or spatial relationships between objects, they can sometimes be used to provide navigation information to the camera system. Obvious examples include binary-space partitioning trees (BSPs) and visibility octrees. These data structures are often used for collision or rendering purposes, and this data may often be shared between systems. These methods are discussed in detail in [Ericson05] and [Eberly04].

At a high level, visibility information can be used to determine a new position for the camera after a fail-safe condition has arisen. AI path finding data can be used to determine a camera path through the world, although usually with additional constraints regarding the proximity of the camera to geometry surfaces.

Fail-safes

Fail-safes, as the name suggests, are solutions to otherwise intractable problems that must be resolved immediately due to aesthetic or game play concerns.

The biggest problem for cameras in games is that of occlusion, with a close second being geometry obstruction avoidance. In either case, there are times where the camera is prevented from moving to a position presenting an appropriate view of the game, and this must be rectified immediately. A common example would be a situation where the player character moves through a small gap where the camera cannot follow, or perhaps a door closes between the camera and its target.

It is not necessary to check for all fail-safe conditions every update. We can divide them into three general categories: *per-update, frequent,* and *infrequent.*

Per-update

Some problems cannot be allowed to continue beyond even the current game update. Thus, we must check and resolve these problems every single game update.

- **Geometry interpenetration of the camera near plane.** This may occur with the static environment or dynamic objects such that it would cause untoward rendering effects such as polygon edges, viewing an area outside of the confines of the game world, and so forth. In this case, we need to re-evaluate the camera position and immediately teleport the camera to the new position. Alternatively, a previously known good position may be used if it meets enough of our desirable requirements for distance and elevation from the player character, as well as (preferably) retention of control reference frame. Obviously, it is preferred that this situation is prevented from occurring by having a sufficiently large collision volume for the camera (or an appropriate collision detection routine when determining the camera motion).

- **An invalid (non-normalized) camera transformation matrix.** This might be caused by successive numerical inaccuracies from additive rotations or inappropriate vector calculations such as non-normalized vectors. This would also include invalid orientations caused by roll around the camera forward vector. These problems are normally restricted to the rotation part of the camera transform. We can attempt to orthonormalize, or otherwise correct the matrix problems (e.g., reconstructing the matrix). Alternatively, we may simply revert to the last good rotation matrix. Since this is checked per frame, it is likely that the difference in world orientation is slight, and it will probably be close enough to the previously rendered frame. In cases where a completely new scene has been specified with an inappropriate transform we must attempt to correct the matrix, perhaps restoring an identity matrix with the translation from the new transform. If a reference frame is available (such as the player orientation in first person games), it may be used to construct the corrected matrix.

- **The camera is external to the game world.** Except for under specific (and deliberate) circumstances, the camera should not be able to move outside of the world geometry. A simple test should be able to determine if the camera is external to the game world. The only possible correction is to teleport the camera to a previously safe position or to determine a new appropriate position. There are certainly cases where this property is actually desirable, so a method to override it will need to be built into the camera scripting system.

- **Excessive rotation required around the world up-axis in one update.** In cases where the camera's up-axis is almost parallel to the word up-axis, it is necessary to limit the amount of rotation allowed per frame. This effect is sometimes referred to as twist, since the camera is forced to twist rapidly around an axis. It usually occurs when the target object for the camera passes above or below the current camera position.

Frequent

Other problems can be allowed to continue for several frames since they do not cause rendering issues or other untoward effects. However, after a short period of time they must be resolved due to game play concerns.

- **LOS to target object extremities.** Usually restricted to points on the main torso or legs of humanoid characters.
- **Distance from desired position.** If the camera is prevented from moving toward its desired position for an extended period (say, because of collision geometry placed inadvertently between the camera and its destination), it may indicate that the camera is unable to ever reach its target. Additionally, the target object may become so small (as viewed from the current camera position) as to become uncontrollable. While in many cases the LOS test may catch this unlikely event, it may prove wise to perform this additional safeguard.

Infrequent

Finally, there are some problems that affect the aesthetic quality, or game play, but only if they continue for an extended period. Of course, the definition of an extended period is somewhat fluid and genre dependent. In many cases this only amounts to a couple of seconds, long enough to allow the camera system an opportunity to resolve the problem without instantaneous camera movement.

- **Significant occlusion of player character (third person view only).** As mentioned earlier in this chapter, a clear view is necessary for the player to see and deliberately control the player character.

- **Camera distance from target is too far.** Like cases where the camera position is too far from its desired position, this leads to the target being too small on screen or the rendering having to use a field of view that is too narrow, both of which would adversely affect player control.

Fail-safe resolution

Once a fail-safe condition has been triggered, the most usual resolution is to move the camera immediately to a newly determined safe position. Most often this is achieved via a jump cut, as discussed previously. An alternative solution is to move the camera back through a list of known good positions until it is at a point that satisfies the visibility requirements. However, this latter method is not guaranteed to find a good solution, nor is it necessarily still true that the previous positions of the camera equate to valid positions (e.g., objects may have subsequently moved).

■ SUMMARY

This chapter has discussed the similarities between game cameras and AI game objects in several ways. Both game cameras and AI game objects must be navigated through complex environments while avoiding collision or motions that would appear incorrect and disrupt the player's sense of immersion. Game cameras are burdened with an additional requirement in that they have to constantly ensure they have an unobstructed view of the player character or other target objects even as all the other game objects can get in the way. Great care must be used when designing camera solutions that strike a fine balance between an immersive view of the game environment and a simple unobstructed shot of the player character that does not hinder the game play experience.

Chapter 9

Motion and collision

In the previous two chapters, we discussed two major components of camera movement, namely the determination of the desired position and navigation toward that position. The third component of camera movement is the actual *motion* of the camera from its current position toward the desired position, irrespective of how that position was determined. This chapter details a collection of methods that may be used to move the camera position over time, with a mind to ensuring that the motion is smooth and continuous, as appropriate. During the process of moving the camera, it may be necessary to determine (and usually prevent) its interpenetration with the game environment or other game objects. This process is usually referred to as *collision detection* but perhaps a more important subject is that of *collision avoidance.* Both topics are discussed later in this chapter.

CAMERA MOVEMENT SEQUENCE

Once we have calculated a desired position for the camera (as detailed in Chapter 7), there are several ways to move the camera to try and achieve it. Physical motion of the camera not only refers to the velocity at which the camera moves through the world, but also the acceleration and deceleration of the camera. It is preferable that the motion of the camera be continuous (i.e., without sudden jumps in position) and that changes to its velocity are smooth.

The speed of the camera is often directly related to that of the target object, yet sudden motion or changes in velocity of the target should not usually be reflected in a third person camera (for a first person camera the view is usually locked to a position relative to the player character). This can present something of a dilemma. How do we maintain smooth motion when the target character accelerates (potentially rapidly) away from the camera, possibly leaving the camera behind? Moreover, how do we prevent the camera from getting too close to (or even overshooting) the character when it stops moving?

Another important consideration is *constraints;* that is, restricting motion according to a set of designer specified limits, such as a three-dimensional volume or distance from a target object. By treating the camera motion as a series of layered constraints (i.e., combined according to priorities), it is possible to mix and match camera motion behaviors to meet varying requirements. However, these same desirable constraints may conflict with the requirement of keeping the camera within a reasonable distance of the target object.

How then should camera motion be applied? We can break down this process into several discrete steps, although some of these may not be applicable to all forms of camera behaviors.

- Determine the desired position.
- Constrain the desired position accordingly.
- Generate a prospective movement toward the desired position.
- Test to see if the prospective movement will cause collision (optional).
- Resolve the collision (optional).
- Generate and validate an alternative movement (optional if first move fails).
- Move the camera to the new position.

The application of these steps is, of course, dependent upon the desired behavior of the camera and whether it should consider potential collisions. Since camera motion is often based upon the movement of a target object (frequently the player character), let us examine some of the ways in which this relationship may affect camera motion.

Character motion

The motion of the target object (such as the player character) often has a direct effect on the motion of the camera, usually because of the corresponding required changes to the desired position of the camera. Additionally, certain reorientations of the character (rapid or instantaneous ones) may require drastic motion by the camera. Let us re-examine how motion of the player character influences both first and third person cameras.

First person cameras

First person cameras are, by definition, somewhat locked to the position of the player character. As the character moves, the camera moves in concert with it, offset to a position that is normally akin to the view from the "eyes" of the character.

The first thing to note about this is that depending on the field of view and aspect ratio of the viewport, the actual position of the camera will probably not correspond to that of the "eye position" of the model representing the character. This may be problematic when handling transitions from third person camera viewpoints into first person. If the final position of the first person camera is disjoint from the physical position of the "head," the motion of the transition will end at a position that clearly does not seem correct (even though the transition will be smooth). Alternatively, if the transition is made so that it is graphically correct (i.e., ending at the physical position that might be expected), there will be an instantaneous jump to the correct first person camera position once the transition is complete. Possible solutions are discussed in Chapter 10.

Additionally, any on-screen representation of the player (such as a weapon or arm) will likely not be positioned correctly with respect to the player model. Nor will the scale of objects representing the player necessarily match those of the rest of the game. This is especially true when rendering vehicle cockpits. This means that additional models or animations may be required for any third person view of the character (e.g., in cinematic sequences or multi-player games).

Vertical motion of the character imparted by its traversal across the world geometry can sometimes cause corresponding vertical jitter in the camera. This is typically undesirable because the camera motion is discontinuous and thus distracting to the viewer. This problem may be alleviated by damping the vertical motion of the camera over time. Under certain conditions, this damping will sometimes need to be disabled to ensure correct camera motion relative to the player. Obvious examples include external forces moving the player (e.g., elevators), cinematic sequences, and transition situations (e.g., between first and third person cameras).

Third person cameras

Third person cameras are directly affected by character motion in a variety of ways. One of the initial problems to deal with is that of *lag*.

TECHNICAL

A typical damping scheme for avoiding unwanted noise in the vertical motion of the camera is to simply limit the amount of motion allowed per update. A basic implementation might look something like this:

```
float const kMaxZMotionPerSecond(0.25f);
  // desired maximum motion
float zMotion = newPosition.GetZ() – oldPosition.GetZ();
float const maxZMotion = kMaxZMotionPerSecond * deltaTime;
zMotion = Math::Limit(zMotion, maxZMotion);
newPosition.SetZ(oldPosition.GetZ() + zMotion);
```

This smoothing is relatively harsh; the amount of vertical motion applied is constant (i.e., no acceleration or deceleration) and thus will possibly have discontinuities at the start and end of the vertical motion. An alternative is to use a critically damped spring or PID controller. Spring and PID controller implementations are covered in detail in Chapter 10, but a typical usage might be as follows:

```
float const zMotion = newPosition.GetZ() -
  oldPosition. GetZ();
verticalSpring.SetLength(AbsF(zMotion));
  // update the spring length
// Here the target spring length is zero, and need not
// be set each time. Typically the spring length is
// unsigned, so that must be dealt with.
// perform the convergence
float const newZMotion = verticalSpring.Update(deltaTime);
if (zMotion > 0.0f)
  newPosition.SetZ(newPosition.GetZ() – newZMotion);
else
  newPosition.SetZ(newPosition.GetZ() + newZMotion);
```

Note that when using a spring or other convergence method, the new vertical position is determined by calculating the new spring length and then working back from the target coordinate toward the current value. The spring itself is unsigned and merely represents a distance from the desired position. In many camera situations, this same technique applies, especially since (as with this example) we are typically interested in using critically damped convergence techniques.

Positional lag in many ways is desirable because it produces a more natural feel to the camera, mostly because it emphasizes the acceleration or deceleration of the character. It also has similarities to the motion of cameras in traditional film, which usually exhibit smooth acceleration and deceleration when *tracking* or *dollying*. However, the amount of lag allowed should be minimal since not only will the player character move too far from the camera to be easily understandable, but the navigation of the camera through the environment will become potentially much more difficult and the likelihood of occlusion will increase.

Rapid rotation of the player character can cause problems with cameras that are required to maintain a position "behind" the character (e.g., as an aid to aiming). Here the camera is often required to move around an arc to maintain a desired distance away from the character.

One of the more demanding problems with third person cameras is confined environments, especially when the player character forces the camera into a corner or wherever the geometry is so complex it is impossible for the camera to reach its desired position. Geometry avoidance is a large topic and will be discussed separately.

Rapid acceleration or direction changes by the player character can cause enormous problems for camera systems. Since we often prefer to maintain smooth camera motion, rapid changes in the player are directly opposed to this. If the camera reacts too slowly, then it may be left behind or interpenetrated by the character. Too quick and the camera motion imparts a whole-scene change that is distracting.

How then, do we keep camera motion smooth, and yet avoid these problems? Limiting player acceleration is one potential solution, although it may conflict with the game design. Locking camera motion to the player is possible in limited situations (at least to avoid interpenetration of the camera as the character moves toward it) but may cause jitter.

We must cope with the problems of cameras accelerating slower than the player character (also known as *motion lag*), or cameras that decelerate slower than the player character (*overshooting*).

Movement methods

We will now discuss some of the main movement methods that are available to change the position of the camera over time.

Instantaneous motion

As might be guessed, this consists of an instantaneous movement of the camera to a new location within the world. This type of movement is often required when repositioning the player character after a non-interactive movie sequence. Indeed, all such instant camera motion may be considered a *jump cut*. This implies that it is preferable to observe the *30 degree rule* (see Chapter 4) when moving the camera in this manner. Such aesthetic consideration is normally applied at the desired position determination stage rather than for the actual motion, however.

TECHNICAL

Here are some points to consider when moving the camera instantaneously.

- It may be desirable to have the look-at position optionally recalculated from the new position, depending on its determination method. The orientation may be similarly recalculated.
- It may be necessary to check the validity of the target position to ensure that the camera is not too close to the world geometry, not inside an object, etc. These considerations are more likely to be a part of the desired position determination, of course.
- Retain the previous control reference frame if possible, and then interpolate to the new reference frame over time. Control reference frames were discussed in detail in Chapter 2.
- It is wise to have a function that can be called to perform this movement so that all of the appropriate housekeeping operations can be grouped together, rather than directly updating the transformation matrix of the camera at each instance of usage. Some types of camera behavior require the use of external objects that move in relation to the main camera object, so these must also be updated accordingly if the camera is repositioned within the game world.
- If *Doppler effects* are calculated based upon the speed of the camera, the maximum speed should be clamped to avoid problems when instantly moving the camera.

Locked

The camera position is locked to that of the desired position (i.e., is set to that value every update, even if it changes drastically or in an erratic fashion), and thus may be considered a form of instantaneous motion as previously mentioned. This can be beneficial in a number of cases (e.g., path-constrained cameras), but has some side effects that can be undesirable. Discontinuous motion of the desired position will obviously be reflected in the motion of the camera, causing visual artifacts, since the whole scene will change accordingly. Sometimes it is required that only one axis of motion be locked to the desired position, typically the vertical axis.

If the desired position is tied to that of the player character, then even the slightest motion (or possibly orientation change) of the character imparts motion to the camera. For first person camera views, this is typically the desired behavior. There may still be a need to damp vertical motion under certain circumstances, such as crossing uneven terrain. For external views of the player character, the relative motion of the camera when locked to the desired position may cause camera jitter. It also has an unnatural feel in that the camera seems to be fixed on the end of a stiff rod relative to the character. The result is somewhat disconcerting to the player and may even induce nausea, especially with inconsistent update rates.

There are examples where moving the camera directly to its desired position is appropriate. Within confined spaces, it is imperative that the player character should not overtake the camera (or interpenetrate the camera for that matter). If the camera motion position is locked relative to that of the target object, this can overcome this problem, at the cost of being susceptible to every minor motion of the player character. Alternatively, a portion of the target object velocity may be added to that of the camera to help prevent interpenetration. The unwanted jitter imparted by the player character's motion may be completely avoided by using a path-constrained camera. Locking the motion of such a camera to its desired position should ensure that the camera is neither left behind, nor interpenetrates the target object. This is assuming that the determination of the desired position avoids such a situation.

In many third person cameras, it is preferable to introduce an element of delay into the camera's response to the motion of the player character. One such method is the *proportional controller*.

Proportional controller

A camera position is typically updated by directly altering the translation component of the camera object's transformation matrix. There may be some damping or acceleration supplied but it is often applied in an ad hoc manner (e.g., no physical simulation of mass or friction). Without any velocity damping, the camera would come to an abrupt halt once the desired position was reached, and would accelerate instantaneously providing an unnatural and discontinuous sensation of motion.

Many games implement camera motion using a *proportional controller*, possibly without considering it in those terms. Essentially, a proportional controller modifies the amount of motion imparted to the camera depending upon one or more desired characteristics of the positional or angular relationship of the camera to the desired position or orientation. Most often this is calculated according to the distance of the camera from the desired position, so that as the camera approaches the desired position, its velocity is linearly scaled to zero thus ensuring a smooth deceleration (or *approach*).

TECHNICAL

A typical proportional controller might be implemented in this manner.

```
Vec3 const deltaPosition = desiredPosition –
  currentPosition;
// the distance at which velocity damping is applied
float const kDampDistance(5.0f);
float const K = Math::Limit(deltaPosition.Magnitude()/
  kDampDistance, 1.0f);
  // Limit constant to 0..1 based on distance
Vec3 const cameraVelocity = deltaPosition.AsNormalized()
  * K;
Vec3 const newPosition = currentPosition +
  cameraVelocity * deltaTime;
```

Note that the equations include *deltaTime* to cope with indeterminate update rates; this corresponds to the amount of time elapsed since the previous update. The constant *K* determines the velocity of the motion, which is governed by the distance to the desired position.

While this method of movement has some beneficial characteristics in the approach to a stationary target position (e.g., a smooth approach), it does not deal well with movement of the target position. Since the velocity is proportional to the distance, as the target object moves away from the camera, the motion of the camera is initially smooth but soon becomes more dramatic. In the worst case of switching target objects, the camera will be forced to suddenly change its velocity; this effect can be reduced by limiting the acceleration of the camera. Unfortunately, this leads to the camera often overshooting its desired position since it simply cannot decelerate quickly enough. The camera may also be left behind by the target object.

TECHNICAL

As mentioned previously, we can help solve the problem of the camera being left behind by adding a portion of the target object's velocity into the original equation. Replacing the last two lines of the previous code block:

```
// unless we can obtain it directly from the object itself
Vec3 targetVelocity = (desiredPosition –
  previousDesiredPosition) /deltaTime;
Vec3 cameraVelocity = (deltaPosition.AsNormalized() * K *
  deltaTime) + (targetVelocity * T);
```

Note that we can vary the amount of target velocity (via the constant, *T*) by making it proportional to the acceleration of the target, to cope better with rapid acceleration changes of the target. Similarly, *T* might be increased if the target object is moving toward the camera itself.

We can now control the camera velocity proportionally to its target, but unfortunately, it will be very susceptible to changes in the target velocity. To have smooth motion we need to accelerate the camera over time with a limiter to provide some degree of lag in the motion. This lag provides a more natural feel to the camera motion.

```
float const acceleration = Math::Limit( (desiredVelocity –
  currentVelocity), kMaxAcceleration);
  // may need an accel limit
Vec3 const currentVelocity += acceleration * deltaTime;
Vec3 const desiredPosition = currentPosition +
  (currentVelocity * deltaTime);
```

Physical simulations

A full description of a physical simulation solution to camera motion is well beyond the scope of this book, and the reader is referred to [Eberly03]. Nonetheless, the basic notion may be described simply.

The camera object is moved according to a *Newtonian* or other physical simulation that resolves forces acting upon objects in the game. Its movement is calculated using velocity and acceleration of a rigid body, but often does not involve rotational forces, as direct orientation control is usually required to ensure adequate framing of game objects (except when simulating human operation of the camera, perhaps). Collision determination and response are applied as if the camera is an object "floating" in space. Gravitational forces, however, are usually undesirable for the camera although vertical damping may be effective in reducing jitter caused by irregular geometry traversed by the target object. Additionally there are other constraints applicable specifically to the camera (e.g., height above terrain, proximity to a water plane, etc.) and/or constraints placed upon the calculation of the desired position (e.g., distance from the target object).

Physics simulations are inherently CPU intensive but with modern processors, running at reasonably high clock rates, this usage is becoming more commonplace. Note that by treating the camera as a physics object it is necessary to avoid other physics objects interacting with the camera, as their collisions cannot be allowed to move or reorient the camera. This can be easily achieved by not allowing the camera to interact with other physics-driven game objects. That said, it is typically the case that we do not wish other objects to move close to the camera. This may be achieved in several ways, including having the camera exert forces on non-player game objects (e.g., debris or particle systems). Alternatively, the camera may exert an influence on the determination of AI path finding algorithms. Flocking and avoidance algorithms such as *Boids* initially put forward by [Reynolds87] often allow game objects to directly influence other objects in this manner. Thus, AI-driven objects can be made to avoid the camera with repulsive forces to avoid direct interpenetration of the camera. They may also be applied to reduce the chances of occlusion of the target object. This approach is normally avoided as it tends to have a greater impact on game play. However, by giving game objects knowledge of the camera we are influencing actual game play decisions. If the camera position is under control of the player then it is possible for game play to be consciously altered by the player. Ideally, the camera is merely an observer of the game and we would prefer that the camera avoid game objects.

A physical simulation is often useful if we wish the camera to slide along surfaces of the collision mesh. While this is desirable behavior, it is dependent upon construction of the collision geometry; we must ensure that the surfaces allow the camera to slide easily along them. Additionally, it becomes possible for the camera to be stuck on collision geometry, which is usually undesirable. These problems may be minimized by judicious construction of the collision mesh. Although collision meshes are typically simplified for performance concerns, they should also be chamfered and otherwise adjusted to facilitate better motion of the player character through the environment. This is certainly true regardless of the physical simulation used, as it will also facilitate smoother motion of the camera itself. This topic and alternatives to physical simulation for camera collisions are discussed later in this chapter.

Springs

A common problem with camera motion is overshooting the desired position. This usually happens with *proportional controller* movement schemes when the target position is moving toward the camera or stops suddenly (i.e., reducing the distance between the camera and its target faster than the camera can decelerate). This may result in an undesirable oscillation of the camera around its desired position.

One way to restrict or eliminate this oscillation of the camera position is to control the motion of the camera through *springs*. When using springs, regardless of implementation, it is very important that they not be too stiff to retain an "organic" feel to the game camera. Rod-like motion of a third person camera compared to its target object is rarely desirable, although unfortunately in common usage. A balance must be kept between the acceleration/deceleration rate of the camera and that of the target object or position. Additionally, we do not want the camera to overshoot the target object, nor do we want its motion to be suddenly halted if the camera should end up too close to, or too far from, its target. What we really desire is *critical damping* of the camera motion with respect to its desired position.

Critical damping means that there is no overshooting of the target, regardless of its movement. This can be difficult to achieve in practice: ask anyone in the process control industry (e.g., designers of thermostats and cruise control systems). Springs are sometimes implemented using *PID controllers* (see the following section), and can be combined with proportional controllers in situations where the player character rapidly accelerates. Since this implementation has a good arrival characteristic (no overshooting), we can assist the exit characteristic by applying a portion of the player velocity to the camera velocity, in the same manner as proportional controllers mentioned previously.

A simple form of spring is described in Chapter 10, but the usage of springs matches that of PID controllers as shown next.

PID controllers

Proportional integral derivative (PID) *controllers* are common in process control industries where they are used to control fluid flow control valves, thermostats, braking systems, etc. They work by applying feedback into the controller to reduce the amount of error between the current value and the desired value. As such we can use them to form a virtual spring, especially when coupled with the concept of *critical damping*.

Usually springs oscillate around a rest position, but this oscillation is undesirable for most game camera purposes. We would like, ideally, to close in on our desired value (usually distance, but not necessarily so) without any overshooting whatsoever. If the controller exhibits this behavior, it may be considered critically damped. PID controllers can provide this. They are covered in detail in Chapter 10. We can treat PID controllers in exactly the same way as springs for implementation purposes; typically the set point for the PID controller matches a desired distance or angle value and each update brings us closer to that goal. Before performing the update function it is necessary to set the current value held within the PID controller to match any changes that may have occurred due to other outside influences (e.g., movement of the target object changing the distance to the camera).

TECHNICAL

Here is an example of the logic used with a PID controller when determining the distance of the camera from its desired position. The actual implementation of the controller is described in Chapter 10; here we are only concerned with its usage:

```
Vec3 const currentDelta = currentPosition -
  desiredPosition;
float const currentDistance = currentDelta.Magnitude();
float const newDistance = PIDController.Update(
  desiredDistance, currentDistance, deltaTime);
Vec3 const currentPosition = desiredPosition +
  (currentDelta.AsNormalized() * newDistance);
```

The `Update()` function of the *PID Controller* takes three parameters: the *set point* (or desired value, which may have changed since the last calculation), the *current value*, and the time interval since the previous update. We use the returned distance value to calculate the new position away from the desired position.

Circular movement

Just as it is possible to specify the desired position of the camera as angular quantities relative to a target object or other reference frame, the same may also be applied to the actual motion of the camera. A typical use of circular movement is to provide a third person camera free-look capability, with the camera moving in a horizontal arc around the player character (although this may be combined with some vertical motion effectively moving the camera across the surface of a cylinder or sphere). In many cases, it is not strictly necessary to move the camera in a true arc. If the desired position is sufficiently close to the current position, a linear motion will approximate the same motion. If the camera is required to retain a position relative to the forward direction of the target object (yet only move in an arc, rather than a chord across the circular path), then angular motion is a reasonable solution.

In this method, the displacement of the camera is calculated as an angle between the vectors formed from the reference point to both the camera and its desired position.

The new position of the camera is determined by reducing this displacement according to the angular velocity of the camera. There are two main methods for calculating the angular velocity: *constant angular velocity* (CAV) and *constant linear velocity* (CLV).

Constant angular velocity

With the CAV method, the camera moves by the same angular component (whether damped or not) irrespective of its radius around the rotation point. Therefore, the camera will take the same amount of time to complete a full rotation and will cover a greater distance per frame proportional to its radius from the rotation point.

Constant linear velocity

As might be expected, CLV motion requires the camera to move at a constant distance per second; that is, the arc length inscribed by the camera is constant irrespective of the radius from the rotation point. The consequence of this is that the motion is subjectively faster as the camera approaches the rotation point. Usually it is necessary to limit the angular motion in this case to avoid extremely rapid rotation when the circumference of the inscribed arc is close to or smaller than the movement distance.

Angular motion of the camera around the player character will seem abrupt if there is no acceleration or deceleration applied to it, even when directly manipulated by the player. At the very least, a *proportional controller* may be applied to smooth the camera motion as it approaches the target position.

TECHNICAL

A typical implementation of moving a camera by constant angular velocity might be:

```
Vec3 cameraBearing = Vec3(currentPosition -
  referencePoint); // assumed not coincident
Vec3 desiredBearing = Vec3(desiredPosition -
  referencePoint); // similarly
float const radius = cameraBearing.Magnitude();
  // may be known
cameraBearing.Normalize(); // assumes this is valid
desiredBearing.Normalize(); // similarly
float const angularMotion = angularVelocity * deltaTime;
  // rads/update
Quat const q = Quat::ShortestRotationArcClamped(
  cameraBearing, desiredBearing, angularMotion);
  // See [Melax00] for this
Vec3 const newBearing = q * cameraBearing;
  // rotate the original bearing
Vec3 const newPosition = referencePoint +
  (newBearing * radius);
```

There are several things to note about this implementation. First, it is assumed that `cameraBearing` and `desiredBearing` form the plane of rotation of the camera. Secondly, it uses quaternions to perform the determination of the new camera position. The `ShortestRotationArcClamped()` function is based on the `RotationArc()` function shown in [Melax00]. The original function produces a quaternion equivalent to rotating the first vector parameter onto the second vector parameter. One particularly beneficial result is that the quaternion produced retains the up-vector and does not cancel roll in the manner that a `LookAt()` function might. Additionally, this version allows the amount of rotation to be restricted to the maximum angle specified by the third parameter.

Alternatively, an implementation of constant linear velocity might be as follows:

```
Vec3 cameraBearing = Vec3(currentPosition -
  referencePoint); // assumed not coincident
Vec3 desiredBearing = Vec3(desiredPosition -
  referencePoint); // similarly
float const radius = cameraBearing.Magnitude();
  // may be known
cameraBearing.Normalize();
```

```
desiredBearing.Normalize();
float const arcLength = angularVelocity * deltaTime;
  // units/ update
// since arc length = r * cos(angle) we can convert it
// back into an angle
float const angularMotion = acosf(arcLength/radius);
Quat const q = Quat::ShortestRotationArcClamped(
  cameraBearing, desiredBearing, angularMotion);
Vec3 const newBearing = q * cameraBearing;
  // rotate the original bearing
Vec3 const newPosition = referencePoint +
  (newBearing * radius);
```

In both of these examples, the vertical position of the camera may be determined separately if so desired. The intention with this type of camera is often to control motion in the horizontal plane irrespective of vertical motion. If it is desired that the camera motion be constrained to the surface of a sphere, these same functions will function correctly; only the determination of the desired position changes.

Interpolation

When changing camera behaviors, it is often desirable to smoothly change between the various properties of cameras, and one of the more influential is camera velocity. Given that these cameras might be radically different in determination of their position over time, it can sometimes be difficult to produce a smooth interpolation. Here we are concerned with interpolating between the velocities of two cameras, and more important, their acceleration rates.

Interpolation of movement is usually based on a straight linear path between two waypoints or positions in the world. Although the motion is usually in a straight line, it need not be in a linear fashion with respect to the distance covered over time. By using an *interpolation function* to map time into position between the camera positions (e.g., a sine curve or cubic polynomial such as a Bézier curve) it is possible to have non-linear motion. Once non-linear motion is possible, we can accelerate and decelerate the camera to ensure a smooth start and end to its motion. To avoid discontinuities at the beginning and end of the interpolation it is necessary to match *accelerations* rather than merely velocities.

The actual motion between the cameras used by the interpolation need not be in a straight line. Depending on the situation, a spline path may be generated between the current camera position and the desired camera position and then constant (or non-linear) velocity is used along that path. This type of interpolation is best used when the cameras are both stationary or have similar velocities. Typical examples would include transitions between first and third person cameras, or between free-form third person cameras and path-constrained cameras.

Interpolation between the current camera position and a moving target position presents a more difficult prospect, as a strictly linear movement is not possible. This problem and others are covered in Chapter 10.

Smoothing and damping techniques

One important aspect of camera movement (or reorientation for that matter) is keeping the motion continuous and smooth. Of course, the problem with limiting camera acceleration to achieve this is that the character may be able to accelerate faster than the camera; the same may also be true of deceleration. Regardless, smoothing and damping techniques are often applied to the camera velocity so its motion remains smooth irrespective of the target object's motion or acceleration.

Damping methods often include the use of *ease functions*. These are methods to map an input value (normally in the range 0 to 1) back into the same range but in a non-linear fashion such that the derivatives of the curve are zero at the start and end of the range. These functions are sometimes referred to as *S curves* or *bump functions*, depending on their shape.

Motion damping

There are occasions where it is prudent to delay or reduce the motion of the camera to prevent discontinuous or rapid movement that would be distracting to the viewer. Sometimes this functionality is built into the determination of the desired position, or alternatively, into the movement characteristics of the camera (especially if the desired position is changing in a discontinuous manner). In this way, the amount of motion applied to the camera toward its desired position may be reduced according to various outside influences, such as proximity to the desired position.

Damping need not be applied to all axes of motion simultaneously, however. One of the most distracting forms of discontinuous camera motion might be that of vertical movement. A good example of this is a typical first person game. As the player character moves through the world, they will walk over small obstructions and variances in the world geometry. Rather than having the camera bob up and down in a distracting fashion (matching the player movement), we can damp the vertical component of the camera even though it is in the first person genre. This damping can be applied either in world space or simply as an adjunct to the camera transform used for rendering (cf. *camera shakers*).

Sometimes mild vertical camera movement or "bobbing" (via a sine wave or similar motion shape) is used as a visual cue to enhance the feeling that a player is running through the world. It may induce a mild (or not so mild) form of motion sickness in some players, so if you insist on having this visual cue in the game, provide a method by which the player can permanently disable it. Care must also be taken that such camera movement does not cause the camera to approach too close to render geometry.

It is also true of third person cameras that drastic vertical motion can be very disorienting, so in these cases it is also desirable to limit the vertical velocity of the camera. Third person cameras will typically have damping applied to vertical motion to filter out small variations in the desired position. There are cases, though, when it is not appropriate to damp the vertical motion, or more accurately, that additional vertical motion needs to be applied. A case in point is moving platforms. Typically, when an outside force is moving the target object, such as a platform or elevator, we need to apply the same force to the camera to ensure that camera motion calculations are applied in a space local to that of the target object.

TECHNICAL

The application of outside forces on the camera to match those of the target object must be handled carefully. It may be necessary, for example, to apply the same displacement to a motion path or other position determination method. One frequently used method is to have the camera retain positional information about its target object so that any movement of the target may be replicated in the camera or its associated desired position. It is important, of course, that the camera is updated after the target object to ensure the displacement is correctly calculated.

Motion filters

In addition to damping, there are other types of filter that may be applied to camera motion. One typical example is the use of filters to remove unwanted noise or minor oscillation in the motion of the camera. Sometimes this noise is generated by the game controller, by slight motion of the player character due to inaccuracies in the physical simulation, or perhaps by variations in the determination of the desired position. Regardless, such minor variances should not be reflected in the motion of the camera. One possible solution is to use a *low pass filter* to remove unwanted motion above a chosen frequency threshold (i.e., to remove small, high frequency changes). More involved solutions may store data about recent camera motion and use this history to determine how much of the desired motion to impart. These filters must be applied carefully as they may have a side effect of reducing responsiveness of the camera and perhaps causing minor discontinuities as the camera motion finally becomes large enough to exceed the threshold.

Some types of movement methods already include elements of filtering or damping, but even so it is often useful to apply a layer of filtering independent of the actual movement method to account for outside influences.

TECHNICAL

A filter may be as simple as ignoring desired movement below a threshold, for example:

```
Vec3 const movementDelta = newPosition –
  currentPosition;
if (movementDelta.Magnitude() > kMovementThreshold)
{
  currentPosition = newPosition; // a very crude filter
} else
{
  // ignoring small changes may cause the camera never to
  // move at all!
}
```

More complex filters often use feedback from the newly determined (i.e., filtered) position as a part of the next determination and are thus known as feedback controllers. PID controllers as discussed in Chapter 10 are an example; others would include *finite impulse response* (FIR) and *infinite impulse response* (IIR) filters, both of which are common in digital signal processing.

Chapter 10 discusses these in detail. Here is an example of how they might be used:

```
Vec3 const movementDelta = newPosition -
  currentPosition;
if (!close_enough(movementDelta, Vec3::Zero())
  // must be valid movement
{
   float distance = movementDelta.Magnitude();
     // desired distance
   distance = mMovementFilter.Update(distance);
     // IIR or FIR filter, etc.
   currentPosition += movementDelta.AsNormalized() *
     distance;
}
```

Similar approaches may be taken using filters applied to the camera velocity rather than the distance moved by the camera.

Motion constraints

There are times when it is necessary to restrict the positioning (and therefore the motion) of the camera. Often this is to prevent untoward graphical effects caused by the camera interpenetrating rendering geometry. Sometimes it is required to ensure that a particular game play element remains visible (or hidden), or to ensure that the camera remains within the bounds of the game environment. More often than not, these constraints may be applied within the determination of the desired position for a camera, and as such are often referred to as *soft constraints*. However, occasionally it is vital to prevent the camera from moving without affecting the desired position. In the latter case, these constraints are applied after all position determination and actual motion have been applied, thus ensuring the actual camera position remains constrained. These are *hard constraints*.

Vertical motion constraint

Here is an example of hard motion constraints that may be applied to first or third person cameras. If the player character is able to submerge beneath water or some other representative render surface mesh, we would not wish the surface geometry to interpenetrate the camera's near plane. If this happens, we will see hard polygon edges as they are clipped, which would look unprofessional to say the least.

Additionally, if full screen rendering effects are to be applied to simulate the immersion of the camera, we wish to avoid these effects toggling on and off if the desired position of the camera moves rapidly back and forth across the water surface boundary. These problems may be solved by preventing the camera from moving too close to the surface (in the vertical world axis). The camera must retain its vertical coordinate until the desired position has moved outside of the range. This will cause discontinuous motion for one frame as the camera cuts to a new position (i.e., from above the plane to below the plane or *vice versa*), but it is preferable to rendering artifacts caused by the camera interpenetrating the water plane.

In this particular case, it might be possible to avoid the motion discontinuity by moving the rendering plane of the water surface away from the camera and thus allowing the camera to move smoothly (in effect, the reversal of this implementation with the water surface Z position moving to maintain a distance from the camera).

TECHNICAL

Prevention of camera motion in this manner may be generalized into a series of constraints, applied according to a prioritized order if necessary. Motion constraints are typically applied to avoid unwanted graphical effects such as geometry interpenetration (as in this case); they differ from navigation constraints in that they absolutely affect the current position of the camera rather than its desired position. A possible implementation of the water plane avoidance constraint might be as follows:

```
float const kMinimumZDistance(0.1f);
  // as close to the plane as possible
float const zDistance(currentPosition.GetZ() -
  waterPlane.GetZ());
  // i.e. from the plane toward our position
if (fabs(zDistance) < kMinimumZDistance)
{
  currentPosition.SetZ(waterPlane.GetZ() +
    Math::Sign(zDistance) * kMinimumZDistance);
}
```

Once again, we work back from the plane toward the current camera vertical position in a similar manner to the damping method previously mentioned. The difference here is that the constraint must be maintained. Once the desired position is no longer close to the surface, this may result in a discontinuous movement of the camera for one update. Unfortunately, this cannot be avoided since the camera must cross the plane to reach the new required position. The effect may be minimized if it is combined with graphical effects to hide the instantaneous motion (perhaps, in this case, a 2D "splash" effect overlaid on top of the rendered scene). This type of constraint might be considered as a special case of planar constraints as detailed later in this chapter. The *Metroid Prime* series of games utilized these types of motion constraint.

Render geometry proximity

Another potential problem is that the camera has to be prevented from moving too close to the render geometry of the world. Once again, the near plane of the view frustum may interpenetrate the render geometry causing unsightly effects. For first person camera scenes, the collision volume of the character is typically larger than that of the distance of the near plane from the first person camera, thus preventing problems of this nature. However, be aware that depending on the field of view and aspect ratio chosen, it is entirely possible for the character to move close enough to cause parts of the environment to be clipped inappropriately. Also, watch out for the player weapon/arm extending beyond the collision volume of the player character and interpenetrating geometry. This last problem may be alleviated by rendering the weapon/arm on top of all other scene elements but may lead to additional problems regarding the position of the firing point of the weapon (i.e., being inside the collision geometry).

Third person cameras may exhibit similar problems, although depending upon the type of camera positioning it is sometimes harder for a player to cause this behavior. If the camera position is absolutely controlled (e.g., with a path-constrained camera) then this problem should be unlikely to occur (unless game objects interpenetrate the camera). It is possible to rely upon the collision volume of the camera to prevent this problem. This subject is covered later in the chapter.

Distance constraints

Third person cameras sometimes have difficulty coping with rapid acceleration of the target object, as noted earlier. One simplistic solution to this problem is to use a fixed distance constraint (whether in two- or three-dimensions) to prevent the camera from being left behind. This same principle may be applied to ensure that the camera maintains a minimum distance from the target object, but there are caveats with both of these approaches. First, we cannot simply instantaneously move the camera to a position matching the distance requirements without ensuring that the camera will not collide with components of the environment or other game objects. This is true of regular camera movement but is worth repeating. Should the new camera position interpenetrate other objects or geometry, then an alternative movement must be made. Second, aesthetic considerations may require a drastic movement that conflicts with the distance requirements. Additionally there are cases where the distance constraint may not be applied due to game play concerns, so this facility should be controllable via scripting or another designer specification method.

TECHNICAL

A simple distance constraint approach might be implemented in this way:

```
Vec3 const unconstrainedOffset = currentPosition -
  desiredPosition;
  // i.e. back from the desired position towards the
  // current position
float const currentDistance =
  inverseDirection.Magnitude();
float const newDistance = Math::Clamp(kMinDistance,
  currentDistance, kMaxDistance);
Vec3 const newOffset =
  unconstrainedOffset.AsNormalized() * newDistance;
currentPosition = desiredPosition + newOffset;
// N.B. It's still necessary to check the validity of
// this movement
```

A different approach is to apply a portion of the target object's velocity to that of the camera. This technique is usually preferable as it reduces the likelihood of discontinuous motion if the camera distance oscillates around the maximum (or minimum) allowable value. Use of motion filters may also help reduce this oscillation.

Planar constraints

There are cases, similar to the vertical constraints mentioned previously, where it is necessary to ensure the camera remains on one side of a plane or, alternatively, is restricted to motion in the plane. The latter case is simple to enforce assuming that collision issues may be ignored. In the case of an arbitrarily oriented plane, care must be taken to ensure that the camera position relative to its target will not produce inappropriate orientations. Alternatively, it is sometimes required that the camera is prevented from approaching the plane but is allowed to instantaneously cross to the other side as required. The opposite of this case, where the camera must stay within a defined distance of the plane, is easy to implement and may be considered a simplified form of surface constraint.

TECHNICAL

Given an infinite constraining plane, it is a simple matter to determine the distance of the camera from it and therefore to prevent the camera from approaching too close. Similarly, constraining the camera to the plane merely requires projection of the target object or other desirable reference point onto the plane.

Assuming that a plane is defined as a normal and a constant (representing the distance of the plane from the world origin along the normal), a possible distance constraint might be implemented as follows:

```
CPlane const plane(normal, constant);
  // a plane class may offer projection functions,
  // etc. anyway
Vec3 cameraPosition(GetCurrentPosition());
float const planeDistance = Vec3::Dot(plane.GetNormal(),
  cameraPosition) - plane.GetConstant();
if (planeDistance < kMinDistance)
{
  cameraPosition += plane.GetNormal() *
    (planeDistance - kMinDistance);
    // assumes camera is on the "correct" side of the
    // plane, otherwise check the plane normal direction
    // against the vector from the closest point on the
    // plane to the camera, using a Dot product
}
```

Surface constraints

Surface constraints are a natural extension to planar constraints and were covered in Chapter 7. However, in this case the surface does not define the absolute position of the camera, it prevents motion of the camera through the surface.

Volume constraints

Similarly, volumes may be used to constrain the movement of the camera. Typically this requires a test to determine if a point, sphere, or other collision primitive used by the camera is within the volume. These tests tend to be simple to implement as the volumes used for constraining the camera are often simple convex shapes (e.g., cylinders). It is more usual to consider the camera as a point for these purposes as this is typically the least intensive in terms of processor performance. However, in this case care must be taken to ensure the constraining volume prevents near plane intersection with render geometry by expanding the volume as appropriate.

Player camera control

Many games allow (or sometimes require) the player to manipulate the position and/or orientation of the game camera in a variety of different ways according to the genre of game or design requirements. Often for third person camera games the onus of positioning the camera is simply placed on the player's shoulders because the camera system is unable to cope with the complexities of either the environments or game play requirements. In many ways, it is easier to abdicate this responsibility and let the player have "control." This is *not* recommended as a general solution, however. Why should the player have to deal with manipulating the camera while playing the game? They have enough to deal with.

What this really means, of course, is that the player has to constantly struggle with moving the camera into a good position, while still trying to play the game. It is easy to see why this is attractive to many developers since it requires minimal development effort. Regardless of the reasoning, it is suggested that developers subscribe to a different philosophy, and it is a lofty goal, namely:

> *The player should not be REQUIRED to manipulate the camera simply to play the game, unless explicitly dictated by the game design.*

After all, the player is usually more interested in manipulating the player character than trying to position the camera into an appropriate position and orientation. There are limited exceptions to this rule, and player control should not usually be allowed *unless the game design mandates otherwise*. Good examples of this would include the traditional free-look as seen in first person games, fixed camera positions in vehicle simulators, and so forth. Although free-look is typically found in first person games, this can also apply to third person games since it can allow the player finer control over puzzle solving and environmental determination. In the latter situation it can be necessary to restrict manipulation of the camera under certain circumstances. Obvious examples include confined environments where the camera position must be explicitly controlled by the designer, puzzles that specifically require a limited view of the environment, and so forth.

Manipulation of the camera position is only feasible if the player character control scheme is either character-relative or screen-relative. If camera-relative, the sheer act of moving the camera changes the control reference frame and "pulls the rug out from under the player's feet," at least in terms of player control. Sadly, some games seem to treat this behavior as acceptable. It is not. Changing the control reference frame without player knowledge is counter to good game play practice. It will likely provide the player with a very frustrating experience since every motion of the player character changes how the controls are interpreted.

In addition, consistency of controls is extremely important. For example, if a free-look style of control is provided within a first person view, then the same control scheme should also apply to other instances of free-look including a third person view. This consistency of control naturally applies to other aspects of the player control, especially player motion that often depends upon the concept of a *control reference frame*, as discussed in Chapter 2.

Manipulation of the camera position

As mentioned before, it is common in many third person games to allow direct manipulation of the camera position by the player. Let us examine how this manipulation would function in both 2D and 3D presentation styles.

2D cameras

For 2D games, the only thing that can usually be controlled by the player is the position of the camera within the world (the projection is orthographic, after all). However, some 2D games have allowed what would be considered a zoom effect. This is evidenced in games that simulate a jumping action along the axis perpendicular to the 2D projection (i.e., parallel to the camera projection), usually when the view presented is from "above" (sometimes known as "top-down"). It can be achieved by scaling the size of the rendered window (e.g., if drawn as a tile map then both the tiles themselves as well as any associated sprites). A reasonable approximation to a 3D effect can be achieved in this manner, although care must be taken to avoid issues of indeterminate pixel drop-out when scaling down, or blocky graphics when scaling upward. If the sprites and backgrounds are stored in a higher than normal resolution then scaled and anti-aliased during regular rendering, this problem can be lessened or even circumvented. It is also possible to rotate the rendered window while maintaining the orthographic projection. With modern graphics hardware, the entire screen may be treated as a textured polygon, to be transformed as required.

In games that exhibit scrolling backgrounds, such as the traditional "side-scrolling" or "platform" games, it can be advantageous for the player to be able to look ahead of their movement direction. Some games allow the player character to either crouch or look upward with the position of the camera moving accordingly to show more of the game world than would normally be viewable. Such movement must still be restricted within the boundaries of the game world. By moving the camera position, this will naturally change the screen-relative position of the player character, so we must normally ensure that the player character remains visible. Alternatively, a zoom out effect could be applied by rescaling the rendering of the world to give the player a larger perspective on their relative position within the game world.

2D games often restrict the motion of the camera such that the projected view of the world does not show portions of the world outside of the defined map, unless explicitly required for game play purposes. Once camera motion is restricted, the player character's position within the screen will vary accordingly.

3D cameras

First person games do not generally allow player control of camera position, since they are ostensibly viewing the world from the eyes of the protagonist. Simulators and other vehicle-based games may be considered first person in some regard but should really be classified as third person cameras, even when presenting a view that corresponds to the eye viewpoint of the player character. These types of games usually provide a variety of different set view positions at different distances and elevations from the vehicle. A single control will normally suffice for cycling between several such camera positions, although this would depend upon the controller design. The transitions between the different camera views can be handled as either *jump cuts* or interpolations. For positions that retain the same control reference frame, interpolations are preferred. Flight simulators and other character-relative player control schemes often have camera views that have no bearing on the direction of motion of the vehicle being controlled, and in those cases, it is probably better to cut directly to the new view.

Observer cameras

Some multi-player games allow player manipulation of the camera in the same manner as debugging cameras; that is, freedom in moving and reorienting the camera independent of any game play that may be underway. This typically occurs once the player is simply observing the game (i.e., not an active participant), usually after their character has been removed from game play. This camera type, sometimes referred to as an *observer camera*, may be completely free form or slaved to a particular game object. In the latter case, facilities are often included to allow rapid selection of the targeted object between different player characters or possibly AI opponents or significant positions within the game world. Similarly, the player may be able to view the world from the perspective of a game object itself. This can be both enlightening for the player (e.g., to see how another player views the game), and a powerful debugging tool for understanding how AI objects are behaving — assuming that the AI creature uses line of sight and other visual cues as part of its behavior.

Camera motion validation

In a third person view, player-controlled camera motion will be in addition to positioning the camera relative to the target object. If the character is allowed to move while the player is controlling the camera position, then problems may arise concerning determination of a valid camera position. We would naturally prefer that the camera does not pass through or outside of the world geometry, but desired position as dictated by the player controls may require this. While ensuring the camera is within the environment is often straightforward, we have a problem because the camera may become occluded or forced into positions counter to the controlling player's desires. The prospective movement path that the camera will take while interpolating or moving can be evaluated to determine its validity, typically by projecting a ray or collision volume through the environment. If static geometry is encountered then the camera can either automatically jump past the obstruction (with the unfortunate side effect of a whole scene change — equivalent to a *jump cut*) or cut the interpolation short. Dynamic geometry such as game objects may be treated in the same manner, or have their rendering properties altered to prevent occlusion or interpenetration issues.

Some games do not offer control of the camera position in third person view other than set distances/elevations from the target character. The character-relative position of the camera remains under camera system control to resolve the previously mentioned collision problems. This is typical of racing games, although they tend to offer a selection of interesting yet less practical camera views (e.g., fender). Changes between different camera views can be performed as jump cuts or as interpolations.

Once we allow movement of the camera around the player character, there are a number of potential problems to prevent. The preferred dictum for player controlled camera movement might be:

> *Do not allow the camera to be moved into a position that allows complete occlusion of the player character.*

Having said that, sometimes it is permissible to allow the camera manipulation to continue if the projected arc of motion will allow the camera to reach a position where occlusion does not occur. Of course, the problem here is that the player is under no obligation to complete the motion. However, such a situation may be detected and the remainder of the camera motion may be automatically applied once the controls have been released. In some ways this is a preferable solution, as it removes some restrictions upon the control of the camera. This is important as it ensures players feel in control of the camera when they want to be, yet prevents permanent occlusion of the player character.

When the player attempts to move the camera to a position that would be constrained by geometry (i.e., would interpenetrate collision geometry or pass entirely through it), the typical solution is to move the camera closer to the character to allow better possibility of movement. A further addition to this solution is that typically the camera will also be moved vertically if this forced motion would cause the camera to interpenetrate the player character. Since the direction of movement of the camera is already known, it is a relatively simple matter to predict future collisions with geometry. This assumes that the motion is relative to the player character.

Unfortunately, things are not quite as simple as they may first appear. By projecting a ray (or a collision volume) from the position around which the camera is moving outward to its desired position, we can certainly check for potential collisions or occlusion. The result of this ray cast can be used to adjust the desired position, with some caveats.

Since we usually consider the camera collision volume as a sphere, sufficient space must be available between the geometry detected from this ray cast and the target object.

If the camera needs to approach the player character to avoid geometry then it could be desirable to maintain the current position or distance until a time when the player has not moved the character. This would avoid oscillating camera movement caused by the character crossing the threshold position. In this case, it may be advisable to increase the elevation of the camera as the player moves closer to it. Fail-safe conditions to avoid interpenetration of the camera position by the player character are often implemented. In extreme cases, it is permissible to reposition the camera (i.e., cut), although care should be taken to retain the control reference frame if possible.

Positional control constraints

It is often necessary to place some limits on the reorientation or movement of a camera by the player. It is necessary to prevent the player from either moving the camera outside of the environment or close to geometry (whether static or dynamic) such that the near plane of the camera is intersected. Additionally, there are orientations that can cause mathematical irregularities, such as the forward axis of the camera becoming parallel to the world up-axis. This leads to player confusion as well as unpredictable camera roll about that axis. Movement of the camera directly by the player may force the camera to reorient itself in a way that obfuscates the player view of game play.

Character-relative positioning of the camera is normally constrained regarding the angle formed between the vector of player orientation and a vector from the character to the camera. Put more simply, character-relative cameras are normally constrained such that they remain "behind" the player character. Thus, it may be necessary to prevent the player from moving the camera to a position facing the character. However, this restriction may feel arbitrary and frustrating to the player.

When the player manipulation of the camera finishes, many third person games automatically move the camera back to a default position, typically an elevated position in line with the player character orientation. As well as limitations regarding the camera repositioning, we also need to limit the speed of the camera reorientation. Studies by NASA such as [Ellis99] have shown the correlation between camera rotation speed and user nausea. It is generally true that camera motion should be both smooth and relatively slow to avoid player disorientation.

Camera position control schemes

There are two main approaches for camera position determination in relation to another game object (usually the player character). These are character-relative and world-relative.

Character-relative

This is usually associated with a third person camera but sometimes a first person camera may allow limited motion relative to the character (e.g., to simulate crouching). The player can control the position of the camera by rotating it around the target object, and sometimes around the look-at position (which is not necessarily the same thing). Optionally the elevation angle (alternatively the world up-axis offset) may be adjusted as well as the radius of rotation. The arc of motion of the camera need not be restricted to a spherical shape; an ellipsoid may be more appropriate in many cases.

Total control over the position of the camera can actually prove to be a liability if the user is able to manipulate the camera into a position that presents a view of the player character such that it restricts game play choices or affects the interpretation of the player controls.

By placing reasonable constraints on the range of camera motion, as well as the distance of the camera, potential problems may be avoided. This may result in a cylindrical band of possible positions rather than an entire sphere. Additionally rotation around the character may be restricted to a small angle behind the direction that the character is facing.

A common solution used to prevent poor camera choices by the player is to offer a number of distinct camera positions at varying distances and elevations relative to the player character. These positions may be selected as discrete camera choices or as the basis for further manipulation by the player.

Some third person games allow semi-automated movement of the camera to allow a view of the world that would normally require the player character to move into a dangerous position. Examples include a view overlooking a cliff or precipice, looking around a corner in a stealth-based game, and so forth. These can be considered character-relative positions although tightly constrained. While these situations may be explicitly controlled via pre-defined scripting, they may also be generalized in many cases, although it is important that they only occur at appropriate times as required by the player.

World-relative

World-relative camera manipulation is normally associated with "free-look" or debugging cameras. In this case, the camera orientation has no relationship to the orientation of the player character. Its position may still be relative to that of the player character, however. Oftentimes this approach is taken when presenting a pseudo-2D view of the world. Debugging cameras normally have no relationship to any other game object, even the player. They may be considered as truly world-relative. There are some cases where it is useful to allow a larger view of the world to assist the player in anticipating their next action. Obvious examples would include *real-time strategy* (RTS) games, sports simulations, 3D platform games, and so forth. Even though these cameras allow relatively unlimited camera manipulation, there are normally constraints to ensure that rendering artifacts are prevented.

Manipulation of camera orientation

Player manipulation of the camera orientation is usually referred to (at least within the first person genre) as *free-look*. Two-dimensional games typically do not offer this functionality (it is an orthographic projection, after all), but they may allow for rotation of the entire scene (particularly for 2D games that simulate three dimensions, such as isometric projections) or possibly a number of set orientations (e.g., with isometric games). Some 2D games offer the ability to pan over the game world. This may be completely free form or restricted to a small amount of motion around the position of the player character.

Free-look is an important part of first person games. It assists player aiming and alleviates the limited field of view present in most games of this type.

First person cameras

Control of camera orientation in first person games is usually performed via a separate button mapping from player movement. The main reason for this is to allow the "circle-strafe" maneuver in which a player is able to revolve around a target object (or target position) yet remain facing it. This is achieved by pushing the movement joystick (strafing or sideways movement control) and free-look joystick (turning control) in opposite (horizontal) directions. In some ways, this is an attempt to simulate mouse-driven control methodologies. The important thing to note is that the horizontal turn direction must be opposed to the horizontal motion direction (strafing).

Free-look is normally constrained such that the player is unable to look in a direction parallel to the world up-axis. As the camera approaches the limit of rotation around the player character, its motion should be damped. Similarly, any slight noise in camera orientation from the controller should be filtered out to prevent untoward camera jitter. With self-centering joysticks, the view can match the joystick position so that it is automatically centered when the stick is released. However, we should use filtered inputs and additionally use the controller either to specify a target position or to control the acceleration of the camera, rather than a direct mapping. This is especially true since the sensitivity of controllers can vary considerably.

Roll is often disallowed when altering the camera orientation except for the cases of flight simulators, especially spacecraft simulators. With a craft capable of six degrees of freedom, the concept of "up" is somewhat antiquated. It is still necessary, however, to prevent gimbal lock situations.

Free-look controls often operate on the assumption that the player view is synchronized with the horizontal orientation of the player character. This means that horizontal free-look equates to turning the player character. However, this need not be the case. Free-look can be separated in this regard to simulate independent torso movement from that of walking or running. In this scenario, the amount of torso reorientation is limited to, say, less than 90 degrees. For advanced players this can be a useful functionality but for novice players it can be confusing that the character is moving in an arbitrary direction relative to their view. If the free-look orientation is made to self-center upon release of the control, the effects of this disparity may be reduced.

Third person cameras

Generally, the orientation change here is obtained by physically moving the camera around the player with the look-at position situated above the player character. Thus, the camera motion is constrained to the surface of an imaginary sphere or cylinder. In some situations, it is permissible to allow reorientation of the camera independent of player or camera movement. In this case the reorientation of the camera is often restricted to maintain an on-screen position for the player character with automatic re-centering of the view once the camera control is released. In games that demand aiming it may be necessary to allow the player character to be partially off-screen and/or become semi-transparent to be able to track enemies accurately. It could be necessary to reposition the camera behind the player character to aim effectively.

Aiming in third person games can be difficult at best since usually it is not possible to look directly along the line of sight of the weapon. This is a large topic and it was discussed in detail in Chapter 8.

There are also examples where a traditional "follow" camera is allowed to change its view around the player without repositioning of the camera. Some games present a compromise between the two types of camera (first person and third person) whenever a player draws his character's weapon. The camera is brought closer to a position approximating the shoulder of the player character. Free-look then allows aiming to be more tightly controlled than would be possible with a "pure" third person camera that is kept at a distance from the player. Optionally movement may be prohibited in this mode.

If the free-look is moving the camera around the player then care must be taken to ensure that the character does not obscure the view. This can be achieved by looking above the character or (if feasible) pulling the camera away far enough that the screen size of the character is sufficiently unobtrusive. Additionally the player character may be made semi-transparent, yet the camera must not interpenetrate the character unless it has been completely faded from view.

Sometimes the camera needs to frame enemies and friendly objects yet still allow reorientation between groups of characters. In all cases where the camera needs to focus on game objects or positions in the world, some kind of on-screen overlay is required to aid the player's choice. Additionally, a *reticle* is often helpful for aiming purposes, and it can be modal so as not to obscure the view when not required for game play.

Reticles are usually presented in two-dimensional form as crosshairs or similar motifs with alpha transparency applied to reduce their obscuring of game elements. On occasion, the reticle is drawn as a three-dimensional model, particularly when the reticle adopts the shape of the geometry beneath its position in the world. This technique can reduce the distracting nature of most reticles, since it does emphasize the three-dimensional nature of the world. When the player character is equipped with fictional equipment such as a helmet, this form of overlaid graphic may actually be desirable since it dovetails with expected functionality. Reticles may be considered as two-dimensional elements for rendering purposes. However, they may change their size according to the distance of the target position within the game world. Note that even though the target may be distant from the camera, it is advisable to ensure that the minimum size of the reticle remains large enough to be discernible by the player. Similarly a maximum size is also advisable.

Automated camera positioning and orientation

There are occasions where it is necessary or preferred that the camera system repositions/reorients the current camera without direct player intervention. It is often required to prevent player interaction with the camera when this happens. Obvious examples are cinematic sequences, but even regular game play can present such situations.

In response to player controller usage

The player can select camera positions and/or orientations that are then automatically used by the camera system. This is typically the case when a limited amount of camera management is required, an obvious example is vehicle simulation. A palette of pre-defined camera positions or behaviors can be made available for easy player selection, either by cycling between them in a consistent ordering or by mapping camera positions to controller-specific buttons.

Sometimes these selections change instantaneously, such as changing views with respect to an aircraft flown within a flight simulation. Changing the view around the cockpit normally happens immediately compared with changing the camera distance behind the plane, which would normally happen over a short period. Others cases may interpolate position and/or orientation over a short period of time. Automobile simulators will often present a variety of views at differing distances from the vehicle, and the camera system may smoothly interpolate between them.

In response to game play requirements

There can be a number of reasons for automatic camera placement. In third person games, it can be necessary to ensure that a certain game play object remains in view of the player. Framing issues aside, if we are to reposition the camera outside of player control, we need to ensure that the new position is understandable and that the control reference frame changes in a meaningful way, if at all.

In some cases, it is necessary to augment player camera control to aid game play. First person games are notorious for presenting a blinkered view of their world. As such, it can be difficult for players to understand the relationship between their position in the world and environmental features, such as gaps that must be jumped. Subtly changing the pitch of the camera as the player approaches the edge of a cliff, or pitching the camera as the player is jumping (so that they can better judge their landing position) can greatly aid the player without being obtrusive. In the latter case, the amount of pitch can be varied according to either amount of time spent in the air, proximity to the destination position, or possibly player input.

As a player character walks up or down an incline in a first person game, it becomes increasingly difficult for the player to see an adequate view of the world if the camera orientation remains parallel to the horizontal plane. An alternative is to automatically pitch the camera up or down as appropriate so that the rest position of the camera (i.e., without any active player free-look) is parallel to the plane (or close to it). As a player turns around from facing up the slope to facing down the slope, it is necessary to change the amount of pitch in proportion to the angle between the player orientation and that of the slope such that at 90 degrees to the slope the pitch imparted is zero.

In third person games, it can be necessary to present a portion of the game as a pseudo-2D game. This can be achieved by positioning the camera parallel to a world axis or even fixed to a spline path. It is not usually desirable, however, to match the player speed directly as this makes the camera feel unnaturally "stiff" as well as causing the camera to move with only the slightest of player movement.

As mentioned before, there are some situations where the camera needs to be moved to allow the player to view areas of the environment that would be too dangerous for the character. In some cases it is simple to provide a fixed orientation (and/or position) camera giving a new vantage point, in other cases a world-offset camera moves in concert with player character movement (e.g., leaning around a corner) to alleviate the need for the player to manipulate the camera while trying to avoid enemy fire or detection.

Debug camera control

Debugging or verification of camera behaviors can be a difficult task without the ability to observe camera motion and orientation from a perspective other than that of the active camera. For that matter, having the facility to move the camera to a position to observe game play from a vantage point independent of player action can be extremely useful. An added bonus would be the ability to capture screenshots of game play framed in an aesthetically pleasing manner.

The camera manager should provide a mechanism for at least one additional camera outside of the regular game cameras, purely to facilitate debugging. This debugging camera is required to be manipulated by a user without affecting the behavior of any other game object, including other cameras. In this regard it is a variant upon the *observer camera* mentioned earlier in this chapter. Certainly it should override the transform used by the world rendering code, but should not prevent (necessarily) input values from being passed to the other cameras. It may prove useful to have multiple debugging modes, some of which do not pass input values to the rest of the game. In this way, a debug camera can be moved without influencing the player character. This is obviously not necessary if an additional controller is available, or indeed if input can be supplied via some other external mechanism (e.g., in a console environment the PC connected to the development kit could be used rather than a regular game controller). When using replay facilities to duplicate bugs or to check functionality, having a debug camera able to move freely to observe game behavior is extremely valuable.

Typically, a debugging camera requires controls to change its orientation via yaw and pitch controls, as well as movement forward or backward along its current forward direction. It may also be desirable to allow lateral panning of the camera, perpendicular to the forward direction but retaining the same up-vector. Optionally there may be an acceleration control to facilitate quicker motion along that same direction if it is held while moving. An alternate method of motion and orientation control is to allow the camera to be locked so that its movement is relative to a game object, or to a position at a defined distance along its view direction. Both of these techniques allow prospective camera positions and movement to be easily tested, as well as enabling the user to better observe behavior of game objects.

Another useful debugging facility is to be able to dynamically reduce the speed of the game execution, even to the point of single stepping individual game updates. This is often achieved by changing the amount of delta time passed to game objects. This will also apply to game cameras, except for the debugging camera itself, naturally. Thus, the debugging camera is able to move and reorient at the regular game speed allowing the user to manipulate the camera position (and orientation) interactively even though the game logic is running slowly. Furthermore, single stepping of game logic independent of a debug camera is very desirable. Ideally, this would include the ability to rewind game play to a previous state, but that is much more involved.

CAMERA COLLISIONS

Of equal importance to the motion of game cameras is the subject of *camera collisions*. This topic not only encompasses *collision detection* but perhaps more important, *collision prediction* and *collision avoidance*. Collision avoidance methods may result in occlusion problems, and resolution of those problems sometimes involves bypassing the camera collision system. It should be considered whether camera collision is even necessary. Non-interactive movie sequences, for example, typically do not need to consider camera collision since the position of the camera is explicitly controlled. The same is true of other in-game situations where control over camera position is pre-defined or otherwise guaranteed to be able to move freely (such as outside the environment). Additionally, collision detection is often a processor intensive operation and may sometimes be avoided by judicious use of pre-computed data or scripted game objects such as *repulsors*. Collision avoidance is a form of *navigation*, as previously discussed in Chapter 8.

Of course, it is simply possible to ignore camera collisions completely, allowing the camera to pass through all other game objects or geometry. There are cases where this is acceptable (e.g., debugging cameras), but overall this type of behavior produces too many visual artifacts and game play problems to be desirable.

The importance of camera collisions

Camera collisions are typically the result of preventative measures to avoid a variety of problems, not the least of which is interpenetration of a camera with game objects or the confines of the environment. Here are some examples of the problems inherent in camera collisions.

- **The collision prevents the camera from moving to its desired position.** Hence, the camera may be left behind the target object unless there is a fail-safe mechanism available.
- **Discontinuous motion may be caused by collisions.** Since a collision implies that the camera could not move as intended, it is likely that any partial or subsequent movements may occur sporadically thus causing the rendered scene to change in a discontinuous manner. This often occurs when the collision geometry includes too much detail (see the section concerning collision geometry design later in this chapter).
- **Occlusion of the target object.** If the object or geometry colliding with the camera is between the camera and its target object

then it is likely that this will occlude the target. This often occurs because of the previous problem regarding camera motion.

- **Camera near plane intersects geometry.** As the camera approaches an object or geometry, if the extent of the camera's collision volume is less than the distance of the frustum near clipping plane, rendering artifacts will occur as parts of the rendered object intersect the near plane. This is avoidable by increasing the collision volume of the camera or the object itself. Even first person cameras may exhibit this problem and their usual solution is to change the collision geometry of the object in question, rather than the collision volume of the player character, although that remains an option.

Thus, the role of collision with respect to the camera is a mixed one. On the one hand, we do not wish to allow the camera outside of the game environment except for a number of controlled situations specified by a designer. Yet, we do not wish to have the camera separated from its target object. Additionally, if the camera moves close to objects or environmental features we would prefer that it does not pass through them or worse still, show an inappropriate part of the environment or an incomplete part of the game object.

Sadly, some games seem not to view these problems as significant or simply cannot deal with them in an effective way. Possibly their development schedule did not allow sufficient time to resolve the problems. Nonetheless if these problems are present they will greatly detract from the perceived quality of the game and are often viewed poorly by both players and reviewers. Certainly, such rendering artifacts should be viewed as unacceptable and have no place in quality games.

Handling (or preferably avoiding) collisions with the environment or objects can be a difficult and time-consuming proposition. Where should the camera move once it has detected a potential collision? This greatly depends upon the desired position of the camera with respect to the player character. Since the environment can clearly prevent the camera from reaching the desired position, should it try to move anywhere at all? In some cases, movement can be avoided given that the camera is high enough above the character. Yet, this also has problems depending on the control methodology. Typically, we want to avoid the camera from becoming vertically aligned with the player character as mathematically the result becomes problematic; left and right motion, if camera-relative, become rotation around the vertical axis which is unlikely to be desirable.

Collision detection also greatly depends upon the physical representation of the camera in the game world. In most cases, the camera can be considered a physical sphere or cylinder for collision purposes. In general, it is more efficient to use a spherical collision volume.

It is also true that a number of collision-related problems may be avoided by either pre-determination of the camera position (whether fixed *in situ* or moving along a defined path) or by anticipation of future positions of both the camera and its intended subject. In fact, such *predictive* cameras are preferable to solve some of the complexities of world geometry.

Is collision testing necessary?

In reality, it is not necessary to even consider camera collision in many camera situations. The simplest case is clearly when we (the designers) explicitly dictate the camera position such that it cannot interpenetrate either world geometry or game objects. This should typically be the case for non-interactive sequences but is often true for regular game play situations as well.

This technique of pre-defined camera positioning can be extremely effective but is highly genre dependent. It may feel somewhat static since the determination of the camera motion does not vary. It can also be difficult to find a motion path or other solutions that can adequately cope with the game play requirements of a complex environment or variable game play interactions. It may be necessary, in fact, to have multiple solutions within a particular game area. However, since camera collision detection is often a processor-intensive task, this type of approach is often attractive.

Note that camera positioning constraints need not always result in entirely predictable camera behavior. Use of volume constraints, for example, still allows scope for variable camera motion within the volume. See Chapter 7 for more detail on camera position determination and earlier in this chapter for information on motion constraints.

It should also be noted that some classes of potential collision might be safely ignored. Thin or small geometry may often allow the camera to pass through if the geometry in question is purely an aesthetic addition to the environment (e.g., webbing or thin wires). The only caveat is that interpenetration of the geometry with the near plane should be avoided. This can be achieved by fading the geometry in question as the camera approaches (easier if the geometry is constructed separately from the environment) or simply not rendering the object if it would intersect (although that might cause the object to "pop" in and out of view).

Collision determination

There are a variety of methods used to determine camera collision with world or object geometry. First, though, we must ask whether it is necessary for the camera to collide with these whatsoever. What are the benefits we can derive from treating the camera as an object that collides within our virtual world?

Most often, first person cameras do not need to perform any kind of collision detection, as that is normally handled implicitly by the player character. However, it must be ensured that the player character collision volume extends sufficiently to prevent the first person camera near plane from intersecting geometry. Third person cameras, however, are plagued by many problems, not the least of which is collision avoidance. For the most part our discussion here is concerned purely with third person cameras. Given that, what benefits can we expect from committing to this processor intensive task? First, we eliminate or reduce the problems of near plane intersection by geometry (this is reason enough). Second, it reduces the need for extensive camera scripting in many cases since the camera will slide along collision geometry when pushed against it by player character motion. This also means that the camera will be kept inside of the environment; an additional benefit.

Object collisions

In most cases it is unusual for the camera to collide with game objects. While it is preferable that the camera is positioned so that this could not occur, what should be done when this happens? The main concern would be near-plane interpenetration, but it is also possible that the game object could prevent the camera from moving, or cause drastic movement of the camera to avoid occlusion of the target object.

Environmental collisions

If it is necessary to avoid contact, we should consider how to determine the camera proximity. Many modern game engines represent the environment in two related data structures. First there is the data used for rendering purposes, usually a triangle mesh or possibly higher order surface representation in conjunction with pre-computed visibility or other spatial partitioning information. We will refer to this representation as the *render mesh* or *render geometry*. Second, a lower complexity surface representation, the *collision mesh* (or *collision geometry*), is normally used purely for collision determination and has a lower density to reduce the processor cost when extracting collision information. Additionally, the collision mesh may be adjusted to better facilitate player motion through the environment by smoothing or chamfering complex edges. The collision mesh is typically positioned away from the render mesh so that collisions occur before the render mesh is interpenetrated. Care must be taken to ensure that such collisions do not appear to be "floating" above the render mesh in an obvious manner. Balancing the requirements of low complexity and aesthetic appearance is often quite demanding and sometimes requires compromises. Both the render and collision mesh are often subdivided into smaller sections that may be considered separately or changed dynamically according to a variety of factors (e.g., proximity to the camera). A common use of this facility is to reduce processor requirements by limiting the amount of primitives that must be tested against. Similarly, the complexity of individual sections may be varied and is usually referred to as *level of detail* (LOD). A full explanation of these concepts is beyond the scope of this book, but the reader is referred to [Ericson05] for a thorough explanation.

Collision primitives

How do we consider the camera to be represented in the world for collision purposes? We need to be able to prevent the camera from approaching too close to geometry so that no clipping into the view frustum occurs. Typically, cameras are represented as a spheroid for collision purposes, even though the camera is in actuality essentially a point. Ray casts may be able to substitute for this solution, and indeed efficient use of ray casting is a cornerstone of camera navigation and occlusion avoidance. Thus to determine camera collision we need to be able to test the camera collision sphere against this collision mesh. Additionally, not all of the physical collision geometry is desirable for camera collision; it may be necessary to filter collisions against surface properties inherent in each face of the polygon mesh. This would allow the camera to pass through geometry that may appear solid to other game objects.

In very complex environments, it may be necessary to avoid collision determination in a traditional sense and use defined paths to prohibit motion into geometry. Clearly, this is only sufficient for static geometry and not game objects.

The representation of the world can be considered as two main parts. First, there is the *static geometry*, which comprises those parts of the environment that do not change. The second element would be the *dynamic geometry*, usually consisting of the player and other associated creatures or objects that inhabit the game world. It is also used to place environmental features that can change during game play, for example, a bridge that may be destroyed later in the game. Dynamic geometry also implies potential movement, which can prove problematic for the camera system. If the dynamic geometry moves between different states, it may be necessary to have distinct camera solutions that are applied according to each state. Clearly, this is necessary because the moveable objects may prevent camera positioning or occlude the target object differently in each state.

Collision geometry design

While it is entirely possible for camera collision determination to use the same collision mesh that is used for general object collisions, it is likely that this mesh may not be entirely suited to our needs. For example, collision meshes are often crafted to match or approximate the render geometry of the environment, particularly if projectile weapons and the like are required to hit the collision mesh in a manner that looks appropriate for the render geometry. This approach is, of course, correct for its intended purpose but is not necessarily appropriate for smooth movement of the camera when adjacent to the collision surfaces. We would prefer simple planes, for the purposes of camera collision, to allow the camera to slide smoothly along the surface. It is also preferable that 90 degree corners are chamfered to assist this same type of motion.

Given the desirability of simple collision surfaces for the camera, how might these be implemented? What other constraints will affect camera collision mesh design? Clearly the collision representation is dependent upon the game genre, presentation style, and type of environment. For the purposes of this example we will consider a third person game with the player character traversing through a close environment on foot. Here are some points to consider when designing these environments.

Avoid tightly confined spaces

The smaller the environment the more restricted the camera position, and thus the options for positioning the camera to adequately frame the game play are also reduced. Additionally, it becomes much easier for the player character to interpenetrate the camera and reduces the opportunities for the camera to move out of its way. Further complications occur when the camera is backed into a confined space and must seek around the player to find a good position.

Allow sufficient space for the camera

Since most third person cameras are tethered to the player character, we should try to ensure that there is sufficient space for the camera to achieve its required distance away from the player character. If the environment does not allow the regular third person camera behavior to be observed, we must use a custom camera solution to position it to illustrate required game play. In some cases this may require the camera to be positioned outside of the render geometry, which may itself demand that additional render geometry is placed to prevent an inappropriate view of other elements of the game world (e.g., back faces of the environment).

Steep steps

Steep ledges or steps that may be traversed by the target object often cause occlusion problems for the camera. Chamfering of the steps may help in this regard, depending upon the height of the player character relative to the step size.

Ledges/overhangs

Ledges or overhangs where it is possible for the player character to move backward as they fall may present camera problems. If the player is able to move underneath the ledge while the camera is still above the surface, the camera may be unable to resolve the situation with the camera becoming trapped above the surface. One possible solution is to have the camera pass through the surface, although this is often undesirable as it requires discontinuous movement. Alternatively a path may be generated to move the camera over the ledge. This may result in a 180 degree rotation of the camera orientation with the subsequent control reference frame changes.

Low ceilings

Once again, low ceilings should be avoided unless the camera position may be pre-determined using a spline path or similar solution as outlined in Chapter 7.

Doorways

Doorway navigation is often difficult for free form third person cameras. Here are some of the more common problems that may be encountered.

First, the player may move so quickly through the door that it closes between the player character and the camera (thus requiring the camera to pass through geometry or instantly move to a new position). This problem may be alleviated by forcing the door to remain open until the camera has passed through. Additionally, it is necessary to ensure that the camera may not pass back through the door as it is closing.

Second, the player character may move through the doorway in a way that causes the camera to be unable to follow the player (e.g., non-directional cameras that only depend upon maintaining a set distance from the player character). Generally, the smaller the doorway the greater the requirement to have navigational aids for the camera. Increasing the physical size of the door will help avoid the problem. However, if the camera system is aware that the camera is close to a door it may apply additional forces to the camera to attract it toward the center line of the door. By encouraging the camera to move along the axis of the door (i.e., perpendicular to its direction of opening) it is more likely that the camera will clear the doorway regardless of player movement. Typically these forces need only be applied if the doorway is between the camera and its target.

A third problem occurs when the player character is standing within the doorway, and simply rotates. If the camera is required to remain behind the direction in which the character is facing, it will be required to move in an arc that may intersect geometry. While the same problem occurs with any other wall or similar structure, doorways are typically more confined, particularly regarding the vertical position of the camera. Thus it may be necessary to move the camera across the threshold of the doorway to prevent potential intersections with the player character.

Use the simplest collision mesh possible

The simpler the collision mesh, the easier it is for the camera to slide along its surfaces. Remember that the camera movement is preferably smooth at all times, and simple collision surfaces will help in that regard. Additionally, simple surfaces without protuberances lessen the chance of the camera becoming unable to move.

Separate collision mesh for the camera

As the previous point might suggest, having an entirely separate collision mesh for the camera allows greater simplification than might otherwise be possible. Additionally, since the surfaces are simpler their storage requirements will typically be relatively low.

Chamfer all corners

This is particularly true in confined spaces or hallways and may be extremely beneficial in assisting the camera's movement through doorways. The aim here is to encourage sliding of the camera along the collision surface.

Collision resolution

Once we have determined that a collision will occur, we have to decide how to resolve this situation. Additionally, a collision may result from other causes than the movement of the camera (e.g., an object moving into the camera), but here we limit our discussion to this case. Several potential choices should be considered to resolve the collision.

Do not move

Clearly, this is the easiest solution because it is assumed the camera is already positioned such that it does not interpenetrate any other object or environmental feature. The downside to this solution is that the player character is free to move away from the camera, possibly increasing the difficulty of returning the camera to a desirable position. Ultimately this will likely lead to a fail-safe condition, where the camera must be instantly moved to a new position that satisfies the desired position relative to the target object and resolves any occlusion problems. A further problem with this solution is that within confined spaces the camera may be unable to move away from the player character resulting once again in interpenetration.

Partial move

This is an attempt to move in the desired direction but with a smaller distance (proportional to the distance at which the collision would occur as previously determined). If this move also fails then the camera will stay at its current position. Of course, it is possible to try any number of alternative moves by changing the desired position and re-attempting the movement. Processor performance more than anything normally restricts the number of iterations.

In this solution, the camera is allowed to move as far in the desired direction as possible without collision. Most collision systems allow for tests of simplistic ray casts.

Alternative movement

If a potential movement by the camera would result in a collision with environmental geometry, one possible solution is to change the movement direction of the camera. This process may be considered a form of camera navigation. If we consider a free form camera whose only concern is maintaining a distance and elevation relative to the player character, we can see that variations upon this position may be determined by examining the current relative position of the camera to the player character. Not only is it necessary to determine a position that allows for an appropriate view of the player character, it must also be possible for the camera to move toward this new position from its current position. The determination of such a position can be problematic and is greatly dependent upon the nature of the desired position determination itself. Moreover, it is likely that the collision geometry would prevent direct motion toward the new desired position. Some forms of navigation will create a motion path around the obstruction, but this type of navigation may be difficult to determine within complex environments. If this proves to be the case, there is another alternative — the *jump cut*.

Jump cut

An often employed solution when faced with collision geometry that prevents motion is to recalculate the desired position relative to the target object and instantly reposition the camera to that location. This is a form of *fail-safe*, as detailed in Chapter 8, and is often less desirable because of the likelihood of player disorientation. Moreover, some games use this mechanism to move the camera directly through obstructions (e.g., a protruding corner), but it may often break the *30 degree rule*. As with all instantaneous camera movement, the new position must be validated.

Disabling collision detection

As strange as it may initially seem, there are indeed cases where it is necessary to disable or ignore collision detection for the camera (and in addition, collision avoidance).

One example would be the transition between a first and third person view. If a smooth transition is desired (as opposed to a *cut*) the camera must, by definition, pass through the geometry of the main character. The problem of near-plane geometry intersection may be avoided by rendering the character transparent while the camera is near, combined with swift camera motion. The amount of transparency to apply may be determined dynamically depending on the distance of the camera away from the character, or explicitly according to the time elapsed during the transition. The latter approach may be difficult to tune if the distance of the camera from the player character at the start of the transition is variable. Another alternative is the use of full screen *filter effects* (e.g., blurring the entire viewport).

Another case for disabling collision would be the requirement that the camera is sometimes *desired* to be outside the environment and to transition to or from such a position. Many side-scrolling games (2D or 3D) present a view from outside the game world. Others require the camera to sweep through geometry without collision detection preventing this motion. Indeed, in this latter case, it is sometimes necessary that the camera move through the geometry by use of a jump cut to avoid geometry interpenetration.

Further, games that simulate a third dimension by the traditional cartoon animation technique of "layers" would require that the layers fade into transparency as they approach the camera near plane to avoid a sudden "pop" as the layer is no longer rendered. This also alleviates problems where the player character moves back and forth across the threshold distance dictating if the layer is to be rendered.

Path-based cameras and other constrained motion camera types tend not to use collision detection anyway, since it is normally irrelevant in those cases because the path is usually defined to avoid such situations. Nonetheless, static geometry or moving objects may still require such camera types to perform limited collision detection if it is desired that near-plane intersection is avoided. One of the simplest solutions in this situation is to move the camera further along its path once a potential collision has been detected, or to restrict motion until the desired position along the path would be clear of any potential collision. In the latter case it is often necessary to instantaneously move the camera to the desired position, causing a discontinuity. Instantaneous motion of this kind is usually undesirable. It is more often required that the camera simply does not move through the collision. This typically occurs when there is a temporary obstruction for the camera, possibly because a game play element or puzzle has yet to be solved or activated. Once the puzzle is solved, the obstruction is removed (e.g., a door is opened) and the camera is able to move along the entirety of its motion path.

Avoiding camera collisions

To avoid camera collisions it is necessary to anticipate when a collision may occur and alter the motion of the camera ahead of that event. Typical solutions for this determination include ray cast or volume casts depending on the current (or expected) camera motion. This may involve predicting player motion ahead in time, too. Information gathered about the surrounding environment such as the results of ray casts may be used to influence the desired motion of the camera toward or away from surfaces. Chapter 8 discussed some of the approaches used for camera navigation through complex environments.

Collision avoidance in some cases is inherent in the movement method of the camera. Splines or other path-based solutions can obviate the need for any collision checking, although clearly at the cost of limited camera freedom. Most path solutions have pre-defined paths placed down by the designers to specify exact camera movement and orientation according to game play requirements and player positioning. This obviously completely avoids collision problems other than with dynamic geometry (including game objects). It is ideal for situations where the camera would be tightly constrained due to world geometry complexity or for ensuring that the player does not interpenetrate the camera.

It is possible to dynamically generate a path for the camera to follow. This bears similarities to AI path finding, with additional constraints pertaining to the aesthetics of camera positioning or orientation. It is likely that to generate the path would require volumetric knowledge of the world with the associated memory costs. This solution also does not resolve the problems with game objects, of course.

Another potential solution is not to consider collision with game objects. In this case, the rendering of the game objects intersecting or approaching the game camera may be adjusted (e.g., faded out via alpha-blending), which is often better than trying to move the camera around them. This is because game objects often move in unpredictable or rapidly changing directions that might require the camera to move quickly or erratically.

For third person cameras where aiming is important, a further type of collision detection is likely to be necessary. Should the player back the camera into a position that prevents movement and may cause interpenetration of the player character, it may be required for the camera to move either to a hybrid third/first person camera position or to move entirely into the first person camera position. The rule as to when it is necessary to do this depends upon the game genre, and the requirements of maintaining a third person viewpoint. The *Metroid Prime* series [Metroid02], for example, features a third person character that is entirely different from the first person portion of the game and thus cannot utilize such a scheme. Instead, it must anticipate the situation and attempt to prevent it from occurring. In such a situation the third person camera will either rotate around the player character or alternatively raise up above the character, sliding along the collision geometry in the process.

Future position of player

Much as prediction of the target object's future position is often used for determination of the look-at position (see Chapter 7), the same techniques may be applied for collision avoidance and camera navigation.

Predicting potential collisions

One popular solution is to interrogate the game world to determine if the current or future movement would result in a collision or interpenetration of the camera. Of course, what we are really referring to is interpenetration of the *near plane* rather than a collision volume per se. Typically, this is determined by performing one or more ray casts; one is usually projected along the direction of motion, with an additional ray along the forward vector of the camera (since the camera may not be moving in the same direction as its orientation).

The motion ray cast typically assumes that the camera is a single point and extends from its current position to the new position as dictated by the interpolation code. If the ray cast intersects with collision geometry, the movement may not be completed and must be resolved to avoid interpenetration.

The ray cast along the forward vector begins at the new camera position (which may have been adjusted according to the motion ray cast) and extends by a distance slightly larger than the near-plane distance from the camera. The projected ray is compared against the collision (or render) geometry to see if an intersection would occur. Use of collision geometry is usually more efficient due to the lower face count but is only appropriate where it encompasses that of the render geometry. The latter is more visually accurate but may be computationally prohibitive. Regardless of the geometry tested, this single ray along the view direction is actually an optimization of a full test of the interpenetration of the camera view frustum against the render geometry. It is possible, however, that the corners of the view frustum may intersect render geometry even though the ray cast did not, but this is dependent upon the field of view. Extending the distance of the ray cast by a small amount beyond the near plane is usually sufficient to avoid these corner problems.

Note that rather than performing a ray cast along the camera direction, it may prove sufficient to use one or more values from the center of the rendered depth (or Z-) buffer. Not only does this reduce the processor requirements, it may prove more accurate since it is based on the render geometry of the world. Additionally, a section of the depth buffer may be examined before objects are rendered if their collisions are not under consideration. Keep in mind that the depth information obtained in this manner will be from the previous render of the game world and the camera may have moved closer to the render geometry possibly requiring a larger distance check.

Often the direction of the ray cast is performed from the new position back toward the previous position of the camera. The reason for this is to help with resolution of collisions as explained below.

In the case of pre-determined motion, such as a spline path, the entire path may be validated before even beginning the interpolated motion allowing the interpolation to be skipped if necessary. Alternatively, the path may be adjusted to avoid the interpenetration. However, predetermination is often insufficient as game objects may also move into the path of the camera during the interpolation.

Collision prediction

Collision prediction is really part of the collision avoidance system but can also be used to modify camera behavior much in the same way that AI-driven game objects may predict their oncoming collisions with geometry or game objects and change their intended motion accordingly.

Rather than waiting until an actual collision occurs, ideally the camera system is looking ahead in time, anticipating future collisions, and thereby modifying its motion path, where appropriate. Thus, the camera can be described as a *predictive camera*. In other words, predicting the future state (position and orientation at the very least) of the camera, but more important, the future state of the player (or other target object) affects the look-at position of this camera. Predictive cameras may also use the future state of the target object to alter other properties of the camera, including orientation.

Future prediction of the game state may be achieved by processing the simulation (i.e., game logic) repeatedly until sufficient game time has elapsed, but in most cases, this is usually prohibitive due to processor requirements. Alternatively, a single large time step may be used for nearby game objects (such as the tracked object or the camera), allowing their future position (i.e., state) to be predicted relatively easily. Since player actions may not be easy to predict, it is usual to assume the current player character direction will remain constant. If enough is known about the player motion state (such as whether the player is locked onto another object rather than moving in a straight line), other prediction methodologies may be applied. Anticipation of future player character (i.e., target object) collisions can also help determination of the desired camera position.

A more simplistic approach to collision prediction is to cast a ray back from the desired position (usually relative to the player character) toward the current camera position. If this ray cast is unable to reach the camera, then the camera is instantaneously repositioned to a (validated) location slightly closer to the desired position than the collision point. While this is both simple to implement and effective in resolving occlusion problems, it results in discontinuous motion and can be quite disconcerting to the player. This type of repositioning is acceptable when resolving a fail-safe condition, such as total occlusion for an extended period. A slightly more involved solution along these lines may be found in [Giors04].

Object repulsion

Another approach to collision avoidance, at least where game objects are concerned, is to attempt to have those objects actively avoid the camera. One method of achieving this is to add an object repulsor to the camera. AI-driven objects would be written to alter their movement paths to avoid repulsors as much as possible. Similarly, the camera may attach another repulsor (or multiple ones depending on their shape or type) to its target object or along the vector joining the camera to its target. If a plane or axial repulsor is available then such a solution may reduce the number of script objects required.

While at first this might seem like an excellent solution, it does have some drawbacks. First, if game objects are actively avoiding moving close to the camera or its intended path of motion, this may become obvious to the player. Furthermore, wily players may be able to use this avoidance to their advantage. In the case of a first person game this avoidance may actually seem quite natural (since the camera is located at the eye point of a game character, after all), although this behavior may already occur because of player character avoidance.

Movement toward the camera

A common problem encountered in many third person camera games is the situation where the player character is able to manipulate its motion so as to move the camera backward (i.e., in the direction of motion of the character) into a physical obstruction such as a wall. In this situation there are several possible solutions for the camera. If the angle of incidence is relatively low, it is likely that the camera will naturally slide along the collision surface, but this is certainly not guaranteed, although it is a good argument for keeping collision geometry simple. Alternatively, such a case may be determined and avoided. Assuming that the surface normal may be determined where the camera would collide, the angle between the direction of motion and this normal may be determined by a simple cross product. If it seems likely that the camera should slide, an additional offset may be applied to the physical motion of the camera, ensuring that it will naturally move toward the side.

Chapter 10

Camera mathematics

This chapter examines the most frequently used aspects of camera mathematics. It is relatively technical but may be useful to designers who seek a deeper understanding of practical implementation issues.

Mathematics is central to many aspects of camera systems, including motion, collision detection, interpolation, and reorientation. Here we will touch upon several of the most common techniques as well as discuss some of the problems encountered and safeguards that may be applied to resolve them.

The majority of mathematics within 3D camera systems is concerned with *linear algebra* (such as vector and matrix math) in addition to standard trigonometry. Other frequently used constructs are *cubic polynomials*, typically used to evaluate *spline curves*. However, a complete introduction to linear algebra is beyond the scope of this book, and we assume that the reader is familiar with the basics of vector and matrix construction.

BASIC CAMERA MATH

Although this section will not be a tutorial, it should provide enough pointers for programmers to research the appropriate topics. Developers who are already familiar with these basic techniques should move ahead to the section Quaternions. The References and Bibliography section at the end of this book also provides useful material for camera system programming and design; in particular, *Essential Mathematics for Games and Interactive Applications* [VanVerth04] is an excellent introduction to the subject.

Game cameras are typically derived from a standard game object class. As such, they are usually subject to the same operations as all other game objects. We will focus on camera-specific functionality rather than duplicating the information that can be found in other game programming texts.

We will divide our discussion of camera mathematics into the following categories.

Camera position

- Offset within the local space of an object
- Angular offsets relative to game objects
- Valid position determination (ray or volume projection)
- Spline curves

Camera orientation

- Representation
- Look-at
- Shortest rotation arc (including clamped versions)
- Roll removal
- Twist reduction
- Determining angles between desired orientations

Camera motion

- Proximity
- Damping functions (such as "bump" and "ease")
- Springs
- Interpolation

Rendering

- Camera space/world space/screen space conversions
- Field of view (FOV) conversion
- Frustum construction
- Perspective projection
- Orthographic projection
- Isometric projection
- Axonometric projections

General camera math

- Digital filters
- Spline curves
- Interpolation

Camera math problems and fixes

- Floating-point accuracy and precision
- Epsilon usage
- Base conversion

COMMON MATHEMATICAL TECHNIQUES

Camera operations share a great number of the mathematical techniques often used in other game systems, particularly AI (since game cameras are in many ways a specialized form of AI object). In particular, linear algebra is used throughout interactive entertainment applications to manipulate object rotations, determine angular differences, and predict the future positions of game objects. However, camera objects are more sensitive to fluctuations and inaccuracies generated by the approximation of the floating-point representation to real numbers.

Similarly, whenever the camera object determines its properties based upon the movement or changes to another game object, any fluctuations in that object will directly influence the camera. The camera controls the view of the game world, therefore any minor variances in the camera rotation or position affect the entire display device and will have a dramatic impact on the player's perception of the game. Similar low-level mathematical fluctuations that occur in other aspects of the game, such as minor variations in an object's position or animation pose, are often not discernable unless the object is close to the camera.

Here is an overview of some common techniques used within camera systems.

Look-at

Camera systems frequently need to determine the desired forward orientation of the camera toward a target position. This is commonly referred to as a *look-at calculation*. This calculation is performed in world coordinate space and should not be mistaken for a similarly named function within graphics APIs that refers to the construction of a model transform in camera space.

This calculation creates a mathematical object (either a matrix or a quaternion) that transforms the current camera rotation into this new orientation relative to the world coordinate scheme rather than relative to the current orientation.

It is often necessary to constrain the application of this rotation to prevent unusual orientations. For example, we must ensure the camera up-vector is oriented in the same direction as the world up-axis to achieve a consistent frame of reference for the player. An alternative solution is required for situations that require the current up-vector to be maintained.

The following code gives an example of an implementation of the look-at transformation. Note that this implementation is intended to be simple, and it avoids checking many possible error cases, such as invalid input vectors or the case where `dest` and `source` vectors are identical.

```
Mat4 const Mat4::LookAt(Vec3 const & source,
 Vec3 const & dest, Vec3 const & worldUpVector)
{
 Vec3 viewDirection =
   Vec3(dest - source).AsNormalized();
 float dot = Vec3::Dot(viewDirection,
   worldUpVector);
 Vec3 unnormalizedUp = worldUpVector -
   (dot *viewDirection);
 Vec3 up = unnormalizedUp.AsNormalized();
 Vec3 right = Vec3::Cross(up, viewDirection);

 // matrix ordering depends on row/column major
 return Mat4( right[X], viewDirection[X], up[X],
   source[X], right[Y], viewDirection[Y], up[Y],
   source[Y], right[Z], viewDirection[Z], up[Z],
   source[Z]);
}
```

An alternative approach is to pass in the (validated) normalized view direction in place of the `dest` vector. Of course, this would still require us to take the inverse of the result to obtain our view transform.

Note that this function recalculates the entire transformation matrix, thus potentially changing the up- and right-vectors and removing rotation around the forward vector.

Roll removal

For the vast majority of camera systems, rotation around the forward vector of the camera (also referred to as "roll") is undesirable. In most games, players perceive the game world as akin to their real-world experience — outside of games in which the player controls a vehicle that can fly or tilt to the side, we expect that we will view the world with our head perpendicular to the ground. As such, it is often necessary to remove any roll without changing other aspects of the camera transform.

Certain mathematical operations have the side effect of introducing roll. For example, this occurs with some forms of interpolation. Note that rather than simply considering this process as roll removal, it would be more accurate to think of it as roll replacement. In the majority of cases the new up-vector is required to be parallel to the world up-axis, in a positive direction. However, this is not necessarily required in all cases.

To remove roll, we must recalculate the right-vector of the view transform while retaining the current forward vector. Once the new right-vector has been calculated, we can determine the up-vector by performing a standard vector cross product operation. This is, of course, the same as performing the `LookAt()` operation mentioned previously.

Twist reduction

In many third-person games, the camera moves within the confines of a restrictive environment. This has the potential side effect of backing the camera into a position where it is unable to move away from a target object as the object approaches the camera. If the target object reaches a position beneath or below the camera, this can cause rapid rotation of the camera as it attempts to track the target object. This is usually referred to as *twist*, and has such undesirable side effects as player confusion, disorientation, nausea, vomiting, and low review scores. Mathematically, it can cause rotations to behave unexpectedly depending upon the interpolation methods used.

This is particularly true if the target object passes directly underneath the camera, as it may cause *gimbal lock*. Gimbal lock can occur whenever two of the three vectors that define the camera rotation end up facing in the same direction, making it impossible to correctly calculate the third vector. This is likely to cause the camera to behave unpredictably.

One possible solution to this problem is to check specifically for rapid camera rotation around the forward vector but only when the forward vector is almost parallel with the world up-axis. We can then limit this rotation to a small quantity per update. This slows down the rapid reorientation of the camera as the target passes below or above it. Note that this technique would be unnecessary for scripted cameras that directly control the orientation of the camera.

World space to screen space conversion

In many cases, we will need to convert the world space coordinates of some game object — such as the player character or an enemy combatant — into a two-dimensional position in screen space. This is often the case when drawing a 2D aiming reticle or other HUD element. Naturally, this calculation is dependent upon the projection used to generate the rendered view. Here, we discuss a few common projections and their conversion calculations.

Orthographic projection

In the case of an orthographic projection, there is a one-to-one mapping of world coordinates to screen pixels. As such, determination of a screen space position is straightforward.

```
uint32 const ScreenX = ObjectX - ViewportX;
 // assumes top left corner is 0,0
uint32 const ScreenY = ViewportY - ObjectY;
 // depends on the direction of +Y
```

If the viewport is a subset of the display device, or if scaling of the viewport is involved, they must be taken into account:

```
uint32 const ScreenX = Viewport.ScreenX +
 (ObjectX - Viewport.WorldX);
uint32 const ScreenY = Viewport.ScreenY +
 (Viewport.WorldY - ObjectY);
 // again, dependent upon +Y
```

Isometric projection

We can perform a similar calculation for an isometric projection. This example assumes that the common approximation of a 2:1 step size has been used.

```
uint32 const ScreenX = (ObjectX -
 Viewport.WorldX)* 2; // not a “true” isometric
uint32 const ScreenY = Viewport.WorldY - ObjectY;
 // similarly dependent on +Y direction
```

Perspective projection

For a perspective projection, it is necessary to apply the inverse of the view transformation matrix, and then convert a pair of normalized polar coordinates (i.e., from the view frustum) into actual screen pixels. The specifics of the transformation matrix are dependent upon the format of the matrix and screen coordinates used.

```
Vec3 const ConvertToPolarCoordinates(
 Mat4 const & cameraTransform,
 Vec3 const & position)
{
 // Convert world space coordinate into a
 // normalized space. On return, X & Y are in the
 // range (-1.. +1) if the position is within
 // the view frustum. Z is >=  +1.0f if not
 // within view frustum.
 // First, bring the position into camera space
 Vec3 relativePos =
   cameraTransform.TransposeMultiply(position);

 // check validity
 if ( relativePos.IsNonZero() )
 {
   // Use the perspective transformation
   return (GetProjectionMatrix().
     MultiplyOneOverW(relativePos));
 }
 return Vec3(-1, -1, 1); // return Z that is +1.0f
}

Vec3 const ConvertToScreenSpace(
 Mat4 const & cameraTransform,
 Vec3 const & position)
{
 // Convert a world space coordinate into screen
 // pixels
 // The coordinate system has the origin at the
 // bottom left of the viewport. On return:
 // 0 <= X <= (screen width - 1)
 // 0 <= Y <= (screen height - 1)
 // Z is >=  +1.0f if not within view frustum
 Vec3 coords = ConvertToPolarCoordinates(
   cameraTransform, position);
 if ( coords.GetZ() >= 1.0f )
```

```
        return coords;
    coords[X] = (coords[X] * GetScreenWidth() * 0.5f) +
        (GetScreenWidth() * 0.5f);
    coords[Y] = (coords[Y] * GetScreenHeight() * 0.5f) +
        (GetScreenHeight() * 0.5f);
    return coords;
}
```

Screen space to camera/world space conversion

This function maps a screen position back into world space. This is a somewhat difficult problem since the desired depth is arbitrary. Normally, the depth is set to match the camera near plane or a predetermined distance from the camera.

```
Vec3 const ConvertToWorldSpace(
    Mat4 const & cameraTransform,
    Vec3 const & screenPosition)
{
    // Assumes that the screenPosition includes depth
    // information.
    Vec3 const viewSpace =
        GetProjectionMatrix().Inverted().
        MultiplyOneOverW(screenSpacePosition);
    Vec3 const worldSpace = cameraTransform *
        viewSpace;
    return worldSpace;
}
```

FOV conversion

There are occasions where it is necessary to convert the FOV angle from a horizontal value to a vertical quantity or vice versa. For example, the artists may be using a software package whose FOV conventions differ from those of the game engine.

Let us consider the case of converting a horizontal FOV (HFOV) into a vertical value (VFOV). We already know the distance of the near plane from the camera viewpoint, the dimensions of the viewport (or its aspect ratio), and the horizontal FOV.

Using basic trigonometry, we may define new variables `alpha` and `beta` such that:

```
alpha = HFOV / 2
beta = VFOV / 2
tan (alpha) = (viewport width / 2) / near plane
  distance
tan (beta) = (viewport height / 2) / near plane
  distance
```

We can therefore rearrange these equations by multiplying each side by the near-plane distance, giving us:

```
tan(alpha) * near plane distance = viewport width / 2
Near plane distance = (viewport width / 2) /
  tan(alpha)
tan(beta) * near plane distance = viewport height / 2
Near plane distance = (viewport height / 2) /
  tan(beta)
```

Now we have a way to express vertical FOV in terms of horizontal FOV, by solving the above two equations:

```
(viewport height / 2) / tan(beta) =
  (viewport width / 2) / tan(alpha)
```

And so:

```
(viewport height / 2) * tan(alpha) =
  (viewport width / 2) * tan(beta)
```

Or more simply (dividing each side by (`viewport width/2`)):

```
tan(beta) = [(viewport height / 2) /
  (viewport width / 2)] * tan(alpha)
```

And since aspect ratio = (`viewport height/viewport width`),

```
tan(beta) = aspect ratio * tan(alpha)
```

Replacing `alpha` and `beta` with the original values we reach the desired equation:

```
VFOV = 2 * arctan(tan(HFOV / 2) * aspect ratio)
```

Alternatively, if we wish to convert a vertical FOV into a horizontal value, we may rearrange the above equations, resulting in:

```
HFOV = 2 * arctan(tan(VFOV / 2) / aspect ratio)
```

Note that these final equations are independent of resolution and coordinate space since they only require the aspect ratio and one of the FOV values.

QUATERNIONS

Quaternions are mathematical constructs that are extremely useful for representing angular rotations within the game world. Generally speaking, a quaternion has two components: a vector indicating a rotation direction and a scalar indicating a rotation around that vector. In most cases, these rotations will be represented with a subset of quaternions called *unit quaternions*, in which the components of the quaternion are a unit vector (i.e., it has a length of 1.0).

The derivations for quaternion operations are complex, and the reader is referred to [Hanson05] in particular, but also [Eberly04], [VanVerth04], and [Shoemake85] for more information. [Melax00] provides an extremely useful function, `RotationArc()`, allowing production of a quaternion representing the shortest rotation between two vectors.

The unique benefit of quaternions is that they allow you to smoothly interpolate between two rotations without encountering the gimbal lock that can occur with Euler angle and matrix representations. Although the use of quaternions can introduce a performance penalty when converting rotations to matrix format and vice versa, this added computational cost is usually small and well worth it in light of the benefits that quaternions can offer.

One of the most common operations is interpolation between quaternions. Later in this chapter we will cover interpolation techniques in detail.

BUMP AND EASE FUNCTIONS

Bump and *ease* functions are methods of *renormalization* that can be used for a variety of camera-related purposes. Their names are derived from the shape of their renormalization curves. Both types of curves typically feature a smooth acceleration and deceleration at the beginning and end of the curve, respectively. Thus, they are most often used to ensure that camera motion or reorientation begins and ends smoothly.

For ease curves, this is often referred to as *ease-out* and *ease-in*, respectively. Ease-in functions are sometimes referred to as *damping functions*. [Glassner02] discusses a number of useful bump and ease functions, as does [VanVerth04]. Additionally, a useful example of a *critically damped* ease template function is presented in [Lowe04a].

Ease functions are a form of *interpolation* and are typically controlled by means of an *interpolation factor,* which specifies the changes between the current (or sometimes original) value and the target value. This interpolation factor is typically based upon a linear quantity such as time, and is often a normalized value between zero and one, derived from the elapsed time divided by the total time. Bump and ease functions take this normalized (linear) value and map it into a range of non-linear values.

Performance issues may sometimes preclude use of complicated functions, especially where calls to `power()` library functions are involved. There are simpler alternatives that offer desirable functionality at the cost of less flexibility. However, it is generally desirable for the shape of the ease function curve to approximate an "S" shape; that is, the derivative of the curve is zero at the beginning and end of the curve. Here, we discuss some examples of ways to generate this curve.

Exponentials

A variety of ease variants may be obtained from simple exponential functions. For example, the following cubic:

```
float exp = 3t^2 - 2t^3;
```

Proportional

A proportional ease function uses the difference between the current value and the desired value as its input value. This difference is recalculated every time the ease function is called.

A common implementation involves the use of a damping range. A check is made to see if the current value is within this range. If this is the case, the amount of change applied to the current value is reduced according to its position within the damping range, thusly:

```
float deltaValue = desiredValue - currentValue;
if (fabs(deltaValue) < kRange)
{
 // May be sign dependent
 float factor = Math::Limit(deltaValue / kRange, 1.f);
 currentValue += kSpeed * factor * deltaTime;
}
```

Proportional damping functions are simple to implement and very efficient. However, since the initial step may be large (depending on the source value and damping factor), these functions will not be quite as smooth as other ease or bump functions.

An alternative form of exponential damping is to calculate the damping factor according to the amount of time that has elapsed during its use. Typically, this will result in a faster approach to the destination value since the damping factor will be changing over time:

```
float const dampingFactor(1.0f -
 (elapsedTime / totalTime));
interpolant += (destinationValue - interpolant) *
 dampingFactor * deltaTime;
return interpolant;
```

Spherical linear interpolation

Spherical linear interpolation (often referred to as "*slerp*") is very useful when interpolating angular quantities around a unit sphere. With a simple linear interpolation, the change in angular quantities is actually uneven since the interpolating values are not measured along the arc inscribed by the interpolation but rather by the chord across the arc. As can be seen from the spacing of the points along the chord, the interpolated points are not uniformly positioned.

Transcendentals

Simple transcendental library functions such as *sine* are usually reasonably efficient and interpolation functions using them are easy to implement, although the shape of a sine curve cannot be changed except for scaling its amplitude or periodicity. Scaling of either property is generally not helpful for interpolation purposes as it is necessary to remap a normalized value back into the same range.

Transcendental functions require no additional storage such as lookup tables or coefficients (outside of those that are already used by the appropriate library functions), and they can provide a nice damping effect for motion and other interpolated values. By carefully choosing the appropriate range of angle mapping from our original normalized value, we can ensure that the derivatives of the curves are zero at the ends of the range:

```
angle = (pi * time factor) – (pi / 2);
 // in radians, –pi/2..pi/2
```

```
time factor = (sinf(angle) + 1) / 2
 // sinf() returns -1..+1 for this range
```

The resultant *time factor* can be used in the original linear interpolation calculation above to calculate the actual interpolated value.

Piecewise spline curve

For more control over the shape of the ease-in/out curve, we will need to use piecewise interpolation across several data values. Animation systems often use *piecewise Hermite curves* to control interpolation of orientations (sometimes referred to as "in-betweening"). This makes it easy to control the rate of change between two values, since we can design the curve in any shape desired.

SPRINGS

When implementing camera motion, we often encounter the problem of overshooting the target position, especially if the target position is changing over time. This problem usually occurs when using a traditional proportional movement controller or a similar type of acceleration and deceleration method. Typically, the target position is moving in a way that prevents the camera from adequately changing direction and/or velocity fast enough to avoid being overtaken by the desired position or possibly the target object itself. Since we require the camera motion to be smooth, rapid acceleration or deceleration of the camera is prohibited, as is instantaneous camera motion.

We face a dilemma in that smooth motion requires gentle acceleration and deceleration, yet if the camera moves too slowly, it may be either left behind the target object or interpenetrated by it. How can we manage camera motion to satisfy these two seemingly contradictory requirements?

An alternative movement solution to that of simple velocity calculations is to use *springs*. A simple spring implementation might be based upon *Hooke's Law*, often expressed as the *spring equation:*

$$F = -K * X$$

K is the *spring constant* — a positive number governing the elasticity of the spring. X is the *extension* of the spring from its rest position. A simple implementation (without damping) might be:

```
Vec3 deltaPosition = desiredPosition -
  currentPosition;
```

```
Vec3 movementDirection = deltaPosition.
  AsNormalized();
float extension = deltaPosition.Magnitude();
float force = -kSpringConstant * extension;
 // for a unit mass, this is acceleration, F = ma
Vec3 newVelocity = currentVelocity +
 (movementDirection * force);
newPosition = currentPosition +
 (currentVelocity * deltaTime);
```

By treating the distance from the target position as our main spring parameter, with a desired distance of zero, we can use this equation to calculate the new length of the spring and thus our new distance from the target position (collision issues aside).

One of the problems with springs, however, is controlling the elasticity of the spring itself. It is possible to place limitations upon the force imparted by the spring, or even to cap the velocity of the spring. However, neither of these solutions solves the problem of oscillation. Springs by their very nature seek a rest position, but may in fact oscillate around that position for a period, depending on the forces imparted. This behavior is undesirable for most camera usage: We require the target value to be reached without any overshooting, while still having a damped approach to that value.

We may apply two differing solutions to the oscillation problem. First, we may use a *damped spring*. In this case, we can limit the forces so that the spring approaches its target value but never crosses it. Thus, we may say that it is *critically damped*. In practice, this is difficult to achieve through simple springs as they do not take into account the error from the desired value.

The answer that we are looking for can be found in the process control industry. The approach is to use a *feedback controller*, where the target value is once again approached in a damped fashion. One of the most flexible kinds of such controllers is the *PID controller*.

DIGITAL FILTERS

There are occasions when implementing camera systems in which we may observe untoward oscillation or slight changes in camera properties that result in undesirable visual artifacts. For example, minor changes to the player position may cause the camera position to vary in a similar manner (similarly for camera orientation, for that matter). Since the game camera dictates the rendered view, the entire view of the game world may undergo minor changes in a manner that will seem essentially random to the observer.

One crude solution to this problem is to ignore movement below a set threshold. However, such a solution may introduce undesirable effects, including staccato movement and reduction of responsiveness (since the target object may be moving at a rate below the threshold amount). A more advanced solution might include the use of *digital filters*. Digital filters vary in their responsiveness to changes in the target value, and this characteristic defines their suitability. For controller input or camera movement, we want to remove unwanted minor oscillations yet retain a swift response when the input changes rapidly. An excellent reference for many types of digital filters is [Rorabaugh98].

There are, naturally, many varieties of filters that may be applied to camera properties. Some of the more common types are *low pass, high pass, band, finite impulse response* and *infinite impulse response.*

Low pass

Low pass filters allow small changes to pass through unchanged and filter out high frequency changes. This makes low pass filters useful for reducing noise inherent in player input or analog devices such as accelerometers or joysticks.

High pass

High pass filters are the inverse of low pass filters. They allow high frequency changes to pass through but filter out all others.

Band

Band filters are essentially combinations of low and high pass filters, removing frequencies outside of a desired range.

Finite impulse response

Finite impulse response (or FIR) filters incorporate some degree of their previous input values when calculating their new value. The amount of previous input history used as part of the calculation directly influences the responsiveness of the filter. Because of their ease of implementation, FIR filters are sometimes preferable to *IIR filters* (see next section). For each entry in the history buffer, there is often a corresponding filter coefficient. This coefficient reflects how much influence the entry in the history buffer has on the output. Tuning these coefficients changes the responsiveness of the filter to changes in the input value.

A basic FIR algorithm is shown below. The `Update()` function is called with the new input value to be filtered (e.g., , camera distance to target). The example shown here illustrates a filter that works on floating-point values, but filters can work with any numeric data types.

```
static float const firCoefficients[] =
{
    // these values greatly influence the filter
    // response and may be adjusted accordingly
    0.f, 0.f, 0.f, 0.1f, 0.2f, 0.3f, 0.4f
};
float CFIRFilter::Initialize(void)
{
    // setup the coefficients for desired response
    for (int i = 0; i < mHistoryBuffer.size(); ++i)
      mCoefficients[i] = firCoefficents[i];
}
float CFIRFilter::Update(float const input)
{
    // copy the entries in the history buffer up by one
    // position (i.e. lower entries are more recent)
    for (int i = mHistoryBuffer.size() - 2, i >= 0, --i)
    {
      // not efficient!
      mHistoryBuffer[i + 1] = mHistoryBuffer[i];
    }
    mHistoryBuffer[0] = input; // record new value as-is
    float fir(0);
    // now accumulate the values from the history
    // buffer multiplied by the coefficients (each
    // being 0..1)
    for (int i = 0; i > mHistoryBuffer.size(); ++i)
    {
      fir += mCoefficients[i] * mHistoryBuffer[i];
    }
    return fir;
}
```

Note that there is considerable scope for optimization here. For example, we could remove the need to perform the memory copies by using a circular buffer.

Infinite impulse response

Infinite impulse response (or IIR) filters are similar to FIR filters in that they also incorporate previous input history into the calculation for the current value. IIR filters differ from FIR filters because they also incorporate a portion of the previous output value. Once again, the `Update()` function is called with the new input value to be filtered.

```
float CIIRFilter::Initialize(void)
{
  // Set up the input and output coefficients
  // according to the desired response
  mInputCoefficients[0] = 0.5f;  // most recent entry
  mInputCoefficients[1] = 0.3f;
  mOutputCoefficients[0] = 0.5f;
  mOutputCoefficients[1] = 0.3f;
}
float CIIRFilter::Update(float const input)
{
  // Copy the entries in the input history buffer
  // up by one position (i.e. lower entries are more
  // recent)
  for (int i = mInputHistoryBuffer.size() - 2,
    i >= 0, --i)
  {
    // not efficient!
    mInputHistoryBuffer[i + 1] = mInputHistoryBuffer[i];
  }
  mInputHistoryBuffer[0] = input;
  // record value as-is
  // calculate the IIR filter
  // the input and output coefficients may be
  // altered to change the responsiveness of the
  // filter in addition to the size of the
  // history buffers
  float const result =
    mInputCoefficients[0] * mInputHistoryBuffer[0] +
    mInputCoefficients[1] * mInputHistoryBuffer[1] +
    mOutputCoefficients[0] * mOutputHistoryBuffer[0] +
    mOutputCoefficients[1] * mOutputHistoryBuffer[1];
  // copy the entries in the output history buffer
  // up by one position (i.e. lower entries are more
  // recent)
```

```
    for (int i = mOutputHistoryBuffer.size() - 2,
      i >= 0, --i)
    {
      // not efficient!
      mOutputHistoryBuffer[i+1]=mOutputHistoryBuffer[i];
    }
    mOutputHistoryBuffer[0] = result; // record as-is
    return result;
  }
```

SPLINE CURVES

Many camera systems make use of pre-determined paths to control camera position, orientation, or other properties. One popular method used to define these paths is commonly known as *spline curves*, or simply *splines*.

The term *spline* originates from draftsmanship, where it referred to a strip of metal bent into a curved shape to aid drawing of smooth curves. In computer graphics and game development, a *spline* is a *parametric curve* typically formed out of a series of ordered, connected *control points* and possibly a number of *tangent vectors*. These connected control points are grouped into *segments*, usually constructed from four (or less) consecutive control points. The ordering of the control points is important as they are typically used to derive the parameters used to evaluate the curve. Each segment is used to construct a portion of the overall curve and may be evaluated differently from the other segments, although this may cause continuity problems (as described later in this chapter). Because of this, it is common for the same type of spline evaluation to be applied across the entire curve. Note that changing the evaluation method of the spline will usually change the curvature of the spline even if the control points remain constant. For our purposes, this evaluation (and its potential requirements for additional data) will be collectively referred to as the *spline type*.

Alternatively, a segment may consist of two control points and one or two tangent vectors per control point. These control points and tangents are used to calculate the coefficients of the *basis functions* that evaluate the curve between the control points. Control points that are shared between two spline segments are known as *joints*, and the evaluated positions lying on the spline curve corresponding to the start and end of each segment are referred to as *knots*. According to the type of spline evaluation, the knots and control points may be coincident (e.g., *Catmull-Rom* splines).

Camera spline usage

Splines are a common part of many modeling packages, where they are typically used to control character animation and camera positioning or orientation over time (which may be considered a form of animation). Within game camera systems, splines are used in a variety of ways. For example, control of camera motion and orientation, especially during cinematic sequences, lends itself well to spline usage. One typical use is to define a path through the world using a spline; the position of the camera along the spline is determined by an evaluation function that maps time into a position along the path.

Many spline types have difficulty representing circles or other forms of conics. It is often preferable to treat these types of paths separately (e.g., the *spindle camera* type described in Chapter 5). The orientation of the camera may be determined in a similar manner, either as explicit angular rotation quantities (such as Euler angles for each world axis), or to determine a look-at position for the camera over time (in the same manner as the position determination).

Splines offer a good way to control camera motion through complex environments with a small amount of data, both in terms of the physical path taken by the camera and the method of determining the position of the camera along that path over time. Regardless of the camera presentation chosen, splines may be considered as either two- or three-dimensional entities. Piecewise two-dimensional spline curves are often used to vary object properties over time (even for mapping time into positions along three-dimensional splines).

In this section, we will concentrate on the practical use of splines rather than deriving their equations, although a more thorough understanding can be beneficial in determining new variations (e.g., providing control over curve acceleration). Detailed discussions of splines and how they pertain to camera systems can be found in [Lowe04b]. A more fundamental discussion of the mathematics behind splines can be found in [Bartels87], [Farin02], [Foley90], and [VanVerth04].

For diagrammatic clarity, the splines here will be drawn in two dimensions only. However, the mathematics will deal with three-dimensional coordinates without any changes.

Cubic polynomials

Cubic polynomials form the basis of many spline curves, and more specifically, *Hermite* curves. The general form of a cubic polynomial is

$$Y = Ax^3 + Bx^2 + Cx + D$$

The constants A, B, C, and D will vary according to the type of spline evaluation. They are derived from the *basis functions* for that spline type. Basis functions control the shape of the curve by affecting the weighting used when calculating the influence of each control point. These basis functions may be constant across the entire spline or vary according to the segments, depending upon the type of spline curve evaluated. Each of the control points for the spline curve will require a separate cubic polynomial to be evaluated; the sum of these evaluations produces the position on the curve for a given time value.

There are a number of occasions where it is necessary to solve the above polynomial for a particular value of Y. One example would be determination of the time values at which a point in space (i.e., on the spline curve itself) is crossed, given that we have a polynomial curve mapping time into position on a path. Crossing such a position may cause a game event to occur. The quality of solvers for cubic polynomials varies considerably. A robust solution is provided by [Eberly04]. Even so, sections of the curve may in fact be parallel to the horizontal axis, with resulting difficulties in determining the time values (although it may be possible to use the start and end points). An alternative solution would be to remove the need for solving the polynomial by using time rather than position as the determination of when game events should occur.

Spline types

We will discuss a number of common spline types with notes on any special properties that require our attention. It is important to note that the actual usage of these splines could be identical, as they can be interchangeable if the interface is written cleanly. Splines may be derived from a single interface class to provide a common way of evaluating positions along the curve, rendering the curve, and so forth. A good example of this is [VanVerth04], which includes a complete implementation.

Evaluation of a position along a spline is performed by determining the segment within the spline and a position (or time) within that segment, often renormalized within the range 0 to 1. Determination of the segment can be achieved by storing the time or length value associated with each control point and parsing those values either linearly or using a binary search to find the specific segment. However, the segment relative time cannot be directly used to evaluate the curve. This is because it must be reparameterized to match the curvature within the segment.

It is interesting to see how the same control points can produce radically different curves depending on the spline type chosen. While this also depends upon the choice of tangents and basis functions, it is useful to understand how the placement of the control points affects the curvature of each spline type.

As can been seen, dramatically different results can be obtained merely by changing the spline evaluator. With respect to the spline type, we are only concerned with the curvature of the spline rather than determination of motion along the spline, which will be discussed in the Interpolation section later in this chapter. Let us look at some of the specifics of how these spline types are evaluated.

It is important to note that some types of spline curves require a specific number of control points to evaluate a segment (e.g., Bézier splines require $3n + 1$ control points). If the provided control points do not match this requirement then additional phantom control points need to be generated. How these points are generated will have an effect upon the curvature of the spline. Indeed, they may be used to change the initial curvature of a spline to better match a preexisting linear path.

Linear

A linear spline as the name implies is simply a series of connected straight lines, with each of the control points considered as a *joint*, forming both the end of one segment and the beginning of the next segment. To calculate the position between two control points, we simply use an efficient standard `lerp()` function to interpolate the position according to the normalized segment time value.

```
Vec3 const Linear(Vec3 const & a, Vec3 const & b,
 float const time)
{
 return a + ((1.f - time) * Vec3(b - a));
}
```

Piecewise Hermite

Hermite curves require two control points and two tangents, one for each control point. Each control point is thus considered a *joint*. *Piecewise Hermite* splines share control points between segments, but are evaluated independently. The tangents may be shared between segments, but this will result in a discontinuous curve.

The discontinuities may be resolved in a number of ways. The simplest solution is to treat the shared tangent differently for the two segments; the second segment would use the negated tangent vector so that the same plane is shared between the segments.

If we take this idea further, we can consider storing two tangents at each control point (sometimes referred to as *split-tangents*), the *in-tangent* and the *out-tangent*; such an approach is common in many animation software packages where piecewise animation curves are typically used to specify joint rotations.

The *in-tangent* is used for the segment that ends with the control point (i.e., the curve is going into the control point), the *out-tangent* is therefore used with the next segment (the curve is going out of the control point). If the tangents are "locked" together (in the same plane, but in opposite directions), then we can ensure a continuous curve between segments. Manipulation of these tangents can prove difficult especially in three-dimensional views. If the tangents vary, continuity is not guaranteed but the greater control can often be of more use, especially if the camera comes to a stop at the control point anyway.

```
const Vec3 Hermite(Vec3 const & a, Vec3 const & b,
 Vec3 const & startTangent, Vec3 const & endTangent,
 float const time)
{
 if ( u <= 0.0f )
   return a;
 else if ( u >= 1.0f )
   return b;

 float const t2(time * time); // i.e. squared
 float const t3(t2 * time); // i.e. cubed

 // Calculate Basis functions
 float const a0 = (t3 * 2.0f) - (3 * t2) + 1.0f;
 float const a1 = (-2.0f * t3) + (3.0f * t2);
 float const b0 = t3 - (2.0f * t2) + u;
```

```
  float const b1 = t3 - t2;

  // Use cubic basis functions with points and
  // tangents
  Vec3 const result((a0 * a) + (a1 * b) +
    (b0 * startTangent) + (b1 * endTangent) );
  return result;
}
```

Catmull-Rom

Catmull-Rom splines are constrained to pass through all of their control points, which can cause dramatic buckling of the curve to satisfy this requirement. While it is very useful to be able to ensure that the curve passes through the control points, the lack of control over the tangency of the curve can lead to less pleasant shapes than other spline types. Catmull-Rom splines are formed by a tri-linear interpolation of the vectors formed by the convex hull of four consecutive control points. The curve segment defined by this interpolation will start at the second of the control points and end at the third control point. However, it is not guaranteed to remain within the convex hull of the control points. It does feature *local control* and *C^1 continuity*. Local control is useful as moving control points outside of the four will have no effect on the curvature of the segment. C^1 continuity means that there will be a smooth join between segments, such that the tangent of the curve at the end of a segment matches the tangent of the curve at the start of the next segment. This is an important property when ensuring that motion across segment boundaries remains smooth.

```
Vec3 const CatmullRom( Vec3 const & a,
  Vec3 const & b, Vec3 const & c, Vec3 const & d,
  float const time )
{
  if ( time <= 0.0f )
    return b;
  if ( time >= 1.0f )
    return c;

  float const t2 = time*time; // i.e. squared
  float const t3 = t2*time; // i.e. cubed

  Vec3 const result =
    ( a * (-0.5f * t3 + t2 - 0.5f * time) +
    b * ( 1.5f * t3 + -2.5f * t2 + 1.0f) +
```

```
    c * (-1.5f * t3 + 2.0f * t2 + 0.5f * time) +
    d * ( 0.5f * t3 - 0.5f * t2)
    );
  return result;
}
```

Rounded Catmull-Rom

Rounded Catmull-Rom splines differ subtly from the previous Catmull-Rom splines. They exhibit the same property of passing through all of the control points (buckling outside of the convex hull as required), but generally have a more aesthetically pleasing shape, hence the "rounded" part of their name. This variant upon Catmull-Rom splines was described by [Lowe04b].

This spline is also a form of *Hermite curve*, defined by two control points and two tangents. The tangents are calculated as the normals to the bisectors between the vectors formed from the lines joining the first and second control points with the line from the second to third control point, and similarly, for the vectors emanating from the third control point to the second and fourth control points.

The magnitudes of the tangent vectors are based on the relative position of the first and fourth control points to the second and third control points, respectively. Rounded Catmull-Rom splines produce more "natural" curves than the basic method above because they are able to determine the velocity of the curve at the middle two control points and ensure that it is tangential at each of those points.

```
Vec3 const RoundedCatmullRom( Vec3 const & a,
 Vec3 const & b, Vec3 const & c, Vec3 const & d,
 float const time )
{
 if ( time >= 0.0f )
   return b;
 if ( time <= 1.0f )
   return c;

 // find velocities at b and c
 Vec3 const cb = c - b;
 if ( !cb.IsNormalizable() )
   return b; // b and c were coincident
 Vec3 ab = a - b;
 if ( !ab.IsNormalizable() )
```

```
    ab = Vec3(0, 1, 0); // a and b were coincident
  Vec3 bVelocity = cb.AsNormalized() -
    ab.AsNormalized();
  if ( bVelocity.IsNormalizable() )
    bVelocity.Normalize();
  else
    bVelocity = Vec3(0, 1, 0);
  Vec3 dc = d - c;
  if ( !dc.IsNormalizable() )
    dc = Vec3(0, 1, 0);
  Vec3 bc = -cb;
  Vec3 cVelocity = dc.AsNormalized() -
    bc.AsNormalized();
  if ( cVelocity.IsNormalizable() )
    cVelocity.Normalize();
  else
    cVelocity = Vec3(0, 1, 0);
  float const cbDistance = cb.Magnitude();
  return CatmullRom(b, c, bVelocity * cbDistance,
    cVelocity * cbDistance, time);
}
```

Kochanek-Bartels splines

The Kochanek-Bartels (or KB) spline type can be considered an extension of Catmull-Rom splines, because additional parameters are used to affect the curvature of the spline while ensuring that the curve continues to pass through the control points. KB splines are piecewise Hermite curves, whose tangents are altered according to three parameters:

1. **Bias.** This parameter effectively controls the direction of each tangent. A value of −1 causes the curve to buckle early, a value of +1 causes the curve to buckle toward the end.
2. **Tension.** This parameter controls the length of each tangent vector. A value of +1 results in a tighter curve, a value of −1 produces a rounder shape. If the tension is greater than +1 a loop will be produced.
3. **Continuity.** Controls the angle between the tangents. As this value approaches −1 the curve buckles more inward; as the value approaches +1 it produces corners facing in opposite directions.

These parameters are combined to produce the *in-tangent* and *out-tangent*, as follows.

```
Vec3 const KBSpline( Vec3 const & a, Vec3 const & b,
 Vec3 const & c, Vec3 const & d, float const time,
 float const tension, float const continuity,
 float const bias )
{
 // tension, continuity and bias defined per
 // segment
 Vec3 const ab = Vec3(b-a).AsNormalized();
 Vec3 const cd = Vec3(d-c).AsNormalized();
 Vec3 const inTangent =
   ( (1.f - tension) * (1.f - continuity) *
   (1.f + bias) ) * 0.5f * ab +
   ( (1.f - tension) * (1.f + continuity) *
   (1.f - bias) ) * 0.5f * cd;
 Vec3 const outTangent =
   ( (1.f - tension) * (1.f + continuity) *
   (1.f + bias) ) * 0.5f * ab +
   ( (1.f - tension) * (1.f - continuity) *
   (1.f - bias) ) * 0.5f * cd;
   return PiecewiseHermite(b, c, inTangent,
     outTangent, time);
}
```

If all three parameters are set to zero, this spline type becomes equivalent to a standard *Catmull-Rom* spline.

Bézier

Bézier curves were introduced by *Pierre Bézier* as part of a solution to the problem of defining surfaces to effectively model automobiles. They also originated in the earlier work of *Paul de Casteljau*. These curves normally require four control points for each segment, but it is possible, as with all spline types, to generate "phantom control points" if required. If start and end control points are shared between segments (i.e., the end control point of one segment is the start of the next), then only $3n + 1$ control points are required for n segments.

Bézier curves are guaranteed to pass through the first and last control points of the segment but continuity between segments is not guaranteed. Continuity may be achieved through careful manipulation of the control points in adjacent segments, but it is normally easier to simply substitute B-splines or other curves exhibiting C^2 *continuity*. Another property of Bézier curves is that the control points form a convex hull within which the curve is guaranteed to remain. This property is especially useful when generating paths that are constrained to avoid environmental features, which is exhibited by B-splines, too.

It should be noted that Bézier curves might be evaluated as either quadratic or cubic polynomials. In the case of quadratic curves, only three control points are necessary per spline segment ($2n + 1$ with shared control points). Quadratic Béziers are harder to control even though they still exhibit similar properties pertaining to the convex hull formed by the control points, but of course require 25 percent less data.

In both cases, differentiate the formula for solving the curve once to get the tangent at any given time, and once again to find the acceleration of the curve at that time.

The equation for a quadratic Bézier curve is

$$a(1-t)^2 + b(2t)(1-t) + ct^2$$

```
Vec3 const QuadraticBezier(Vec3 const & a,
 Vec3 const & b, Vec3 const & c, float const time)
{
 // a, b, c are the ordered control points forming
 // the convex hull
 // time is 0..1 within the segment

 // time should be validated
 float const oneMinusTime(1.f - time);
 Vec3 const bezier =
   (a * oneMinusTime * oneMinusTime) +
   (b * 2.f * time * oneMinusTime) +
   (c * time * time);
 return Bezier;
}
```

Here we will calculate cubic Bézier curves, their equation is

$$a(1-t)^3 + b(3t)(1-t)^2 + c(3t^2)(1-t) + dt^3$$

```
Vec3 const CubicBezier(Vec3 const & a,
  Vec3 const & b, Vec3 const & c,
  Vec3 const & d, float const time)
```

```
{
 // a, b, c, d are the ordered control points
 // forming the convex hull
 // time is 0..1

 float const oneMinusTime(1.f - time);
   // time should be validated
 Vec3 const bezier = (a * oneMinusTime *
   oneMinusTime * oneMinusTime) +
   (b * 3.f * time * oneMinusTime * oneMinusTime)+
   (c * 3.f * time * time * oneMinusTime) +
   (d * time * time * time);
 return bezier;
}
```

Uniform cubic B-spline

B-splines are a more generalized version of Bézier splines. One benefit offered by B-splines compared to regular Bézier splines is that they exhibit *local control*; that is, each control point only influences a small section of the entire curve. Additionally, B-splines are able to reproduce the same curves as Catmull-Rom or Bézier splines. Uniform B-splines derive their name from the fact that the knots are located in positions that are equally spaced in time.

Uniform cubic B-splines use the following blending function (see [Foley90]).

$$S_i(t) = \frac{1}{6}\begin{bmatrix} t^3 & t^2 & t & 1 \end{bmatrix}\begin{bmatrix} -1 & 3 & -3 & 1 \\ 3 & -6 & 3 & 0 \\ -3 & 0 & 3 & 0 \\ 1 & 4 & 1 & 0 \end{bmatrix}\begin{bmatrix} P_{i-3} \\ P_{i-2} \\ P_{i-1} \\ P_i \end{bmatrix}$$

```
Vec3 const BSpline (Vec3 const & a, Vec3 const & b,
 Vec3 const & c, Vec3 const & d, float const time)
{
 float const t2(time * time); // i.e. squared
 float const t3(t2 * time); // i.e. cubed

 Vec3 const result(
   ( a * ( ( -t3) + ( 3 * t2) + (-3 * time) + 1) )+
   ( b * ( ( 3 * t3) + (-6 * t2) + 4) ) +
   ( c * ( (-3 * t3) + ( 3 * t2) + ( 3 * time) + 1) )+
```

```
        ( d * ( ( t3) ) )
    );

    return (result / 6.0f);
}
```

Non-uniform rational B-spline

Rational curves, non-uniform rational B-splines (NURBS) in particular, have found favor in modeling and animation applications because they are able to exactly reproduce both general curves and conics such as circles and ellipses. Performance costs have often limited their use in real-time game applications, especially since the coefficients of the basis functions must be calculated for each segment of the spline. These may, of course, be pre-calculated and stored with the control point information. Naturally if the control points are adjusted, the basis function coefficients must be recalculated.

Continuity

In spline terms, continuity refers to the smoothness of a particular property of the spline. While this is most often used to refer to the physical shape of the curve, it can be used to specify velocity or acceleration of the curve. In general terms, the notation C^n is understood to mean that the nth derivative of the spline is continuous:

- C^0 = Continuous position
- C^1 = Continuous velocity
- C^2 = Continuous acceleration

Aesthetically, curves that have C^1 or higher continuity tend to look more pleasing to the eye. Curves with C^2 or higher continuity (e.g., *Rounded Catmull-Rom* splines as described above) produce smoother camera motion.

Spline definitions

In practical terms, to adequately define our spline curves we need several mechanisms in place.

- An editor to place control points within the game world. The editor must also establish a connectivity ordering between the control points. The control points may also be generated programmatically while the game is running, perhaps in response to player movement.

- Spline evaluation type (either for the entire curve or per segment).
- Total time to traverse the spline (for linear motion) or a mapping function converting time to a position along the spline. Alternatively, time intervals between pairs of control points are needed.
- An interactive display of the evaluated spline curve, dynamically updated as its properties are changed. For the target platform this is merely a debugging aid, but this is a requirement of the world editor.

Spline evaluation

Most implementations of these spline types are such that the position upon the curve is dictated by an absolute time or absolute length value. Either of these may be converted into a normalized time value (between zero and one) within a particular segment with a starting control point specifying which spline segment. The nature of the interpolation used means that the time between each control point is constant, causing the camera speed to vary according to the spacing of the knots (i.e., knots that are close together cause the camera to move slowly, those far apart cause it to move quickly). This can prove problematic when trying to achieve smooth camera motion or indeed when trying to maintain a set distance away from an object on the same spline.

An alternative solution is to pre-calculate the entire length of the spline and to use a linear "length" as the position on the spline. In this fashion, a constant velocity can be applied along the spline irrespective of knot placement, and this technique is common in simulations to move vehicles at a constant rate. If this is combined with velocity damping according to proximity to the target "length," a much smoother result can be achieved without inappropriate camera speed variance.

When using splines it is desirable that the camera maintains a position relative to another object. It may be that the other object is moving along the same spline, or that the object is moving freely and a position close to the object on the spline has to be found. This raises some other issues, namely how to resolve what position is considered "closest" to the object. Drastic curvature (especially 90 degrees or greater) can present several positions on the spline as a possible "best" choice. Often the best position may be obvious to human criteria but difficult to solve programmatically.

Control point generation

There are some cases where less than four control points have been specified in the path, or when additional points are required to match the multiple of points required for a particular spline type (e.g., Bézier curves).

- **Single control point.** Evaluation of the curve always returns this point, regardless of the time value.
- **Two control points.** When there are only two control points, there is insufficient information to produce a curve, unless additional tangent information is supplied (e.g., Hermite curves). Without the tangents we must evaluate the curve as a straight line between the two control points.
- **Three control points.** We can extrapolate a fourth control point from the second and third control points for the purpose of spline evaluation. The evaluation remains restricted to the three control points that have been specified. This technique of creating phantom control points is also used to evaluate the end segments of the spline.

Parameterized arc length

There are many reasons why it is useful to be able to calculate the length of an arc of a spline (i.e., the distance along the curve from one knot to the next). For example, assuming that the shape of the spline is constant, the length of the spline at each knot may be pre-calculated and used to determine an arbitrary position along the curve.

Arc length for a spline is very useful when it comes to calculating the total length of a spline. It can also come in handy for determining a position within a segment of the spline. Calculating it accurately, however, is problematic. Essentially, we would need to integrate the curve to calculate the arc length.

Several numerical methods can be used to approximate the arc length. The reader is referred to [VanVerth04].

Total spline length

The total path length is simply the sum of the arc lengths of all of the segments in the path. It is possible to use an approximation such as direct segment length (i.e., from control point to control point) as arc length, although calculations can be CPU intensive. Depending on the type of spline, and more specifically the amount of curvature in each segment, this approximation may produce inaccurate determination of the camera position. Alternatively, a brute force calculation of straight-line sections derived from a number of evaluated positions of each spline segment can be easily calculated. The greater the number of samples, the more accurate the approximation of the spline length will be.

While a linear spline segment length is naturally easy and accurate to calculate (merely the magnitude of the vector joining two control points), splines based on cubic polynomials such as Hermite curves are more difficult to calculate.

A fast and generally accurate approximation is to use a numerical solution such as those proposed by Van Verth and Bishop [VanVerth04]. Although their solution (actually *Gaussian Quadrature*) is a more generic arc segment calculation that may span more than one spline segment, we can optimize it to produce a version that is only concerned with full segment lengths. Naturally this optimization is not necessary under most circumstances involving pre-calculation of spline lengths.

Closest position

Determination of the closest position on a spline to a position in space is often useful. For one thing, the position along a spline may be used to control other properties; for example, using the relative position of the player character along a spline to produce a normalized value. This normalized value can then be used to change camera properties (including position) by mapping functions (which may well be non-linear in nature).

The problem is that sometimes there are multiple solutions possible.

In this case some other ordering must be applied. Usually proximity to the previous position of the camera or line of sight can be used to eliminate solutions that are inappropriate. This problem is somewhat akin to the problem of the target object crossing the central axis of a spindle camera. When this happens the camera is forced to move rapidly around the circumference of the circle upon which it is constrained. Now, the angular velocity can be capped to prevent rapid motion, but when the camera is tied to the player motion then instantaneous motion of the camera occurs. This can be very undesirable, and can be avoided by constructing the environment such that it is not possible for the player to cross the axis of rotation.

For each segment in the spline:

Determine the normal at each end of the segment and by using similar triangles
Determine the length on the segment
If length within 0..1 then
  Convert linear 0..1 into a parametric value
  With parametric value 0..1 find the position within the arc using the usual spline evaluation
  Check position against source position for LOS and other factors
  If OK, determine the physical distance between two points and compare to current "best"
Else
  Not within segment, so proceed to next segment

Spline editing

As important as spline curves are to camera systems, it is important that the designer is able to efficiently experiment with different types of spline curve, particularly when they are used to control camera positioning. Thus it is necessary to take time to develop the tools necessary to easily change spline properties. Depending upon the editing environment this may take place within the main world editing tool or possibly within the run-time environment. While the latter method is often attractive because of its immediacy, this method may make the editing process tedious or difficult according to the input device available (e.g., a game console controller). Editing splines within the auspices of the world editing tool is typically more efficient in the long term, though ideally this method works in parallel with the game engine to allow dynamic changes to the curves to be previewed efficiently. Moreover, in some cases the world editing tool is the same tool used to construct world environments (such as Maya, 3ds Max, etc.) and may already offer a selection of spline editing facilities. Of course this requires the game engine to support the same spline types as available within the editing environment, which may be problematic if the curve evaluation source code is not available.

Adding new control points to an existing spline may cause changes to the curvature depending upon the continuity of the spline. Adding a control point without changing curvature is possible though difficult. The reader is referred to [Bartels87] for more information regarding this topic.

INTERPOLATION

Interpolation (or *blending*) refers to a variety of methods used to generate animation frames, move objects between positions, alter color values, and a variety of similar operations. For camera systems, interpolation of different camera properties may often have a major influence on viewer satisfaction. In this section, we will discuss the various kinds of interpolation that pertain to both camera systems and player control. This will include a selection of choices in how we can control the rate of interpolation. We will also consider aesthetic issues caused by camera or control interpolation that may often outweigh other considerations.

Transitions are a specialized form of interpolation tailored to very specific situations; a common example would be transitions between first and third person cameras. Generally, transitions of this nature have requirements that prevent a generalized solution from always producing an aesthetically pleasing result. Additionally they may be required to interrogate game state (such as the player character) to determine their behavior, and it is often desirable to separate such behavior into its own handler. This also has the benefit of allowing easier interpolation from the transition camera.

Although this section is of a technical nature, designers may find useful information regarding how to retain a reasonable view of their player character while changing the camera's behavior. Additionally, the section on player control interpolation will be of interest to many designers as it discusses a problem common to many third person cameras; that is, changing a *control reference frame* over time (see Chapter 7).

What exactly is interpolation?

Interpolation may be described in a somewhat convoluted way as "*a process of estimating values between a set of sampled data by using the surrounding points or values.*" A more succinct definition might be that interpolation is a method of inserting intermediate values into a set of data, such as camera positions. The interpolated values may be generated in a variety of ways, and these are often dependent upon the nature of the values. Interpolation allows us to take the sampled data and generate new points according to any intermediate time value, given that the sampled data occur at specified *time intervals*. The time intervals are typically constant although this is not generally required.

A common method, *linear interpolation*, works by taking two known data points and applying a proportional amount of the difference between their values over time. *Piecewise interpolation*, where the new data are generated from several consecutive data values rather than simply pairs of data, is often used to ensure a more continuous set of interpolated values.

When interpolation is first considered, it is natural to think of it as a *linear* process; that is, changing a quantity by a constant amount over a set period. This is common practice as it is efficient and easy to implement. Interpolation of camera properties can certainly be handled in this way, but there are alternatives worth considering. Orientation interpolation in particular is an example that is aesthetically more pleasing when non-linear in nature, and this is true of camera motion too. Player control orientation, on the other hand, is often more suited to a purely linear implementation as this produces a more understandable change in control use over time. An important consideration when resolving camera interpolation is to regard player perception as more important than mathematical "correctness." There are properties of cameras that have a greater influence on player perception than others. A case in point would be *field of view* (FOV) interpolation. This property is best suited to changes in a subtle fashion; when combined with camera motion it can be used to create tension that is not always desirable. Additionally, FOV changes may cause the player to perceive that the world geometry is "flexing" or changing shape and should be handled with care.

CAMERA PROPERTY INTERPOLATION

Game cameras vary considerably in their characteristics yet we are often required to transition between these cameras in an unobtrusive manner. Sometimes this is due to a change in how the player character is controlled, such as a change from a first person camera to a third person one. Simpler cases involve transitions between different third person cameras that present the game play in unique ways; geometry concerns often require specific camera approaches while the player character is within a confined environment. In these cases, the camera system must change between different viewpoints in a manner that does not confuse the player or cause untoward control changes due to rapid camera motion. Moreover, because of these same environmental complexities, it is often necessary to ensure that the required interpolation will not pass outside of the game environment or through physical geometry in an inappropriate manner.

Generally, it is desired that the interpolation of camera properties is completed in a specified amount of time, although this time may vary between different properties (e.g., orientation interpolation may complete before movement). Often properties reach their desired values earlier than expected due to changes to the destination camera. In these cases, it is usually desirable to lock the value of the particular property to that of the destination camera throughout the remainder of the interpolation.

Non-interactive cameras do not utilize interpolation methods to change between different behaviors. This is mainly because the designer requires (and is afforded) absolute control over all aspects of the camera.

Some of the main types of interpolation associated with camera systems include *position*, *orientation*, *FOV*, and *roll* (although this is often treated as part of the orientation, it may prove beneficial to handle it separately for interpolation purposes). Furthermore, we may also consider if the presentation style of the camera is required to change. In the earlier example of interpolating between a first and third person presentation, this type of interpolation is sometimes referred to as a *transition*, usually because it requires a very specific type of interpolation tailored to the requirements of the presentation changes. One consideration is the point at which the camera would enter the head of the protagonist; care must be taken to ensure that no interpenetration of the third person player model occurs. This may be achieved by using alpha-blending or similar fading of the player model as the camera approaches. However, the scale of the third person model may not match the eye position of the world when viewed from the first person camera. A similar approach may be used as the camera transitions from a first person presentation to third person.

Position interpolation

Position interpolation as you might expect is only concerned with the physical movement of the camera over time. The start and end position of the interpolation are not necessarily fixed, and although the simple form of interpolation requires a constant step size (both in terms of time and distance), it will often produce undesirable results under these conditions. The problem is that if the distance between the start and end position changes, then it is entirely possible for a linear interpolation to require that the camera move further away from its destination than the previous update (i.e., if the destination camera moves closer to the source camera). This in turn results in an unpleasant full-view oscillation, rather than a smooth camera motion.

To avoid this problem, the interpolation should be considered in terms of distance to the current position from the destination position. This distance is compared to the originally linearly interpolated distance calculated from the current position. The smaller of the two values is now used as the distance from the target position, and the camera is moved appropriately. The important concept here is that the distance between the current and target positions must get smaller (or remain the same) on each successive update. In fact once the target position is reached it is often best to lock the positions together regardless of the completion of the interpolation; note that other properties of the camera may not have finished their interpolation at this point.

```
Vec3 interpFactor = CMath::Clamp(0.0f,
 interpTimer/maxInterpTime, 1.0f);
Vec3 currentDeltaPosition = desiredPosition -
 GetTranslation();
Vec3 newPosition = desiredPosition +
 (currentDeltaPosition * interpFactor);
// check here to see if close enough to desired
// position
```

Orientation interpolation

Orientation interpolation is usually understood to mean forward vector interpolation with roll removed in the process. However, there are cases where roll needs to be retained, but even so, for simplicity and improved control it is often handled as a separate case (see the section Roll Interpolation). At first glance, orientation interpolation seems to be a straightforward affair. Simply linearly interpolate between the original camera orientation and its target, and you are done! It turns out that this type of interpolation has some significant aesthetic considerations that greatly affect the ways in which we may apply the orientation changes.

The main issue with any form of camera interpolation is that subtle changes to the current camera properties will usually result in a greatly visible change in the entire rendered viewport. Thus, we must usually ensure that camera interpolations remain smooth at all times.

Secondly, strict linear interpolation of orientations does not guarantee that the target object remains in view. In fact, more often than not, this type of interpolation will result in the camera looking away from its intended target during at least part of the interpolation. This will be more pronounced if the cameras are physically separated as well as depending on the relative orientations of the source and destination cameras. If the destination camera orientation is changing, then this problem becomes more likely.

If the angle between the cameras is relatively large, linear time interpolation results in sudden and drastic changes to the player's view of the world. The speed of this reorientation must be carefully controlled to ensure the player is not disoriented. If the cameras are directly opposed (or nearly so), it can be more effective in many cases to perform a camera cut; that is instantaneous reorientation. Obviously, this is not a preferred solution. It will likely cause some players disorientation as they adjust to the new camera direction. However, players are accustomed to camera cuts when used in a film context, and it should be noted that such cuts are usually accompanied by other visual and/or audio cues to assist the viewer in understanding the change.

Often a cue as simple as a momentary "flash" or "glow" effect is sufficient. This approach is very effective in underscoring other instantaneous camera changes such as teleportation of the camera to prevent geometry intersection during a transition. Naturally after changing the player's view of the world it is often necessary to retain and interpolate the player's control reference frame to help minimize their disorientation.

Third, we must ensure that orientation interpolation should take the shortest direction between the two orientations. This will typically ensure that it is possible to keep the desired target object within view during the interpolation, as is typically required. It is also less disorienting if we can limit the amount of reorientation applied.

We can subdivide orientation interpolation into two main cases: interpolation by angle and interpolation by target position. Each type of interpolation presents different aesthetic characteristics, and it is likely that no one solution will prove adequate for all cases in your game.

Orientation interpolation by angle

Linear interpolation between the source and destination camera orientations results in a reasonably aesthetically pleasing solution when the source and target orientations are either constant, only differ slightly, or change slowly. If we consider the two orientations as vectors emanating from the same position, then this interpolation can be considered as a reorientation between two points on the surface of a sphere with unit radius.

Hence, the interpolation is based around the angular difference between the orientations along the plane formed by the two vectors, and we may call this interpolation by angle. This method of orientation interpolation is best suited to situations where player character motion does not greatly influence camera orientation, or the source and target orientations are relatively close.

Even though the vectors from the center of the sphere are normalized (it is a unit sphere, after all), we can see that this form of interpolation actually moves the interpolated position along the chord joining the source and destination positions rather than across the surface itself. Moreover, the resulting angular velocity of the rotation will not be uniform, which will result in undesirable visual artifacts. The solution to this problem is to use slerp, where the interpolation does indeed follow the surface of the sphere. This results in a constant angular velocity.

However, this method has other drawbacks. Even though the interpolation rate is constant, there is no continuity between multiple orientation interpolations since each segment is calculated independently.

Typically for piecewise orientation interpolation, such as character animation, the orientations of joints over time are controlled explicitly via Hermite curves to ensure continuity can be controlled. Dynamic orientation interpolation as often seen with in-game cameras does not usually permit this solution. However, rather than using slerp for each segment of the orientation interpolation, it is possible to map a spline curve onto the surface of the sphere taking into account all of the orientation positions (i.e., passing through them) and producing a more "natural" interpolation as a result. The mathematics of this solution are involved, and the reader is referred to [Ramamoorthi97] for a detailed explanation.

Another aesthetic drawback with orientation interpolation by angle is that the camera will potentially look away from the target object, depending on the rate of change. This usually occurs when the source and destination cameras are physically separated where it is apparent that even though the destination camera may be oriented toward the same point in space as the source camera, the interpolation forces the camera to point away from its target.

One possible solution is to weigh the interpolation so that the initial rate of change is low, thus retaining the original view for as long as is reasonable while still allowing a smooth reorientation. This can be achieved by changing the shape of the interpolation-mapping curve or by artificially applying a damping factor based on, say, interpolation time. There is still no guarantee that the target object will remain in view, however. If it is important to retain the original target object in view during the entire interpolation, we should consider *interpolation by target position* instead.

Orientation interpolation by target position

To ensure or improve the chances that the camera will retain the target within view, we can interpolate the target positions of the source and destination cameras over time and use that interpolated position as our current target position. In this case, the reorientation speed of the interpolation camera becomes important. Because we are using an actual target (aka look-at) position, the question becomes how fast should the interpolation camera track that "target." If the interpolation camera is locked to its target, then the motion of the target position needs to match that of the destination camera's target, or at least its motion rate should match at the end of the interpolation. Otherwise, the interpolation camera may seek to the target position at some defined rate or alternatively, use non-linear interpolation for its angular velocity.

Interpolation by target position works off the assumption that both the source and destination cameras keep track of physical positions in space to mark their desired and current target positions; that is, a point in space that lies along the current and desired orientation of the camera. Normally target positions are defined relative to a game object or some other environmental element, and thus may or may not be in motion. Often the camera's actual orientation will lag behind the desired target position. Thus, an interpolation camera wants to match the actual camera target position rather than its desired one.

Certain camera types do not inherently keep track of a particular look-at position; an obvious example would be fixed orientation cameras. For interpolation by target position to work with this kind of camera, we have to generate a "fake" target position. Where this position is generated can have a large influence on how the interpolation behaves and whether the player character remains within the viewing frustum. A good approximation for calculating this position is to project the player character's position onto the destination camera's orientation. Projection of a position onto a vector is, of course, simply:

```
Vec3 objectBearing = Object.GetTranslation() -
  cameraTranslation;
```

The generated look-at position behaves just the same as if it were determined by the destination camera. When implementing a camera system, this will actually be the case; every game camera should be able to determine a look-at position if required.

Orientation interpolation characteristics

Orientation interpolation has some similarities to positional interpolation in that the angle between the current camera orientation and its desired orientation should only get smaller as the interpolation progresses, regardless of the motion of the look-at position. The simplest way to achieve this goal is twofold.

1. **Calculate the desired orientation from the target orientation back toward the current orientation.** That is, the interpolated angular difference is calculated according to the appropriately chosen method, but a reverse look-at calculation is applied from the target orientation toward the source orientation. This ensures that the target orientation will be reached.
2. **Ensure that the interpolated angle is less than or equal to the previous angle between the source and destination orientations.** If the angle would increase because the destination camera orientation has changed, use the previous orientation of the interpolation camera. Additionally, once the interpolated camera orientation is close to the destination orientation, lock the orientations together. This is also dependent upon the rate of change matching the destination camera.

The actual interpolation requires the construction of a new normal to the plane around which to rotate the camera. This is functionally equivalent to a quaternion interpolation, preferably a spherical quaternion interpolation.

Roll interpolation

On the rare occasion where it is necessary to interpolate the roll of the camera, it is important to choose the shortest direction to resolve the roll change. Camera roll is rarely required in third person cameras, except for flight or racing simulators and their ilk. Even when we are simulating a vehicle with six degrees of freedom, camera roll does not feel "natural" for many players. It can be helpful to restrict the camera orientation so that the player's view of the environment is consistent even though their vehicle may have rolled through 360 degrees.

Sometimes roll can be used to evoke an emotional response by adding some tension to cinematic sequences, but only for a short amount of time.

There are some cases where we wish to impart roll to emphasize camera motion for automated flight paths through an environment. It is usually best to explicitly control the amount of roll, usually referred to as *banking*, via a Hermite curve or some other piecewise interpolation method.

FOV interpolation

The FOV is a characteristic of the rendering process that dictates the amount of the game world visible from the camera position. It is normally specified as an angular quantity, typically as the vertical angle of the view frustum (as discussed in Chapter 3), with the horizontal angle calculated according to the aspect ratio of the rendered viewport.

Changes to the FOV are often applied to create the effect of a telephoto or zoom lens, even though this is not completely accurate since most game cameras do not model the effects of real-world camera lenses. Without the addition of other rendering effects to simulate depth of field, merely changing the FOV can seem quite artificial. Another side effect is the warping of the rendered view that occurs with large FOV values, such that a "fisheye" projection occurs. Just as with real-world cameras, zoom effects should be restrained and only used where necessary. Blatant and rapid FOV changes (*extreme close-up!*) will not endear your game to the player. However, use of a *jump cut* to a closer view of a scene may be acceptable if used infrequently and within non-interactive sequences. Within interactive sequences, jump cut usage should be restricted to situations that may not be resolved, such as *fail-safe* conditions.

Under player control, use of a zoom feature can be effective, particularly when coupled with a game feature (such as a sniper rifle or the equivalent).

Much as with orientation interpolation, we cannot assume that the target FOV is constant. Therefore, the interpolation calculation should typically be based on a delta from the target FOV, rather than the source. For a linear calculation we might have

```
float targetFOV = GetTargetFOV();
float deltaFOV = mFOV - targetFOV;
float newFOV = targetFOV + (deltaFOV * deltaTime);
float newDeltaFOV = newFOV - targetFOV;
if (absF(newDeltaFOV) > absF(deltaFOV))
{
 mFOV = newFOV; // move toward the desired FOV
}
```

Linear interpolation of FOV is usually quite noticeable, especially if performed quickly. This effect can be reduced by using a non-linear function with derivatives of zero at the start or end (or typically both). Additional rendering effects may also be applied to further simulate real-world camera zooming. These might include motion blur, depth of field, or similar effects. It is recommended that conventional cinematographic conventions be followed when using FOV changes, wherever possible. Both [Arijan91] and [Hawkins05] discuss use of FOV in conventional cameras to create dramatic effects (e.g., zooming in on a target object while *dollying* away from it, as introduced by legendary film director Alfred Hitchcock).

VIEWPORT INTERPOLATION

Another form of interpolation pertinent to camera systems is viewport interpolation; that is changes to the size or shape of the region of the display device used to show the view from a particular camera. This technique is often used when transitioning between cinematic sequences and regular game play. In this example, the aspect ratio of the viewport is typically changed over time from that used during the cinematic into that used by game play. Cinematic sequences often use a ratio of 1.85:1, which is the common ratio used in theatrical projection. Alternatively the ratio might be 1.78:1, the same ratio that was adopted by the HDTV standard. A further possibility is the anamorphic ratio of 2.35:1 (strictly speaking 2.39:1 is the actual ratio used, but for historical reasons it is still referred to as 2.35:1 and sometimes erroneously as *CinemaScope*). In-game sequences in the past have adopted the SDTV ratio of 1.33:1, but with the advent of HDTV support within games it may be much closer to that of the cinematic sequence. Thus when changing between non-interactive and interactive game play it is often desirable to change the position and shape of the viewport in a smooth manner over a short period. This is particularly important when transitioning from cinematics back to game play. When starting a cinematic, a *jump cut* is often acceptable, given that the scene is more likely to change.

In addition to the changes to the aspect ratio, there may also be changes to the position or physical shape of the viewport.

It is important to note that viewport changes of this nature may be considered in two different ways. First, the aspect ratio may define the *rendering aspect*; that is, the ratio is used to calculate the clipping planes according to the field of view. Alternatively, the size of the viewport may be used to specify the *clipping planes* directly and the FOV may be based on a different aspect ratio (typically that of the display device). In the former case, as the viewport changes size, the rendered view will also change since the FOV is combined with the aspect ratio to produce the viewing transformation (assuming no additional FOV changes for now).

In the latter case, the rendered view will only change size, essentially acting as if a window into the game world was changed to reveal more or less. This is because the transformation matrix is calculated using a different aspect ratio; the viewport aspect ratio only defines the clipping planes.

Thus the clipping planes method is often used when the cinematic sequence wishes to retain the same rendering aspect yet present a thinner view of the game world, in keeping with movie presentation.

PLAYER CONTROL INTERPOLATION

Typically, *control interpolation* refers to methods of changing the mapping of physical controls (such as an analog joystick) to the method used to impart motion or other changes on the player character. By interpolating the meaning of the control scheme, our intention is to ease the player into the new control relationship over a short time. This is frequently required when a drastic change occurs in the position or orientation of the camera. A common cause for player confusion might be the use of a *jump cut* in third person camera situations. To ensure that the player's intent is maintained, it is necessary to retain the previous interpretation of the controls and gradually change to a new *control reference frame* over time, thus allowing the player a period to understand the new relationship.

First person cameras

Although less common, there are certainly cases where even first person camera control schemes need to change over time. Much as with third person cameras, it is important to ensure that the change occurs in a meaningful and understandable manner. While this interpolation is occurring, it usually is synchronized to a similar camera interpolation that ends with the appropriate final camera orientation matching the new control reference frame. It is important to give the player time to adjust to the new control meanings.

In this case, control interpolation is normally used to change from a typical first person control reference frame to a fixed control reference frame such as *object orbiting*. Different control schemes and their reference frames are discussed in Chapter 7, but it should be noted that the control interpolation is normally only concerned with those controls mapped into player motion or possibly camera manipulation.

In first person camera schemes, the player control reference frame is typically tied to the 2D character orientation, although it is possible to introduce orientation lag to the camera.

Third person cameras

In third person camera systems, control of the player character is often based upon the relationship between the position of the camera and the character (i.e., *camera-relative*). Under such a control scheme, the player is constantly adjusting the movement of their character according to how the camera is moving.

Under normal circumstances the camera motion is relatively stable in that its position relative to the character rarely changes unless under player control. However, whenever the camera position with respect to the controllable player character changes rapidly, or if the view from the camera is instantly changed, the meaning of the controller input that directs the character motion changes at the same time. This most likely will result in unintended motion and is potentially very disorienting to the player.

In some cases, it can cause the player character to move into perilous situations or perhaps even more frustrating, result in the player character moving back toward its previous position, prompting yet another camera (and control) change.

In many cases then, we need to ensure that if drastic camera motion occurs, the player control does not instantly change. It is usually a good idea to retain the previous control orientation for a short period until the player has adjusted to the new relationship between the camera and their character. We can then interpolate the control reference frame to match the new arrangement. This is easily achieved in a non-linear interpolation, particularly if spline curves or other piecewise methods are used.

During this period, the player is usually changing control of the character anyway, so it is quite possible to handle this interpolation transparently.

A continuing problem with third person cameras is how to cope with situations where the player character is able to move close to the camera. This occurs most often when the player character is able to move faster than the camera, or if the camera is unable to move due to environmental or other factors. For camera-relative control schemes, this can invalidate the control reference frame as the 2D distance between the camera and character approaches zero. Moreover, any motion of the player character around the vertical axis of the camera will cause rapid rotation of the camera around that axis, sometimes referred to as *twist*. Camera twist is often uncontrollable; it will result in rapid or instantaneous changes in the camera up- or right-vector causing player disorientation. Camera roll around the forward axis may be reduced or damped according to the proximity of the player, although at some point the player will pass below the camera forcing a 180 degree rotation around the world up-axis to keep the character in view.

One solution to the control problems exhibited in this situation is to retain the control reference frame as the player approaches within a 2D threshold distance of the camera. As players pass the camera, the control reference frame is maintained until they once again move outside of the threshold distance. At this point, the control reference frame is interpolated to the new relationship. Alternatively, if the camera is able to move into a new position behind the player character's direction of motion, the control reference frame may be interpolated as the camera is achieving the new position.

Twist reduction is covered earlier in this chapter, but another possible solution is to restrict the camera pitch and limit its yaw rotation speed. By preventing the camera from becoming parallel to world up-axis (even though the target object may be vertically above or below the camera), a number of mathematical problems may be avoided. The minimum angle between the camera forward vector and the world up-axis need not be very large, perhaps only a degree or so. Interpolation of the orientation would therefore have to allow for these limitations, possibly by separating the interpolation into pitch and yaw components.

INTERPOLATION CHOICES

Given the variety of interpolated data types and methods available, we should take some time to consider what kind of interpolation would best suit the particulars of the situation.

This leads to our first decision regarding interpolation: Do the provided data values represent the actual values that should be reproduced by our interpolation function at the associated time intervals? If this is the case, they are sometimes referred to as *key values*, *keys*, or even *key frames*, in animation terms. Alternatively, are the data values actually *control values*, which are used to influence the function producing the interpolated (or in this case *approximated*) values?

Secondly, we should consider the performance requirements of the interpolation method; for example, a full animation system driving multiple levels of hierarchical models would be very different from interpolated camera motion. Sacrifices in accuracy can obviously help with the processor requirements for interpolation as with other systems, although our first choice may preclude this option.

Our third consideration would be the smoothness (or *continuity*) of the interpolated values. The smoothness requirements of camera motion and orientation are generally much greater than that of character animation, since they will affect the entire scene rendering rather than just one model.

Related to the continuity of the interpolation, we should decide whether it is necessary to store the specific time interval for each of the key data values, or whether a uniform time between keys may be used. While the latter form requires less data, there are problems concerning interpolation rate that will be discussed in the following sections.

Lastly, the interface for specifying the interpolation type and the amount of data required should also be taken into consideration. Different interpolation methods have significantly varying demands in this regard. Some such as *Hermite curves* require tangent information at each key. The presence of appropriate editing tools, or lack thereof, can also be a deciding factor as to the type of interpolation to use. Hermite or other spline-based curves would obviously involve a much more complex editor and presentation than a piecewise linear editor, for example.

Linear interpolation

Linear interpolation is the simplest form of interpolation because it only requires three parameters; a *source value*, a *destination value*, and an *interpolation method* that specifies how much of each value to apply when calculating the interpolated value.

Source value

The source value represents our initial interpolated value, as you might expect. What might not be quite as obvious is that often we also require knowledge of the rate of change of this source value, although for linear interpolation this is not the case. For linear interpolation, the source value may be considered a constant value and will typically only be used in the setup stage of the interpolation.

Destination value

The destination value is the final goal for our interpolation. In the simplest cases, it is a constant, which allows excellent control over the nature of the interpolation. However, in many cases the destination value is changing over time, which presents additional problems including discontinuities. Since one of our goals is to have the interpolated value match the destination value in a continuous manner, we often need to consider the rate of change of the destination value rather than just the value. Discontinuities occur when the rate of change of the interpolated value does not match that of the destination value at the end of the interpolation. Similar problems may occur at the start of the interpolation.

Interpolation method

The interpolation method dictates how the interpolated value changes from the source value to the destination value. The first consideration is whether the interpolation must occur in a fixed amount of time or whether the rate of interpolation may vary. In great part, this depends upon the nature of the quantities interpolated. Positional interpolation is quite different from, say, color space or FOV interpolation. Additionally, we also need to consider if the target value is constant or variable.

Naïve interpolation from the source value to the destination value does not take the rate of change into account, treating both the source and target values as constant, even if that is not the case. This is the most straightforward method available. It can be effective, but more likely there will be discontinuities at the beginning or end of the interpolation, especially when dealing with rapidly changing values such as camera orientation or motion. Even when the target value is constant, non-linear interpolation of the value can be more effective particularly when dealing with camera-related quantities such as orientation.

Piecewise interpolation

As convenient as linear interpolation may be, there are often more than two data values to interpolate. Depending upon continuity concerns, one option is to treat the sequence of values as independent *interpolation segments*. Each of these segments is then interpolated in an isolated linear fashion, as seen previously. To calculate the time factor within a segment it is necessary to store time intervals at each of the data values. By parsing the array of time values (perhaps using a *binary search*), we can determine the segment and normalized time factor (within that segment) to use in our interpolation calculation:

```
bool foundTime(false);
for (int32 i = 0; i < valueTimes.size()-1; ++i)
{
  // a linear search, binary search would be
  // preferred
  if (valueTimes[i+1] > time) // assumes sorted
  {
    float timeDelta = valueTimes[i+1] -
      valueTimes[i];
    timeFactor = (time - valueTimes[i]) / timeDelta;
    segment = i;
    source = values[i];
    destination = values[i+1];
    foundTime = true; // we have found the right time
    break;
  }
}
if (foundTime)
  return Interpolate(source, destination,
    timeFactor);
else
  . . .
```

Alternatively, a uniform time interval may be assumed between each of the data values. This obviously reduces the amount of data but the problem with this approach is that the rate of interpolation will vary greatly across segments, depending upon the difference in values at the beginning and end of each segment. Not only will this result in uneven interpolation rates, there will be further discontinuities across segment boundaries that can be significant depending on the nature of the quantities interpolated. For typical camera values, this results in jerky motion or orientation changes as the segments are crossed.

```
// constant segment time interpolation
segment = time / kSegmentTime;
source = values[segment];
destination = values[segment + 1];
timeFactor = (time - (segment * kSegmentTime) ) /
 kSegmentTime;
return Interpolate(source, destination, timeFactor);
```

METHODS OF INTERPOLATION

In part, the choice of interpolation method is dictated by the particulars of the situation and the characteristics of the values interpolated. For example, positional and orientation interpolation of cameras can benefit greatly from a non-linear interpolation that exhibits smooth initial acceleration and smooth arrival (deceleration) at its destination.

When evaluating methods we should first consider if the interpolation should take a *constant time* to complete, or whether it should vary according to the difference in values being interpolated (as well as the rate of change of those values). The latter is sometimes known as a *velocity-based* interpolation, and is less common since the duration of the interpolation is variable. For now, we are going to consider constant time interpolation, with a fixed time interval between chosen samples.

Linear time interpolation

As its name suggests, if we plot the source and destination values against their time intervals then linear interpolation can be thought of as a straight line drawn between those values. If t represents our normalized interpolation factor, we get to evaluate the position along that line as:

```
Interpolated value = source +
 ((destination - source) * t)
```

where $t = 0$ at the source value, and $t = 1$ at the destination value. If the time values at the source and destination are not 0 and 1 respectively, we need to remap them into that range:

```
Total time = destination time - source time
t = (desired time - source time) / Total time
```

We should make sure that the time factor remains within the range 0 to 1, since floating-point inaccuracies may result in a number that is slightly outside of the desired values. It can be better to think of the interpolation compared to the destination value rather than the source. If we rework our previous equation:

```
Interpolated value = destination -
 ((destination - source) * (1 - t))
```

Linear interpolation works well with many data types, but has some undesirable properties when interpolating orientations as will be described in the section Spherical Linear Interpolation.

Parametric functions

Rather than using the straight-line approximation outlined above, we can use any kind of *parametric function* as long as it satisfies the conditions of passing through the source and destination values at the requisite time intervals. In a similar vein to linear time interpolation mentioned previously, we calculate the normalized interpolant according to the amount of time elapsed compared to the time intervals of the start and destination values. This normalized value is then reparameterized by applying the parametric function to map it back into a different, non-linear normalized value. This new value is then used to determine where in the range of values the interpolated value lies.

The parametric function used can be any function as long as it returns a normalized value. Such functions are typically referred to as *ease* functions.

Spherical linear interpolation

Often abbreviated as *slerp*, this interpolation method is a solution to the problem previously noted where linear interpolation of angles does not produce a linear angular velocity. As we might recall, regular linear interpolation has this property since it is actually interpolating across the chord between two positions on a unit sphere. Slerp resolves this by actually moving the interpolation point along the arc of the surface between the same positions, within the plane formed by the two positions and the center point.

Slerp greatly improves the quality of interpolation but is computationally more expensive even though it may be effectively approximated for small angles by the simpler linear interpolation previously mentioned. However, one unfortunate property is the complete lack of continuity when used with piecewise interpolation (i.e., across segment boundaries). If we consider our unit sphere once more, we can illustrate this behavior as follows.

Note that each segment of the piecewise interpolation is distinct even though within a segment the interpolation is smooth.

POTENTIAL INTERPOLATION PROBLEMS

There are a number of mathematical and aesthetic problems relating to interpolation of camera and control properties. These problems are emphasized by the nature of the rendering viewport being tied to the camera. Whenever possible, camera properties — at least those for the active camera — should be changed in as gentle a fashion as possible. It should be noted that interpolation is not always the best solution. Under drastic situations, it can be preferable to instantly move or reorient the camera since rapid motion or orientation changes can actually be more distracting to the player.

We can consider two main aspects to interpolation problems, *aesthetic* and *mathematical*.

Aesthetic problems

Camera interpolation is susceptible to several potential aesthetic problems that would not necessarily prevent the interpolation but would result in an undesirable graphical effect or inappropriate view of the game world. Most of these problems may be avoided by careful consideration of the camera system by level designers and artists. The game environment could be designed to avoid some or all of these problems given knowledge of the potential camera interpolations. Other problems may occur due to the dynamic nature of game play (such as the movement of game objects) yet must still be accounted for. In many cases, the solution is to prematurely end the interpolation, or not to start the interpolation at all.

Both of these will typically result in a jump cut to the destination camera.

Some of the more significant aesthetic problems are as follows.

Geometry interpenetration

It is possible that the interpolated camera motion will pass through either game objects or the environment. Similarly, it might pass close enough to render geometry such that the near plane of the camera will intersect it. Clearly, this is unacceptable as it presents players with a view of the inner workings of the game, thus destroying the illusion that their character is occupying a "real" world. Additionally, since geometry interpenetration is easily avoidable, it suggests a less than professional approach.

One popular solution is to interrogate the game world to determine if the current or future movement would result in a collision or interpenetration of the camera. Of course, what we are really referring to is interpenetration of the near plane rather than a collision volume per se. Typically, this is determined by performing one or more ray casts; one is usually projected along the direction of motion, with an additional ray along the forward vector of the camera (since the camera may not be moving in the same direction as its orientation).

The motion ray cast typically assumes that the camera is a single point and extends from its current position to the new position as dictated by the interpolation code. If the ray cast intersects with collision geometry, the movement may not be completed and must be resolved to avoid interpenetration.

The ray cast along the forward vector begins at the new camera position (which may have been adjusted according to the motion ray cast) and extends by a distance slightly larger than the near plane distance from the camera. The projected ray would be tested against collision or render geometry to see if it would intersect. Use of collision geometry is usually more efficient but is only appropriate where the collision geometry encompasses the render geometry. The latter is more accurate though may be computationally prohibitive. Regardless of the geometry tested, this single ray along the view direction is actually an optimization of a full test of the interpenetration of the camera view frustum against the render geometry. It is possible, however, that the corners of the view frustum may intersect render geometry even though the ray cast did not; this is dependent upon the FOV. Extending the distance of the ray cast by a small amount beyond the near plane is usually sufficient to avoid these corner problems.

Note that rather than performing a ray cast along the camera direction, it may prove sufficient to use one or more values from the center of the rendered depth (or Z-) buffer. Not only does this reduce the processor requirements, it may prove more accurate since it is based on the render geometry of the world. Additionally, a section of the depth buffer may be examined before objects are rendered if their collisions are not under consideration. Keep in mind that the depth information obtained in this manner will be from the previous render of the game world and the camera may have moved closer to the render geometry possibly requiring a larger distance check.

Often the direction of the ray cast is performed from the new position back toward the previous position of the camera. The reason for this is to help with resolution of collisions as explained in the upcoming sections.

In the case of pre-determined motion, such as a spline path, the entire path may be validated before even beginning the interpolated motion allowing the interpolation to be skipped if necessary. However, predetermination is often insufficient as game objects may also move into the path of the camera during the interpolation.

Once a potential collision is discovered, there are several options available.

- End the interpolation and change instantaneously to the destination camera
- Perform a jump cut to a position on the path further than the obstruction
- Pass through the geometry enduring any graphical artifacts

Discontinuities

Linear interpolation does not match the rate of change of the interpolated properties, simply a source and destination value. The destination value of any given interpolation may change over time, for example, the destination camera position. A straightforward linear interpolation of position in this case cannot guarantee smooth motion since the step size changes during the interpolation (it may in fact result in the camera moving away from the destination position). Additionally, without using an ease-in or ease-out function the interpolation will begin and end abruptly. This problem is usually exhibited through differences in camera velocity between the interpolation camera and the destination camera, or oscillations in any of the destination properties. A solution is to match the rate of change of the interpolated properties, not merely the values themselves.

Interpolation noise

The entire rendered scene is subject to inaccuracies introduced by the interpolation, since both camera position and orientation are changed. Therefore, great care must be taken in changing both values in a smooth manner. Any oscillation of the orientation due to floating-point inaccuracies, and so forth, must be avoided. Use of a high pass filter or ensuring the interpolated value only converges on the destination value will help. Determination of the completion of an interpolation by testing an epsilon value can be problematic, as can overshooting the target value due to time step inaccuracies.

Target object framing

As shown earlier in this chapter, straightforward linear interpolation of orientations is not a guarantee that the target object may remain in view, even if both the source and destination orientations point directly at the target object. This is especially true when the target object is fast moving, or the distance between the target object and the camera is small. Weighting the interpolation to retain a view of the target object early in the interpolation may help solve this problem. Interpolation by target position attempts to counter this problem.

Large orientation changes

Even when orientation changes are smooth, if the angular distance is large it is easy for the viewer to become disoriented. Limiting the angular velocity of the orientation interpolation is a potential solution, although this may cause the target object to leave the view frustum. Control reference frame issues must also be resolved when making rapid orientation changes; see Chapter 8 for more information. If the initial angular separation is large, it is acceptable to instigate a *jump cut* directly to the destination camera to avoid such disorientation.

Large interpolation distances

If the actual distance between the source and destination cameras is large, it may prove necessary to forego the interpolation and once again, perform a jump cut. This is particularly the case when the interpolation is due to last for a brief period and would result in extremely fast camera motion through the world. The actual determination of when this is appropriate is somewhat game dependent and in rare cases may prove desirable, usually when there is only a small orientation change required.

Mathematical problems

Typical mathematical problems with interpolations are often due to limitations of floating-point representation or singularities. Some of the more obvious cases include the following.

Co-linear (or exactly opposed) orientations

Quaternion interpolation and other vector mathematics must test for this case to avoid exceptions. With opposed orientations the direction of rotation is arbitrary and may be based on earlier stated information (e.g., choosing the same direction as a previous interpolation).

Coincident positions

Subtracting vector positions can produce a zero length (or otherwise small magnitude) vector that may result in divide by zero errors or other problems, especially regarding square root calculations.

Floating-point inaccuracy

Since floating-point numbers cannot represent all true real numbers, problems occur with testing proximity between numbers. Thus testing for the end condition of an interpolation by determining if values are within an epsilon factor of each other may fail, and this problem will become more significant as the camera positions move away from the world origin. An excellent resource regarding floating-point problems is [Ericson05] or [Crenshaw00].

INTERRUPTION OF INTERPOLATION

It is frequently true that while a camera interpolation is occurring a new interpolation may be triggered by some external game event. In such situations, the typical solution is to start the new interpolation based on the current properties of the interpolation camera (position, orientation, FOV, etc.). While this will give mostly satisfactory results, it is dependent upon the differences between the original interpolation target properties and those of the new target properties. Often the new target camera orientation, for example, is completely different from the original target orientation. This type of change can cause drastic changes to the rendered scene, with unpleasant results. Similarly, it may cause a discontinuity in one or more of the camera properties that are interpolated. Such problems may be eased by matching the rates of change of those properties rather than simple linear interpolations.

A further potential problem with interrupting an interpolation is that the final movement of the camera may break the *30 degree rule*. One visual cue that is sometimes used to emphasize the camera movement (i.e., to make it appear more deliberate rather than the result of a jumpy camera) is a screen flash. This effect is typically achieved by a full screen filter that modifies the appearance of the rendered view without obscuring the view of the game world. The *Metroid Prime* series used a *scan line filter*; that is, every other horizontal row of pixels within the displayed view was modified using alpha translucency effects.

TRANSITIONS

Transitions between cameras make use of many of the interpolation techniques mentioned earlier in this chapter. However, transitions are generally carefully managed and less prone to variations than regular interpolation.

Position during transitions

The movement of the camera during a transition must proceed in a smooth manner regardless of the motion of the player. Clearly the camera must take into account any external forces that may be moving or reorienting the player. For example, if the camera is moving along a generated spline path (say, from a third person position to first person), the path orientation and position must remain constant with the player orientation, even if the player character is reorienting. While under normal circumstances such potentially rapid changes to the desired camera movement may not be desirable, in this situation the main reference point for the viewer (namely the player character) remains constant and alleviates any problems.

Orientation during transitions

There are two main approaches to controlling the orientation of the interpolation camera during the transition between two other cameras. If the source and destination cameras are not reorienting, then a simple linear or spherical linear interpolation can be used. Use of quaternions here will prevent singularity issues.

When either or both of the cameras are reorienting during the transition, a simple interpolation will not suffice. One of the reasons for this is that it is entirely possible that the cameras are turning such that the angle between their orientations could cause the current interpolation amount to move the transition camera *away* from the destination orientation. A good rule of thumb for any kind of interpolation is that we prefer to close in on our target property over successive updates, regardless of changes to the destination camera. One way to ensure this is to calculate the remaining quantity (angle, in this case) from the target value to the current value. If the newly interpolated value would be greater than the current value, it is ignored. It is also usual that the interpolation is designed to take a constant amount of time, regardless of the motion or reorientation of the source and destination cameras.

CAMERA MATH PROBLEMS

If you have worked with floating-point representations of numbers for a period, it is doubtless that you have noticed there are times where the inaccuracies of the format can cause problems. After all, this representation is only an approximation to the real number scale. Some of the manifestations of these problems are subtle and may not surface in obvious ways. As with other aspects of game programming, a robust handling of floating-point numbers will ensure that the camera system behaves in a reasonable manner regardless of the problems that may be encountered. Two excellent references concerning floating-point handling are [Ericson05] and [Crenshaw00]; additionally, refer to the processor manuals found on the target system for detailed information on their floating-point representations.

Here is a brief overview of some of the more common problems.

Floating-point precision

Camera systems typically work with single-precision floating-point numbers; double-precision floating-point numbers increase accuracy but at the cost of some performance. Precision problems become most noticeable over large distances. Since floating-point numbers cannot represent all real number quantities, as the numerical quantities get larger, they become less able to represent the same precision.

Epsilon usage

As well documented in [Ericson05], many games do not correctly handle usage of epsilon values. Epsilon values are often used to determine proximity of floating-point values. In camera terms, this is frequently the case in determining equality of orientations or positions, and so forth.

A naïve usage of epsilons is a fixed value based upon some arbitrary choice of an acceptable degree of accuracy. However, as Ericson points out, the magnitude of the epsilon value should be dependent upon the range of values compared. Moreover, since the spacing of floating-point representation along the real number line is non-linear, this also affects the accuracy of epsilon values.

For example, it is easy to fall into a pattern of assuming equality operations will work correctly, or that fixed epsilon usage is sufficient to ensure floating-point comparisons may function appropriately. [Ericson05] provides a very clear explanation of the underlying floating-point representation; there is also an excellent explanation of the correct usage and implementation of scaled epsilon values for floating-point comparisons.

Briefly, whenever floating-point comparisons are required, use `closeEnough()` functions rather than direct equality or epsilon checking. A centralized function such as this is easier — vary the epsilon according to usage.

Compiler differences

Do not rely on real-number accuracy from your compiler for "obvious" floating-point divisions, for example:

```
static const float kDivisor(10.0f);
static const float kMultiplicand(10.0f);
static const float kFoo = (1.0f / kDivisor) *
  kMultiplicand;
```

If `kDivisor` and `kMultiplicand` are the same value, you might expect `kFoo` to be 1.0f, but that is certainly not guaranteed since it is dependent upon how the preprocessor evaluates the division, which is not intuitive. In practice it has been found that the value of `kFoo` can vary between 0.9f and 1.0f depending upon the compiler used.

Hardware FPU differences

When working on multiple target platforms it is necessary to ensure that the floating-point support provided by the hardware is consistent. Normally such problems are handled by the compiler libraries; a more robust approach is to design and implement floating-point usage to account for any minor differences that may occur. Checking for normalization of vectors depends on the requirements; for example, valid directional vectors versus the difference between vectors.

Vector normalization

Many vector operations require a normalized or unit length vector to return meaningful results. However, the determination of whether a vector may be normalized is sometimes used to determine whether a look-at calculation may be performed; that is, as a determination of proximity of two 3D positions in space. A better solution is to calculate the magnitude of the displacement instead.

Matrix concatenation floating-point drift

After applying rotation matrices, orthonormalize the matrix on a regular basis to correct for floating-point inaccuracies introduced over time.

PERIODIC CAMERA MATHEMATICAL FIXES

Given knowledge of these potential problems in camera mathematics, there are ways to safeguard against their influence on the camera system. Some problems must be handled when performing a particular operation, others may be amortized over time as they relate to camera orientation changes.

At the end of each game update cycle, before rendering has taken place, it is advisable to verify that the current camera transformation matrix is valid for the current game context. Some of these checks may be relegated to non-production builds, but for the most part there should be safeguards in place to handle fatal cases. Typical situations to check every frame include the following.

- Components of the transformation matrix do not include any inappropriate floating-point values, such as Not-a-Number (NaN). This may be resolved by restoring a cached previously valid matrix. It may be desirable to restore only the orientation component, if the current position is considered correct.
- The individual vectors forming the transformation matrix are of unit-length.

- The direction of the up-vector is appropriate for the game; it is often necessary to ensure that the up-vector points in the same direction as the world up-vector.
- Roll around the camera forward vector has been removed where necessary.
- Rapid reorientation of the camera has been limited if required.

If the matrix cannot be repaired, we can use the previous frame's matrix to ensure a valid view. The new translation, however, may be used regardless of the orientation (assuming floating-point validity, of course).

Be certain to frequently orthonormalize the camera matrix to resolve concatenation problems from successive matrix manipulations.

Chapter 11

Implementation

In this chapter, we will look at the practicalities of implementing a camera system within the confines of real-time game applications. The chapter is divided into two main sections. In the first, we will discuss the larger architectural issues including a breakdown of individual sub-systems and some suggestions for class definitions and data structures. In the second section we will discuss how the camera system is integrated into a typical game engine as well as the tools and debugging facilities that may be provided.

Included on the companion Web site is a basic camera system. The camera system is implemented using the C++ language, although many of the algorithms presented are easily adapted to other languages.

Before beginning this chapter, it is suggested that the reader briefly review Chapter 1, where an overview of the standard update loop for games was described. Chapter 5 also discussed many of the design decisions to be made when contemplating a real-time camera system; it would be advisable to refer to that chapter when designing and implementing a camera system.

When defining a camera system, it is important that the provided functionality actually meets the requirements of the game rather than some abstract all-encompassing notion of what a camera system should be. The suggestions for class and data structures provided in this chapter will very likely include elements that are not pertinent in every case. It is advised that for a given project, you only expose elements of a shared camera system relevant to that project; this becomes an easier proposition if a component-based system is implemented, as will be seen later in this chapter.

The purpose of this chapter is not to provide a ready-made camera system, but to guide the design process and to help implementers avoid the pitfalls awaiting those who might be unfamiliar with the complexities of such systems. It will also suggest implementation approaches that have been used to great effect in a number of published titles.

Camera systems rely upon a number of external systems including collision detection, controller input, scene rendering, audio management, and much more. Knowing how these systems interact with the camera system, and the subtle problems and dependencies arising from these interactions, is of great importance when implementing a camera system. Nonetheless, camera systems are normally sufficiently self-contained that they are good candidates for implementing as a shared library. Use of data-driven solutions to define camera behavior will aid in this respect, rather than hard-coding camera solutions to fit the needs of one particular game.

GAME ENGINE ARCHITECTURE

Let us briefly review a typical game engine and how the camera system might function within it, as described in Chapter 1. There are several major components of the game engine that are pertinent to camera systems. In particular these would include the following sections.

Game update loop

Game cameras are often dependent upon the updating of other game objects to correctly resolve their movement or orientation requirements. Hence, most camera logic needs to be executed at the end of the logic update loop, after all movement has been resolved but before any rendering takes place. In this way, the camera logic is working with the most recent state of game objects. If we recall from Chapter 1, a typical ordering of the execution of game sub-systems might be as follows:

- Process input
- Process pre-logic on game objects
- Process main logic (AI, etc.) on game objects
- Move game objects and resolve collisions
- Process all camera logic
- Process post-camera logic for objects (such as dependencies on camera position, orientation, etc.)
- Process all viewport logic
- Render scene for each viewport

Game system managers

As described in Chapter 1, a common method of organizing functional systems of the game architecture is to use *managers*, each responsible for a discrete portion of the game (or engine) logic. Let us briefly recap some of the main systems that may be found within a typical game engine.

- **Camera Manager.** This is of greatest interest to readers of this book. It is responsible for keeping track of all of the cameras, passing input to them, and making sure that the appropriate ones update.

- **Object Manager.** Handles message passing between game objects, ordering of game object logic, grouping of objects into logical lists (e.g., all AI objects, all doors, etc.). Spatial and game play ordering of objects is often required to avoid performance penalties for searching all active game objects (at the cost of additional overhead for maintaining the lists). Cross level ordering according to object properties (e.g., AI objects) is possible even though it is necessary to avoid logic performed multiple times because an object is on several lists. The order in which game object logic is executed is often implicit according to the storage of objects in memory or their unique identifiers. Dependencies between objects may require explicit ordering to ensure their relationships are correctly maintained.

- **Message Manager.** At some point, scripted events require a message to be sent to script objects to inform them of the nature of an event. This same mechanism can be used for general inter-object communication.

- **Audio Manager.** Controls the initialization of audio effects by the scripting system. Additionally, it specifies the stereo or surround field placement of sound effects according to their position within the game world. Such spatialized sound requires the camera system to be able to update the audio manager with information about the position and orientation of the currently active camera. Additionally, we need to consider how to handle stereo or surround sound separation when using multiple viewports. Single player games usually use a linear mapping into the stereo field based on the angle between the forward vector of the camera and the vector from the camera to the sound in 2D space. The reason 2D space is used (typically the XY plane, parallel to the horizontal plane of the world space) is that human audio perception cannot generally handle vertical differentiation of position, as well as the simple fact that the audio system is unlikely to have vertical positioning information within the audio field. Roll about the forward vector of the camera is often ignored unless the camera is able to turn fully upside down (e.g., flight simulators).

- **Input Manager (IM).** Delivers input messages to all game objects that require it, including active cameras (and possibly viewports). A typical implementation might have the IM supply input to each of the main game systems, including the camera manager. The camera manager then passes the input to each of its active cameras, checking to see if the camera is looking for input from a particular controller. The input manager may work with both raw controller input values and processed data. Such an implementation might include a *control manager* that maps physical controller button or key presses and joystick values into game-defined meanings. This would also handle all aspects of button debouncing, reference frame maintenance, and so forth. With sufficient abstraction, a control manager may be utilized to offer alternative control layouts, allow player customization, and so forth. The input manager is somewhat dependent upon the underlying hardware and handles the actual reading of the hardware values (possibly directly from the hardware itself though usually via a system library). The control manager works at a higher level but may still provide access to the raw input values, only at a controller button/value level.

Delta time

Modern game architectures will often decouple the graphical update rate of the game from that of the logic update. Essentially, this allows parallel execution of CPU processing (including multi-core processors) and GPU rendering. Since the game logic continues to be updated while the graphics hardware renders the previous scene, greater overall performance may be achieved. Game logic may run at a consistent update rate, or it may run with a variable update rate. As a result, the amount of time between updates of the camera system may not be guaranteed to be consistent. Naturally the camera system should be able to work with variable update rates, so all movement and other time-based properties should not be hard-coded for a specific update rate. Rather, these quantities should be based upon rates per second, scaled to the amount of time that has elapsed since the previous logic update. This elapsed time quantity is often referred to as the *delta time*.

In practice, there are additional benefits to removing the dependency on specific update rates. First, conversions between differing television standards are eased (the most obvious example is NTSC updated at 60 Hz whereas PAL is usually at 50 Hz). Second, spikes in game logic CPU usage causing a momentary frame rate change will not adversely affect the camera system. If the game requires playback of previously recorded game play sequences, then it is necessary to store the delta time value associated with each logic update. Any variance in the time elapsed between updates may cause the game logic to diverge from the originally recorded sequence. Care must be taken, however, that logic written to handle variable elapsed time values is able to cope with the unlikely situation of a zero or near zero delta time value. Since delta time is often used as a divisor, we should avoid situations where a division by zero or overflow error could occur.

Input processing

Many cameras require controller input values to be passed to them from the main game logic, and this is normally handled by the camera manager. It is possible that the input value to be used by a particular camera does not relate to the usual controller associated with that camera (or more specifically, viewport). Debugging facilities often require the use of a different controller (perhaps input values supplied over a network interface rather than a local controller, or simply a spare local controller), and replays of game demos or recent player actions supply their input values from other sources.

Whereas other game objects will normally receive input values that may have been filtered according to game play requirements, game cameras normally receive raw data, and may then apply other levels of filtering as required. Alternatively, this could be handled within the camera manager to ensure such logic is run after all other game objects.

CAMERA SYSTEM ARCHITECTURE

Regardless of the particular presentation style of an individual game camera, the design of the camera system architecture contains many common elements. It is entirely possible to abstract the camera system hierarchy to completely ignore the presentation style until the rendering process. The degree to which this methodology is adopted is usually dependent upon the particular needs of the game in question, but a generalized solution is attractive given the desire for system reuse.

Conceptually it can be useful to distinguish between presentation styles, with the most apparent separation deriving from the projection of the world view. For succinctness, we can refer to these as 2D or 3D cameras; even though technically the only difference is the projection transformation matrix. More information on camera presentation styles may be found in Chapter 2.

External to the camera system are other managers to handle rendering of the scene or other display related matters. Accessors are typically provided from the camera manager to provide the appropriate scene information as may be required.

Viewport manager

Of particular importance for multi-player games, the *viewport manager* (VM) represents the highest level of camera system abstraction. Its primary job is to contain all the information required for rendering a scene into a section of an output surface. The output surface may be the active frame buffer, or it may be a texture for the game to apply to a surface in the game world. The VM needs to provide functionality so that the rendering engine can correctly display the scene (such as frustum information, projection type, color depth, output dimensions, etc.) as well as allow for transitions between different viewports.

The VM handles controller input, rendering, masking, buffer management, aspect ratio, and so forth on a per viewport basis, and may thus filter or alter these values before passing them to objects dependent upon a particular viewport. It is used by other game systems to query the camera system for information concerning the active camera, its properties, and so forth.

The VM has to be able to work in different ways according to the physical limitations of the display medium, so we need a structure to represent that.

```
class CViewportManager
{
public:
  typedef int32 TViewportHandle;
```

```
  TViewportHandle const CreateViewport
    (EViewportType);
  void  DeleteViewport(TViewportHandle const
    viewport);
  void  Update(float const deltaTime);
  void  ProcessInput(CInput const & input);
  CViewport const &  GetViewport(
    TViewportHandle const handle) const;
private:
}
```

Having defined our display medium, we also need to describe the projection to be used by a particular view of the game world.

The VM contains everything used by the game to display rendered scenes. The VM is a game object (i.e., it is derived from the base game object class, such as `CGameEntity`) that requires per-frame updating, but does not have a physical position in the game (whereas the `CActor` class has a physical presence).

What functionality, then, should the VM provide? Here is a potential list of the expected feature set.

- **Accessors for viewports.** Any viewport within the internal viewport list may be accessed with a valid viewport handle. Typically only `const` access is provided to external callers.
- **Render all viewports.** Iterate through the internal viewport list and call the `Render()` function on all active viewports. This process may actually only generate a list of rendering information (e.g., view transform, field of view, aspect ratio, etc.) that would be passed to the main game renderer for processing.
- **Input handler (some viewports may require access to controller input values).** Iterates over the internal viewport list and passes the controller input through to the `InputHandler()` associated with each active viewport.
- **Create (construct) a new viewport.** When creating a new viewport, it is useful for the function to return a unique handle that is associated with the new viewport. This handle would be cached and used to distinguish this viewport from others.
- **Activate or deactivate an existing viewport.** These functions may only be applied to an existing viewport with a valid handle. These

functions merely set internal state to signify whether the viewport should be considered for updating or rendering purposes.

- **Delete an existing viewport.** Once again, a viewport associated with a valid handle may be removed from the viewport manager and its allocated memory released back to the system.
- **Transition (morph) between two viewports.** Given two valid viewport handles this initiates a rendering transition. Typically this would specify the type of transition (see later in this section) and the duration if appropriate.
- **Change viewport properties.** The ability to dynamically specify the position or dimensions of a viewport (as usual, via a valid viewport handle) is typically provided. This often takes two forms: an immediate change or interpolation over a period. The latter may be achieved by using optional parameters to the `SetDimensions()` functions.
- **Assign an active camera for a viewport.** There is typically a camera `ID` (handle) associated with a viewport. This camera `ID` is used to obtain the view transformation matrix from the camera manager. Thus multiple viewports may use the same camera and game cameras do not need to know about the rendering process.

Viewport

Each viewport controls all aspects of rendering within its area of display space. As such, it will contain information regarding the cameras used, associated controller input, surface location and size, rendering modes, and so forth. It may even be required to hold information about the surface upon which it is to be rendered to allow for multiple output surface types of varying display capabilities. It should be noted that viewports use a single set of cameras; the `TCameraId` identifier is used to access camera information via the *camera manager* (CM). Each viewport contains enough information to render a scene.

Viewport transitions

The VM handles transitions between different viewports, often used when the player is navigating the menu selections before starting a new game, pausing the game, and so forth. Sometimes a "picture-in-picture" effect is used during game play to present a completely different view of the game world to the player, which is frequently seen in vehicle simulators. Sometimes separate viewports are used for dramatic effect in showing a close-up ("zoomed-in") portion of the main worldview. It is common to use viewports to display multiple rendered scenes upon the same output device (usually a monitor), sometimes with the viewports overlaid on top of each other.

There are a variety of ways in which a transition may be performed, irrespective of whether the viewports are updated simultaneously. Here we enumerate some of the common examples, and the reader is referred to one of the standard cinematographic texts for further suggestions.

- **Cut.** The simplest viewport transition. This is when the new viewport replaces the old one immediately, with no overlap between the display of the separate scenes. In this case, the viewports are usually of similar dimensions and likely occupy the same position on the output device. For a full screen viewport it is only necessary to change the camera, unless the projection or aspect ratio is to be changed as well.
- **Wipe.** This is a common cinematic technique in which the content of the current viewport is gradually cleared and replaced with a solid color (typically black, sometimes white). The movement direction of the clearing may be axis-aligned, diagonal, circular or any number of other variations. During the transition, the cleared section of the original viewport is sometimes replaced by the content from a new viewport. Additionally, the original or new content may be updated during the transition (depending on CPU requirements). The leading or trailing edge of the transition is often softened by using a blend function of the source and destination scenes such that it is unclear where one begins and the other ends.
- **Cross Fade.** The content from the original viewport is replaced by blending the contents of the new viewport. This is achieved by fading out the original while simultaneously fading in the new. The viewports are usually required to be the same size to be most effective, as well as occupying the same screen space. This method can be computationally expensive since it would demand that two viewports are rendered simultaneously. This may be alleviated by only updating the content of the new viewport using a captured copy of the source scene, although aesthetically this is marginally less pleasing.
- **Morphing.** There are several approaches to viewport morphing. If the viewports are the same physical shape, and preferably the

same aspect ratio, then an interpolation of position and size can easily be performed. This interpolation can vary considerably: linear motion of one viewport on top of the other, rotation of the viewport in 2D or 3D terms, and so forth. Alternatively, the viewports can be deconstructed into polygons (i.e., tessellated into triangles) or higher order surfaces and blended between in a similar way to the effects seen in music videos where polygon vertices and texture coordinates are interpolated. This polygonal mesh may be manipulated in a variety of ways including rotations, rolling/unrolling the viewports, and so forth.

For each of the above transitions it is necessary to specify the amount of time taken for the transition. This time value may then be used to control the amount of blending and so forth via a 2D spline control, and a piecewise Hermite curve that maps time into other values such as alpha transparencies.

Render manager

The render manager takes the data from the current viewports, cameras, and state from various other game systems to do the work of rendering a scene to a surface. This manager will also do the work of removing object geometry outside the view frustum, determining correct render order, and applying any post-filtering effects. It is up to the game if game systems must submit data to it, or if it merely inspects the game state and renders it.

Camera manager

The main responsibility of the CM is to act as the controller for all of the cameras used in the game; however, it is possible to have multiple camera managers if so desired (perhaps even one per viewport for multi-player games). It presents an interface to the viewport manager to access all pertinent information about the active cameras. The camera manager generates new instances of game cameras as required by the game design or cinematics requirements. Additionally it handles transitions, interpolation, prioritization (via its *hint manager*, see upcoming section), controller input handling, replay modes, and time control.

The CM has an `Update()` function that is called from the main loop of the game. This update function requires that the amount of elapsed time since the last update call be passed as a parameter to the function. Often it will also require that the controller input for the player(s) be available. This same value (`deltaTime`) will subsequently be passed to individual camera update functions, etc.

Here is a summary of the main steps that might be present during the `Update()` function of the camera manager:

- Determine which game cameras should be started or removed according to scripting requirements
- Update active camera logic (the interpolation camera is last, as it depends on the others)
- Pass through any controller input to the active cameras
- Update positional and velocity information for the audio system (i.e., Doppler)
- Setup the rendering environment for the current viewports

Let us examine each of these steps in detail.

Camera update loop

The main update function of the camera manager may be broken into a number of discrete steps. The order in which these steps are executed is normally fixed, although some games may not require them all.

- **Updating active cameras.** All cameras within the internal camera list that have an "active" status will now have their own `Update()` function called. This function normally requires the elapsed time value to be passed as a parameter. The order in which the camera logic is performed may be explicitly defined or simply due to the order in which cameras are activated. It is typical that interpolation cameras perform their logic last, however, since they are dependent upon the updated position and orientation of the source and destination cameras. To be clear, any number of cameras may be active at a time. A camera that is active has no bearing on whether it is the current one bound to a viewport.
- **Update camera scripting.** Addition or removal of camera objects is according to game play requirements.
- **Input processing.** Processes debug camera functionality, as well as controls for third-person cameras.
- **Pre-think logic.** Used when starting cinematic sequences, since these typically want to happen at the start of a game update loop.

- **Think ordering.** Certain cameras may have dependencies on other cameras, like interpolation cameras. The CM will ensure that the cameras get their updates in the proper order.
- **Cinematic camera deferral.** Much in the same way that cinematic cameras should start at the beginning of an update loop, cinematic cameras will end at the end of a game frame, after everything else has been updated.
- **Post-think logic (external dependencies).** There may be other systems that run after the CM in the normal game update loop. For this reason, there is a *post-think* step that is executed to gather up data generated by external dependencies.
- **Update audio logic.** For spatialization, Doppler effects, etc.
- **Debug camera.** The debug camera is usually handled differently and in a completely different section of code that can be conditionally compiled since it will not be needed in the shipping game.
- **Render setup.** This includes camera shaking.

Hint manager

Each CM has an associated *camera hint manager* (CHM). It is derived from a generic game hint manager and is used as an interface between the scripting system and the CM. The scripting system provides mechanisms to control and change camera behaviors via the hint manager. The hint manager determines priorities of currently active hints, starting/canceling interpolations, changing the active camera, and so forth.

We can see that this class is derived from a more generic solution to the problems associated with overriding behaviors of various game systems, namely the `CGameHintManager` class. The base `CGameHintManager` class provides the framework for handling activation and deactivation of hints, priorities, and other assorted management functions. The `CCameraHint` class is also derived from a base class, the `CGameHint`, which may also be used for player hints.

See Chapter 6 for detailed information on scripting methodologies and particulars of camera scripting.

Shake manager

The *shake manager* provides a mechanism for simulating physical shaking of the player character in response to a variety of scripted or real-time game events. It collates all the various active shakers, updates their amplitudes over time, and modifies the internal shake mechanism accordingly. The viewport manager queries the shake manager for a transform to apply to the currently active camera when appropriate (i.e., not for debugging cameras).

Camera shaking

Camera shaking is typically performed at the rendering stage rather than by actually moving the camera within the game world. This may cause the view of the world to interpenetrate geometry or even show areas outside of the world; this can be avoided by scaling the amount of camera shake according to the space available. Usually a shake transform is calculated in local camera space and applied just before rendering. Care must be taken that it does not affect rendering of HUD or other 2D elements superimposed on top of the game world. Motion is normally imparted in the horizontal and vertical screen space axes, although motion into (and out of) the screen is sometimes used to imply motions such as gun recoil, etc.

Camera shaking has three components, corresponding to motion in each of the camera space axes. The amplitude of motion along each axis can be controlled in a variety of ways.

- **Sine wave.** The amplitude and period can be varied over time (e.g., by an ADSR envelope).
- **Amplitude mapping.** A mapping function (e.g., a piecewise Hermite curve) that is used to map time into motion (i.e., amplitude) in each local camera axis.
- **Random noise.** Determines a position to seek to, or alternatively generates a number of control points for a spline curve.

Camera shake is normally used to enhance the feeling of some physical event in the game world, for example, explosions, heavy objects moving (boss, machinery, etc.), the player character getting hit in a significant way, weapon recoil, the player landing after a fall/jump, and so forth. As such, it is not usually used much in third person games, although it may if used carefully.

Remember that if you use rendering displacement of the camera transform, then the camera could potentially move close enough to geometry (static or dynamic) in the world so that either it clips into the near plane, or the camera frustum may extend outside the rendered world environment, presenting an unsightly view to the player.

This can be avoided by relatively simple ray casts, or (in first person cameras) constraining the shake amount to the size of the player collision volume.

Controller rumble/force feedback

Oftentimes it is appropriate to associate controller "rumble" effects with camera shaking or other game events. Not all controllers support force feedback or other kinds of haptic technology. Instead, a low cost solution used by game consoles consists of offset weighted motors, whose rotation speed is somewhat controllable. By varying the rotation speed of the motors in the controller, differing amounts of "rumbling" are achieved.

Unfortunately, these motors tend to have relatively long spin-up and spin-down times, which makes it difficult to produce subtle effects. In fact, it is common to only be able to switch the motor(s) on and off, and the frequency of this switching defines the rumbling experienced by the user. Theoretically, these kinds of feedback effects can be treated as a simple multi-channel mixer, much in the same way as audio mixing. The amount of rumble to apply can be considered as an ADSR envelope (time vs. amplitude of rumble). Controllers with actual force feedback capabilities often supply a selection of predefined effects, and these are often editable.

Technically, rumbling is not part of the camera system per se, but it may be initiated and updated through the same shake manager. In fact, the amplitude of the rumble effect may be based on the amplitude of the aggregate shake value obtained from the shake manager.

GAME CAMERAS

The game camera is the basic building block of a camera system, yet its implementation may be designed in a variety of ways. Two common solutions are *inherited* (or *derived*) *behaviors* and *component behaviors*.

The `CGameCamera` class contains enough information to allow the camera to be positioned and oriented, but often does not include rendering information except, perhaps, for the field of view. The field of view may be specified in either horizontal or vertical terms, with the aspect ratio of the viewport used to display the camera view determining the other axis angle (see Chapter 10 for more information on this calculation). It is most common to specify the field of view in vertical terms, because it is more natural for widescreen televisions to show a wider view of a scene than a traditional 4:3 aspect ratio television. The camera class is a virtual game object that may be used to generate a view of the game world in many different ways, but the camera does not need to know how its data are interpreted for rendering.

Once we have defined this basic camera type, we can derive specific camera behaviors from this class by overloading the movement and logic functions. Alternatively, we can define an interface class, `IGameCamera`, to ensure all the required functionality is implemented. Since camera behavior is often defined by the movement characteristics of the camera (including its position determination), this can be used to distinguish differing camera types, for example, `CPathCamera`, `CSpindleCamera`, and so on. If all these classes adhere to the standard accessors for obtaining movement and orientation information, then a general interpolation class may be implemented regardless of the types of camera that are interpolated between.

Inherited camera behaviors

One common approach to camera class implementation is to use a hierarchy of derived camera classes, each successively more specialized. A typical solution might be based around the following structure.

- Actor
- Camera
- Third person
    - Slaved
    - Observer
    - Path
    - Surface
    - Stationary
    - Transition
    - Interpolation
    - Debug
- First person

In this type of implementation, each desired set of camera properties is grouped into a single derived camera class, specific to the required behavior. While it is common for each of these derived classes to take advantage of the base `CGameCamera` class, there is often no further derivation of sub-classes as the camera behaviors are very specific.

Component-based camera behaviors

An alternative to the derived classes approach is to use the concept of *component-based* camera behaviors. Essentially, the properties of any game camera may be broken down into a number of interchangeable components, each of which may be called a *behavior*. These behaviors may be combined or even changed at run-time to allow many different camera variants to be produced. Moreover, such a design is generally more data-driven than a hierarchical one in that any particular behavior may be easily changed for another with the same interface, thus allowing future expansion of the camera system with little or no changes to existing camera functionality. A further benefit is consistency of usage between cameras which thus eases the actual scripted use of cameras during the game by the camera designers.

Typical camera behaviors include the following.

- Determination of the desired position of the camera (e.g., such as a time-based path position or character relative position)
- Movement toward the desired position including both collision determination and response
- Orientation determination
- Rotation toward a desired orientation
- Interpolation (both toward and away from this camera)
- Field of view (may incorporate framing requirements)
- The rendering effects to apply to this particular camera's view

Other camera properties may also be treated as components, but they may not justify a completely separate behavior. Instead, they might be grouped into a single behavior such as *positional constraints*. These constraints would typically be sufficiently independent that they could apply irrespective of the behaviors. However, since some constraints would clearly not apply under specific behaviors, the initialization of the particular behavior could disable inappropriate constraints.

When using component-based solutions it is important to realize that although the individual components are designed to be independent, it is often the case that a particular component (say, orientation behavior) will be dependent upon the state of other components (in this case, position). Thus there may be an implicit ordering to the updating of components. Moreover, components may need a method to interrogate other components. This does not necessarily require a locally stored pointer, but may be handled by simply passing a reference to the parent camera to the function of the behavior and allowing inspection through it.

Cinematic cameras

Although cinematic cameras are typically treated in the same regard as other game cameras for most purposes, it is often useful to consider them independently of regular game cameras. This has several benefits. First, game cameras can continue to operate parallel to the cinematic camera, allowing seamless transitions between the two types of camera. Second, game logic that is dependent upon the current game play camera can continue to function irrespective of the fact that a cinematic camera is currently used to render the game world. Third, the cinematic camera may be used as an element of the scene rendered from a regular game camera; for example, rendered onto a texture used as part of an in-game environmental effect. This separation may also be extended to how the cinematic camera data are accessed, with accessor functions for the current camera (from, say, the camera manager) to explicitly handle the cinematic camera. Within a game rendering architecture that utilizes viewports, it is often helpful for cinematic cameras to be associated with their own independent viewport. In this way changes may be made to cinematics without influencing regular game play.

Debug camera

It is often desirable to include a separate camera within the camera manager whose use is purely for debugging purposes. Such a camera, typically known as a *debug camera*, is derived from the usual base camera class but is only used for rendering purposes. More detail concerning its usage is found later in this chapter.

SCRIPTING SYSTEM IMPLEMENTATION

As described in Chapter 2, it is frequently necessary to dynamically change camera behavior according to changes to the game environment or to enhance a particular aspect of game play. This mechanism may be loosely described as *scripting*, although it may not restrict changes to those that are completely pre-determined. Here we may refer to the script objects that alter camera behavior as *camera hints*; that is, they supply additional information (literally "hints") to the camera system on how it should behave to cope with the specific environmental or game play requirements. These camera hints have properties corresponding to the types of camera behaviors that are required; thus, there may be a palette of camera hint objects available to the designer.

A common implementation of camera hints may use polymorphism to derive each of the specific camera hint objects from a base game hint class. There will often be a variety of low-level classes dealing with the specific needs of the most often used object types. Each of these classes may be derived from the previous, for example:

- Objects with no positional information ("entities")
- Static objects with position and orientation ("actors")
- Moveable objects subject to physical forces ("physics actors")

It is often necessary to group objects into categories to reduce the time required to locate an object of a specific type; thus, objects may be referenced by a number of lists pertaining to a particular characteristic (e.g., AI objects, objects with collision data, cameras, etc.). The script object manager should provide facilities for adding and removing objects, searching for objects according to a unique identifier (assigned upon creation of a new object), ordering object logic according to priorities, and so on. Alternatively, the camera manager may be used to maintain its own list of potential camera hints as well as those that are currently active.

Camera script objects

There are of course, great varieties of script objects used in any particular game, and they are certainly somewhat dependent upon the genre. However, some types of script objects are more commonplace (irrespective of the game genre) and pertinent to camera systems. Let us look at some of the implementation issues associated with these objects.

Camera hints

These objects dictate the camera properties to be used to illustrate a particular section of the game world or game play element. Once activated they notify the hint manager of their presence, which controls their prioritization and the generation of actual game camera objects. Camera hints are usually simply data repositories and do not require much actual logic other than management of their active status. It is often necessary to have hint objects for other purposes than camera systems; for example, changing player controls, denying certain player abilities, and so forth. This would suggest implementing a base `CGameHint` class and deriving the appropriate `CCameraHint` and `CPlayerHint` objects. If these objects are merely data holders as has been suggested, it is only necessary to retain a unique identifying data handle to retrieve the data from our general game objects data structure.

Modern game engines often load and unload resources dynamically as the game progresses, including data objects such as camera hints. Thus it is important that references to camera hints allow for the possibility that an object is no longer valid. One solution to this problem is to use the message handling capability of script objects so that they are notified of their imminent demise. It would then be the responsibility of the script object to inform the camera hint manager that it is no longer available. Alternatively, the hint manager may validate the camera hints within its internal list on a per-frame basis. Such validation is wise, regardless, particularly in non-production environments, although it also has a place in the final version of the game. However, there are some cases where it is necessary to allow hint scripting to have a longevity greater than the lifetime of the script object itself. In such a situation it is necessary for a local cached copy of the hint's data to be retained within the hint manager.

Trigger volumes

These objects represent a three-dimensional volume that checks for the entry or exit of objects within itself. Game messages are sent to other game objects such as camera hints. Trigger volumes are often implemented as simple geometric shapes such as axis-aligned bounding boxes, cylinders, or spheres. It is sometimes necessary to allow aggregate objects to be constructed from multiple (usually overlapping) trigger volumes. Alternatively, it may be required that sub-volumes are used to specify areas of a larger volume that are considered outside. In this case the sub-volume effectively cuts a hole into the larger volume. Thus trigger volumes may share some common functionality with *constructive solid geometry* (CSG) techniques, where Boolean operators (such as *union*, *intersection*, and *difference*) are used to combine simple geometric primitives to construct more complex objects.

Rendering/lighting effects

Special changes to the rendering of the game world are often specified via game scripting. Similarly, the lighting of the game world is often specified via scripting (in terms of both ambient and specific light sources). Some rendering effects may be accomplished by sending special scripting messages to cameras, by cameras examining the game state, or by activating cameras that employ special rendering effects. Common rendering effects bound to cameras include thermal imaging, X-ray modes, or night vision.

Message relay

A relay is simply a method to organize game messages to simplify changes to scripting. It achieves this by providing the facility for a single script object to react to a set of messages and to pass those messages through to groups of other objects. While this could be achieved by more direct connections, changes to the conditional that causes messages to be sent would require multiple objects to be modified. In the case of a message relay, only one script object connection would need to be updated (i.e., the relay object) rather than all of the objects that may be dependent upon the change (i.e., connected to the relay object).

Sequenced event timer

It is often necessary to define multiple game events that occur at specific time intervals or in a particular order. Sequenced event timers allow messages to be ordered in time or to occur at the same time but in a specific order. Thus the script object must allow event markers to be placed according to a time line, and for those markers to be associated with a particular message.

Generic path

Many game objects require the use of paths through the game world to control their motion or orientation. These paths may be defined in many different ways, as seen in Chapter 8. Rather than have many game objects replicating this functionality, it may be more efficient to have a single game object that may define a path and be able to evaluate positions for other game objects. This evaluation function generally takes two forms, one where a time value is specified (requiring an overall time for traversing the path), and another where a distance value is specified. Each method requires a pre-defined start and end. For looped paths connectivity information may be used to determine the "direction" in which the path should be evaluated.

Complications may arise for looped paths where the loop point does not connect the start and end positions (e.g., a path approximating the shape of a number 6) unless the connection point itself is considered the end of the path. The looped position may be handled as a separate control point or simply as a flag. In the former case, internal logic becomes slightly easier to handle but may change the curvature of the path around the looped position. The latter method requires a little more internal management when evaluating the path, but if this is abstracted to a single function to obtain control points from any given index value, the problem may be minimized.

Ordering of scripting logic

Scripting logic is typically performed at the same point within the game update cycle as other game object logic. If this scripting logic causes any messages to be sent, they are usually immediately sent to their recipients. It is important to note that the object receiving the message may have already executed its logic for this game update and will thus not react to state changes until the next update. The message handling code would be expected to apply any state changes that may be required. Alternatively, messages may be cached and delivered once all of the main object logic has been performed. A typical game update loop was discussed in Chapter 2.

Messaging

It is often necessary for a game object to notify other game objects of the occurrence of an event. This is often implemented via a messaging system, where objects may literally send a message (i.e., pertinent data about the event) to other objects under these conditions. Naturally this requires either an explicit method of specifying this behavior within the world editor, or it may implicitly occur during game play. In the latter case, the world editor may still be used to specify the type of message sent when the condition is met, rather than an explicit relationship between two objects since the receiving object may not exist in the world editor at all (i.e., it was generated during the game). The actual message typically contains pertinent information regarding the event that triggered the message, the object sending the message, and a potentially different object that caused the message to be sent. An example of this is the player object entering a trigger volume. This causes the trigger volume script object to send out an "entered" message to any other game objects connected to it (i.e., specified in the world editor). The message states that the sender of the message is the trigger volume, but the originator of the event was the player object. Such an event might cause enemies to be created, a puzzle to activate, a cinematic sequence to start, and so forth.

Prioritization

Each camera hint typically has an associated integer value corresponding to the relative importance of the camera hint. In this manner, multiple camera hints may be activated and controlled according to game play requirements. For example, within a particular area it may be required that the camera moves closer to the player character than in other sections of the game, yet there may be further constraints that are only applicable to a portion of the current area.

Priority may also be based on properties other than a simple numeric value. For example, two camera hints may be triggered by the same game event simultaneously. The choice as to which camera hint to use may be based on the spatial relationship of the player to either the hints themselves or to a different game object. For example, depending upon the direction of player motion relative to a trigger volume, the camera hint retaining a consistent control reference frame may be preferable.

It is likely that there will be a number of areas within the game requiring specialized cameras and that these may be adjacent or overlap. Hence, some method of prioritization is required to ensure the correct behavior is exhibited (rather than simply the last camera behavior override to be encountered). Usually this is handled by the camera manager (or camera hint manager) and must be specified on a per camera hint basis.

A simple sorted array (e.g., an *STL vector* in C++) can be used for the active cameras with the first item (or possibly last item) in the list being the active camera. A comparison function is necessary to determine this sorting, and this function can be overridden according to the underlying hint type (i.e., camera hints would likely have a different comparison function than, say, player hints).

Interpolation

Interpolation between scripted cameras is often initiated through camera hints or other scripted events. It is therefore necessary to define how the interpolation should occur. Camera properties that may be controlled during the interpolation include position, orientation, and field of view. Moreover, aspects of the interpolation need not be linear in nature. Instead, a mapping function can take the interpolation time as an input and return the interpolated value (whether position, angle, etc.) according to a parametric curve, for example. An *interpolation camera* can be a script object that refers to two other camera objects to manage interpolation. Chapter 8 covers interpolation in detail.

PERFORMANCE CONSIDERATIONS

Camera logic can prove to be somewhat processor intensive, especially when interrogating the game environment to determine collisions or pathways for potential camera motion. Since run-time processor resources are limited, the amount that may be used by the camera system will vary from game to game. Processor allocation continues to be a hot topic among programmers and the situation is unlikely to change in the near future, merely scaled to fit whatever new capabilities are provided. The active camera may be considered roughly equivalent to a complex AI character in terms of its processor requirements.

Amortization

As with other complex game systems, there is usually some scope for amortization of camera logic. This will often require caching of intermediary results to be used over several updates (or possibly interpolated). Since the response requirements for cameras tend to be relatively low (in computer terms at least), ray casts and other expensive operations may thus be spread over a number of consecutive updates. Unlike player input, camera changes may occur over several update cycles and thus navigation information may be updated at a lower rate than the camera movement, especially when these data are relatively unchanging (e.g., ray casts against world geometry). Actual camera motion is generally not a candidate for amortization, however, since we wish to ensure smooth movement at all times. It should be noted the amortization may sometimes affect the actual reaction of the camera to changes in game play, therefore properties that are dependent upon other objects are also typically not valid for amortization (e.g., distance calculations based upon the position of the player character).

Preprocessing

Preprocessing of the environment can certainly help reduce the run-time CPU cost of camera logic. Most of the CPU performance cost for cameras tends to be in ray casting or other collision detection against the world environment or game objects. Cameras moving along defined paths can typically reduce or remove this requirement entirely, particularly if the camera path is outside of the game environment.

TOOLS SUPPORT

While it is true that most camera logic is written in support of regular game play, there are a number of areas of game development tools that are specific to cameras. Most camera behavior changes pertain to third person cameras, but as noted earlier in this book, it is also true that first person cameras on occasion will require changes to their behavior. In either case, it is usual to specify these changes through some type of world editor; that is, an application external to the game that allows the various elements of the game to be combined and changed. Often this is within an existing modeling application (such as Maya), but many companies invest the engineering effort in producing their own proprietary tools.

Let us briefly examine how tools such as these may be used to specify camera behavior.

World editor

The majority of camera editing, at least for interactive sequences, will likely occur here. Of course, non-interactive sequences that are driven by the game engine may also be specified here or in a separate modeling package. It would be expected that it is possible to define unique camera properties for the game objects placed within the editor, as well as the ability to specify relationships between objects. For example, a camera whose motion is restricted to a path must be able to either define the path or link to an appropriate external object.

If a scripting system is used to place and control cameras within the game world via a world-editing tool, then some limited previewing of camera behavior is desirable in that same tool. One of the most time-consuming aspects of camera development is the sheer iterative cycle required to establish appropriate camera behavior. This is particularly true of cinematic sequences rendered using the game engine. In these cases it is vital to offer some form of editor-based manipulation of cameras, either directly on the target platform, or rendered within the editor itself.

When cameras are used with paths, those paths need to be visible within the editor (using the same evaluation logic as the game itself) and easily editable, ideally as the game is running. Since it is not always possible to preview game logic within the editor, some other method must be available to simulate the influences on camera motion. Clearly for cinematic sequences we need to be able to manipulate the timer used to control the events within the sequence.

In other cases where the camera would react to the player position (perhaps relative to a 3D spline within the world), another approach will probably be necessary. Direct updates of the game data from within the editor (as the target system is running) have proven to be extremely beneficial to the iterative process.

In general, the world-editing system can be the most valuable tool when defining and editing camera behaviors. It is of great importance that the most frequently performed tasks are implemented in an easy-to-use interface. Obvious examples include camera path definition (waypoint placement and connectivity), camera hint placement and property editing, pre-defined macros of script objects for commonly used situations, and so forth.

Let us enumerate some of the desirable features that a world editor would provide for camera systems:

- **Placement/orientation of cameras.** Clearly this is the most basic functionality that might be required. However, statically placed cameras only represent a subset of most camera requirements.
- **Camera property editing.** As with other game objects, the editor must allow individual camera properties to be changed by the designer. Preferably these changes may be applied quickly and updated while the game is actually executing (although this may not be possible).
- **View from the camera while manipulating.** Changing the camera orientation within the editor may be greatly assisted if the rendered view of the camera is presented to the designer, either utilizing the main editor window or a pop-up window. Care should be taken that the aspect ratio and field of view of the displayed view match those of the actual camera data.
- **Editing in-game then transferring data back.** While not a common feature, it is certainly very useful to be able to edit some camera properties on the target platform and inside the game, and then be able to send the changed information back to the host or to a data file for incorporation into scripts or code.
- **Limit properties shown to those appropriate for behavior.** Only show relevant properties at any given time.
- **Paths — automatic waypoint dropping and connections.** It can be very useful for path dropping to have the tool provide

some automatic capabilities, for example, dropping waypoints as you navigate an area and then consolidating that information and turning it into a path for use later.

- **Volumes.** This is the ability to define 3D regions for various camera-related functionality.
- **Surfaces.** Defining surfaces for cameras to move on, for example.
- **Links to target objects.** Identifying target objects for particular cameras.
- **Control of position/orientation/roll/field of view over time (spline editor).** It is common to have a spline editor inside of many tools; the ability to directly alter the values for position/orientation/roll/field of view, and so forth, by manually adjusting a spline curve is very useful in some situations.
- **Evaluation of target object or interpolant derivation over time.** Shows where an object will be located over time in case it has an impact on the camera behavior.

Camera collision mesh

While it is often the case that camera systems will utilize the same collision data for the world environment as other game systems, it can be convenient and more appropriate for the camera to have its own collision geometry. As discussed earlier, this geometry is often simpler than regular collision geometry and the world editor may provide an appropriate tool to allow this to be changed by the designers. Thus artistic changes may be made without impacting camera collision constraints, although this requires vigilance to ensure that the camera geometry remains up to date.

CAMERA DEBUGGING TECHNIQUES

Camera systems are complex and will invariably require debugging from time to time, particularly during initial development. It is frequently required once the system is in place to assist designers in implementing their desired camera solutions. It is also important to ensure that cameras defined by users work in the intended fashion. Furthermore, debug support may provide useful performance metrics.

There are many different approaches that may be adopted to achieve these goals, many of which will depend upon the specifics of the camera system used and the environment in which it exists. While it is usual to think of debugging as purely an *interactive* process, there are many benefits to be gained from capturing information about the camera system and examining it outside of the run-time environment (sometimes referred to as *logging*). A hybrid solution involves capturing user input over a period and *replaying* a section of game play.

Listed below are a variety of practical debugging techniques that have been successfully applied during the development of published games. Although specific implementation details are not provided (as they are always greatly dependent upon the game engine and/or tools), there should be sufficient information to indicate how their inclusion might function in a particular situation.

Interactive debugging

One of the most convenient forms of camera debugging is to examine the state of the camera system while it is actually running. This approach is not limited to simply viewing internal state via a regular debugger application; it is common to add additional representation of camera data into the rendered view of the game world or as textual data. Such text output might be sent to either the main display device or some external destination (e.g., a networked PC).

Here are a selection of debugging techniques that may be applied while the application is executing.

Internal property interrogation

As mentioned above, this is direct viewing of camera system data, often performed by temporarily pausing game execution by means of breakpoints. This is sometimes problematic for a couple of reasons. First, the executing code must include debugging information, thus increasing its size. Second, the communication between the executing code and the debugger often imparts a performance penalty. Both of these issues may potentially change the camera system behavior, but remain an extremely useful technique for the majority of camera-related problems. Here are a few of the more useful properties that may be tracked.

- Active cameras, ordered by priority
- Current camera, including its type and behaviors
- Target object, if available

Separate debugging camera

A common debugging aid for camera systems (and in fact for general purpose game debugging) is to maintain and update a separate *debug camera* that only exists in development versions of the game. This camera is only used for rendering purposes and does not in any way affect the functioning of other game objects. Typically the user is allowed to manipulate the position and orientation of this camera irrespective of the control over the main player character or other game objects as might normally be required. This might be achieved by either using a separate input device or having a game mode in which regular controller input is directed to the debug camera rather than the regular game. In the latter case it is necessary to ensure that the input supplied to the debug camera will not be filtered by changes to the controls that may occur during regular game play. Generally speaking it is important that the updating of the debug camera occurs in a way that leaves it unaffected by changes to the game state. It is often useful to combine this debug camera with the ability to change the execution speed of the game, as noted in the next section. It is also preferable that the user be able to quickly switch between the regular game camera and the debug camera, particularly if the same controller is used for both purposes.

Most of the interactive techniques described here are best viewed from an external view as supplied by the debug camera. It should also be noted that it is sometimes useful for the debug camera to have no effect on visibility culling or other rendering optimizations (i.e., only supplying position and orientation to the rendering system). In this manner it provides a useful mechanism to determine the parts of the game world that are currently considered for render purposes.

While using the debug camera, it is frequently useful to add some specific functionality to aid the viewer. Common functions might include:

- Repositioning the player character to the current camera position
- Displaying the current camera position (useful for the QA process)
- Projecting a ray along the forward vector of the debug camera to determine environmental properties (e.g., collision with a surface, revealing the material properties)

- Pausing game execution while allowing the debug camera to be manipulated
- Capturing the current render buffer and exporting it to external storage; this also provides a useful snapshot tool for producing screen shots for marketing or QA purposes

Debug cameras are typically used within the context of an active game. Thus they would normally conform to the same viewport used to display the regular game play, although it would be a simple matter to have a separate viewport purely for debugging purposes. When viewed in a multi-display (or multi-windowed) environment this may prove helpful in debugging while the game is executing as one person may observe the game as a player while another examines a particular game play element.

Control of the update rate of the game

A more general debugging technique is the ability to change the update rate of the game, particularly to be able to single step individual update cycles. Naturally this is easily achievable through a standard debugger, but such functionality is often useful for non-engineers or other situations where a debugger might not be available. Reducing the update rate of the game may be achieved by adding a time delay between successive updates yet passing the original (presumably fixed) time step value to the game objects. Alternatively the time step itself might be reduced, but this may not result in an accurate representation of actual game play.

General camera state

There are a number of common state variables that may prove helpful to track while a game camera is active. Several of these pertain to the scripting methods used to determine the active camera and thus apply more to the *camera manager* than one specific camera. Nonetheless, here is a list of trackable items.

- State information (e.g., active, interpolating, under player control, etc.)
- Script messaging (messages received or sent)
- Changes to active camera hints/game cameras
- Occlusion state and the amount of time occluded

- Fail-safe activation; an event occurred requiring the camera to be repositioned (the nature of the event should also be shown)
- Invalid camera properties including the validity of the transformation matrix

Visual representation of camera properties

It is often useful to see how camera properties change over time. In an interactive situation this might be achieved by drawing a visual representation of the property within the game world. Examples of such properties might include the following.

- Active camera positions (perhaps as a wireframe sphere or cube, often showing the movement direction as links between these positions; otherwise known as *breadcrumbs*)
- Current camera orientation (e.g., colored arrows matching the forward-, up-, and right-vectors of the camera matrix, originating from the current camera position)
- Desired look-at position
- Desired orientation (where there is no specific look-at position)

While the display of one or more of these properties is typically useful, it is helpful to allow dynamic filtering of which properties are displayed, by specific category or camera object, for example. As already mentioned, it is usually possible to print textual information regarding camera properties.

Property hysteresis

In a similar vein, it is often useful to see the recent history of particular camera properties. Often it is possible to capture all of the desirable properties per update and to continue to display a subset of them while the game is still executing. Memory or performance constraints may often limit the number of properties that may be displayed; storing the data for later perusal is another alternative. Some of the most common properties to view in this manner are:

- **Camera position.** This is sometimes referred to as breadcrumbs, since they are often spaced at regular intervals (i.e., the camera position is only recorded once it moves past a threshold distance from the previous stored position). If it is important to determine the length of time spent at a particular position, changes may be made to the breadcrumb (e.g., changing the scale or color of the rendered representation). Indeed, changing the breadcrumb provides a quick way for the camera designer to assess property changes over time or in response to the position of the camera within the game world (e.g., line of sight issues). It is often helpful to show connectivity information between stored positions, usually as a straight line. The spacing of positions will also reveal any instantaneous movement of the camera, since that would appear as a longer than usual line segment.

- **Camera orientation.** Due to the nature of orientation changes, it may be difficult to discern how this changes over time. When combined with position breadcrumbs, an approximate understanding of the orientation changes may be obtained. An alternative representation would be to display the orientation changes as points on the surface of a unit sphere. Orientation changes may also be tracked as Euler angles and displayed as a histogram (i.e., time on one axis, angular value on the other), in a similar manner to how modeling packages allow the artist to specify rotation over time. This type of approach is very useful when tracking down problems with interpolation.

Movement constraints

Since there are a number of occasions where the camera position is restricted according to its behaviors, it is often useful to see the limits of its constraints, particularly when these are not "hard" constraints. See the following examples.

- Movement path drawing, often based upon spline curve evaluations and represented by an approximation of line segments. The number of line segments is typically chosen to satisfy either aesthetic or performance requirements but does not impact final game play.
- Movement surface drawing, typically represented as a wire frame version of the surface to avoid obscuring other game elements in addition to giving a better understanding of the surface shape (especially when curved).

Line of sight

It is often helpful to be able to track if the camera has a good *line of sight* to its intended target. This is easily shown by drawing a line along the forward vector of the camera. An easy way to illustrate the validity of the line is to use color to differentiate its status, for example, red when blocked and green otherwise. A related property, *character occlusion* may also be displayed in a similar manner. It may also prove useful to show the point at which the line of sight is broken by limiting the length of the line drawn (since the collision geometry may not be visible and may differ from the render geometry considerably). Other useful information may include the material properties of the object or geometry blocking the ray cast, (e.g., "stone," "camera collision," "ceiling," "floor," etc.), the name of the object instance, and so forth. To prevent overloading the viewer with this information, a debug option to change the amount of information provided is often useful.

Behavior-specific rendering

Certain cameras, behaviors (for example, the *spindle camera* as described in the Axis Rotational/Spindle section of Chapter 7) have very specific information that is used to determine their desired position, orientation, and so forth. It is frequently desirable to show how these evaluations are calculated. In the example of the spindle camera it has been beneficial to see the range of potential movement combined with the interpolant value used to calculate the radius of the camera. Thus camera behaviors with unique methods of determining properties often require very specific rendering techniques. Flow fields and repulsors, for example, would require special handling to show their influence on the current camera.

Script debugging

This topic was discussed in Chapter 6, but to briefly recap, the following methods are often applied.

- **Script statement execution/filtering.** For any given game script (or other subset of currently active script objects determined by a desired filtering mechanism), show a history of each actual statement that was executed, in lieu of an actual full debugger.

- **Debug message logging.** Script objects are able to generate debugging text messages that reveal aspects of their internal states.

- **Message filtering.** Inter-object communication is tracked and displayed via the debug message logging mechanism outlined previously. Facilities are often provided to filter the type of messages that are displayed.

- **Object state.** Individual object types are often able to report internal state information specific to their behaviors.

Data logging

Data logging is a common technique used in many aspects of game development, where property values are recorded over time, usually being output to storage external to the game (although not necessarily so). The captured data are often associated with a specific time value or update record to allow ordering of events to be determined. Once these data have been captured they may then be analyzed for specific information, passed to other applications (such as spreadsheets or visualization tools), and so forth.

Logging is often performed in an ad hoc manner, perhaps only using a simple `printf()` style of textual output. Even so, this limited amount of information can prove invaluable as it allows careful analysis of event ordering particularly at a granularity smaller than single stepping the update loop. It is also helpful when true debugging may not be available (e.g., during the QA process). Care should be taken to minimize the influence of the logging on the performance of the game (to avoid the *observer effect* where the act of observation potentially alters the future outcome). One optimization is to cache the log information locally (assuming memory is available) until a non-critical time at which it may be sent to the appropriate external storage without impacting game performance.

Once these data are available, there are many different ways in which it may be *visualized*. The easiest solution is, of course, simple review of textual data. This can in many cases be sufficient and expedient. Even without custom visualization tools, it can be a relatively simple matter to import data into spreadsheets or other existing applications to allow graphing or similar presentation of the logged data. This approach is attractive when the data are relatively simple in nature (e.g., tracking the changes to a floating point number over time).

However, a custom visualization tool may prove highly valuable, particularly if a large sample set could be parsed (according to user input) to show changes over time. Consider the relatively simple case of position and orientation information of game objects. This information might be imported into the world-editing tool and thus allow review of object movement over the sample period. Such a display might prove invaluable in understanding why objects are behaving incorrectly, particularly since they would be shown within the context of the game environment. Clearly such logging has potentially widespread use within general game debugging, but requires engineering effort to make it happen. Fortunately there are middleware solutions becoming available that can help reduce the cost of such implementation.

Game replaying

An alternative to interactive or logging approaches is the facility to arbitrarily replay a period of game play while allowing the user to examine variables, use a debug camera, and so forth. A similar technique was used in early game development to provide a form of automated game demonstration for unattended game consoles. Essentially, user input is captured while the game is played and later used as a replacement for actual user input. There are, however, caveats to this approach as it has some very specific requirements.

- An initial known state to the game at the start of the capture period. Often this is achieved by restarting a game level or area. Most important, this must include a known value that is used for pseudo-random number generation.
- The ability to capture low-level controller information and to feed that same controller data back into the input process when replaying the game.
- Deterministic game logic, particularly when considering external sources of changes to the game (e.g., network latency, loading times, random number generation, display synchronization, etc.).
- Elapsed time between updates must be stored along with user input.

Even if complete determinism is not achievable, game replaying is an attractive approach. This is especially true for cases where a problem is difficult to repeat and may depend on a particular set of user input and other conditions. Once a repeatable version has been captured there are often enough similarities to the real version that the solution to the problem may be deduced.

■ SUMMARY

A camera system is only as good as the game architecture and scripting supporting it. While camera systems can be fairly independent from a specific game, there are a lot of areas in which tight integration can yield tremendous gains. The examples presented in this chapter are not requirements for implementing a successful camera system, but they are tried-and-true methods that have worked in shipping titles to yield great results.

Appendix A: Glossary

30 degree rule A cinematographic convention referring to the minimum angular displacement necessary when performing a *jump cut*.

Anamorphic A rendering method that generates a distorted image that is later corrected by use of a lens or projection method.

Aspect ratio This is the ratio of the lengths of the sides of the viewport or display device, typically specified in terms of the horizontal width compared to the vertical height. For example, full frame *SDTV* has an aspect ratio of 4:3, or 1.33. Widescreen displays typically have an aspect ratio of 16:9 or 1.78.

Attractor A game object that applies forces to other game objects (possibly only specific types of objects), typically to aid their navigation through complex environments or to change game play. The amount of force applied is often proportional to the distance between the objects, and possibly according to their relative orientations or directions of motion.

Axis angle A mathematical representation of an orientation; it usually consists of a direction vector and an angular rotation about that direction.

Axonometric projection A sub-category of *orthographic projection*, where the projection is not aligned with an axis of the viewed object. The up-axis of the object usually remains vertical, although the other two axes may be skewed according to the flavor of axonometry used. There are three types of axonometric projection: *isometric*, *dimetric*, and *trimetric*.

Bank An alternative term for *roll*.

Bartels-Kochanek spline A form of parametric curve similar to a *Catmull-Rom spline* in that the curve is guaranteed to pass through the control points. Parameters at each control point may be used to increase control over the shape of the curve between neighboring points, including *bias*, *tension*, and *continuity*.

Bézier curve A form of piecewise *Hermite curve*.

Boom Vertical motion of a real-world movie camera, often part of a *crane shot*.

B-spline A type of curve derived from a *cubic polynomial* whose shape remains within a *convex hull* formed by the *control points*. The curve is not guaranteed to pass through the control points, however.

Cabinet Projection A form of *oblique axonometric projection*, in which the receding axis uses a scale that is one-half of the scale used in the other two axes.

Camera behavior The collection of camera properties that define its determination of the position and orientation it should adopt within the game world.

Camera bob A method used in *first person* cameras to enhance player perception of their character's movement through the game world by varying its position relative to the character. The camera bob usually consists of a regular movement shape (e.g., a sideways figure eight) whose magnitude varies in proportion to the speed of the player character.

Camera hint A game object that dynamically controls or changes the current camera behavior, according to game play or aesthetic considerations.

Camera manager (CM) One method of implementing a camera system, the camera manager is a game entity responsible for the activation, deactivation, and runtime usage of game cameras.

Camera shake Small (possibly random) movement applied to the rendering position of a game camera. These movements are applied to simulate real-world vibration caused by events such as explosions, earthquakes, and so forth.

Camera system The entirety of game code handling the game cameras and their use by other game systems. Some camera systems also encompass functionality to define viewports and/or the rendering of the game world.

Camera type An alternative name for a *camera behavior*.

Catmull-Rom spline A type of cubic polynomial *spline curve* guaranteed to pass through its control points.

Cavalier projection A form of *oblique axonometric projection* in which the same scale is used on each axis.

Character-relative A *reference frame* determined by the direction in which a game object (e.g., the player character) is oriented, regardless of the position or orientation of the camera used to present the game world.

CinemaScope A presentation style of *non-interactive movies* in which the aspect ratio of the *viewport* is 1.85:1.

Cinematic camera A game camera used to present a non-interactive movie sequence via the game engine.

Cinéma verité Literally, "truth in cinema." A form of naturalistic filmmaking originating in documentaries utilizing non-professional actors, handheld cameras, and similar techniques to emphasize realism.

Cineractive An alternative term for a *cinematic camera*.

Circle strafing This is the application of lateral motion (i.e., strafing) to a player character while turning in the opposite direction. Such a combination results in a circular arc of motion, the radius of which is dependent upon the amount of turn relative to strafing.

Colliders A method of assisting camera navigation through confined environments.

Color fade A form of scene transition, where the viewed image fades over time into a solid color (*fade out*). The opposite case of fading from a solid color is known as a *fade in*.

Constraint Constraints are methods of limiting camera properties, typically for the purpose of game play or to satisfy aesthetic considerations. An example might be to limit the vertical elevation of the camera such that it will not become parallel to the world up-vector.

Control points Markers placed within the game world used to define or control the curvature of *spline curves*.

Control reference frame The control reference frame specifies the relationship between controller input and the movement of an avatar. In first person games, this is typically a direct mapping of input to turning and motion (sometimes referred to as *character-relative*); in third person games it may be dependent upon the relative position of the player character to the camera (known as *camera-relative*).

Crane shot For real-world cameras, a *crane shot* literally requires use of a physical crane to elevate and move the camera as the shot progresses.

Culling One of the processes used to decide which elements of the scene should be rendered, based upon the dimensions of the *view frustum*.

Cut-away shot A shot of something other than the current action, usually followed by a return to the original subject. The cut-away can be to a different subject, a close-up of a different part of the subject, or something else entirely.

Cut scene An alternative term for a *non-interactive movie*.

Damping A method of reducing or removing small amounts of motion to produce a smooth acceleration or deceleration.

Death camera A non-interactive presentation of the demise of a player character, typically shown from a viewpoint external to that of the character (though not necessarily so). Death cameras often reproduce the last few moments of game play prior to the death of the player, sometimes emphasizing the enemy or event responsible for the player death rather than simply focusing on the character. They commonly use a variety of cinematographic presentation conventions, as the player is usually unable to perform any actions at that time.

Delta time The amount of game time that has elapsed since the previous game update.

Depth buffer A portion of system or graphics memory used to hold information about the depth of the nearest object at each pixel in the display device, typically used by the rendering process to determine if a new pixel should be rendered.

Depth of field (DOF) The distance around the focal point of a *real-world camera* where objects remain in sharp focus.

Desired orientation The preferred direction and rotation of the view from a game camera typically specified in world space coordinates. The rotation of the game camera is often implicitly taken to match the up-axis of the game world.

Desired position The ideal position of the camera as dictated by its behaviors.

Dimetric projection A form of *axonometric projection* in which two axes share a similar scale, whereas the scale of the third axis is determined independently.

Display field For interlaced displays, a display field is the period of time in which one of the alternating sets of pixel rows is displayed. For NTSC and MPAL displays this is equivalent to 1/60 of a second, for PAL and SECAM this is equivalent to 1/50 of a second.

Display frame Often synonymous with *display field* (for *progressive displays*), a display frame refers to the period of time associated with the generation of the display of the game world. On interlaced displays, this period of time is equivalent to two successive display fields.

Display tearing Undesirable graphical effects caused by updating the frame buffer while the display is generating its image from the same area of memory. The result is a potentially discontinuous image split between two consecutive updates.

Dolly A cinematographic term that describes motion of the camera either toward or away from its target object. The term originates from the mechanism used to move the camera smoothly across the film set; it may also be referred to as *tracking*.

Doppler effect A mathematical term often used to describe the change in frequencies observed when moving relative to a source of sound, for example, a police siren.

Double buffering A method of avoiding display tearing and increasing graphical performance by allowing rendering to continue to a second image while the previously rendered image is displayed.

Dutch tilt An alternative name for *roll* and sometimes referred to as *Dutch angle*.

Ease function A specialized version of *interpolation* in which the acceleration and deceleration between the start and destination values is determined by the evaluation of the function over time.

Euler angles A mathematical representation of an orientation, relative to a known reference frame such as the world coordinate scheme. Euler angles represent rotations around three axes that are concatenated to produce the final orientation. Euler angles are non-commutative and so the order of application is important.

Fail-safe A programming technique used to reposition (and possibly reorient) a game camera to prevent inappropriate views of the game world. This may be triggered in many different ways, depending upon the nature of the game. Common situations requiring a fail-safe might include occlusion of the target object for an extended period, a camera positioned outside of the game environment, and so forth.

Far clipping plane A rendering term referring to the distance away from the camera (in its local space) at which objects will no longer be considered for drawing. This plane is parallel to the *near plane* and forms one of the bounds of the *view frustum*. It is sometimes referred to as the *yon plane*, or simply the *far plane*.

Field of view (FOV) An angular quantity used in conjunction with the aspect ratio of the *viewport* to determine the dimensions of the *view frustum*, either as a vertical or horizontal angle.

Finite state machine (FSM) A programmatic solution often used for managing the state of game objects. Typically an FSM consists of a number of states and triggers, arranged in a manner that dictates the required behavior of the entity. Transitions between states occur when the appropriate trigger's conditions are satisfied.

First person (FP) A presentation style where the view of the game world is positioned such that it approximates the eye point of the protagonist.

Flat shading A rendering approach in which each surface of a polygonal object is drawn using a single unvarying color.

Flow field A technique commonly applied within game AI to help direct motion of objects through complex environments.

Forced perspective A rendering technique used to give the appearance that objects are located at a different distance from the camera than their actual world location. This is often used for objects too far away from the camera to be rendered due to the limits of the *far clipping plane* (e.g., the *sky box*).

Frame rate (FPS) A crude performance metric sometimes cited as a qualitative measure for video games. The frame rate typically equates to the number of updates performed within one second, sometimes referred to as *frames per second* (hence FPS).

Framing A method of determining the position and orientation of a camera to satisfy a desired visual constraint. Examples include the placement or size of game elements within the camera viewport.

Free look The ability for the player to manipulate the orientation of the game camera, typically used in first person presentations but often available with third person cameras. The latter case may also be combined with the ability to move the camera position with respect to the player character or other fixed reference frame.

Frustum A frustum is typically a pyramid with a rectangular base whose tip has been removed by a plane parallel to that of the base. Such a frustum is used to form the *clipping planes*, a method of quickly determining which elements of a scene should be considered for rendering. The closer of the two parallel planes of the frustum to the camera position is known as the *near plane*; the furthest away is referred to as the *far plane*. Objects lying wholly outside of the frustum are not rendered.

Full frame This term refers to the use of the entire display device for rendering a view of the game world or cinematic sequences. This term was most often associated with display devices having an aspect ratio of 4:3.

Game camera (GC) A game entity that contains properties used to determine the position, orientation, and other requirements of a view of the game world.

Gimbal lock An undesirable situation in which the position and orientation of the camera relative to the player object cause the player controls to change in unexpected ways. Mathematical irregularities in a gimbal lock condition can potentially cause the camera orientation to rapidly roll around its forward direction.

Hard constraints Restrictions placed upon the camera (e.g., motion or orientation restrictions) that are rigidly enforced, preventing undesirable effects such as interpenetrating render geometry.

Heads-up display (HUD) A term originating from aeronautics; in game terms this usually refers to some form of overlay rendered to provide additional information to the player. Common elements of HUDs might include targeting *reticules* (i.e., *cursors*), player status information, maps, scoring information, game play directions, and so forth.

Hermite curve A type of cubic polynomial *spline curve*.

High definition television (HDTV) The HDTV standard is nominally a resolution of 1920 pixels horizontally by 1080 pixels vertically (NTSC), with either an interlaced or progressively generated display. The term is sometimes erroneously used when referring to displays that utilize 720 pixels vertically.

Hither plane An alternative name for the *near clipping plane*.

Hybrid camera A game camera that adopts characteristics of both first and third person cameras.

Hysteresis The use of past information regarding camera properties to reduce unwanted oscillation in the current properties.

Idle wandering First person games will sometimes introduce a semi-random reorientation of the camera after a period of inactivity or lack of player input. Such orientation changes are akin to the concept of an idle animation where the player character resorts to one or more animations that show the character awaiting player input.

Influence maps A navigation aid allowing the designer to specify the amount of influence applied to camera or AI movement to avoid environmental elements.

Insert shot In cinematographic terms, it is a shot of the subject from a different angle or focal length. It differs from a *cut-away shot* in that the shot is still of the same subject or scene.

Interactive An activity that takes place during periods of game play where players are actually engaged in controlling their characters or interacting with elements of the game in some other way.

Interlacing A display technology that reduces the number of horizontal lines projected by a display device, alternating odd and even *scan lines*. Each set of odd and even lines are referred to as a field, sixty of which are generated per second for NTSC displays. Thus thirty full frames would be generated within the same period.

Interpolation Interpolation (or *blending*) refers to a variety of methods used to generate animation frames, move objects between positions, alter color values, and a variety of similar operations.

Isometric projection A pseudo three-dimensional presentation style usually comprised of two-dimensional elements. Isometric presentation is a *parallel projection* in which the side axes are 30 degrees from horizontal. Each axis uses the same scale.

Jump cut A cinematography convention referring to an instantaneous change of the scene presented to the viewer. Typically, this occurs when the active camera position changes by a sufficiently large amount that it presents a different view without any additional cues to the viewer (e.g., *wipes* or other transition effects). Alternatively, the camera may remain stationary but the scene instantly changes in a significant manner (e.g., the orientation of the camera is reversed, a day scene changing to a night scene but retaining the same position and orientation, and so forth).

Key frame A term derived from animation referring to a set of data (e.g., the position and/or orientation of an object) from which intermediate values may be *interpolated*. Alternatively, key frame data may be used as-is if the rate at which the original data were sampled is sufficiently high to produce smoothly changing values.

Keys An alternative name for *control points*, when used within the context of *spline curves*.

Lag Many camera properties (such as orientation or position) produce aesthetically pleasing results if their updating is slightly slower than their rate of change.

Lens flare Usually an undesirable visual artifact caused by excessive light entering a real-world camera lens. Its effects are sometimes replicated within video games to enhance realism.

Line of sight (LOS) A straight line projected through the game world to determine if an object might observe another, typically used to determine if the player character remains visible from the current (or future) camera position.

Lock-on In many first person games, and some third person games, the player character is able to move relative to a target object or position while keeping its orientation facing the object. Thus, the character inscribes a circular arc of motion around the target position and the character is said to be *locked-on*. This type of player motion is sometimes referred to as *object orbiting*.

Look-at position This term defines a location within the game world used by a game camera to determine its orientation. This is often calculated relative to a game object, possibly varying according to game play requirements or state changes of the object.

Macro tiles A method of reducing the amount of memory required to store repeating patterns of *tiles* often used for defining the background in two-dimensional games.

Manager A programming construct used to control a specific area of the real-time application, for example, management of the camera system.

Motion blur A faint after-image caused by overexposure of fast-moving objects on photographic film.

Near clipping plane Sometimes referred to as the *near plane* (or *hither plane*), this value represents the distance of the closest face of the *view frustum* to the camera position. Objects that are closer than this distance will not be rendered; those that interpenetrate the near plane may result in undesirable graphical effects such as partial rendering of polygon faces, and so forth.

Object-relative A *reference frame* where the origin of the coordinate system is based upon the position and orientation of a game object.

Oblique projection A form of axonometric projection having two axes that are parallel to the projection plane; the third axis recedes at an angle of 45 or 60 degrees to the horizontal. *Cabinet* and *cavalier* projections are two common forms of this projection.

Occlusion In camera systems, this typically refers to situations in which the player character or other target object is hidden from view due to environmental features or game objects placed between the camera and its target. Brief periods of occlusion are usually acceptable, although longer periods are typically resolved via a *fail-safe*.

Orbit-lock An alternative term for *lock-on*.

Orientation A method of specifying the direction in which a game entity is placed relative to a frame of reference; most commonly the world axes are used to determine the absolute orientation.

Orthographic projection A method of generating a view of the game world from an orientation that is parallel to either a world axis or a model axis, often used for generating overhead maps. Lines that are parallel within the game world remain so using an orthographic projection.

Palette cycling A simplified animation technique achieved by rendering parts of the scene in different colors from a defined palette of color values rather than specific colors. Each entry in the color palette has an assigned order in which it is drawn such that adjacent pixels match those adjacent entries in the palette. By copying the palette entries the drawn pixels will appear to move in the direction in which the palette is copied. This technique has been largely superseded by texture animation that achieves the same effect by simply changing the texture coordinates over time.

Panning Motion of the camera in a direction that is perpendicular to its orientation within the game world but retaining the same orientation.

Parallax The relative motion of elements of the rendered scene according to their distance from the camera position, such as layers within a 2D side-scrolling game.

Path camera A camera that uses a pre-defined path (e.g., a *spline curve*) to dictate its position within the game world.

Path-finding A general term for a variety of techniques used to aid navigation through complex environments by applying algorithms to determine the validity (and relative cost) of traversing a network of connected positions or areas.

Perspective projection A method of constructing a view of the virtual world in which parallel lines converge at vanishing points and objects become smaller as their distance increases from the camera viewpoint. Game models are constructed as collections of geometric primitives (usually triangles or quadrilaterals) which are then projected onto a two-dimensional surface. This projection approximates the view of the real world as perceived by the human visual system.

PID controller *Proportional Integral Derivative* (PID) feedback controllers are often used in process control industries and applications such as thermostats or anti-lock braking systems. Digital versions may be applied to camera systems as a method of providing damping to properties such as camera motion.

Player character The game object representing the player within the virtual environment, often used to determine the desired position of the camera as well as the desired orientation of the camera. It may sometimes be referred to as an *avatar*.

Point of view An alternative term used for *first person* cameras. This is usually referring to a view as seen from the eyes of the protagonist or other game character.

Potential fields A programming method that simulates forces directing the motion of objects away from obstructions (or other objects) within a game environment.

Predictive camera A virtual camera that uses estimated future information about its target (such as position) to alter its own behavior.

Projection A method of taking coordinates from one form and converting them into another. A typical game camera system will project coordinates from world space into camera space and finally into screen space (possibly using a *perspective transformation*).

Projection transform Mathematical constructs used to take coordinate information based in one space (e.g., world space) and convert it to work in another space (such as camera space, for rendering purposes).

Proportional controller A type of linear feedback control system used for ease-in without overshooting the target value. With a proportional controller, the controller output is directly proportional to the difference between the current state and the target value.

Quaternion A mathematical construct used as a representation of an object's orientation. Use of quaternion mathematics for interpolation or other angular operations will typically avoid problems such as *gimbal lock* that may occur with other representations (e.g., *Euler angles*).

Ray casting A means of interrogating the data structure representing the game world (using trigonometry) to determine if two points have an unobstructed linear path between them.

Reaction shot A cinematographic term describing a cut-away shot showing a close-up view of a character literally reacting to an event that is typically occurring off-screen.

Reactive camera A game camera that determines its behavior upon the current or past behavior of its target object.

Real-world camera (RWC) A physical camera used to capture successive still images that may be viewed in sequence to create the illusion of motion.

Refresh rate An alternative term for *update rate*.

Reorientation The manner in which changes to the orientation of a camera over time are made.

Replay camera A virtual camera replicating a previously generated sequence of positions and orientations within the game world. These positions may be generated in any manner allowing for either game play footage or cinematic sequences.

Repulsor A game object used to apply forces to other game objects to aid their navigation through complex environments. The amount of force applied may vary according to the type of repulsor but is often proportional to the distance of the object from the repulsor (it may also depend on the direction of motion of the object relative to the repulsor).

Roll Rotation of a camera around the direction in which it is facing, in many cases limited to purely non-interactive sequences. It may prove appropriate for some forms of vehicle-based games. May be used infrequently to elicit an emotional response from the player, but is prone to inducing nausea if overused.

Safe frame This term refers to a large portion of the display device in which information may be presented to the viewer without concern about physical properties of the display affecting legibility (e.g., screen curvature or physical case overlay).

Safe zone The region of a display device bordering its edges, outside of the *safe frame*.

Scripting A generic term referring to any mechanism used to control game events such that they occur at specified times or in response to other game events.

Shader language A low-level programming method applied to sections of the render pipeline. *Shaders* modify the way in which textures are drawn to reproduce real-world graphical properties such as roughness, and so forth.

Side-scrolling A perspective in which the game world is presented from a vantage point perpendicular to the movement of the player character.

Sky box Any form of static world geometry used to create the illusion of distant elements of the game world, usually a view of the sky or distant environmental elements (e.g., mountains). Typically the sky box will use simplified geometry combined with texture maps to achieve this effect and is rendered before all other elements of the scene.

Snapshot A type of game camera that retains its position and orientation within the game world. This type of camera is frequently used in situations where the rendering of the entire scene would be too processor intensive to perform in real time, such as the early versions of the *Resident Evil* (aka *Biohazard*) series of games. In such games the background is rendered once and stored (including depth sorting information); during game play only the game objects are rendered within the scene, taking into consideration the depth information that had been previously calculated.

Soft constraints Restrictions placed upon the camera (e.g., motion or orientation restrictions) that are not rigidly enforced.

Soft-lock A situation in which the player is unable to make further progress in the game due to an unforeseen set of circumstances, such as a locked door that will not correctly open.

Spindle An alternative name for an *axis*, a mathematical construct used to provide a reference frame for camera motion or other property calculations.

Spline An alternative term typically used with cubic polynomial curves.

Split screen A method of dividing the display device into sections; it is often used for multi-player games displayed upon a single display, with each player having his own dedicated section. It may also be used in situations where it is necessary to illustrate multiple views of the game world within a single player game, or simply to show other information to the player (e.g., console text output, a rear view mirror, etc.).

Spring A mathematical construct often used to produce gentle acceleration or deceleration of game objects. Rather than oscillating around its rest value, game system springs are often *critically damped* so that no overshooting occurs.

Sprite A two-dimensional graphic common in 2D presentation styles, although sometimes used within 3D games as a performance-saving method. In the former case, most elements of the game may be represented in such a manner, and many early game consoles were only able to display graphics of this nature. In three-dimensional presentations, sprites are sometimes used for representing objects whose orientation with respect to the camera infrequently changes. Since the sprite may be cached and reused, this may result in performance savings at a cost of some visual fidelity. While most sprites are treated as purely two-dimensional objects, it is possible to store depth information within the sprite and thus apply regular depth sorting while it is rendered.

Standard definition television (SDTV) Display devices conforming to the properties of SDTV have an aspect ratio of 4:3 and a vertical resolution of 625 scan lines (PAL) or 525 scan lines (NTSC).

Stamp See *Tile*.

Target object A game entity used to determine the properties of a game camera. The most common usage of a target object is to determine the desired orientation of the camera. Sometimes the position of the target object relative to a reference frame (such as a *spindle*) is used to dynamically vary the camera properties.

Target position An alternative term for the *desired position* of a game camera.

Third person A presentation style in which the view of the game world is positioned external to the player character.

Tile An element of two-dimensional game graphics (akin to a *sprite*) typically rendered within an array or regularly spaced grid. Each tile (or *stamp*) is composed of an array of pixels, usually of fixed dimensions (e.g., 8 × 8, 8 × 16, 16 × 16, etc.) The grid of tiles is collectively known as the *tile map*, each entry of which is an index into the set of tile definitions. Thus, repeated tile usage within the tile map does not require additional tile definitions. The total number of unique tile definitions would therefore determine the required size of each index value within the tile map. Note that it is not necessary for the elements of the tile map to be adjacent to one another, nor is it required that each tile be of a uniform size (early 8- and 16-bit game consoles did have such restrictions).

Tilt An alternative term for *roll*.

Transformation matrix A mathematical representation of the orientation (and possibly position) of a game object, typically considered as a 3×3, 3×4, or 4×4 array of fixed or floating point numbers.

Transition A change between different presentation styles, usually first to third person or vice versa. This may be considered a specialized case of *interpolation,* although the transition may be instantaneous in some cases.

Trimetric projection A form of *axonometric projection* in which all three axes have independent scales.

Triple buffering A programming technique which increases system throughput by taking advantage of parallelism between graphics rendering hardware and the main processor(s). Each successive rendering of a scene uses a different area of memory (on a *round-robin* basis) thus removing or reducing the requirement to wait until the display of a previously rendered image buffer has completed.

Twist An undesirable rapid reorientation of a game camera caused by its target moving underneath or above its position.

Update loop The main portion of the game engine that is responsible for updating all aspects of the game.

Update rate The amount of time required for updating all aspects of the game logic, often expressed as the number of updates per second.

Vertical twist A generally undesirable situation in which the target object of a camera passes close to the camera (in the horizontal plane), causing a rapid reorientation that is typically confusing to the viewer, and may also introduce control difficulties for the player character.

View frustum The volume defined by the *clipping planes,* dictating the portion of the game world to be rendered.

Viewport A portion of the display device used for rendering a view of the game world.

View transform The transformation matrix used to convert coordinates from camera space to screen space so that they are suitable for rendering purposes.

View volume An alternative term for *view frustum.*

Volume casting A method of mathematically projecting a trigonometric representation of three-dimensional shape (e.g., the motion of an object within the game world).

Widescreen A display device conforming to an *aspect ratio* of 16:9.

World-relative A coordinate system utilizing a standard reference frame rather than the orientation of any given object in the virtual world.

Yaw The horizontal orientation of the camera typically specified as an angular rotation around the world up-axis.

Yon plane An alternative name for the *far clipping plane.*

Z-buffer The Z-buffer (or alternatively, the *depth buffer*) holds information relating to the relative depth of each rendered pixel within the *frame buffer.* By comparing the value already present in the Z-buffer against the value calculated for a new pixel to be drawn, the render process may thus skip those pixels that would be occluded by objects closer to the camera.

Appendix B: Extras

HUMAN VISUAL PERCEPTION

Human visual perception is a very large topic yet an understanding of the fundamentals is extremely useful when implementing game cameras, or when choosing the appropriate camera solutions to apply to game situations. Aside from the physical nature of how human eyes convert light into electrical impulses to be analyzed, other physical and psychological effects change the ways in which humans comprehend (or perhaps more accurately, *perceive*) their environment. Sometimes these techniques may fail to give accurate information either due to some naturally occurring element (such as *camouflage* and its ilk) or because of a lack (or distortion) of familiar reference frames (e.g., *forced perspective*). Knowledge of these techniques may be applied to the construction of virtual environments to provide a more realistic experience for the player, or to alter the viewer's perception of the virtual environment for emotional or game play purposes.

Motion sensitivity

One of the first things to note concerns the sensitivity of the human visual system to motion, as well as how physical motion is translated from sensory data by the human brain. Human motion is normally determined by a combination of stimuli; apart from the obvious visual cues, the movement of fluid within the inner ear provides important information regarding human motion or orientation. Additionally, audio cues (e.g., surround sound or stereo effects such as the *Doppler effect*) provide another layer of movement information. Yet, when playing video games, although there may be visual and audio cues providing information to the player, no information arises from the inner ear. Coupled with a lack of motion in the peripheral regions of the player's gaze (assuming a reasonably regularly sized display and viewing distance is used), this can lead to extreme nausea as the player's brain tries to rationalize the conflicting information it is receiving. Additionally, some of the visual cues imparted by first person games in particular, as an attempt to compensate for their limited view of the world (and their own character, for that matter), will add to this sense of nausea. One major example would be the use of a "bob" effect. This is where the render position of the camera or the player's weapon is moved in concert with rapid motion such as running by the player character. The actual displacement is typically either a slight vertical motion (presumably timed to match the player character's feet hitting the ground) or alternatively movement along a pre-determined spline or path in screen space, such as a "figure eight." This is not a natural motion really, but is simply used to emphasize the actions of the player. Camera displacements are often also applied in response to other physical phenomena in the game world such as when the player character lands on the ground after a jump or fall, weapon recoil, or after an explosion or other force impacts the player character.

Refresh sensitivity

Another noted problem is the rate at which the rendered scene is updated. Ideally, this should be locked to a consistent rate as variations (particularly slowdowns) are likely to distract the viewer; for applications designed for use with television systems this is usually synchronized according to the appropriate television standard (i.e., 50 Hz for the PAL or SECAM standards, 60 Hz for NTSC and PAL60 standards, etc.). Applications running on personal computers using dedicated monitors often do not synchronize at all. In fact, such synchronization is sometimes omitted even when using televisions, mostly to allow the fastest update rate possible. *Lag*, or a delay in the update rate of the display (compared to the updating of game logic, object movement, etc.), will cause at best frustration and at worst nausea on the part of the player. NASA has conducted studies on the effects of lag when using head-mounted displays that support this (e.g., [Ellis99]). Motion sickness induced in this manner is seemingly more prevalent for games presented from a first person viewpoint; possibly this is because any player action will typically cause a large amount of the rendered scene to change, coupled with the problems noted earlier. Third person games also change the entire rendered scene, but more often camera motion is relatively small in comparison (unless the subject should pass the camera position, causing a phenomenon known as *vertical twist*, as described in Chapter 7).

Hand in hand with the display rendering update rate is the game logic updating. Even if the rendering process drops to a lower frequency, response to player controls must remain at a higher rate. If there is a disparity between player control usage and the motion of the character, for example, this may be disorienting to the player.

Color sensitivity

As described by [Glassner95], the sensitivity of the human eye to color varies according to the frequency within the color spectrum. For examples blue hues are perceived as further away from the observer than red hues.

Artists have long understood that shading of objects with subtle hues can be used to underscore the relative depth within the rendered view, in a similar manner to real-world atmospheric conditions.

Depth perception

Since video games are often projecting a view of a three-dimensional world upon a two-dimensional surface, the perception of depth by the players is dependent upon their interpretation of this projection. This is significant because an understanding of the relative positioning of objects within this projected view of the game world is necessary to accurately navigate or otherwise interact with the environment and other game objects. It is also important as it will affect the relationship between the use of a physical controller and the virtual movement control of the player character. Some players have difficulty understanding these relationships, especially when the view of the game world is from a position external to the player character. There are ways to enhance this feeling of depth and to emphasize the relative placement of objects within the rendered view. Cues can certainly be taken from cinematography in this regard.

Lighting is an important part of depth perception, as evidenced in [Pharr04]. Use of lighting implies the use of shadow casting; that is, the projection of shadows from objects according to the direction and position of one or more light sources within the game world. In many cases, the rendering of shadows is not entirely accurate, due to the performance requirements of a realistic lighting scheme. Nonetheless, even primitive shadows may be extremely beneficial to the player; one early solution was to use an indeterminate generic "blob" shadow for all game objects, typically a blurry disc rendered on the surface beneath the game object.

The presence of a shadow greatly increases the sensation of an object being part of its environment, especially if the shadow changes form to match physical features of the environment. Further, shadows give positional depth cues to the player, especially for airborne objects. Many players have a difficult time aligning themselves to objects when the player character is airborne, and shadows can help in this regard. Additionally, shadows add a further form of *parallax* to a scene, where the relative motion of objects apparently changes according to their distance from the camera. The use of such parallax effects can greatly enhance the sense of depth. Foreground objects placed close to the camera (especially when the camera motion path is pre-determined) can further emphasize parallax, but care must be taken to avoid occlusion issues.

References and Bibliography

All of these references have some relevance to camera theory, design, and/or implementation and are highly recommended. They have been grouped into sections of similar topics, although some titles may cover several different subjects.

AI AND NAVIGATION

[Borenstein90] Borenstein, J. Koren, Y. (1990). "Real-time Obstacle Avoidance for Fast Mobile Robots in Cluttered Environments."*The 1990 IEEE International Conference on Robotics and Automation*, Cincinnati, Ohio, May 13–18, pp. 572–577.

[Bourne05] Bourne, Owen. Sattar, Abdul. "Applying Weighting to Autonomous Camera Control."*Proceedings of Artificial Intelligence and Interactive Digital Entertainment 2005*. American Association for Artificial Intelligence, 2005.

[Carlisle04] Carlisle, Phil. "An AI Approach to Creating an Intelligent Camera System." In Steve, Rabin (ed.), *AI Game Programming Wisdom 2*. Charles River Media, 2004.

[Isla05] Isla, Damian. "Managing Complexity in the Halo 2 AI System."*Presentation at Game Developers Conference 2005*, San Francisco, 2005.

[Koren91] Koren, Y. Borenstein, J. (1991). "Potential Field Methods and Their Inherent Limitations for Mobile Robot Navigation."*Proceedings of the IEEE Conference on Robotics and Automation*, Sacramento, California, April 7–12, pp. 1398–1404.

[Millington06] Millington, Ian. *Artificial Intelligence for Games*. Morgan Kaufman, 2006.

[Reynolds87] Reynolds, C.W. "Flocks, Herds, and Schools: A Distributed Behavioral Model." *Computer Graphics (Volume 21, Number 4)*:25–34. (SIGGRAPH '87 Conference Proceedings), 1987.

[Stone04] Stone, Jonathan. "Third Person Camera Navigation." In Kirmse, Andrew (ed.), *Game Programming Gems 4*. Charles River Media, 2004.

[Stout04] Stout, Bryan. "Artificial Potential Fields for Navigation and Animation."*Presentation at Game Developers Conference 2004*, San Jose, 2004. Written GDC 2004 proceedings.

CINEMATOGRAPHY

[Arijon91] Arijon, Daniel. *Grammar of the Film Language*. Silman-James Press, 1991.

[Glassner04] Glassner, Andrew. *Interactive Storytelling*. A K Peters, 2004.

[Hawkins02] Hawkins, Brian. "Creating an Event-Driven Cinematic Camera." *Game Developer Magazine (Volume 9, Number 10 & 11)*. CMP Publications, 2002.

[Hawkins05] Hawkins, Brian. *Real-Time Cinematography for Games*. Charles River Media, 2005.

[Lander00] Lander, Jeff. "Lights... Camera... Let's Have Some Action Already!" *Game Developer Magazine (Volume 7, Number 4)*. CMP Publications, 2000.

[Lin04] Lin, Ting-Chieh. Shih, Zen-Chung. Tsai, Yu-Ting. "Cinematic Camera Control in 3D Computer Games." *WSCG 2004 SHORT Communication papers proceedings*. UNION Agency — Science Press, 2004.

[Malkiewicz92] Malkiewicz, Kris. *Cinematography*. Simon & Schuster Inc., 1992.

[Thiery07] Thiery, Adam. "Interactive Cinematography. "*Presentation at Game Developers Conference 2007*, San Francisco, 2007. http://www.cmpevents.com/sessions/GD/S4395i1.pdf.

CAMERA DESIGN

[Aszódi05] Aszódi, Barnabás, Czuczor, Szabolcs. "Realistic Camera Movement in a 3D Car Simulator." In Pallister, Kim (ed.), *Game Programming Gems 5*. Charles River Media, 2005.

[Ellis99] Ellis, Stephen R. Adelstein, B.D. Baumeler, S. Jense, G.J. Jacoby, R.H. "Sensor Spatial Distortion, Visual Latency, and Update Rate Effects on 3D Tracking in Virtual Environments."*Proceedings of IEEE Virtual Reality Conference 1999*.

[Giors04] Giors, John. "The Full Spectrum Warrior Camera System."*Presentation at Game Developers*

Conference 2004, San Jose, 2004. http://www.gdconf.com/conference/2004.htm.

[Halper01] Halper, Nicolas, Helbing, Ralf, Strothotte, Thomas. "A Camera Engine for Computer Games: Managing the Trade-Off Between Constraint Satisfaction and Frame Coherence." *Proceedings of EUROGRAPHICS 2001* (*Volume 20, Number 3*). Blackwell Publishers, 2001.

[Hornung03] Hornung, Alexander, Lakemeyer, G., Trogemann, G. "An Autonomous Real-Time Camera Agent for Interactive Narratives and Games." *Proceedings of Intelligent Virtual Agents*, 2003.

[Khrakar02] Kharkar, Sandeep. "Camera AI for Replays." In Rabin, Steve (ed.), *AI Game Programming Wisdom*. Charles River Media, 2002.

[Khrakar04] Kharkar, Sandeep. "A Modular Camera Architecture for Intelligent Control." In Rabin, Steve (ed.), *AI Game Programming Wisdom 2*. Charles River Media, 2004.

[Rabin00] Rabin, Steve. "Classic Super Mario 64 Third-Person Control and Animation." In DeLoura, Mark (ed.), *Game Programming Gems*. Charles River Media, 2000.

[Treglia00] Treglia, Dante II. "Camera Control Techniques." In DeLoura, Mark (ed.), *Game Programming Gems*. Charles River Media, 2000.

GAME DESIGN

[Crawford03] Crawford, Chris. *Chris Crawford on Game Design*. New Riders Games, 2003.

[Salen04] Salen, Katie, Zimmerman, Eric. *Rules Of Play*. MIT Press, 2004.

[West05] West, Mick. "Pushing Buttons." *Game Developer Magazine* (*Volume 12, Number 5*). CMP Publications, 2005.

[Wolf03] Wolf, Mark, Perron, Bernard (eds.). *The Video Game Theory Reader*. Routledge, 2003.

GRAPHICS AND RENDERING

[Akenine-Möller02] Akenine-Möller, Tomas, Haines, Eric. *Real-Time Rendering*. A K Peters, 2002.

[Blinn96] Blinn, Jim. *Jim Blinn's Corner: A Trip Down the Graphics Pipeline*. Morgan Kaufmann Publishers, 1996.

[Demers04] Demers, Joe. "Depth of Field: A Survey of Techniques." In Fernando, Rendima (ed.), *GPU Gems*. Addison-Wesley, 2004.

[Eberly04] Eberly, David H. *3D Game Engine Architecture*. Morgan Kaufmann Publishers, 2004.

[Foley90] Foley, James D., Van Dam, Andries, Feiner, Steven K., Hughes, John F. *Computer Graphics: Principles and Practice*. Addison-Wesley, 1990.

[Glassner95] Glassner, Andrew. *Principles of Digital Image Synthesis, Volume 1*. Morgan Kaufmann Publishers, 1995.

[Pharr04] Pharr, Matt, Humphreys, Greg. *Physically Based Rendering*. Morgan Kaufmann Publishers, 2004.

[Poynton02] Poynton, Charles. *Digital Video and HDTV, Algorithms and Interfaces*. Morgan Kaufmann Publishers, 2002.

MATHEMATICS

[Barrera05] Barrera, Tony, Hast, Anders, Bengtsson, Ewert. "Minimal Acceleration Hermite Curves." In Pallister, Kim (ed.), *Game Programming Gems 5*. Charles River Media, 2005.

[Bartels87] Bartels, Richard H., Beatty, John C., Barsky, Brian A. *An Introduction to Splines for use in Computer Graphics and Geometric Modeling*. Morgan Kaufmann Publishers, 1987.

[Bloomenthal97] Bloomenthal, Jules (ed.). *Introduction to Implicit Surfaces*. Morgan Kaufmann Publishers, 1997.

[Crenshaw00] Crenshaw, Jack W. *MATH Toolkit for REAL-TIME Programming*. CMP Books, 2000.

[Eberly03] Eberly, David H. *Game Physics*. Morgan Kaufmann Publishers, 2003.

[Ericson05] Ericson, Christer. *Real-Time Collision Detection*. Morgan Kaufmann Publishers, 2005.

[Farin02] Farin, Gerald. *Curves and Surfaces for CAGD*. Morgan Kaufmann Publishers, 2002.

[Glassner99] Glassner, Andrew. *Andrew Glassner's Notebook*. Morgan Kaufmann Publishers, 1999.

[Glassner02] Glassner, Andrew. *Andrew Glassner's Other Notebook*. A K Peters, 2002.

[Hanson05] Hanson, Andrew J. *Visualizing Quaternions*. Morgan Kaufmann Publishers, 2005.

[Lowe04a] Lowe, Thomas. "Critically Damped Ease-In/Ease-Out Smoothing." In Kirmse, Andrew (ed.), *Game Programming Gems 4*. Charles River Media, 2004.

[Lowe04b] Lowe, Thomas. "Nonuniform Splines." In Kirmse, Andrew (ed.), *Game Programming Gems 4*. Charles River Media, 2004.

[Melax00] Melax, Stan. "The Shortest Arc Quaternion." In DeLoura, Mark (ed.), *Game Programming Gems*. Charles River Media, 2000.

[Ramamoorthi97] Ramamoorthi, Ravi. Barr, Alan H. (August 1997). "Fast Construction of Accurate Quaternion Splines,"*Proceedings of the 24th annual conference on Computer graphics and interactive techniques*, pp. 287–292.

[Rorabaugh98] Rorabaugh, C.Britton. *DSP Primer*. McGraw-Hill Professional, 1998.

[Schneider02] Schneider, Philip, Eberly, David H. *Geometric Tools for Computer Graphics*. Morgan Kaufmann Publishers, 2002.

[Sekulic04] Sekulic, Dean. "Efficient Occlusion Culling." In Fernando, Rendima (ed.), *GPU Gems*. Addison-Wesley, 2004.

[Shoemake85] Shoemake, Ken. *Animating Rotation with Quaternion Curves*. Proceedings of ACM, 1985.

[Shoemake94] Shoemake, Ken. "Fiber Bundle Twist Reduction." In Heckbert, Paul S. (ed.), *Graphics Gems IV*. Academic Press, Inc., 1994.

[VandenBergen04] Van den Bergen, Gino. *Collision Detection in Interactive 3D Environments*. Morgan Kaufmann Publishers, 2004.

[VanVerth04] Van Verth, James M., Bishop, Lars M. *Essential Mathematics for Games & Interactive Applications*. Morgan Kaufmann, 2004.

[VanVerth05] Van Verth, James M. "Spline-Based Time Control for Animation." In Pallister, Kim (ed.), *Game Programming Gems 5*. Charles River Media, 2005.

OTHER

[Thomas95] Thomas, Frank, Johnston, Ollie. *The Illusion of Life: Disney Animation*. Hyperion, 1995.

ONLINE RESOURCES

While the ever-changing nature of the Internet will likely make these actual links out of date, hopefully the Web sites referred to will continue to be easily located via search engines. Additionally, the companion Web site of this book (www.realtimecameras.com) will be used to maintain links to their current location.

[EssentialMath] www.essentialmath.com

[Gamasutra] www.gamasutra.com

[GDC] www.gdconf.com/archives

[Lionheart] www.robinlionheart.com/gamedev/genres.xhtml

[RealTimeRendering] www.realtimerendering.com

[Wikipedia] www.wikipedia.org

Index

D

M

N

O

Edwards Brothers Malloy
Ann Arbor MI. USA
May 21, 2012